PRAISE FOR *Driving While Brown*

"Long before Donald J. Trump, there was Joe Arpaio, the Bull Connor-esque sheriff notorious for his mistreatment of immigrants and Latinos in Arizona's largest county. But the authors of *Driving While Brown* have masterfully documented the previously unknown story of the Latino activists who organized to bring him down and help turn Arizona into a new battleground state. Investigative journalism, storytelling, at its best."

Alfredo Corchado, author of *Midnight in Mexico* and *Homelands*

"This is combustible nonfiction: an irresistible subject, a white sheriff so consumed by the perceived threat of brown immigrants that he'll defy the federal judiciary. Add two of the best reporters in the Southwest—really, anywhere—and you get a searing, decades-long portrait of racism in America and the criminal justice system that has perpetuated it, and the deconstruction of an ignorant and self-absorbed elected official who is very much like the president who pardoned him. To read this book is to understand America in the twenty-first century."

Walter V. Robinson, Pulitzer Prize winner, leader of the *Boston Globe*'s Spotlight Team that inspired the Academy Award–winning film *Spotlight*

"*Driving While Brown* reads like a novel and is at once a rich, intimate portrayal of the excesses of immigration enforcement in one locality in the country as well as an analysis of the forces and power dynamics that make these repressive practices possible in the rest of the country."

Cecilia Menjívar, Dorothy L. Meier Chair in Social Equities and Professor of Sociology, University of California, Los Angeles, and President, American Sociological Association, 2021–22

"In *Driving While Brown*, Greene Sterling and Joffe-Block expertly fill in the blanks and connect the dots to build a compelling, comprehensive narrative of the immigration battles that have defined and redefined Arizona, offering a window into the ethnic and racial animus in the United States today and the transformative power of hope and purpose shared by younger generations. This is a book for our times."

Fernanda Santos, author of *The Fire Line: The Story of the Granite Mountain Hotshots* and former Phoenix bureau chief for the *New York Times*

"Arpaio is, if it's possible, even Trumpier than Trump. This splendid book is a lively portrait of a demagogic anti-immigration crusader and the people who helped bring him down. But the authors have nonetheless let Arpaio's own voice be heard, and they have listened carefully to people on both sides of the immigration debate that seems certain to rage for decades to come."

Adam Hochschild, author of *Lessons from a Dark Time and Other Essays*

"*Driving While Brown* is an engaging chronicle of hate disguised as populism, from its short shelf life to how it inspired courageous activists to stand up, push back, and launch a movement that's remaking our political landscape."

Ricardo Sandoval-Palos, PBS Public Editor and coauthor of *The Fight in the Fields: Cesar Chavez and the Farmworkers Movement*

Driving While Brown

The publisher and the University of California Press Foundation gratefully acknowledge the generous support of the Anne G. Lipow Endowment Fund in Social Justice and Human Rights.

Driving While Brown

SHERIFF JOE ARPAIO VERSUS THE LATINO RESISTANCE

Terry Greene Sterling and Jude Joffe-Block

UNIVERSITY OF CALIFORNIA PRESS

University of California Press
Oakland, California

First Paperback Printing 2022

Library of Congress Cataloging-in-Publication Data

Names: Greene Sterling, Terry, author. | Joffe-Block, Jude, 1982– author.
Title: Driving while brown : Sheriff Joe Arpaio versus the Latino
   resistance / Terry Greene Sterling and Jude Joffe-Block.
Description: Oakland, California : University of California Press, [2021] |
   Includes bibliographical references and index.
Identifiers: LCCN 2020047408 (print) | LCCN 2020047409 (ebook) |
   ISBN 9780520294080 (cloth) | ISBN 9780520389809 (paperback) |
   ISBN 9780520967356 (ebook)
Subjects: LCSH: Arpaio, Joe, 1932– | Immigration enforcement—
   Arizona—Maricopa County—History.
Classification: LCC JV6483 .S846 2021 (print) | LCC JV6483 (ebook) |
   DDC 363.28/20979173—dc23
LC record available at https://lccn.loc.gov/2020047408
LC ebook record available at https://lccn.loc.gov/2020047409

Manufactured in the United States of America

29 28 27 26 25 24 23 22
10 9 8 7 6 5 4 3 2 1

To the truth seekers

Contents

Preface

In June 2017, Joe Arpaio, the former sheriff of Maricopa County, Arizona, was feted in a hotel ballroom in Scottsdale. It was his eighty-fifth birthday. The mostly white and elderly guests sipped drinks from the cash bar and bid on the raffle prize, a gun that shot pepper gel, flares, and rubber bullets.

A birthday cake decorated with chocolate badges sat on one table. A slotted cardboard box called a "wishing well" perched on another. Guests were encouraged to deposit a donation into the wishing well to help pay the legal bills of the man once known as America's Toughest Sheriff, who would soon go to trial for criminal contempt of court. Arpaio had violated a judge's order to stop arresting unauthorized immigrants who had committed no crimes and turning them over for deportation.

We attended Arpaio's birthday fundraiser as journalists researching this book. We sat with several guests at a round table with a red, white, and blue Fourth-of-July-themed centerpiece. One woman with gray hair and blue eyes glared at us as though we couldn't be trusted. She told us she had picked corn as a teenager in the Midwest. Now, she said, unauthorized immigrants had taken those corn-picking jobs from Americans. She told us she knew also, on good authority, that unauthorized immigrants stole videos from video stores. The solution was to throw "illegals" out of the country, which is why she supported Joe Arpaio.

Arpaio, a slightly hunched, bespectacled man dressed in a blazer and slacks, and his wife, Ava, wearing a black dress and flats, stood near the birthday cake. He whacked at the candle flames with a knife, like Zorro, and then blew them out.

At the time, President Donald Trump had been in office for six months. As usual, Arpaio told the crowd he was an early supporter of Trump's candidacy, thus branding himself as a crucial player in the ascendance of the far-right wing of the Republican Party and the Trump presidency. He noted, too, that both he and Trump were under attack. He'd become convinced that he and Trump were both victims of a conspiratorial liberal news media and shadowy Obama holdovers in the federal government.

Arpaio singled us out, as he often did when we attended his events and press conferences, as journalists writing a "hit piece" book about him.

"I've got to be careful," he said, pointing at us.

"They are hoping I get convicted and go to jail so they sell more books."

He was referring to his criminal trial, scheduled later that month. Should a judge find Arpaio guilty, there was a remote possibility that the former sheriff might do time in a federal prison.

We had no stake in the outcome of the trial. And because Arpaio frequently labeled us as hostile journalists at his events, we were used to the audience reaction—glares, mostly, and surprised, uncomfortable laughter.

We understood, too, that Arpaio was manipulating his audience to paint himself as a victim of the news media. In fact, he craved media attention and had spent his career seeking it out. Privately, he was friendly to us. Over the four years we reported this book together, and for several years before that in our individual capacity as Phoenix-based journalists, Arpaio granted us interviews at a number of places—in his home, in his office, in his Tent City jail, before and after press conferences, in airports and airplanes, at a film festival, at election night parties, and throughout the 2016 Republican National Convention. People often asked us how we'd gotten so much access to such a well-known, polarizing figure in American politics. The answer was simple. We asked for interviews and we showed up at events. Our goal was to understand Arpaio's motivations and include his perspective. We wanted to tell his side of the story in connection with a central narrative in this book—his immigration crackdowns as Maricopa County sheriff. We also sought his reactions to the Latino-led movement that was determined to bring him down.

Arpaio was eager to share his talking points. We understood he did not always tell us the truth. We confronted him with inconsistencies. We also confronted him with the misery and terror he'd caused immigrant families and American citizens of Latino descent. His agency had engaged in systemic racial profiling and had enabled the deportation of tens of thousands of immigrants, sometimes permanently. When asked about this, he shifted the blame to the immigrants themselves for being in the country without papers.

This book is not a biography of Joe Arpaio. Instead, it is a story about the human consequences of his relentless immigration enforcement in Maricopa County. It tells the story of two movements on opposite sides of the immigration policy divide. It is about a coalition of Maricopa County residents, many of them Americans of Mexican descent or born in Mexico, who rose up against Arpaio. They include Lydia Guzman, Carlos Garcia, Alfredo Gutierrez, Danny Ortega, Mary Rose Wilcox, Antonio Bustamante, and Sal Reza. And it is about Arpaio himself, along with his political allies Russell Pearce and Andrew Thomas, his deputies and staffers, the conservative journalist Linda Bentley, and loyal supporters like Kathryn Kobor and Barb Heller, who felt the United States was threatened by unauthorized immigrants and were comforted by the sheriff's crackdowns.

As the bitter immigration divide pioneered in Arizona spreads and as the country grapples with discriminatory policing against communities of color, this book is about what Arizona can teach the nation. The resistance chronicled in these pages shows how one community confronted civil rights violations—in the courts, on the streets, and in the media.

The people you will meet on these pages struggled to define American identity in a time of demographic change. They share their conflicts, hopes, failures, and victories, and through their voices we may come to understand the strength and weaknesses of the federal judiciary, the consequences of local enforcement of federal immigration law, and what happens when abuse of power goes unchecked as an elected official violates the constitutional rights of one segment of his constituency in order to satisfy the desires of faithful voters.

This book is divided into three parts.

The first part, Origins (1846–2006), explores the genesis of Arizona's immigration-themed social justice fights, which traces back to cycles of racism and resistance in the state. Arizona's present-day Latino-led resistance movement descends from civil rights battles waged by Mexicans, Mexican Americans, Chicanos, and immigrants throughout the last century. It took its lessons from earlier resistance to the racism rooted in the Mexican-American War and the eugenics movement of the 1920s, as well as from unions demanding equality for Mexican American workers in Arizona mining towns, the farmworker advocacy of Cesar Chavez and the Chicano movement of the 1960s, the fight against California's Proposition 187, the day labor rights movement in Arizona, and the 2006 national immigrant rights marches.

The second part, Battles (2006–2016), chronicles the height of animus over immigration in Arizona. As fear and resentment toward unauthorized immigrants spread across Arizona, Arpaio pivoted to becoming an immigration enforcer. As he overstepped the constitution by taking increasingly aggressive steps to round up unauthorized immigrants in Maricopa County, Lydia Guzman and other activists collected evidence to sue him in court for racial profiling. Their movement gathered together coalitions, gained national momentum, and found ways to get the media to capture the story. As the legal tension built, Arpaio tested the authority of the federal judiciary.

The final part, Changes (2016–2019), follows Arpaio's fall from grace after losing his re-election for sheriff and being found guilty of criminal contempt of court. He was rescued by President Donald Trump, who issued his first presidential pardon to save him. But even as Trump's national immigration policies imitated Arizona-style efforts to punish and deport unauthorized immigrants, Arizona was moderating. Federal courts tempered the state's immigration laws. Demographic change reshaped the state's electorate. Younger activists in Arizona, most of them immigrants themselves, became the new face of the movement against restrictionism.

The people who lived through much of this history, who felt it and witnessed it and learned from it, give voice to this book.

We thank them.

Authors' Note

Events and scenes in this book were either witnessed by us, described to us in interviews, drawn from public records, videos, or archival documents, or reported in the media.

Since we could not interview all the leaders of the dueling movements at the heart of this book, we chose to interview a selected group of sources who told us what shaped them, what they risked, and why they kept fighting for so long.

We interviewed more than one hundred people over the last decade and reviewed thousands of public records, court filings, archival documents, social media posts, videos, emails, and newspaper clippings. We attended court hearings, birthday parties, community meetings, marches, press briefings, conferences, and demonstrations.

Sometimes we jointly interviewed sources. Other times, we individually interviewed sources. We use "told us" and "we" when referring to one or both of us.

All quotations in this book were either directly heard by us during interviews, described to us by people who heard the quotes themselves, documented in public records, detailed in media reports, and subsequently fact checked. When we write a person's thoughts, those thoughts were conveyed to us by that person.

When we quote the writings of others in public records, personal journals, emails, or letters, we do so with the original punctuation and spelling.

A detailed accounting of our research can be found in the chapter notes. The Appendix provides two tables describing the federal court cases and laws named in this book.

We use the terms Mexican, Mexican American, Hispanic, Chicano, Indigenous, and Latino in their historical contexts or according to the preferences of people we interviewed. We chose to default to the term Latino in other instances, because that is the term used in the *Melendres* lawsuit, which is central to this book. Latino was also the most commonly accepted term people used to self-identify during much of the time period described on these pages. We understand that Latinx is more gender inclusive, and has come to be preferred by many for that reason. We also respect the fact that those from Latin America who self-identify as Indigenous do not always consider themselves Latino.

Under current conventions, the terms Latino/Latinx are not tied to a racial category, but rather to an ethnicity. We use the word "white" as shorthand for Caucasians who do not claim Latino ethnicity, although we recognize using "white" in this way is imperfect since many people who identify as Latino are racially white.

We could not identify a specific, commonly used term or phrase to describe the movement to halt unauthorized immigration. We chose to use the word "restrictionist" to describe laws, policies, and people embracing this goal, as well as the mission of restricting legal immigration to very low levels.

We use the word "migrant" to describe people who have recently entered the country or are in transit and "immigrant" to describe the foreign-born who reside in the United States. We use "undocumented" and "unauthorized" interchangeably to describe immigrants who crossed the border without proper documentation or overstayed a visa.

We added accent marks, or didn't, to names and surnames of people in this book in accordance with their individual preferences.

The Maricopa County Sheriff's Office under Joe Arpaio conducted several different kinds of immigration enforcement actions detailed in this book. These included patrols on rural roads to intercept vehicles shuttling incoming migrants from the border, roundups of immigrant day laborers, and worksite raids. Deputies also swarmed neighborhoods, pulled over cars for minor traffic violations, and arrested those who could not prove they were lawful immigrants. Those operations were known by several names. The sheriff's office called them "saturation patrols" and "crime suppression operations." Some critics called them "community raids." We have chosen to refer to them as "sweeps."

Many times, Arpaio reacted to perceived slights from his foes with actions that his critics and court records refer to as "retaliation." We use "retaliation" in that context, and because the evidence supports a pattern of behavior that suggests it. This said, we want to make it clear that Arpaio has always denied retaliating or abusing his power.

The dates on the chapter titles reflect the time span for core events covered in those chapters.

Selected People in This Book

IMMIGRANT RIGHTS MOVEMENT

Elias Bermudez

Antonio Bustamante

Maria Castro

Carmen Cornejo

Petra Falcón

Katherine Figueroa

Carlos Garcia

Dennis Gilman

Alejandra Gomez

Alfredo Gutierrez

Lydia Guzman

Viridiana Hernandez

Dr. Sylvia Herrera

Father Glenn Jenks

Annie Lai

Jason LeVecke

Daniel Magos

Dr. Angeles Maldonado

Manuel de Jesus Ortega Melendres

Danny Ortega

Julie Pace

Randy Parraz

Dan Pochoda

Roberto Reveles

Salvador Reza

"Samuel" (pseudonym)

Andre Segura

Cecillia Wang

Ray Ybarra Maldonado

Stanley Young

RESTRICTIONIST MOVEMENT

Linda Bentley

Buffalo Rick Galeener

Barb Heller

Kris Kobach

Kathryn Kobor

Pam Pearson

Tim Rafferty

Valerie Roller

George Sprankle

Jim Williams

MARICOPA COUNTY SHERIFF'S OFFICE (MCSO)

Lisa Allen

Detective Ramon Charley Armendariz

Sheriff Joe Arpaio

Captain Steve Bailey

Chris Hegstrom

Chief Deputy David Hendershott

Captain John Kleinheinz

Sergeant Brett Palmer

Sheriff Paul Penzone

Executive Chief Brian Sands

Chief Deputy Jerry Sheridan

Len Sherman

Lieutenant Joe Sousa

ELECTED OFFICIALS IN ARIZONA AND MARICOPA COUNTY

Governor Jan Brewer

Congressman Ruben Gallego

Attorney General Terry Goddard

Phoenix Mayor Phil Gordon

Governor Janet Napolitano

State Senator Russell Pearce

County Supervisor Don Stapley

State Representative Raquel Terán

County Attorney Andrew Thomas

County Supervisor Mary Rose Garrido Wilcox

Attorney General Grant Woods

LEGAL AND LAW ENFORCEMENT COMMUNITY

David Bodney

Tim Casey

Paul Charlton

Maricopa County Superior Court Judge Gary Donahoe

Former Mesa Police Chief George Gascón

Michele Iafrate

Tom Liddy

Michael Manning

Stephen Montoya

Julie Pace

FEDERAL JUDGES

U.S. District Court Judge Susan Bolton (*United States v. Arizona, Valle del Sol v. State of Arizona, United States v. Arpaio*)

U.S. District Court Judge Mary Murguia, later appointed to the Ninth Circuit Court of Appeals (*Melendres v. Arpaio*)

U.S. District Court Judge Roslyn Silver (*United States v. Maricopa County*)

U.S. District Court Judge G. Murray Snow (*Melendres v. Arpaio*)

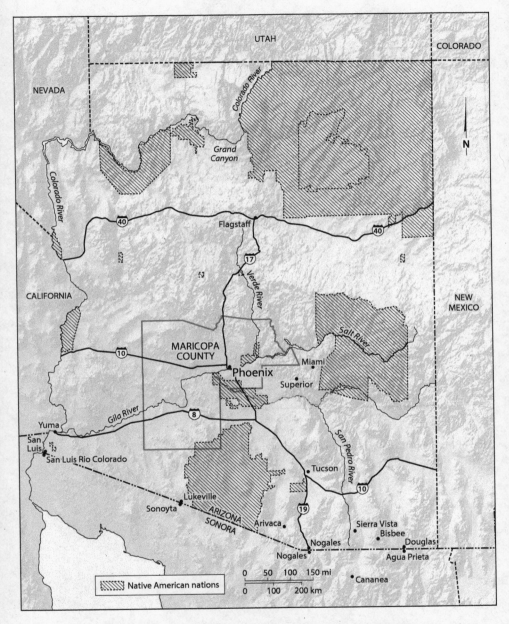

Map of Arizona, showing Maricopa County and the United States–Mexico border. (Map drawn by Bill Nelson)

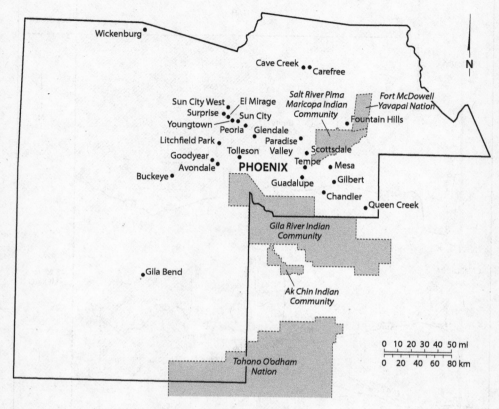

Map of Maricopa County, Arizona. (Map drawn by Bill Nelson)

Prologue

LYDIA AND THE SHERIFF, 2017

The window shade was drawn, giving the artificially lit room a bunker-like feeling. Outside cameras fed video of an empty porch onto a monitor above a desk, where an eighty-five-year-old man bit glumly into a meaty deli sandwich.

It was August 8, 2017. Joe Arpaio, the former sheriff of Maricopa County, Arizona, knew he would soon be sentenced for his crime. And even though a prison sentence was a long shot for a federal misdemeanor, the very idea that it was a remote possibility angered and unnerved him.

He had stacked printouts of personalized Google alerts and emails, along with a few fan letters, on his desk. They were comforting proof to him that he was still famous and his supporters had not abandoned him.

He'd long branded himself as "America's Toughest Sheriff," the guy who forced many inmates in his jails to live and sleep in uncomfortably hot tents, wear pink underwear, buy their own salt and pepper, eat gloppy, tasteless, and sometimes moldy food, and undergo other hardships geared toward getting more press.

As sheriff, he'd apprehended and jailed and sent tens of thousands of undocumented immigrants into deportation proceedings in Maricopa County. He had become known to those who opposed him as much more than an "immigration hardliner" or "border hawk." His critics viewed him, instead, as a twenty-first-century patriarch of the restrictionist immigration movement, which is rooted in a dark history of eugenics and white supremacy dating back at least to the early decades of the twentieth century.

As Arpaio developed his brand, it helped him keep his office into his eighties. It also embroiled him in a history-making class action federal lawsuit, in which Latino drivers successfully sued Arpaio and his agency, the Maricopa County Sheriff's Office, for racial profiling. This lawsuit, in turn, had resulted in court-ordered reforms, including an explicit judicial order forbidding Arpaio or anyone in his agency from detaining undocumented immigrants who had not been accused of crimes and turning them over to federal authorities for deportation. Arpaio had disobeyed the court order for seventeen months, two federal judges ruled, which led to a criminal contempt of court guilty verdict on July 31, 2017, and an upcoming sentencing that October, which could include up to six months in a federal prison.

Even though the sentencing was still a few months away, people wondered what might happen. Would Arpaio get off with a fine or probation? Or would the marshals shackle Arpaio and lead him out of the courtroom? Would they distribute his mugshot on the internet? Would he be marched in front of the cameras in a perp walk? Would Arpaio be confined to a prison cell . . . with a cellmate?

He had long professed his innocence. He viewed his conviction as the end result of a conspiracy by former President Barack Obama loyalists, still embedded in the United States Department of Justice, which had successfully prosecuted him in a Phoenix courtroom.

I'm the victim, he had told us more than once.

On this August day, we were perched, as usual, in a couple of small chairs facing his large desk. Arpaio was telling us about his plan to get President Donald Trump's attention. Two dried-out ballpoint pens commemorating his twenty-five years as a federal narcotics agent sat on his desk. A name plaque read: *Sheriff Joe Arpaio, America's Toughest Sheriff.* He sat in a high-backed black executive office chair. His office, a corner suite on the first floor of a building he owned in Fountain Hills, the town where he lived some 30 miles northeast of Phoenix, was a museum-like tribute to himself. Shelves in the hallway leading to the bathroom were crammed with police-themed tchotchkes—coffee mugs, hats, bobblehead dolls, and a "border wall brick"—all of which reminded him of his twenty-four years as sheriff of the nation's fourth most populous county, now home to about 4.5 million people.

Carefully arranged framed newspaper and magazine articles, photographs, and letters of commendation dating as far back as the 1960s hung on all the walls. He'd positioned the most important photos so he could point to them from his desk—a picture of a younger Arpaio mugging with President George W. Bush, another of Arpaio with thinning, slicked back graying hair shaking hands with President Barack Obama, and several of Arpaio posing with Donald Trump as a candidate and newly elected president. He'd endorsed Trump early. Once, at a campaign event, a photographer caught a moment in which Trump wrapped his arm around Arpaio, who half-smiled, coyly. Later, Trump autographed the picture: *I Love You Joe! Donald Trump*.

After Arpaio had endorsed Trump, the sheriff had identified with him.

Trump, fourteen years younger, was Arpaio's "only hero." They traveled "the same highway." They would "never surrender" as they battled forces that tried to bring them down—mainstream media, big government, leftist judges, open borders liberals, or any combination thereof.

They both understood the "immigration problem."

Arpaio had told us once that should he be convicted, he didn't need to be rescued with a presidential pardon. He could take care of himself.

But we sensed his bravado failed him after he was convicted. After marching shackled immigrants in front of the media in "perp walks," he understood what might lie ahead for himself. Only Donald Trump could rescue him. The president reportedly had asked his appointee, United States Attorney General Jeff Sessions, if he could drop the prosecution of Arpaio. Sessions had refused, and the case went to trial. The president had planned to pardon Arpaio should he be found guilty. But more than a week had passed since Arpaio's guilty verdict, and Trump had stayed mum.

Arpaio pinned the president's unresponsiveness on White House aides who didn't like Arpaio and thus didn't tell Trump about Arpaio's predicament. So Arpaio had strategized to get the president's attention.

A few days before, the former sheriff had spoken with Jerome Corsi, a conspiracy theorist who, like Trump and Arpaio, had repeatedly alleged that Barack Obama had a fake birth certificate. Corsi wrote for the right-wing extremist website InfoWars.

The website ran videos featuring Alex Jones, another conspiracy theorist who maintained, among other things, that the 2012 massacre of children at Sandy Hook Elementary School was a fabricated event meant to undermine the gun rights of Americans. InfoWars also published pieces that embraced anti-immigrant views.

The president read InfoWars.

Arpaio knew this, and so likely did Corsi, who wrote an InfoWars story about Arpaio's pressing need for a presidential pardon. The piece was headlined "'Where Is Trump?' Sheriff Arpaio Asks."

"After being convicted of criminal misdemeanor contempt, former Maricopa County Sheriff Joe Arpaio has come out swinging, arguing the judge was biased and asking why President Trump is abandoning him, considering Arpaio was an early campaign supporter whose conviction reflects the determination to enforce immigration laws the Trump Justice Department is now exhibiting," Corsi wrote.

Other media took the InfoWars plea mainstream. *The Arizona Republic,* the largest newspaper in Arizona, reported Arpaio would accept a presidential pardon. So did Politico.

Arpaio sat back and waited.

Four days after Arpaio told us about his scheme to get Trump's attention, white nationalists gathered for a "Unite the Right" alt-right, neo-Nazi protest in Charlottesville, Virginia. The protesters included white supremacists and the Ku Klux Klan, who had long supported Trump and his pro-white, anti-Muslim, anti-brown-immigrant rhetoric.

They had gathered in Charlottesville to protest the removal of a monument honoring Confederate hero General Robert E. Lee.

Even after a white supremacist plowed his car into the crowd of counterprotesters, killing one woman and injuring dozens of others, President Trump caused a controversy when he said there were "very fine people on both sides."

If Trump were to choose this post-Charlottesville moment to do what he planned to do anyway—issue his first presidential pardon to Joe Arpaio, so admired by white supremacists for his unsparing immigration sweeps—

the pardon could accomplish multiple goals. It could save his friend. It could divert media attention away from Charlottesville. And the very act of pardoning a man so well regarded by the extreme right-wing of the party could signal to Trump's base that the president was still on their side.

As Joe Arpaio sat in his house in Fountain Hills, Lydia Guzman stood with thousands of protesters who'd gathered around the Phoenix Convention Center, where President Donald Trump would soon hold a rally. It was late afternoon, August 22, 2017. The hot, sloping sun tinted the white walls of Saint Mary's Basilica the color of desert honey. Guzman snapped photos with her Android smartphone. So many people had turned out to protest the president's response to the Charlottesville violence and also the possible presidential pardon of Joe Arpaio. People on crutches, on walkers, in wheelchairs, on foot, on bikes. People of different ethnicities, disabilities, sexual identities, religious faiths, political persuasions, and ages. They filled Monroe Street, sat on the Herberger Theater steps, and gathered around life-sized bronze sculptures of dancers. Some chanted. Others beat drums. They waved American flags. The thick air smelled of shampoo and sweat. People fanned themselves with baseball caps, sun hats, and signs.

THINGS ARE NOT ALT-RIGHT IN THE USA!
NO NAZIS! NO KKK! NO WHITE SUPREMACISTS!
HELL NO, DON'T PARDON JOE!

Ever since Trump's election, Guzman felt, the vitriol against immigrants and minorities once so rampant in Arizona had spread across the country. Joe Arpaio's friendship with Donald Trump had been one reason, among many others. But standing in the crowd, seeing the diversity of ethnicities and ages, she felt the Latino-led civil rights movement she had helped lead had won the narrative, in Arizona at least. Recent polling showed about 50 percent of Arizonans opposed an Arpaio pardon. Only 21 percent supported it.

Just one month earlier, Guzman had been inside the Phoenix Convention Center where Trump now spoke. She'd been one of several local Latino activists feted by UnidosUS, the national Latino civil rights nonprofit once known as the National Council of La Raza.

The nonprofit had boycotted Arizona and Maricopa County several years before, when Sheriff Joe Arpaio was using restrictionist state laws as a justification to round up, criminalize, and turn over unauthorized immigrants for deportation.

Now, Arpaio, the patriarch of Arizona's anti-immigrant movement, had been voted out of office in 2016 and faced prison time—key symbolic victories for the Latino-led movement that had risen up against Arpaio and the state laws he'd relied on. UnidosUS had chosen to have its 2017 conference in a city it once boycotted. This was a sign of the growing influence of Arizona's Latino activists as role models for resistance to the anti-immigrant animus that had spread across the country with the Trump presidency.

Yet on this August afternoon, in the very same building where Guzman and other Arizona activists had been honored by UnidosUS, the president promoted the same anti-immigrant narrative they'd battled for years in the courts, on the streets, and in the hearts and minds of Arizonans.

Guzman watched men and women in American flag shirts and American flag baseball caps enter the convention center to attend the rally. Not that she'd ever care to, but she figured if she wore Old Glory couture, she would be accused of defacing the American flag.

Instead, she wore an embroidered brown tunic, black pants, and sensible black walking shoes. A short woman with carefully coiffed waves of black hair framing her round face and large dark eyes, she looked put together, confident and calm, but she felt ragged inside. All the speculation over the possible presidential pardon of Joe Arpaio had left her out of sorts. For days, she'd tried to bolster the spirits of her friends and allies in the Latino community who worried Arpaio might get pardoned. Arpaio was no longer sheriff, everyone knew, but a presidential pardon for illegally rounding up Latino immigrants would be a symbolic slap in the face to the movement that had struggled for years to stop the local sheriff from violating the civil rights of brown-skinned Americans and Latino immigrants.

She'd been one of many in the movement who had taken on Arpaio when he was so powerful people were afraid of him. She had helped Latino drivers successfully sue the sheriff for racial profiling. That lawsuit had led to the guilty verdict that Arpaio hoped would be wiped away by the president.

Guzman knew many in her community yearned to see Arpaio get a taste of the humiliation he'd meted out to Latinos. Arpaio in a mugshot.

Arpaio in handcuffs. Arpaio behind bars, if only for a day. But now, Guzman thought, it looked as if Trump would rescue Arpaio with a pardon before he was even sentenced.

She figured the president might well pardon Arpaio that afternoon, just to humiliate the movement.

"The fact that he was going to come to Arizona in our face, under our noses to do this, I think that was the biggest insult," she told us. "It was more like he was taunting us . . . and we couldn't do anything about it. I felt helpless."

Joe Arpaio watched the protest that Guzman attended on his large-screen television in his home on a cactus-stabbed hill in Fountain Hills. He saw the president, his hero, stroll out on a stage as speakers blared "God Bless the USA." Among the thousands in the convention center, many shook red *Make America Great Again* posters, blue *Drain the Swamp* posters, and white *Veterans for Trump* posters.

"Ava," Arpaio told his wife, "he's going to say my name."

And soon, Trump did.

"So was Sheriff Joe convicted for doing his job?" Trump asked the crowd.

The crowd chanted, "Pardon Joe! Pardon Joe!"

"I think he's going to be just fine, okay?" the president smiled.

"But," he added, "I won't do it tonight, because I don't want to cause any controversy."

Outside the convention center, phones lit up with text messages detailing Trump's hints that likely he would soon pardon Joe Arpaio. Guzman knew it would happen. And when it did, it would feel to her as though all the movement's years of hard work were being discounted by Trump's pen. And the suffering she'd witnessed—wrongfully detained and deported immigrants torn from their families—would be discounted too.

Really, she hated to say it, because he was always nice to her face, but she secretly thought of Joe Arpaio as a cockroach. For decades, the movement had tried to sweep away Arpaio and everything he stood for.

But for now at least, he'd sidled into a dark space, out of reach.

I Origins

1848–2006

1 An Immigrant's Son

1923–1993

He didn't talk about it.

Ciro Arpaio never said why he abandoned his red-roofed village, cloistered in the hills of southern Italy, and the people he loved.

Or at least that's what his son, Joe, told us years later, when he was an old man and couldn't remember much about what his father told him. Or chose not to.

But there were plenty of reasons tens of thousands of poor Italians like Ciro wanted to come to the United States. Italy was adjusting to the aftereffects of World War I—new borders, economic and social shifts, explosive nationalism, and a volatile authoritarian prime minister, Benito Mussolini. Whatever his motive, in 1923 Ciro jumped aboard the *Presidente Wilson,* a workhorse steamer that shuttled Italian immigrants to the United States of America. Ciro was twenty-two years old. The *Presidente Wilson* wasn't designed to slice through the Atlantic full throttle, panting acid smoke. But there was no choice. The *Presidente Wilson* had to beat ten other immigrant ships to New York Harbor. If it didn't, the passengers aboard might be deported back to Italy due to restrictive immigration quotas for southern and eastern European immigrants, considered undesirables.

Judge magazine cartoon by Louis Dalrymple disparages Italian immigrants, 1903. The restrictionist stereotype of immigrants as craven invaders carried over into the twenty-first century. (New York Public Library)

Luckily for Ciro Arpaio, on July 1, 1923 the *Presidente Wilson* beat the ten other ships in transit and was the first in line for immigration processing at Ellis Island. The ship's victory rated a front-page article in *The New York Times*, sharing space with a story about contractors needing more migrant workers and a piece on the Ku Klux Klan, a powerful white supremacist, anti-immigrant group that had gone mainstream in recent years.

When the *Presidente Wilson* arrived in New York Harbor, the foreign born made up close to 13 percent of the population in the United States—near the all-time peak. Many Americans felt crowded and anxious. Italian immigrants and other immigrants from southern and eastern Europe had long been viewed as criminally inclined, disease-spreading, job-stealing, shifty, swarthy-skinned invaders.

President Warren Harding had tapped into this animus when he signed the 1921 Emergency Quota Act. The law severely restricted immigration from southern and eastern Europe, and was followed in 1924 by an even more restrictive immigration quota law.

These laws were stoked in part by the nation's embrace of eugenics, a popular "science" that fused Victorian anthropology with white supremacy. Eugenicists believed northern and western European Protestants, along with their descendants in the United States, belonged to the most advanced race of human beings on earth. They feared eastern and southern European immigrants, like Italians, might mongrelize and diminish what they considered the superior race.

Influential American eugenicists lobbied hard for immigration restriction, earning the name "restrictionists," a term that would be revived in the twenty-first century, when the foreign born again occupied over 13 percent of the American population.

After Ciro, a short, thickset man with determined eyes and wavy dark hair, was processed on Ellis Island, he eventually settled in Springfield, an industrial town on the Connecticut River in western Massachusetts. He dabbled in door-to-door sales, then got into the grocery business. Within a few years, he co-owned a grocery store called Del Vecchio and Arpaio Wholesale Italian Grocers.

He likely met Josephine Marinaro, the daughter of the publisher of Springfield's Italian language newspaper *L'Eco della Nuova England*, when he placed grocery ads in the newspaper.

Josephine had immigrated from Italy at the age of three with her family. When she met Ciro, she was a kindergarten teacher—and a solid woman with dark hair and eyes, a broad nose, and thin lips. Ciro probably seemed to be a good provider. Even as the Great Depression destroyed other men, he prospered in the grocery business. The two married in 1931, when Josephine was twenty-two and Ciro was thirty. A year later, their son, Joseph Michael Arpaio, was born.

Nine days later, Josephine died. The Springfield City Clerk listed post-childbirth pulmonary edema as the cause of Josephine's death. A Springfield newspaper reported her demise as "sudden."

After living with his maternal grandparents for three years, young Arpaio and his father moved to a small apartment on the second floor of a house on Cedar Street, right across from the Springfield Cemetery. A housewife on the first floor watched over Joe while his father toiled away at the grocery store. At night, Ciro came home so exhausted he fell asleep in his chair, ignoring his son.

The immigrant's son, who would one day become an iron-hearted immigration enforcer, had a mutt named Pepper, who followed him to school. He made snow angels in the backyard during the winter and played cowboy with his toy six shooters in the summer. He walked to a local movie house to watch Westerns. Sometimes, he sat on the front porch and stared at the cemetery and listened to ball games on the radio.

Ciro married a telephone operator named Rose when Joe Arpaio was twelve. He didn't always get along with Rose. The stepfamily dynamics were made even more difficult when Ciro and Rose had a son, Michael.

Joe Arpaio had a difficult time in school. He struggled to get passing grades and often bore the brunt of anti-immigrant taunts: *Dago! Wop! Guinea!*

He took it, pretended to ignore it. Because that's what you did back then, he told us.

Arpaio chose not to go to college. Instead, he enlisted in the Army after graduating from high school in 1950. And after his three-year tour in France as a medical clerk ended, he set out to show the world he was somebody.

He applied to be on the U.S. Border Patrol but told us he flunked the entry test. In four years, he had three jobs. First he was a beat cop in an African American neighborhood in Washington, D.C., where he said he whacked people with his nightstick. "I was a pretty aggressive cop," he told us. "Made more arrests than anybody in the precinct. Not that I was prejudiced. I wasn't prejudiced." He wanted to become a detective, but after nearly four years he hadn't been promoted and, as he put it in *Joe's Law*, "the promotion rolls were backed up" and "I was pretty constantly aching somewhere on my body, from one encounter or another." So, he moved on to the police force in tiny Las Vegas, Nevada, where, he often claimed, he arrested Elvis Presley for a traffic violation and took him down to the station house to meet the guys. After six months in Las Vegas, Arpaio moved east again, signing up as a narcotics agent for the Federal Bureau of Narcotics, where he would stay for twenty-five years.

We came to understand that Arpaio learned, in the small drug enforcement agency then overseen by the Treasury Department, a lot of things that would inform his tenure as a Maricopa County sheriff. He learned how to assume a fictitious role. He learned how to self-validate by inserting himself in the news. And he learned how to create chaos on the United States–Mexico border to achieve a political goal.

In the early days, Arpaio dreamed up tough-guy characters for his undercover work and jumped into those roles with gusto. One of his partners in Chicago, Bill Mattingly, told us he and Arpaio went undercover passing themselves off as pimps looking for drugs to buy for their "junkie whores."

To play these roles the duo tooled around in fancy cars that authorities had seized from suspected crooks. Arpaio smoked a cigar and dressed in flashy sports coats. He purchased five-dollar "nickel bags" of heroin for the whores, after which he and Mattingly placed the low-level dealer into the back of a car and threatened years of prison if the dealer didn't name his supplier. This earned Arpaio the bureau nickname of "Nickel Bag Joe."

"If you're a real good liar, you were a good undercover agent," Mattingly said.

Back at the office, Arpaio typed up the reports late into the night. By then he had a wife. In 1957 he and Ava Lam, a clerical worker he'd met in Washington, had married in a simple civil ceremony in Chicago. Ava aspired to be a hairdresser and found Arpaio to be a "little Italian cutie."

Mattingly met Ava at an agency Fourth of July picnic. He thought she was sweet and pretty, and he worried that Arpaio ignored his wife and spent too much time away from her. He would sometimes say, Joe, go home to Ava, it's late.

Early in their marriage, Ava asked her husband to call her every night, so she wouldn't worry. "I don't want to sit and worry. I only want to know you're safe. I don't care what you're doing, where you are. I want to know you're safe. That's all," she told us she recalled telling her husband.

He called, and she didn't complain about his long hours.

Ava didn't mind that her husband wasn't much help caring for their first child, Rocco, a boy named after Rocco Marchegiano, better known as

"Rocky Marciano," the Italian American boxer. Her husband only babysat once and never washed a dish, cooked or made a bed, she told us.

"He was too busy, had to sleep when he was off, 'cause he did work a lot of hours," she told us.

Then she added, "It's okay."

The Arpaios settled into an American enclave in Istanbul after Arpaio was transferred to Turkey in 1961. It was a prestigious post, because Turkey was key to an international heroin trafficking network and one of a handful of countries where the Federal Bureau of Narcotics stationed agents overseas. Ava was alone much of the time with their toddler son.

Back in Springfield, Massachusetts, Ciro was alone, too. When he was sixty, in 1961, his second wife died of cancer. By then, Ciro was a prominent member of the Springfield Italian American community. His younger son, Michael, was still in high school. His older son, Joe, told us he knew his father, "coming from the old country always believed in education" and was disappointed that his first-born hadn't gotten a college education.

Then, in 1963, Ciro read a story in a Springfield newspaper, headlined "Ton of Opium Seized in Turkey." The only person named in the story was "Joseph Arpaio, special narcotics agent," who reported the opium bust was the "largest ever made in Turkey and one of the largest in the world." Arpaio told us his dad was proud of him, and had showed the article around Springfield.

From then on, Joe Arpaio sought validation in the media.

While still in Turkey in the early 1960s, Joe Arpaio got in a gun battle. His three accounts of the deadly shootout in Turkey are inconsistent: first in a newspaper interview, then in testimony before a United States Senate subcommittee, and last in his two cowritten memoirs. The differing versions of the shootout story reflect Arpaio's tendency to mold a story to fit the audience.

Arpaio first told the deadly shootout story publicly in 1982, shortly before his retirement from drug enforcement and two decades after his tour in Turkey. In an interview with a Phoenix reporter, Arpaio spoke carefully. He said back in the 1960s, when he was in Turkey, he and five

Turkish police officers got in a gun battle with Turkish drug dealers. "Four of the Turks got away, and the other was shot to death," Arpaio told the reporter. He didn't say who, exactly, shot the man. But he did say he and the Turkish cops were charged with murder, and the charges were eventually dismissed.

He referenced the shootout again in 1989, during a hearing before the International Narcotics Control Caucus of the United States Senate, chaired by then-Senator Joe Biden. This time, he said he killed two Turks. According to transcripts of his testimony, Arpaio, in the context of critiquing the efficacy of the State Department working abroad with drug enforcement agents, blurted out to the senators: "A paradox: one of my weekly gun battles in the mountains of Turkey where I killed two Turks, two dope peddlers, and I was indicted along with four other police officers for murder. I sent a cable through State Department channels and nothing happened. Three weeks later, they finally decided, 'Gee, we had better do something with Joe.' Of course, I resolved the matter. My indictment was dismissed, and the other police officers had to stand trial; but they were found not guilty. Let me add we were in the line of duty."

He changed his story a third time in his two memoirs, coauthored with Len Sherman. In both books, written in Arpaio's first-person voice, the passages describing the shootout are the same, word for word. The books note "two people were killed" during the gun battle Arpaio was involved in. The books cast Arpaio as a victim of internal Turkish political squabbles and detail how the American ambassador and Turkish leaders interceded and got Arpaio off the hook. "The charges were dropped," the books say, "and the press didn't get a chance to smear the story all over the front pages."

"I can't say I lost much sleep over the whole affair," Arpaio says in his memoirs. "It's not that I was glad the dealers had been killed. I wasn't. But it happened, and more often than on one occasion."

We asked Arpaio several times if he'd ever killed anybody. He answered: "Not that I know of, although in Turkey I used to have gun battles, I think one . . . gun battle I did hit one or two of the dope peddlers only because I am the only one that had the gun. A thirty-eight I guess." He added hastily that he had never killed anyone in the United States. Another time, he told us, "In Turkey I've had some gun battles. I don't know who killed who. . . . But I never killed anybody."

Joe Arpaio learned more about the United States–Mexico border—and its potential for political exploitation—when he was assigned to drug enforcement in the Washington, D.C. metro area. In the nation's capital, he and other drug enforcement officials "regaled" Nixon with "war stories" about drug interdictions. In 1969, Nixon ordered Operation Intercept—a blockade of border-crossing stations on the United States–Mexico border. The blockade was trumpeted by the Nixon administration as a means to keep Mexican drugs out of the United States, but it was actually an expensive publicity ploy intended to showcase Nixon's war on drugs and intimidate Mexico into complying with it. Among other things, Mexican leaders did not want Americans to aerially spray Mexican marijuana fields with herbicides.

That fall, Arpaio helped orchestrate the three-week border blockade for the Department of Justice, which by that time oversaw federal drug enforcement.

Long lines of honking cars and trucks waited for hours to enter the United States as immigration authorities and narcotics agents individually searched four and a half million children, men, and women. Some were strip-searched. Officials even inspected women's hairdos.

Arpaio told us he observed the chaos from an airplane, along with G. Gordon Liddy, a Nixon advisor who later served more than four years in prison for his role in the 1972 burglary of a Democratic National Committee office in the Watergate Hotel.

While Arpaio witnessed the border bedlam from the sky, Antonio Bustamante felt it on the ground. Bustamante was a senior at Douglas High School, a tall honor student who played football. The sister border towns of Douglas, Arizona and Agua Prieta, Sonora, situated in rocky, semi-arid grassland, were intertwined economically and culturally. It wasn't unusual for Douglas residents to have relatives in Agua Prieta and vice versa. Just about everybody in Douglas, like Bustamante, was of Mexican descent and spoke Spanish.

"Commerce came to a standstill," Bustamante told us.

"Mexicans cursed Nixon, and American border residents thought their government in faraway Washington was being run by idiots."

The blockade lasted three weeks.

At the time, Bustamante had never heard of Arpaio. Decades later, he would vocally oppose restrictive immigration policy in Arizona. And as an activist, he would see similarities in style between Operation Intercept and Arpaio's neighborhood sweeps and traffic stops that ensnared so many American citizens of color and Latino immigrants in Maricopa County.

"Same techniques. Same attitude! Ignorance, disrespect, and narcissism," Bustamante told us.

The Nixon administration was pleased with Arpaio and sent him to Mexico City in 1970 as regional director of the Bureau of Narcotics and Dangerous Drugs for Latin America. By that time, the Arpaios had a second child, Sherry, a girl. They moved into a Mexico City suburb with mid-century homes surrounded by high walls.

Ciro visited his son in Mexico. He saw the signs of his son's success. The classy house. Ava's maid. The Nixon administration valued Arpaio so much that Richard Kleindienst, Nixon's deputy attorney general, would jet into Mexico City and consult with Arpaio over conspiracies and undercover operations. And every now and again the Mexican attorney general dropped by for whiskey and pie. Arpaio sensed his stern father was impressed, even though he said nothing.

Ciro died in 1974 of pancreatic cancer. Arpaio told us he bought his father's headstone and buried Ciro between his two wives.

By then, Arpaio was stationed in Boston. He'd served in Chicago, Istanbul, Mexico City, San Antonio, Texas, and the Washington, D.C. metro area—close to two decades investigating conspiracies, going undercover, and managing regional operations. The Federal Bureau of Narcotics had morphed into the Federal Bureau of Narcotics and Dangerous Drugs, which had become the Drug Enforcement Agency, known as the DEA.

And with only four years left before he could retire, he chose Arizona as his last DEA post.

In 1978, when Joe Arpaio first stepped into the DEA office in downtown Phoenix, the city center was an archipelago of modest skyscrapers, old hotels, abandoned movie palaces, dive bars, pawn shops, rundown bungalows, and vacant dusty lots.

Maricopa County, which encompassed the Phoenix metro area, was larger than the state of New Jersey and home to about one and a half million people. The Arpaios, like so many newcomers, chose to live in the northeast valley. Ava eventually set up a travel agency in Scottsdale, one of the wealthiest suburbs ringing the city. Scottdale was known for its orderly wide streets, expensive shopping malls, resort hotels, art galleries, golf courses, and a western-themed downtown that evoked the cowboy movies Joe Arpaio had watched as a kid in Springfield, Massachusetts. Beyond the metro area, irrigated fields of pima cotton, sweet alfalfa, and orchards of fragrant orange and lemon trees gave way to the beige and pink sands of the Sonoran Desert.

As the new DEA agent in charge of the Phoenix region, Arpaio was challenged by two Mexican American colleagues who claimed he was a vindictive racist. Phil Jordan, who headed the Phoenix office of the DEA before Arpaio took over, told us he publicly criticized Arpaio for sabotaging relationships between Mexican and American drug enforcement agents. Jordan told us Arpaio subsequently initiated an internal DEA investigation. The probe centered on allegations that Jordan had leaked secret information to a journalist and had used the office copy machine to duplicate a cookbook for his girlfriend. Jordan was stripped of his rank and confined to a desk job. Months later, the DEA found the allegations had no merit. When we asked about this, Arpaio wouldn't deny he kickstarted the investigation, but he wouldn't confirm it, either.

Laura Garcia, the only Mexican American woman agent in the Phoenix DEA office, clashed with Arpaio after she called a city fire marshal about explosive chemicals carelessly and illegally stored in the DEA office in downtown Phoenix. Garcia was pregnant. She had reason to worry about chemicals in her workplace. *The Arizona Republic* learned of the chemicals and wrote a story about it. Garcia told us that following publication of the article, Arpaio seemed to go against her. In her memory, Arpaio disparaged her race and ethnicity during Monday morning meetings, sent her on useless and exhausting travel assignments, and ordered his underlings to go through her car and then write up an investigative report about her having two parking tickets.

"You should be home having babies and cooking tortillas," she remembered Arpaio telling her.

She toyed with suing Arpaio for harassment but told us she couldn't find a lawyer willing to take the case because Arpaio was a powerful man and she was just a woman. She told us she complained to the Equal Employment Opportunity Commission, but the agency didn't take her seriously. She left the DEA and moved to another state.

Arpaio remembered the conflict very differently years later. He strongly denied making the tortilla comment. He said that at the time he and Garcia had their differences, there were rumors that the DEA would be absorbed by the FBI. At a meeting he warned his staffers not to be caught "shacking up" because the FBI would have none of that kind of behavior, which prompted Garcia to file a complaint. The Equal Employment Opportunity Commission got in touch with him, and told him to "be careful." And then Garcia left the agency and life went on.

Joe Arpaio retired from the DEA when he was fifty, in the summer of 1982. He was feted at a dinner at the Mountain Shadows resort in Paradise Valley, a wealthy Phoenix suburb. *The Arizona Republic* sent its society reporter to cover the gala. Over roast beef, cooked carrots and broccoli, Senator Dennis DeConcini, a Democrat, praised Arpaio. "Other lavish tributes," the newspaper wrote, came from prosecutors, cops, FBI agents, and federal immigration officials.

He figured the world would forget him because that's what happened when people retired. No one would remember the kid from Springfield, the kid the bullies called *Wop, Dago,* and *Guinea,* the kid who didn't go to college but made it big anyway. No one would remember the undercover work, the conspiracies, the pimp with junkie whores, the ton of opium seized in Turkey, the border blockade called Operation Intercept. No one would remember Joe Arpaio.

Well, he wasn't ready to be forgotten. Not quite yet.

Arpaio rarely mentioned the decade he worked at his wife's business—the Starworld Travel Agency in Scottsdale, which she opened in 1980. Days after he retired from the DEA, in 1982, an ad appeared in *The Arizona Republic* announcing Arpaio's transition to Starworld Travel Agency. The ad included a photograph of Arpaio staring tentatively at the camera through aviator glasses, as if unsure of a travel agent's proper demeanor.

A Tough Cop... An Effective Sheriff

JOE ARPAIO
Republican for Sheriff

Front panel of Joe Arpaio's 1992 campaign brochure for his first Maricopa County Sheriff's Office race.

The Starworld Travel office, decorated with travel posters and furnished with large desks, sat in a Scottsdale strip mall near Handlebar J, a touristy Western steakhouse. Ava sold cruise and plane tickets, but Arpaio would not master his wife's computer, which held schedules, itineraries, and vouchers. Ava told us her husband helped with advertising and delivering tickets.

"I emptied the wastebasket, counted the money, got customers," Arpaio said.

After a few months at Starworld Travel, Arpaio ran for the Phoenix City Council. At the time he was a registered Democrat. On the stump, he suggested driving the homeless out of town or locking them up in jail. It foreshadowed what some viewed as his politically opportunistic treatment of vulnerable populations. Arpaio lost that election, and returned to the travel agency, where he hawked reservations for space flights that never happened.

After ten years at the travel agency, Arpaio ran for Maricopa County sheriff in 1992. He later said he had a "a hard time working for my wife so I ran for sheriff. You have my wife to thank for that." He defeated the incumbent Maricopa County sheriff, Tom Agnos, in the Republican primary. Agnos had mishandled an investigation of a shooting at a Buddhist temple that had killed nine people. By then, Maricopa County's population had surged to a little over two million. The United States Census reported "non-Hispanic Whites" accounted for about 77 percent of the county population, while Hispanic residents made up 16 percent. The remaining 7 percent were people defined as Black, American Indian, Asian and Pacific Islander, or Other.

As a politician, Arpaio connected with Silent Generation retirees who'd migrated to Maricopa County from the snowy American Midwest, with working-class white families, and with mainstream conservative voters who were fearful of a record-breaking violent crime wave that peaked in the United States in 1991.

Arpaio told voters who craved law and order that he would keep them safe. His drug enforcement career made him seem especially qualified to be the top lawman in the county. His campaign literature warned that current mismanagement of the sheriff's office "could be a source of wasted tax dollars because of multi-million dollar lawsuits." He promised to stay for just one term, should he be elected.

He was endorsed by the editorial board of *The Arizona Republic,* the county's most influential conservative voice. The newspaper insisted Arpaio could reform the "clownish sheriff's department."

Kathryn Kobor, who would remain an Arpaio loyalist for decades, told us she always voted for him because he was one of the few politicians who listened to people like her. She and her working-class family had moved to Arizona when she was four, in 1947. Her father, a former gas station attendant, at first had dug ditches in a Maricopa County citrus orchard. Eventually her parents got jobs at Motorola, a high-tech company and one of the state's largest employers. They'd prospered and purchased a home.

Like so many Phoenix old-timers, Kobor would recall the Phoenix of her youth as an idyllic oasis. Within the sleepy city, she waded in tree-shaded irrigation ditches and sipped lime Cokes in drugstore soda fountains. Kobor felt safe in Phoenix, even at night, when she and her sister walked home from the bus stop after taking in a movie. But as the years passed, Kobor no longer felt safe. Phoenix was a big city now, and Kobor trusted Arpaio to lock up criminals and restore law and order.

"I've followed Joe Arpaio for years and he's actually my hero," she later told us.

As an undercover narcotics agent, Arpaio had been adept at inventing new personas for himself. Now, as the newly elected sixty-year-old top lawman in Maricopa County, he transitioned from the role of travel agency co-owner who emptied wastebaskets to a tough Western sheriff. This new role—a heroic lawman who kept the town folk safe—comported with the Westerns he'd seen as a kid. Ava began calling him "Sheriff Joe."

"I think the first thing I said when we got awake in the morning was, 'Hi, Sheriff,'" she told us.

"So even in bed I'm working. Think of that," Arpaio replied.

His job requirements didn't always sync with his newly invented character. He couldn't gallop after horse thieves. He was tasked instead with administering a large agency. His main job involved oversight of county jails, where many inmates had been convicted of relatively minor offenses—like prostitution or drunk driving—and were serving sentences of less than a year. The remaining jail inmates awaited their day in court. Many were too poor to pay their bail. Some were ultimately convicted of serious crimes and served the remainder of their sentences in the state's prison system.

Besides administering the jails and transporting inmates from jail to court, Arpaio's department was expected to police county communities that did not have their own law enforcement agencies. But state law gave Arpaio vast power to keep the peace anywhere in the county, even in cities and towns with their own police forces that didn't particularly want him there. Arizona sheriffs are elected officers. While their budgets are controlled by county supervisors, sheriffs cannot be fired.

I'm the sheriff, Arpaio often said. No one tells this sheriff what to do.

2 The Valley Girl

1967–1997

In the early 1980s, as Joe Arpaio wrapped up his DEA career, a young California middle schooler was styling her feathered black hair like Farrah Fawcett's on the popular television show *Charlie's Angels*. Like her besties, Lydia Guzman dressed surfer-style—Hawaiian-style flowered shirts, seashell necklaces, and Vans slip-on canvas shoes. She went to a predominantly white Catholic school in the San Fernando Valley, and never thought much about her ethnicity.

Until one weekend beach trip, when Spanish-speaking Latino laborers whistled at Guzman's tall, blond, bikini-clad friend.

"I hate Mexicans," the girl said.

"But," she told Guzman, "you're different."

Guzman realized, for the first time, that she really was different, at least in the San Fernando Valley. She was an American citizen who spoke Spanish almost as effortlessly as she spoke English and felt at ease in Mexican immigrant, Mexican American, and white American cultures.

And that ability to navigate several different worlds with confidence and grace would shape her, many years later, into a high-profile civil rights activist who would draw both criticism and respect for her pragmatic approach in her relentless battles with a cycle of immigration restrictionism imposed in the first two decades of the twenty-first century and embraced by a man she would grow to detest—Sheriff Joe Arpaio.

Guzman, thirty-five years younger than Arpaio, was just as driven. Both Arpaio and Guzman had been shaped by strong-minded and strict immigrant parents. They both sought parental approval and didn't get it very often, so they looked for it elsewhere. Arpaio's hunger for approbation would lead him into the universe of the anti-immigrant alt-right. Guzman's need to be somebody took her in an entirely different direction.

Rafaela Avila, Guzman's mother, grew up in the Mexican state of Zacatecas. She told us she wasn't allowed to attend school past sixth grade because she was a girl. Instead, her father put her in charge of their village store when she was thirteen to test whether she had a talent for business. She proved her worth by turning an impressive profit in a short period.

As a teenager in the early 1960s, Avila fell in love with a handsome village boy who serenaded her outside the family home. For reasons Avila would never understand, her father forbade her from marrying the boy and dispatched his heartbroken daughter to Los Angeles, California to live with a female cousin.

Years later Lydia Guzman half-jokingly told us: "I guess we come from a long line of awful parents, including myself."

Avila told us she believed that her duty, as a daughter, was to obey her parents, even if doing so would bring years of sorrow. After travelling north, Avila stayed with her mother's relatives in Tijuana and eventually obtained a Mexican passport and tourist visa. She entered the United States legally at the San Ysidro, California port of entry.

Her visa expired but she stayed in Los Angeles, where she soon married Robert Guzman, a bilingual Mexican American. Their first child was a boy. Because Avila had an American husband and son, she had a good chance of qualifying for a green card that would give her legal permanent residency in the United States, along with a pathway to citizenship. Although she would eventually get her green card, she missed her first appointment at the Immigration and Naturalization Service office in Los Angeles, because on that day she gave birth to her second child, Lydia.

Avila told us she labored at low-paying, grueling jobs while her husband worked in a machine shop. Eventually, she hired on with a poultry processing plant, quartering iced chicken carcasses on an assembly line. She found it dangerous and disgusting, but it paid well. She hoped to save enough money to buy a house and perhaps one day own a restaurant.

She was pregnant with her third child when the cutting machine at the poultry plant sliced off her right index finger. She wept over losing the finger, but told us she hired a lawyer who got her a two-thousand-dollar workers' compensation award.

Avila used her severed finger payout to kick-start her successful career as a landlord and entrepreneur. She pooled the payout with money she borrowed from relatives, bought four small houses on a weedy lot in Glendale, just north of Los Angeles, and cleaned them up. She lived in one house with her family and rented out the others. Avila and her children would forever be grateful for the workers' compensation seed money that set them on the path to the middle class. Guzman was constantly surprised by her mother's grit. "She had that whole American Dream thing going on in her head," Guzman told us. "Don't take 'no' as a final answer. Never let them say 'no' to you."

Home life was chaotic and tense. Avila and Robert Guzman didn't get along but went on to have three more children. Guzman tried to relieve the household stress by playing the family clown.

As a child, Guzman was largely oblivious to racism, although once she and her siblings were blamed for a lice outbreak at their private Catholic grade school, which was attended mostly by white students.

When Guzman started middle school, the family moved to a suburban bedroom community in the San Fernando Valley. Here, Guzman picked up the pervasive lilting "Valley Girl" accent to fit in with her classmates.

Toh-tah-ly *awe*-some!

Guzman's parents split up shortly after she finished middle school.

The separation took a financial toll on the family at first. By then Avila had bought a former drive-in restaurant called Jerry's Orange. The menu included American hamburgers and Mexican enchiladas. Avila was proud of the place, but she sold it after the split-up. And she could no longer afford Catholic school tuition. She moved the kids around, and they bounced from one public high school to another. Finally, in 1985, Avila moved to Pomona, California. Guzman enrolled in Pomona High School for her senior year.

Unlike Guzman's prior schools, Pomona was more ethnically diverse. Guzman changed her style to fit in with the other Latina students. She wore hoop earrings and sprayed her hair with Aqua Net. She lined her large brown eyes with a thin black Sharpie marker and drew in precise arched eyebrows with a different Sharpie meant for marking china.

Her favorite class was Civics, where she learned about the Watergate scandal that led to President Richard Nixon's resignation. "No man is above the law," her teacher said. Understanding that slice of American history would always feed Guzman's optimism as an activist in Arizona, even in the darkest times. From the Watergate narrative, she learned that if there was corruption, it would be exposed. If there was wrongdoing, justice would ultimately prevail.

And she sensed it was her calling to be a part of that process.

Guzman wrote for the school paper and dreamed of becoming a journalist. As a high-school senior, Guzman and other Latino teens helped canvas Latino neighborhoods to register voters.

She volunteered on the city council campaign of Nell Soto, a longtime Democratic activist. Growing up, Soto had felt discriminated against as a Mexican American even though her family had lived in Pomona for generations. She hoped to become the first Hispanic woman on Pomona's council. In the 1987 election, Pomona's black and Latino voters turned out in such force that Soto won decisively. Guzman, still a teen, was inspired by Soto's victory.

As a young adult, Guzman would see that, thanks in part to earlier voter registration efforts, Pomona voters approved city council districts that enabled more equitable elections. Minority candidates won more seats in the years that followed. Guzman took it as a sign that empowering voters worked.

Guzman wanted to attend college to study journalism. But she didn't believe her mother, who prided herself on what she had accomplished with only a sixth-grade education, would understand. In Guzman's memory, recruiters from California State University at San Bernardino popped by Avila's house and asked her to cosign student loans, but Avila refused. Guzman told us her mother had been influenced by a friend who warned her Guzman might drop out and get married and leave Avila with the tuition bills. Avila had a different memory—she told us at the time she didn't own a house to serve as collateral for loans to pay Guzman's tuition. She didn't know if her daughter understood her financial position.

As Guzman walked the college recruiters out, she was crushed, and embarrassed for wasting their time. For years, the lost opportunity would bring tears to her eyes. She would tell herself: "I could have become someone."

Avila wasn't rich, but like many immigrants, she was driven to work hard. After her divorce, Avila regained her financial footing by buying four used pickup trucks in Mexico and starting a small import-export business. The trucks hauled Mexican crafts and pottery up to the United States and returned to Mexico loaded up with Jordache jeans, electronics, and linens.

Guzman felt her industrious mother wanted her to make money, too, and forget the unpaid community work that Guzman was drawn to. Avila told us she didn't mean to convey disapproval—she was proud of her daughter's civic engagement.

"In a way I admired her, in a way I resented her," Guzman told us.

Guzman tried to stay away from her father to avoid upsetting her mother. But occasionally, the father and daughter stole away for visits. Over Chinese food one night, her dad passed on lessons he'd learned during his brief involvement in the Chicano student movement in the 1960s, which had left him disenchanted with the efficacy of marches and protests. "It is one thing to go out there and yell," he counseled his daughter, but he had come to believe change was effectuated "inside the walls of the building—not outside." From then on, Guzman sought ways to get inside the building, to work within the system. It's where she would feel most comfortable. And effective.

When Guzman was twenty-two, her first daughter, Ashley, was born. But the relationship with Ashley's father didn't work out. A few years later, she married a Los Angeles Police Department officer.

The two bought a three-bedroom house in Palmdale, a desert bedroom community separated from Los Angeles by the San Gabriel Mountains. Inspired by the changes she had seen in Pomona, Guzman decided the following spring, at the age of twenty-six, that she wanted to represent

Latino residents as a Palmdale city councilwoman. Her husband ran for mayor. They both lost.

Before Guzman could think about her next political move, immigration restrictionists helped get a voter initiative called Proposition 187 on the 1994 California ballot. The proposed law asserted, among other things, that Californians suffered "economic hardship" and "personal injury and damage caused by the criminal conduct of illegal aliens in this state."

The initiative promised to ban unauthorized immigrants in California from accessing state-funded public services, including education and non-emergency healthcare. It required state employees to inform federal immigration authorities about unauthorized immigrants who applied for benefits. This included undocumented immigrant parents who registered their children, who also lacked papers, for school. The proposed law also required local law enforcement to "fully cooperate" with federal immigration officials. The policy proposals embedded in Proposition 187 would become a template for future restrictionist laws in other states, including Arizona.

"They were creating fear and hate, and a narrative that immigrants were here to drain the system," Guzman would recall years later.

"That was the biggest insult."

A well-organized restrictionist nonprofit, the Federation for American Immigration Reform, widely known as FAIR, was key in crafting and disseminating messaging that portrayed undocumented immigrants as invaders who preyed on American citizens by taking their jobs and consuming services that raised their taxes. It was a recycled message from the 1920s, when politicians influenced by the eugenics movement used the immigrants-as-invaders theory to change the nation's immigration policy.

The founder of FAIR, a Michigan eye doctor named John Tanton, sought to dramatically reduce immigration into the United States. Under the guise of environmentalism and population control, he and his followers revived the eugenically influenced anti-immigrant sentiments of the early twentieth century, earning the name "restrictionists." Tanton didn't deny his affiliations with modern eugenicists and white supremacists, and didn't apologize for it, either. He simply claimed his cause needed to build coalitions to succeed.

In 1986, seven years after Tanton founded FAIR, millions of unauthorized immigrants got green cards thanks to a new immigration law signed by President Ronald Reagan. That same year, Tanton wrote a memo to attendees of a secret restrictionist conference. He pointed to multicultural California as a doomed state. "In California of 2030, the non-Hispanic Whites and Asians will own the property, have the good jobs and education, speak one language and be mostly Protestant and "other." The Blacks and Hispanics will have the poor jobs, will lack education, own little property, speak another language and will be mainly Catholic. Will there be strength in this diversity? Or will this prove a social and political San Andreas Fault?"

Two years later, in 1988, Tanton's memo, which painted Mexican immigrants and their American citizen progeny as over-breeders and inferior to whites, was leaked to *The Arizona Republic*. The newspaper printed excerpts. At the time, Tanton, through a nonprofit called US English, was spearheading and funding Official English, a ballot measure to make English the official language of Arizona. Under the proposed initiative, members of the public could sue state employees if they heard them speaking another language on the job—like Spanish.

But Tanton's memo, widely viewed as racist, provoked such outrage in Arizona that Tanton claimed to step down from his leadership post. Immediately after the memo was printed, supporters of Official English, including conservative activist Linda Chavez and celebrity journalist Walter Cronkite, distanced themselves from Tanton, who seemed unconcerned about being branded a racist. He told *The Arizona Republic* it only amounted to personal attack and a "concession" that he had won the argument.

A small margin of Arizona voters—about a half of 1 percent—passed the Official English ballot measure.

Despite the pushback, Tanton continued to peddle his eugenically-themed rhetoric. "I've come to the point of view that for European-American society and culture to persist requires a European-American majority, and a clear one at that," he wrote in 1993. Under Tanton's leadership, FAIR spun off or incubated like-minded think tanks and nonprofits, including NumbersUSA, the Immigration Reform Law Institute, US Inc., and the Center for Immigration Studies. Each entity promoted immigration restrictionism for an intended audience. FAIR was aggressive and political, pushing for changes in immigration laws through grassroots activism and lobbying, while the Center for Immigration Studies marketed the same agenda in public policy reports.

As Californians debated Proposition 187, FAIR bankrolled sixty-second radio spots that claimed the proposition's opponents wanted "an open-ended commitment to pay for services that like a magnet attract a never-ending flow of illegal immigrants to our state."

"If you hear something over and over again, people tend to believe it. You know, if you tell the lie repeatedly people will believe it," Guzman told us. She viewed Proposition 187 as a direct assault on California's entire Latino population, and that included American citizens like her. She would never forget that California's Republican governor Pete Wilson championed Proposition 187 in his re-election bid.

Shortly before the November election, Guzman marched with about seventy thousand people in Los Angeles to protest Proposition 187. The crowd was so massive Guzman couldn't hear the speeches. But she was delighted to learn musicians had played a mariachi rendition of "The Star-Spangled Banner." It was one of the largest marches in city history.

Then, on Election Day, a stunning 59 percent of California voters approved Proposition 187.

From that point forward, Guzman saw the world differently. She felt her community was up against a powerful movement that was swaying voters toward anti-immigrant and anti-Latino sentiment. And those forces just might succeed, if Latino Americans got too comfortable and didn't fight back.

Immediately, the Mexican American Legal Defense and Educational Fund and the American Civil Liberties Union sued to prevent the new law from taking effect, calling it unconstitutional. Their court challenge succeeded.

This gave Guzman faith in the courts. Civil rights litigation could stop anti-Latino policies in their tracks. She would cling to that lesson years later, hang on to it when nothing seemed to go right for the Latino community in Phoenix.

Guzman wanted to do her part to prevent similar measures from ever happening again. She knew thousands of Southern California immigrants were eligible to naturalize, thanks to Reagan's 1986 amnesty. She joined a new coalition of immigrant rights groups who helped Spanish-speaking immigrants apply for citizenship in order to vote. Guzman threw herself into naturalizing as many of these immigrants as she could in Palmdale.

The backlash to the defunct Proposition 187 would eventually be credited with catalyzing Latino civic engagement in California and making the state a Democratic stronghold.

By 1997, Guzman and her husband had a toddler son, James. Work obligations and financial stresses had tested their marriage. Eventually, they couldn't pay the mortgage for their Palmdale home and lost it. Not long after, they split up.

At the time, Avila had already settled in Maricopa County, where she bought and fixed up rental units and flipped houses. Guzman moved from California with her two children to be with her mother. She resolved to make a fresh start in a new city, in a new state.

Just a few weeks before Guzman arrived in Arizona in August 1997, a five-day immigration raid had taken place in Chandler, a Phoenix suburb. Up until then, Chandler was best known for a giant Christmas tree made entirely of tumbleweeds.

Now it was known for terror.

Chandler police had teamed up with Border Patrol agents and raided heavily Latino neighborhoods in the downtown area, which was slated for redevelopment. They demanded immigration papers from men, women, and children who appeared to be of Latino heritage.

Four hundred thirty-two undocumented immigrants were arrested in the sweep. Police records didn't say how many American citizens or foreign nationals with green cards or valid visas were detained.

A few months after the crackdown, Arizona Attorney General Grant Woods, a Republican, wrote in a published report: "Numerous American citizens and legal residents were stopped on multiple occasions some within short distances for no other apparent reason than their skin color or Mexican appearance or use of the Spanish language." By targeting Latinos, the attorney general concluded, police and immigration authorities had engaged in unconstitutional policing.

Holding her son, James, Lydia Guzman stands with daughter, Ashley, in the driveway of their home in Palmdale, California in the mid 1990s. (Courtesy Lydia Guzman)

Guzman had come to the same conclusion. After settling in at Avila's house, she loaded her son, James, into a car seat and drove to central Phoenix to the office of the Mexican American Legal Defense and Educational Fund, known as MALDEF.

She was a beautiful young woman, with a thick head of shoulder-length black hair and large dark eyes. With James in tow, she marched into the MALDEF office, introducing herself politely. "I'm here to help," she said.

She enrolled in the nonprofit's leadership workshop and soon made friends with key community leaders. Among them was a lawyer named Danny Ortega, who, along with lawyer Stephen Montoya and others had battled Tanton's FAIR and Official English in the 1980s. In Ortega's view, the new law was "a full scale attack" on the Latino community. Ortega and Montoya were victorious when the Arizona Supreme Court eventually struck down Official English because it violated the constitutional rights of state workers and people who used state services.

Guzman attended Ortega's workshop on challenging racism, titled *¡Coraje!* The Spanish word meant, to Ortega, heartfelt anger. "It was not just a matter of politics—it was a matter of passion to take the necessary risks to fight this ugly animal," Ortega told us years later.

It didn't take long before Guzman gave her own workshop, in which she shared lessons learned from the epic Proposition 187 fight in California. Racists could target Arizona with more ugly voter initiatives and laws, she warned. Activists needed to register Latino voters to defend against them. She titled her presentation "Vienen Tiempos Duros."

Hard times are coming.

Joe Arpaio hadn't been sheriff long when he met Lisa Allen, who was thirty-six years old and reported for a CBS affiliate in Phoenix. He hired her as she was quietly casting about for a job after she was told she was getting too old to report on television.

She didn't look old, though. She was well put together, with a bubble of blond hair, makeup that accentuated her large eyes and lips, and bright outfits that made people notice when she walked by. On one of her first days at the sheriff's office, Allen wore an uncharacteristically conservative getup—slacks and a simple top—and toned down her blush, lipstick and eyeliner, just like the other women in the sheriff's office.

"What happened to you?" Arpaio asked her. "When I hired you, you had makeup on. You look different. Just be yourself. Don't worry about trying to fit in with these people."

She had the skills to deliver what he craved: the attention of journalists, which he had begun seeking three decades before, after his father complimented him on being in the newspaper.

Allen told us she understood Arpaio wanted to be the "star" and it was her job to make him one. In the 1990s, Arpaio and Allen hatched one "news story" after another. First, in 1993, Arpaio erected "Tent City"

—a warren of thirty-seven frayed Korean War era surplus tents that housed sentenced inmates. At Allen's suggestion, a large blinking neon VACANCY sign was affixed to a water tower on stilts that hovered over the tents. The sign winked at tented inmates, who shivered during cold winter nights and sat listlessly on their cots, their necks wrapped in wet towels, on baking summer afternoons. By 1997, more than 560 male inmates lived in Tent City. They shared a total of eight showers, eleven sinks, eight permanent toilets, and twelve portable toilets.

Arpaio often took journalists, politicians, and interested members of the public on tours of the Tent City jail. Reporters sometimes asked about the inmates' obvious misery, and Arpaio would frown, explain he didn't make the law, he only enforced it, and criminals got exactly what they deserved. He seemed to like these televised combative exchanges and controversies that he could control. He told us it didn't matter if he got good or bad publicity. The end result was that press interviews enabled him to talk directly to "the people"—his base of voters who liked his tough approach toward inmates.

If local reporters became fatigued by one jailhouse story, Allen and Arpaio came up with another one. Everything merited a story, including moments when Arpaio banned jailhouse coffee, cigarettes, and salt and pepper. Journalists reported how Arpaio served inmates aged green bologna for lunch, cut daily inmate meals down to two, then served unseasoned vegetable proteins instead of meat. He initiated chain gangs as a disciplinary option and invited reporters to photograph queues of inmates in clownish striped prison chinos, connected to one another by leg chains, standing on sidewalks near busy streets spearing litter into plastic bags.

Arizona law allowed county sheriffs to have volunteer posse groups. Arpaio turned the posse into a theatrical army, sending mostly middle-aged, white participants on missions that included chasing down prostitutes or parading with holstered pistols through shopping-mall parking lots.

Arpaio's greatest stunt may have been requiring inmates to wear pink underwear. The boxer shorts, in particular, were such a hit with fans that Arpaio autographed them at charity auctions.

His popularity soared. In 1996, *The Arizona Republic* called the sheriff a "GOP kingmaker" as Republican candidates vied for his endorsement that election year. His approval rating a few months later, the newspaper reported, was "a stratospheric eighty-five percent."

But the GOP kingmaker didn't always efficiently manage his agency. Inside the sheriff's office, some former staffers would say, the culture was toxic. Underlings jostled for Arpaio's approval. Even members of the media relations office, which Arpaio valued highly because staffers there got him on television, were not spared. In the early years of his administration, Arpaio exacerbated animosity between two prized public information officers, Lisa Allen and Deputy John Kleinheinz.

Kleinheinz told us he despised Allen's jailhouse publicity stunts, because he felt they cheapened the reputation of the sheriff's office. And Allen, years later, would paint Kleinheinz as duplicitous and opportunistic.

Once the two quarreled so bitterly Allen wept. (Neither would remember what they fought about.) Kleinheinz hightailed it down to Arpaio's office. He told the sheriff he'd made Allen cry.

Within a few minutes Arpaio's phone rang. The sheriff picked up, and pressed the speaker button. It was Allen. She didn't know Kleinheinz was in Arpaio's office, listening on the speaker phone as she told Arpaio about their fight. And she didn't know that as she told her story, Kleinheinz watched Arpaio making faces mocking her.

Arpaio eventually converted a corner of his office into a television-ready set. He set his desk in front of a backdrop decorated with his law enforcement memorabilia, including the nightstick from his beat cop days in Washington, D.C. On one side of the desk, an enormous rustic sign read:

TENT CITY, VACANCY, TODAY HARD LABOR—HAIRCUTS—BOLOGNA SANDWICHES—35 CENT MEALS—EDUCATIONAL TV—PINK UNDERWEAR—HIGH OF 122 DEGREES—DRUG TESTING. NO SMOKING—MOVIES—COFFEE—GIRLIE MAGAZINES. IF YOU DON'T WANT TO DO THE TIME DON'T DO THE CRIME.

Arpaio kept a tally of his media interviews. He instructed staffers to collect all newspaper and magazine articles about him, along with videos of his television appearances. Clippings and videos were stashed in cardboard boxes, which Arpaio locked in his private closet.

"I don't see anybody dying around here," Joe Arpaio told Morley Safer, a reporter for the CBS program *60 Minutes*, during a tour of Tent City.

During the interview, he seemed concerned with his weight, and told Safer he had undergone "fifty enemas" and was on a brutal low calorie diet. He complained that a local cartoonist had drawn him as a "five hundred pound sheriff."

It was 2001, and Arpaio was wildly popular. "If I was appointed I would have been fired seven years ago," Arpaio told Safer, referring to his unfettered power as an elected sheriff. "Because in government the famous word is 'You can't do this. You can't do that. We're going to be sued.'" But Arpaio *was* facing legal troubles. Consultants for the federal justice department were investigating Arpaio's disorganized, understaffed jails. Inmates were subjected to excessive use of force, one consultant said. Another found lack of adequate monitoring of inmates in restraint chairs and noted a high number of inmate grievances about violent guards. Private lawsuits filed by families of inmates who had died in restraint chairs or were beaten to death by guards or other inmates were starting to make news.

International and national journalists often failed to report on the controversies surrounding the jails and the documented suffering of people confined in them. It was difficult for reporters to resist the weird, grandfatherly charms of the man who had come to be known as America's Toughest Sheriff.

In the early 2000s, Joe Arpaio regularly showed up at El Portal, a Mexican restaurant that drew a robust lunch crowd of powerbrokers, politicos, and journalists. Furnished with muscular, dark wooden tables and chairs, the eatery was decorated with portraits of civil rights heroes like Cesar Chavez and Martin Luther King, Jr., and was famous for its homemade cocido, a Mexican stew made of beef rib, vegetables, and potatoes. It was Arpaio's favorite meal there.

Mary Rose Garrido Wilcox co-owned the restaurant with her husband, Earl. At the time, Wilcox was also the only Latina, the only woman, and the only Democrat sitting on the Maricopa County Board of Supervisors, which oversaw Arpaio's budget.

Both Arpaio and Wilcox had won their first county elections in 1992. They were sworn into county government together. They were friends. Early on, Arpaio gave Wilcox an unusual compliment.

"You look so much like my mother in her pictures," Wilcox would remember Arpaio told her. "I could never get mad at you."

Earl Wilcox, a tall man who loved basketball, had grown up in the same south Phoenix barrio where El Portal was situated. As a neighborhood activist, he ran a basketball gym for kids. Sometimes, Arpaio dropped by the gym and brought the kids hot dogs from the jailhouse kitchens.

"He would come and we would highlight him with the kids," Mary Rose Wilcox told us. "I remember one time he even made a three-point shot from mid-court."

Wilcox appreciated Arpaio's vows to keep her heavily Latino district safe. And she respected Arpaio for not wanting to waste law enforcement dollars by apprehending undocumented immigrants and handing them over to federal officials for deportation.

But then, after fifteen years of friendship, Arpaio would change. He would begin targeting unauthorized immigrants, instead of protecting them. His relationship with Wilcox, his Mexican American political ally who looked so much like his mother, would turn into a sour feud. It would end with what Wilcox would view as a retaliatory law enforcement investigation and a baseless criminal indictment.

Wilcox would recognize Arpaio's immigration crusade as the latest iteration of the cyclical persecution of Mexicans, and people presumed to be Mexican, that had plagued Arizona for generations.

Close to a century and half before Joe Arpaio was elected sheriff, the roots of anti-Mexican animus had been planted in Arizona. In 1848, during the Mexican-American War, the United States crushed Mexico and assumed ownership of huge swaths of Mexico's northern provinces—parts of Alta California and territory that would become Utah, Colorado, Nevada, New Mexico, Texas, Wyoming, and Arizona. This victory prompted thousands of land-hungry Americans to settle in what was once Mexico. They pushed Mexicans already living there aside, and some took over their properties and businesses.

Tensions escalated in Arizona Territory in the 1860s, after settlers in southern Arizona joined the Confederate States of America. After the

Confederacy lost the Civil War, its sympathizers stayed on in Arizona, and would help shape the state's politics and prejudices.

The United States government wanted to open up land for new settlers, so it sicced former Civil War soldiers on Native Americans in Arizona Territory, slaughtering many and driving others into reservations. As white settlers confined Native Americans to reservations, they knew they still had to contend with another group they viewed as problematic—"Mexicans."

In a popular 1878 guidebook for prospective Arizona settlers, writer Richard Hinton described "Mexicans" as "quite primitive" and "patient and industrious, despite their shiftless way."

"Mr. Mexican is picturesque, indeed, as his swarth face and rolling eye, keen, yet slumberous of aspect, looks furtively at you from beneath the broad and dirty sombrero, while he leans lazily against a dirty adobe wall wrapped in his dirtier serape," Hinton wrote.

Newcomers poured into Arizona, including Southerners who helped settle Maricopa County, especially a small farming community they called "Phoenix." The tiny town was named after the mythical bird that was burned alive, only to be reborn from its own ashes. Since Phoenix sprouted atop long abandoned Native American settlements, the name made perfect sense. But to some former confederates in Arizona, "Phoenix" meant a lot more. It was post–Civil War code for the rebirth of the South and all it had stood for.

By 1870, 240 people lived in Phoenix. About half were considered "Mexicans" at that time. In territorial Arizona, recent immigrants from Mexico and Mexican American citizens were both dubbed "Mexicans." Some of these "Mexicans" had been born in the territory when it was still part of Mexico. These new Mexican American citizens had voting rights and were legally considered white.

But whites moving into the new territory from other parts of the United States did not view their fellow Mexican American citizens as equals. So another word slithered into the race-based lexicon of the American Southwest—"Anglo." Anglo was a synonym for "white" that excluded "Mexicans." A racial caste system developed in Arizona. First came whites, then "Mexicans" of any category, then on the lowest tier, Native Americans, African Americans, and immigrants from Asia.

In 1912, the year Arizona became a state, stories in *The Arizona Republican* newspaper, the predecessor to the *Arizona Republic*, published articles reflecting how many Anglos in the town viewed all "Mexicans"—as knife-flashing drunks, attackers of white women, thieves, desperados, killers, and radical revolutionaries.

That same year, Arizona's first state legislature passed a law requiring all would-be voters to pass a literacy test by reading the United States Constitution in English. The test disenfranchised many Mexican American citizens.

Anglos in Phoenix created local zoning restrictions that forced "Mexicans" and other people of color to live in segregated neighborhoods. These were almost always located in undesirable areas, like south Phoenix. Here, after violent rainstorms, the Salt River could bolt out of its banks, unleashing brown floods capable of washing away trees, crops, homes, horses, and people.

Alfredo Gutierrez was born into the anti-"Mexican" climate in 1945. Miami, Arizona, some eighty miles east of Phoenix, clung to shrubby hills overlooking the Inspiration copper mine, an enormous open-pit excavation with dusty, yawning jaws. Gutierrez lived with his family in the segregated mining town. His childhood was shrouded by an unspoken fear of deportation, even though everyone in his immediate family was an American citizen.

But American citizenship offered no protection from deportation, Gutierrez knew. His father, Samuel, was among more than one million Mexican immigrants and Americans of Mexican heritage deported to Mexico in the early 1930s, during the Great Depression. President Herbert Hoover assured voters the deportations cleared the way for "real Americans" to get jobs.

Samuel returned to Miami to work in the mines in the early 1940s. He became a union activist, part of a gutsy labor movement in Arizona copper mining towns that was rooted in early twentieth century radicalism.

It just didn't feel safe to Samuel in Miami. He was on edge. The deportation cycles kept coming. About a decade after Samuel returned to his home, in 1954, President Dwight Eisenhower's administration launched Operation Wetback. Named after the popular slur for Mexican border

Samuel Gutierrez (top row, left, closest to sign) as a teenager with a group of "Mexican" youth who participated in activities at the segregated YMCA in Miami, Arizona in 1928. Samuel was deported a few years later. Alejandro Trujillo (left, standing) was the director of the "Mexican YMCA." (Courtesy Dr. Christine Marin, Lupe Trujillo Marin's collection)

crossers, the deportation program was meant to mollify Americans who complained that unauthorized Mexicans took their jobs during an economic downturn. It was also intended to pressure Texas farmers to stop hiring undocumented Mexican workers and contract instead for laborers from Mexico through the Bracero (manual labor) work visa program. The Eisenhower administration claimed it rounded up and deported more than one million unauthorized Mexican nationals.

This time around, Samuel's union, the International Union of Mine, Mill and Smelter Workers, known as Mine Mill, helped the so-called "Mexican" miners resist the deportations. There was a system in place— lookouts spotted law enforcement vehicles winding up the hill and alerted town criers who ran through the canyons, passing along the warning.

Alfredo Gutierrez's worldview—and his future activism fighting restrictionism in Maricopa County—were shaped by his growing up in a mining town with a strong union. He believed labor unions were important allies in civil rights battles, because he'd seen his father's union dismantle segregation, piece by piece. The union helped desegregate his school, where once teachers taped his mouth if he spoke Spanish. The union even forced the desegregation of the YMCA swimming pool.

And importantly, he told us, the union secured equal wages for Mexicans, who'd always earned less than Anglos and European immigrants.

Animated, with a runner's wiry build and thick curly hair, Gutierrez grew up to be a nimble thinker and fearless, eloquent speaker. After serving in the Vietnam War, marrying, and working briefly at the mine, Gutierrez enrolled at Arizona State University.

Gutierrez's arrival at ASU in the 1960s coincided with a surge in Chicano civil rights activism throughout the American Southwest. He connected at the university with other young people of Mexican heritage who had grown up in copper mining towns. Many, like Gutierrez, had experienced similar discrimination as Mexican immigrants, and he closely identified with them. They too had seen how strong unions made good partners in battles for equity and social change. They called themselves Chicanos and joined the movement of the same name. Their leadership would influence civil rights activism in Arizona for decades, and would shape the resistance that rose up against Joe Arpaio and Arizona's restrictionist immigration laws in the twenty-first century.

Gutierrez, like most Mexican American students he met at ASU, felt uncomfortable at the sprawling, predominantly white campus in Tempe. Many of his friends were the first in the family to attend college. "Almost all of us were on some form of financial aid and had pretty serious economic woes," he told us.

Chicano students often gathered in the shade of a large tree near the main library. That's where Gutierrez met Mary Rose Garrido, the future Mary Rose Wilcox, who would serve Joe Arpaio cocido at her restaurant before their ugly falling out.

She and Gutierrez became fast friends. She'd grown up in Superior, another Arizona copper mining town. She had seen the Mine Mill union win better health benefits and safety regulations for the majority Mexican American workers.

Garrido shared Gutierrez's sense that discrimination against Mexicans and Mexican Americans alike was more accepted in Maricopa County than in their hometowns near the mines. In Phoenix, some restaurant owners still advertised their burritos and enchiladas as "Spanish food," operating under the theory that locals would not eat Mexican food. Mexicans still lived in segregated neighborhoods. Mexican American kids were still tracked into high school vocational education classes instead of college prep courses. The ASU students from mining towns vowed to lead a movement to oppose this status quo.

In part to fight this systemic racism, they founded the Mexican American Student Organization, which later became the ASU chapter of the national Movimiento Estudiantil Chicanx de Aztlán, or MEChA.

Gutierrez visited Phoenix Union High School—a large downtown school—to protest the school's policies of guiding Mexican American students into vocational education classes. That's where he met Danny Ortega, a friendly scholar and athlete who would grow up to be a prominent civil rights attorney and Lydia Guzman's friend and mentor. Before he met Gutierrez, Ortega hadn't paid much attention to civil rights. He just wanted his teachers to like him and his Mexican immigrant parents to be proud of him.

"I was like Mr. Mainstream," Ortega told us.

Gutierrez and his fellow student activists opened Ortega's eyes to inequities in his high school—the dearth of teachers and administrators of color, the aging buildings, tracking that excluded Mexican American kids from college preparatory classes and the out-of-date learning materials. Ortega hadn't thought about those things before. Meeting Alfredo Gutierrez, who "represented a radical Chicano to the utmost" profoundly influenced Ortega.

As his last year at Phoenix Union drew to a close, Ortega was selected to give a commencement address. Administrators previewed his speech and approved it. But Ortega abandoned that draft. Instead, with the guidance of Gutierrez and other Chicano activists, he delivered a scolding oration that hammered Phoenix Union's unfair educational system for minorities.

Danny Ortega (at podium) was president of the MEChA chapter at Arizona
State University in the early 1970s. Sonny Najera (behind from left) sits
with Joe Eddie Lopez, who was a Maricopa County supervisor at the time.
(Courtesy Rose Marie Lopez and Joe Eddie Lopez and the Chicano/a Research
Collection at Arizona State University)

"The first to war. The last to get jobs. Dilapidated buildings. I mean, I did it all," Ortega told us.

Ortega regretted deceiving school administrators. But the bold move signified to him that "whatever it took to get our message out to create change, we were willing to do." He enrolled at ASU and became MEChA president.

Gutierrez left ASU before graduating and dove into off-campus activism. He continued pushing for reform of educational policies in Arizona schools. He spoke out against the Arizona Republican governor, Jack Williams, who signed a law preventing the farmworker union activist Cesar Chavez from organizing strikes during harvest season. Gutierrez witnessed Chavez fasting in a Phoenix church in protest of the anti-strike law, and got to know Antonio Bustamante, who was a student at Stanford University. The former Douglas High School football player had lived through Operation Intercept, the chaotic 1969 border blockade engineered in part by Joe Arpaio. Now Bustamante was Cesar Chavez's bodyguard.

In 1972, when he was twenty-six, Gutierrez was elected as a Democrat to the Arizona Senate. Two years later, Gutierrez became senate majority leader. Burton Barr, the conservative Republican house majority leader, approached Gutierrez one day at the Arizona capitol and said, "You are one of the smartest Mexicans I have ever met."

"No, no, I am one of the smartest guys you ever met," Gutierrez shot back.

He knew some Arizona politicos thought of him as a Mexican, in the old-fashioned way. As an inferior. "I think that people were thinking terrible things, but they didn't dare say it because their bill would be dead," Gutierrez told us.

"Hell, yeah. I knew what was going on behind my back."

He clashed with his mentor, Cesar Chavez, in the 1970s. Gutierrez heard from Chicano friends that Chavez sympathizers were beating up undocumented immigrants at the Arizona-Mexico border, hoping to discourage the migrants from entering the United States and possibly scabbing for lettuce growers in the midst of contract negotiations between growers and the United Farm Workers Union.

The thought of physically attacking undocumented Mexicans dredged up visceral rage in Gutierrez. As the son of an unfairly deported father, he

Antonio Bustamante (left) and Cesar Chavez at the United Farm Workers headquarters in La Paz, California on November 8, 1973. Bustamante served on Chavez's road
staff and was his bodyguard for five months. (Courtesy Antonio Bustamante)

felt a strong bond with Mexican immigrants. But in the 1960s and 70s,
Gutierrez understood not all Mexican Americans felt the same way.

"I think it is fair to say across the board that the families who had been
deported were very supportive of those who were coming over," Gutierrez
told us. "I think where the distinction arises is with the second, third,
fourth generation Latinos who viewed those who were coming across as
endangering their place, endangering their ascendency into white
American equality. There were a number of very eloquent leaders who
made that point, Cesar amongst them."

In his memory, Gutierrez asked Chavez over lunch at a Phoenix hotel to
stop his sympathizers from beating up undocumented immigrants at the
border. Chavez at first denied there were border beatings. Then he scolded
Gutierrez. Chavez told him scab migrant workers jeopardized the progress

of his fair-wage negotiations with growers. Chavez stormed out of the restaurant. Ultimately, Gutierrez would feel he won the argument after Chavez publicly supported amnesty for people who were undocumented.

"Cesar had gone from being virulently anti-immigrant to having an epiphany and changing completely—he did a one-eighty," Gutierrez told us.

As Alfredo Gutierrez was making a name for himself in the Arizona Senate, Danny Ortega graduated from the College of Law at ASU. It was 1977. He was twenty-five. He got his first job at Community Legal Services, a legal aid firm, where he defended low income Mexican American and immigrant clients facing evictions.

Ortega's new colleagues told him about police clashes with Mexican migrant farmworkers in Peoria, a small agricultural town some thirteen miles northwest of Phoenix. At the time, some farmworkers were trying to organize unions, and tensions ran high in the small town.

A Mexican farmworker with a green card, which gave him permanent legal residency in the United States, told Ortega's colleagues a troubling story. The farmworker recalled he and three friends had driven to the Peoria post office to pick up mail. They'd just started to drive home when they were pulled over by a Peoria police officer.

The officer asked for immigration papers. When two backseat passengers had none, the officer hauled them to the Peoria jail.

The farmworkers said it happened again and again. Police stopped and questioned immigrants in grocery store parking lots and arrested those suspected of being undocumented. On one night, police cars roared through the orchard where farmworkers slept, red lights flashing and sirens wailing. Farmworkers scrambled up orange trees and hid. "Run like rabbits!" a cop yelled from his police car.

Once farmworkers wound up in the Peoria jail, police turned them over to Border Patrol to be deported. They were never charged with crimes. But the Peoria police chief figured that because it is a federal misdemeanor to cross the border without papers, immigrants without papers must be criminals.

"People were being stopped because they were brown, driving while brown," Ortega told us.

The situation upset Ortega for two reasons. First, his father had been a farmworker, so he took it personally. And second, he understood that even as an American citizen with a law degree, as long as his black hair and brown skin could subject him to extra police scrutiny, he would never truly have equal rights in the United States. He wouldn't be equal if racial profiling was allowed. No Mexican American would.

"We saw this not only as an attack on the undocumented community. But we saw it as an attack on us, simply because of the features of our skin and our hair color and our language," Ortega told us.

In 1978, Ortega's colleagues at Community Legal Services took on the farmworkers' case for free and sued the city of Peoria. They joined forces with the Mexican American Legal Defense and Educational Fund (MALDEF) and filed a federal lawsuit called *Raul Gonzales v. City of Peoria*.

The lawsuit would become one of the most important American cases about the limits of local police enforcement of federal immigration law. It would impact police interactions with both immigrants and American-born Latinos in Western states for decades to come. And it would shape key legal fights between immigrant rights activists and restrictionists in the courts.

In the *Gonzales* lawsuit, Ortega's colleagues argued the Peoria police tactics were unconstitutional. Local cops, they contended, didn't have the authority to enforce federal immigration law. And Peoria police, the attorneys said, had violated the farmworkers' Fourth Amendment constitutional rights, which guarantees equal protection, by making improper stops and arrests without reasonable suspicion of a crime—in effect, unfairly targeting them for their Mexican appearance.

Federal courts—both at the district and appellate level—ruled the farmworkers failed to meet the high bar necessary to prove that Peoria's police practices demonstrated an ongoing pattern of intentional discrimination. But the language in the Ninth Circuit's 1983 ruling gave Arizona's nascent immigrant civil rights movement a victory nonetheless. The judges agreed with the farmworkers that local police do not have authority to arrest undocumented immigrants just because they lack immigration papers.

The appellate court opinion established that undocumented immigrants are not criminals, though restrictionist lawmakers and advocates would continue to insist otherwise. Instead, according to the appellate court's ruling, immigrants in the country without a valid visa are "unlawfully present," which is a *civil* violation of federal immigration law. And according to the ruling, only federal immigration officers can enforce the civil provisions of federal immigration law.

By the time the Ninth Circuit opinion came out in 1983, Ortega had started his own law firm. He would go on to build a robust immigration law practice, thanks to his seemingly inexhaustible energy level, his bilingual skills, and his participation in legal education shows on three different Spanish language radio programs in Phoenix.

Immediately he and other immigration lawyers used the precedent from *Gonzales* to advocate for their clients wrongfully harassed or stopped by local police without cause.

"That [decision] was one of the biggest weapons we had in dealing with the police," Ortega told us. "We used it all the time."

After serving as Cesar Chavez's bodyguard, Antonio Bustamante graduated from Stanford University, then went on to get his law degree from Antioch School of Law in Washington, D.C. As a young criminal defense lawyer in Tucson, he stumbled on the Ninth Circuit *Gonzales* opinion while researching an immigrant client's case. "I've known all my life, cops, when they feel like hassling somebody who is brown, they will start poking around into their authority to be here under immigration law," he told us. "And I realized when they do that, that's usually unconstitutional."

Nearly thirty years later, the legal precedent set by the 1983 *Gonzales* opinion would play a critical role in an epic legal battle that would pit Danny Ortega, Antonio Bustamante, Lydia Guzman, Mary Rose Wilcox, Alfredo Gutierrez, and so many others against a powerful restrictionist adversary: Sheriff Joe Arpaio.

4 Restrictionism Takes Root

2003-2005

For years, Lydia Guzman thought her mother was an American citizen. But then one day, Rafaela Avila confessed she wasn't.

The revelation happened sometime between 2000 and 2003, when Guzman was director of voter outreach for the Arizona secretary of state. Her job included encouraging voter participation. But ironically, her own mother hadn't taken the first step to vote—becoming a citizen.

Avila had qualified for citizenship for decades. But instead of applying for citizenship, she was satisfied with being a legal permanent resident, or a green card holder. But legal permanent residents couldn't vote, which bothered Guzman.

"Mom, do you realize that I help thousands of people become citizens? And I thought you were a citizen. I can't believe it," Guzman said. "We're gonna fill out your [citizenship application] form, right now."

Avila complied.

Guzman secretly arranged to speak at Avila's citizenship ceremony a few months later. During the ceremony in the federal courthouse, she stayed out of her mother's line of vision, but peeked at Avila sitting among her fellow new citizens holding little American flags.

When Guzman spoke at the podium, Avila's eyes teared up. Then she whispered in Spanish to the woman sitting next to her, *¡Es mi hija!* ("She's my daughter!").

Guzman told us it was a rare moment in which she felt her mother's pride and approval.

By then, Guzman had moved out of Avila's house in Phoenix and bought her own, a small white three-bedroom house in Glendale, a western suburb of Phoenix. The house was a point of pride for both mother and daughter. After her failed marriages and financial troubles in California, Guzman felt she'd started to make something of herself in Arizona. Her voter outreach work at the secretary of state's office was fulfilling, time consuming, and paid her bills. Still, she couldn't shake a simmering anxiety about the future, a sense of foreboding that the same race-based hate-filled propaganda that had washed over California with Proposition 187 would soon come to Arizona.

She was right.

In 2004, Russell Pearce, a ruddy-complected, white-haired, thickset member of the Arizona House of Representatives, claimed with scant evidence that unauthorized immigrants used taxpayer-funded state benefits and voted illegally in elections. He championed a restrictionist ballot initiative, Proposition 200, as a way to stop the "illegals" from their alleged thievery.

Like California's Proposition 187, the Arizona initiative required state officials to verify the identity of those applying for public benefits. If state workers discovered unauthorized immigrants, the law required them to report the immigrants to federal authorities, on threat of criminal charges if they failed to do so. And the measure required all Arizona residents to submit citizenship documents to register to vote as well as show identification at the polling place.

Proposition 200 was backed by FAIR, the same nonprofit founded by John Tanton that had backed Arizona's Official English measure and California's Proposition 187. FAIR reportedly contributed upwards of 450 thousand dollars to the effort to pass Proposition 200. A self-described European American separatist and Tanton associate, Virginia

Abernathy, served as chairwoman of the Proposition 200 national advisory board.

In Arizona, Russell Pearce likened unauthorized immigrants to invaders.

"I am not mean-spirited about anything," Pearce told us. "I have grandchildren that are Hispanic. My best friends growing up were Hispanic as well. In fact, all my neighbors were Hispanic at one point, almost."

Pearce became a Maricopa County sheriff's deputy in 1970. Seven years later, he lost part of his finger in a bizarre shooting incident in Guadalupe, a small town bordering Phoenix that was settled by Yaqui Indians from Mexico, Mexican Americans, and Mexican immigrants.

Pearce told us he was patrolling Guadalupe late one night when he noticed a boy standing near the Tastee Freez with a Maricopa County Sheriff's Office patch sewn onto the seat of his pants. "I was in the process of removing the patch from the butt of his pants," Pearce told us. At that moment, he noticed some teenage gang members walking down the street, carrying paper bags containing six packs of beer, accompanied by a Doberman. He told the boy with the patch on his pants to "step in the [police] car" and tried to arrest the other kids for underage possession of alcohol. That's when one of them ordered the Doberman to attack Pearce, he told us, and a scuffle ensued, which ended up with another kid grabbing Pearce's revolver and shooting Pearce. The bullet, he said, sped through his finger and lodged in his back. Pearce told us the boys "had already made a pact that night to kill a deputy." More than forty years later, some Guadalupe residents still question what happened that night.

Pearce ascended to the post of chief deputy for newly elected Joe Arpaio in 1993, but left after just a year. By then, Arpaio had decided to run for sheriff again, despite a promise to serve only one term. Pearce was the likely competition. Both men told us that is why Arpaio asked Pearce to leave. After a controversial tenure in the Motor Vehicle Division of the Arizona Department of Transportation, Pearce was elected to the legislature in 2000. Four years later, he helped get Proposition 200 on the ballot.

To Lydia Guzman, Proposition 200 endangered the voting rights of low income and minority citizens and inaccurately stereotyped unauthorized immigrants as welfare leeches. This was largely due, in her view, to FAIR peddling flawed research that inflated the taxpayer burden of unauthorized immigration. It particularly galled her when she heard restrictionists testifying at hearings in the Arizona state legislature, citing a 2004 FAIR report claiming taxpayers paid more than one billion dollars to bankroll public benefits consumed by unauthorized immigrants and their American citizen children. She felt the FAIR report didn't factor in contributions immigrants made to the state economy. Guzman knew the statistics were misleading, but because they were presented in an official-sounding report, many Arizonans believed them. "We felt impotent in a way. We felt, like, helpless," she told us.

She worried about what she viewed as xenophobic rhetoric creeping onto cable news. Then-CNN anchor Lou Dobbs lamented "the invasion of millions of illegal aliens . . . bringing with it a health-care crisis." On Fox News, Bill O'Reilly said undocumented immigrants stole public benefits.

By then, Guzman was no longer working at the secretary of state's office. She had been ideologically incompatible with the new secretary of state, a conservative Republican named Jan Brewer who supported Proposition 200. That was the beginning of a clash between the two strong minded women that would last for years.

Guzman quickly got another job, because she had to feed her kids, then nine and fourteen, and pay the mortgage on her house. She became state director for the Southwest Voter Registration Education Project, a non-partisan Latino voter engagement nonprofit.

She felt pulled in so many directions. The kids needed her. Her daughter, Ashley, now a high school freshman, resented her for being unavailable. Guzman chastised herself for not spending more time with her two children.

But in 2004, she couldn't say no when Democrats asked her to run for the Arizona Senate in her Republican-favored district. She knew she had little chance of winning. Her name would appear on the same 2004 Arizona ballot as Proposition 200.

She got to know Alfredo Gutierrez, the Chicano activist and former state senator, during the fight against Proposition 200. By then, he had been out of the state senate for eighteen years. He spent the late 1980s and the 1990s as a high-profile lobbyist, then retired and returned to activism. In 2002, he ran a fiery, progressive campaign against centrist Janet Napolitano in the Democratic gubernatorial primary and lost. After that, he became a Spanish language radio host for a Phoenix radio station connected to his mentor Cesar Chavez's farmworkers union.

On the air, in his tiny sound room at the radio station, Gutierrez put on his headset every day and often spoke out against Proposition 200. Immigrants stopped by the radio station, dropping coins and dollar bills in five-gallon jugs, their contributions to battle the proposition.

Off the air, Gutierrez helped lead a coalition of business people, political leaders, and local activists battling Proposition 200. Two white Republicans— Grant Woods, the former Arizona attorney general who had investigated the 1997 Chandler raids, and Julie Pace, an employment lawyer—were selected as spokespeople for the anti-Proposition 200 movement. Gutierrez and others theorized whites might vote down Proposition 200 if they understood from other whites how it would inconvenience them. For instance, elderly whites who didn't have driver's licenses would not be allowed to vote if they didn't have any handy identification.

The anti-Proposition 200 campaign focused on not outraging white Arizonans. Drawing on lessons learned from California's Proposition 187 fight ten years earlier, Proposition 200 opponents advised their allies not to carry Mexican flags or use the word "racist."

Guzman wanted to use her platform as a state senate candidate to speak out against Proposition 200. But she told us, "the Democratic party silenced me"; she couldn't "touch Prop 200 with a ten-foot pole" in her campaign. In her memory, party officials told her, "Don't talk about that [Proposition 200] because it is going to hurt you. You will be seen as a leftist radical."

She later came to question this approach. "I think I should have alerted more people that the tide of hate was coming," she told us.

Election day ended up being miserable for her. Proposition 200 passed by ten points. Guzman also lost her state senate race by ten points. George W. Bush, a Republican, carried Arizona easily and was re-elected president. And a young restrictionist, Andrew Thomas, who'd made "Stop Illegal Immigration" his central platform and yard-sign slogan, won the Maricopa County attorney race by seventeen points. She didn't think much about Joe Arpaio's re-election as Maricopa County sheriff. The "GOP kingmaker" sailed into his fourth term by beating two challengers with a margin of twenty-six points.

At least, Guzman told herself, there would be one happy memory from that evening. Her mother, a brand-new American citizen, had voted for the first time. And she'd voted for her daughter. It made Guzman proud and happy, even as she wondered why Avila had resisted becoming a citizen for so long.

Shortly after the election, Danny Ortega and the Mexican American Legal Defense and Education Fund tried to stop Proposition 200 from taking effect. The federal lawsuit failed. Ortega told us the strategy was to block the law because it might "slow the tide for what we thought might be coming."

Shortly after the election, Russell Pearce's son Sean, a Maricopa County sheriff's deputy, was serving a warrant in a Phoenix suburb when he was shot by an unauthorized Mexican immigrant. "My son was shot and critically wounded in the line of duty by an illegal alien wanted on homicide. Almost died. I've been shot and critically wounded in the line of duty . . . I've got a long list, a long list of people who've died and from illegal aliens that shouldn't have," Pearce told us.

Sean Pearce was still recovering from his wounds when his father arrived at the copper-domed state capitol in Phoenix for the new legislative session in 2005. By then, several Republican moderates had lost their seats, and the Republican-dominated legislature was more extreme than in years past. Russell Pearce began introducing an ambitious restrictionist agenda by sponsoring several state immigration bills, which sought, among other things, to deny bail to jailed unauthorized immigrants and authorize local police to make immigration arrests.

Pearce cosponsored one historic measure that passed with bipartisan support. The Arizona Human Smuggling Law made it a state felony to smuggle unauthorized immigrants into Arizona for profit.

It was the first state law that empowered local law-enforcement authorities to arrest smugglers, who could then face prosecution in Arizona courts. Most of the lawmakers who backed the law pegged it as humanitarian legislation, protecting migrants preyed upon by cruel smugglers. Even the local Spanish language newspaper, *La Voz*, applauded the Human Smuggling Law. "We believe this law is good and necessary," the editorial board wrote. "We know full well that coyotes [smugglers] are directly responsible for hundreds, perhaps thousands, of undocumented deaths."

One Latino state lawmaker warned the legislation might be misused to target Arizona's immigrants, but no one took much notice. The law wasn't widely viewed as anti-Latino or anti-immigrant.

At least not then.

5 Arpaio Transformed

2005–2006

By 2005, Joe and Ava Arpaio were both in their seventies and had moved into a new house in Fountain Hills, a wealthy town of about twenty thousand residents some thirty miles east of Phoenix. It was a small house with a garage big enough to hold Arpaio's prized candy-apple red four-door Cadillac DeVille, which Ava believed one day would be valuable because her famous husband had owned it. Their living room balcony looked down on the town's namesake fountain—a tall plume of water that periodically shot up from the center of an artificial lake consisting partly of treated effluent.

Sometimes, Ava gazed out her kitchen window and saw a javelina nursing her young in the desert garden. Or a rattlesnake sunning itself. Ava and her husband both liked Fountain Hills, a tranquil spot far away from the city. Of the town folk, 96 percent were white and most voted Republican. What's more, the town contracted with the Maricopa County Sheriff's Office for policing services. And John Kleinheinz, Arpaio's former media relations staffer, was now a sheriff's office captain in charge of the Fountain Hills district.

In 2005, *The Fountain Hills Times* wrote about the Maricopa County Sheriff's Office's volunteer posse. The story did not mention Arpaio but included a photograph of Kleinheinz and a few posse members. Kleinheinz viewed it as good press for the posse—until he got a marked-up copy of the article from Arpaio. "Where was I?" Arpaio scrawled underneath the photo.

Kleinheinz tacked a clipping of the article on his office wall as a reminder of what he had come to view as Arpaio's ego-driven leadership.

Arpaio was a Fountain Hills celebrity. Residents appreciated law and order. With Arpaio in town, they felt safe playing golf or strolling along the banks of the artificial lake. Nonwhites weren't always welcome, though. Kleinheinz told us locals frequently complained about people of color infiltrating Fountain Hills. People would ask him: "Why are there Mexicans walking down our street? Why are there blacks in this town?"

After Arpaio and Ava moved to Fountain Hills, their son, Rocco, had assumed more responsibilities at Starworld Travel. Ava had long hoped to retire and travel with her husband to places like Australia, New Zealand, and Paris. Arpaio didn't like vacations, though. And sometimes, Ava, who had planned other people's vacations at the travel agency for years, told herself there was really no need for a vacation. She already lived in a beautiful place. Plus, she told us, if her husband was happy, well, she was happy, too. Arpaio did not want to retire. He had no hobbies. He had no close friends. "Friends," he once told us, "I don't even know what that word means, I got to look at a dictionary what a friend . . . what the terminology of a friend is."

A sliver of moon lit the dark desert when Patrick Haab, a twenty-four-year-old Army reservist, parked his red Mazda at a roadside rest stop just off Interstate 8 in southwestern Maricopa County. It was April 10, 2005. Haab was returning to his home in a Phoenix suburb from San Diego, California. He had packed two guns and 134 rounds of ammunition for the trip.

Just south of the rest stop, a well-traveled migrant trail sliced north from Sonora, Mexico. Border Patrol agents stopped people attempting to cross the southwestern border more than one million times in 2005. About half of the arrests took place in the Arizona desert or just next door in an eastern stretch of southern California. The migrants crossed on foot because they couldn't get visas that would permit them to legally enter the United States.

Their journey often followed a pattern. Usually, guides known as "coyotes" led the migrants through the punishing Arizona desert. They often trudged for miles, skirting government checkpoints and scanning the landscape for Border Patrol agents. Drivers awaited them at designated pickup spots, including the rest stop where Patrick Haab parked his Mazda.

After getting out of his car, Haab walked into the nearby desert so his black Labrador retriever could relieve itself. That's when Haab saw six men running from the desert toward a white Chevrolet Suburban parked at the rest stop. Haab and his dog gave chase. The dog nipped at one man's pants. The men jumped into the Suburban, where a driver was already at the wheel. Haab pulled his gun, pointed it at the Suburban, and got the keys from the driver.

Then Haab dialed 911 and falsely identified himself as an off-duty officer for the United States Army Special Forces. "Yeah, I've got a Suburban full of illegals out here on highway eight at a rest stop," he said. "I just stopped at the rest area here and, uh, went out in the field to let the dog out and, uh, saw five or six of them came barreling across the field and jumped into the Suburban . . . they all got backpacks and everything. They're pretty sweaty smelling."

"So they're all just sitting there minding you, huh?" asked the dispatcher.

"Yeah. I've got a, I've got a firearm," Haab answered.

"Should I just keep them in the vehicle," he asked the dispatcher, "Or splay 'em out on the ground?"

"Ya know, I can't tell you one way or another," the dispatcher answered. "Do whatever you feel is appropriate."

Haab opted to splay the men on the ground.

When Arpaio's deputies arrived, Haab changed his story. He now claimed the migrants had rushed him, he had feared for his life, had drawn his gun in self-defense, and had made a citizen's arrest.

The terrified migrants denied they'd rushed Haab, and deputies didn't buy his story either. As one deputy phoned someone to pick up the dog, Haab was arrested on suspicion of seven counts of aggravated assault with a deadly weapon. He was booked into a Maricopa County jail.

At a jailhouse press conference, Haab claimed he was acting in self-defense and Arpaio's deputies had wrongly arrested him. Haab, who falsely identified himself as an Iraq War veteran to the media, became an instant celebrity among restrictionists. A local locksmith who felt Haab was unjustly jailed posted Haab's ten-thousand-dollar bail. Strangers sent Haab donations.

A growing number of Arizonans were fed up with what they viewed as their elected leaders' indifference toward illegal immigration. They were convinced their government treated unauthorized immigrants better than it treated American citizens like themselves. A few Arizonans decided to monitor the border for "illegals." And at the time Haab was arrested, a nascent border vigilante movement called the Minuteman Project patrolled the Arizona desert.

Haab insisted he didn't have a clue about the highly-publicized Minuteman Project that was taking place on the very night he cornered the migrants at the rest stop. And he denied affiliation with the civilian vigilantes.

Dressed in camouflage, some Minutemen scoped out migrant trails in search of unauthorized immigrants. They kept in close touch via their staticky walkie-talkies, communicating with military jargon.

Valerie Roller, a blue-eyed grandmother and a technical support specialist for a cable company, and her husband, George Sprankle, a military veteran and former construction worker, told us what it felt like to be part of the Minuteman Project. They had heard reports from restrictionist nonprofits about unauthorized immigrants swarming across the border and had worried about how the immigrants would damage the country by using up resources. They decided to take a stand, and took their Harley-Davidson motorcycles down to the Arizona-Mexico border, between Bisbee and Sierra Vista. They stayed at a motel, where they befriended other like-minded Minutemen. And in the morning, they made their move.

"We actually lined up along [the border] to show that bikers, if we could secure the border, why couldn't the government. And it was more symbolic than anything else," Roller told us.

Following Haab's arrest, Arpaio condemned border vigilantism. "We should never take the law in our own hands," the sheriff huffed.

Years later, he told us he remembered Haab had pulled a gun on the migrants and "put them on the ground" because "they looked Mexican and illegal." He said he still stood by his decision to arrest Haab. "You don't pull a gun . . . on people because they look like they are here illegally. By the way they were here illegally. I took a lot of heat on that."

Arpaio misjudged the political weight behind Haab's celebrity and what it signaled—a restrictionist movement taking root in his prized base of voters. Angry county voters wrote letters to newspaper editors, branding Arpaio as unfit for office because he was too easy on "illegals" and too hard on American patriot heroes like Patrick Haab.

Looking back on Haab, Arpaio told us: "He was a hero and I was the bad guy."

Andrew Thomas, the newly elected Maricopa County attorney, used the Haab controversy as a way to distinguish himself as a champion of the increasingly popular restrictionist movement. Thomas hadn't had much practical legal experience, but he had graduated from Harvard Law School, which he considered repressively liberal. He authored several pieces in conservative publications and wrote books. He proposed unconventional fixes for the criminal justice system, including displaying criminals in public in open-air holding pens, presumably to face the scorn of their peers.

But Thomas didn't view Haab as a criminal. He maintained Haab was justified in drawing his weapon and pointing it at the migrants. Then he dropped the charges against Haab. And while it wasn't unusual for a county prosecutor to drop charges after Arpaio's deputies made arrests, Thomas's actions on such a high-profile case embarrassed, humiliated, and insulted Arpaio, a former Arpaio colleague told us.

Three months after Arpaio weathered a torrent of criticism for arresting Patrick Haab at the highway rest stop, Arpaio went out of his way in the summer of 2005 to help Isabel Acosta, a twenty-nine-year-old undocumented Mexican immigrant who lived in Maricopa County. At the time, Acosta's former boyfriend and father of her two children was accused of killing her parents and brother. After the murders, he fled to Mexico with the two kids.

Arpaio and Carlos Flores Vizcarra, the Mexican consul general in Phoenix, arranged for Acosta to obtain special permission to travel to

Mexico to retrieve her children and return to the United States. Arpaio even said he'd help Acosta get legal status so she could stay to testify against the ex-boyfriend.

"If critics want to complain I'm smuggling aliens across the border to save two kids, so be it," Arpaio told one reporter at the time. To another he explained, "I take heat when I go to the toilet, so it doesn't matter. But our mission was to solve this murder and I wanted those two kids back. They're citizens of the United States."

Arpaio vowed more than once he would not lock up dishwashers and other unauthorized immigrants who were simply in the county to work menial jobs. And he and the Mexican consul general became fast friends. They even went on a chummy walk-through of the Tent City jail. And soon, the two created an avenue for Mexican authorities to join Arizona authorities in an organized effort to thwart future cross-border kidnappings. Not long after that, the consul general invited Arpaio to be a guest of honor at a consulate event. Danny Ortega and Lydia Guzman attended too, stood next to each other in the auditorium and applauded Arpaio. Ortega viewed the sheriff as level-headed and sensible. Guzman thought he was a great man.

In a few short months, they would despise him.

Like Joe Arpaio, Danny Ortega at first didn't understand the sophistication and strength of the restrictionist movement. That changed in November 2005, when Ortega was asked to speak at an immigration-themed conference sponsored by the county attorney, Andrew Thomas. Some activists had declined Thomas's offer to speak at the conference, but Ortega accepted, hoping to engage those with differing views. He was surprised, though, when he entered the convention hall at a Scottsdale hotel. Hundreds of conventioneers swarmed the reception hall, stopping at booths sponsored by restrictionist nonprofits and like-minded Minutemen.

"Oh my God, this is bigger than I ever imagined," Ortega told us he remembered thinking.

In addition to Russell Pearce, Ortega's fellow panelists included Kris Kobach, the legal mind of the movement to crack down on undocumented immigrants. Kobach was affiliated with FAIR's legal arm, the Immigration Reform Law Institute. Kobach told us he had not played a direct role in

Arizona's Proposition 200 campaign. But he was determined to curb illegal immigration and alleged unauthorized immigrant voter fraud. He helped defend portions of Proposition 200 and a similar Kansas law from legal challenges.

Over several years, Kobach would help craft numerous state laws and city ordinances meant to make life so difficult for unauthorized immigrants they would be compelled to "self-deport." Kobach would play a role in key Arizona immigration policies and would become an immigration policy advisor to both Arpaio and Donald Trump.

Square-jawed and broad-shouldered, Kobach was polished. He had degrees from Harvard University, Oxford University, and Yale Law School. As a young lawyer, he advised the justice department on immigration and counterterrorism; critics said he instituted policies that ethnically profiled Muslims. Thanks to his influence, the justice department reversed longstanding policy and took the position that local police could make immigration arrests as long as state law permitted it.

According to Kobach's interpretations of the law, local and state police had "inherent authority" to enforce all aspects of federal immigration law. The way Kobach saw it, local police could arrest immigrants simply for the civil violation of being in the country without papers.

Kobach shared his views on the panel with Danny Ortega at the Scottsdale conference. No slouch on case law, Ortega cited the Ninth Circuit's 1983 opinion in the Peoria farmworker case that said only federal authorities could arrest immigrants for civil violations of immigration law, to refute Kobach's assignment of "inherent authority" to local and state police.

The audience of about five hundred people vigorously applauded for Kobach. Ortega earned only a splatter of lonely claps from a single table.

After the convention, Andrew Thomas focused on making good on his campaign promise to bust unauthorized immigrants. The blue-eyed, baby-faced county attorney with the red moustache chose to vigorously prosecute the state's new Human Smuggling Law when it took effect in the summer of 2005. And he simply couldn't do it alone, not in the grand style he imagined.

He and Joe Arpaio needed each other.

Many legislators said publicly the Human Smuggling Law was intended only to help local police arrest human smugglers, not their cargo of migrants. But Thomas wanted to prosecute the migrants, too. In Thomas's view, migrants who paid smugglers to sneak them into the United States were actually conspiring with the smuggler.

He reasoned that if migrants paid a smuggler, they were guilty of an aggravated felony: conspiracy to violate Arizona's Human Smuggling Law. Once convicted of an aggravated felony, migrants were almost always deported. And they weren't likely to return legally, since felony records often disqualified them from obtaining visas to enter the United States.

What's more, Thomas theorized, arrested migrants would rat on their smugglers in an effort to reduce the jail sentences they would have to serve before deportation. This, Thomas projected, would result in more smuggler convictions.

Thomas laid it all out in a legal opinion for the sheriff.

By doing so, he handed Arpaio the political cover to reinvent himself as an immigration enforcer. And his deputies now had legal grounds to arrest migrants on felony charges for conspiring to smuggle themselves.

Arresting people for conspiracies clicked for Arpaio, a former drug enforcement agent. "If you find a dope peddler in the car and you see five people in the back seat, they're involved in that conspiracy. They are part of that transaction," he told us years later. "So when you get a smuggler in the car and you got ten smugglees—illegals—in the car who paid the smuggler three thousand dollars to come across the border, hey, they're part of that. See, I don't have to be a Supreme Court justice to figure that out."

In March 2006, Maricopa County deputies stopped two vans caravanning through lonely flats punctuated by twisted bushes and the occasional thirsty farm. One van sported the logo of an upscale Phoenix furniture store but, suspiciously, carried Sonora license plates. More than fifty migrants were inside the vehicles, and almost all were arrested on suspicion of conspiring with a smuggler to smuggle themselves into Arizona. The men and women ranged in age from their early twenties to midforties. They wore baseball caps, jeans, jackets. Most admitted they'd paid the smuggler for their passage. Arpaio invited reporters to film and photograph the migrants in pink handcuffs as they arrived at the jail.

"I'm not going to go around on street corners and pick them up because they look like Mexicans," Arpaio promised at the time. But he vowed to continue arresting smugglers and migrants involved in a conspiracy.

Some legislators publicly voiced outrage at the Arpaio-Thomas interpretation of a law they had voted for as a means to arrest predatory smugglers.

Even so, Arpaio's standing rose with his former critics who'd chastised him for his handling of the Haab and Acosta episodes. He later denied that his about-face was tied to political opportunism. Instead, he insisted he began arresting migrants because the new law directed him to do so. In other words, he was simply a cop following the law and his county attorney's legal advice.

Arpaio would claim in his second memoir that he, not Thomas, cooked up the migrant-smuggler conspiracy idea in the first place.

Decades of changes in American immigration policy shaped the political context for Arpaio's transition to immigration enforcement in 2006. The nation at the time was slowly moving toward another cycle of anti-immigrant sentiment that mirrored the xenophobia of the 1920s that had almost prevented Joe Arpaio's father from making it into the United States.

Back when Joe Arpaio was a federal drug enforcement agent in San Antonio, Texas, Congress implemented the first major immigration policy shift in his lifetime. The Immigration and Nationality Act of 1965 nixed 1920s-era national-origins quotas intended to favor northern European immigrants. The new law now allowed immigrants to enter the country based on their skills and relationships to American citizens and legal permanent residents. Employers could also sponsor immigrants. The law allowed American citizens to sponsor spouses, parents, and minor children without any numerical caps.

Yet even though the law was billed as an effort to ease national origin quotas from Europe, Asia, and Africa, it capped immigration for the first time from Canada, Latin America, and the Caribbean. Eventually the law would limit Western Hemisphere immigration to at most twenty thousand visas per country. This cap did not apply to spouses, parents, and minor children of American citizens.

Decades later, the 1965 law had unintended consequences, scholars would find. It ended up dramatically shifting the nation's demographics because immigrants of Asian and Latin American descent eventually sponsored more relatives than their European counterparts. This caused unease in some cohorts of the dwindling white majority.

The 1965 law also resulted in an unexpected uptick in illegal immigration on the nation's southern border. The combination of new quotas in the Western Hemisphere, along with an end to the Bracero program in 1964, forced some Mexicans and Latin Americans who could not get a visa to seek other ways to get into the country.

When Arpaio was working with Ava at Starworld Travel, President Ronald Reagan signed the 1986 Immigration Reform and Control Act. The law increased border enforcement, imposed sanctions on employers who hired undocumented workers, and clamped down on illegal crossings by increasing the Border Patrol's staffing. The law also gave legal status to about 2.7 million unauthorized, mostly Mexican, immigrants already in the country. Some conservatives in the twenty-first century, including many Arpaio admirers, would later criticize the so-called "Reagan amnesty" for encouraging illegal immigration. In political calls to action, they would wave signs that said, "Remember 1986!"

In 1996, when Joe Arpaio was touted as America's Toughest Sheriff and delighted fans by passing out autographed pink boxer shorts, President Bill Clinton, a Democrat, signed a sweeping immigration law that further criminalized immigrants.

The 1996 law ensured that more immigrants with legal status would be deported if they committed a growing list of felonies, known as "deportable felonies." The federal law made it nearly impossible for unauthorized immigrants with felony convictions to remain in the country. It also cut government benefits available to both documented and undocumented immigrants, and fattened the Border Patrol with five thousand new agents. The 1996 law set up the legal structure for local-federal immigration enforcement agreements called "287(g) partnerships" that would later give Arpaio tremendous authority to enforce federal immigration laws.

Even before the new law was passed, the Clinton administration began clamping down on illegal immigration by adding fencing and strong lighting to some busy border hotspots. This had the effect of routing migrants to more remote stretches of the border. Immigration officials presumed that the fierce Arizona desert would serve as a natural barrier, deterring migrants from crossing. Instead, in the years that followed, hundreds of thousands of unauthorized migrants felt they had no choice but to hazard Arizona's southern deserts. Thousands died on the journey. Desert animals scattered their bones across the desert, and many human remains would never be identified.

As border crossings became more treacherous, Mexican immigrants who had once migrated cyclically to work in the United States now felt stranded in the United States. The risk and cost of cyclical border crossing was too high. A growing number of unauthorized Mexican immigrants began building their lives and raising families in the United States.

For some Arizonans, the increased diversity was a welcome change.

For others, it wasn't.

Many of Arizona's undocumented immigrants settled in Maricopa County, where it was becoming increasingly common to hear Spanish on the streets of Phoenix. Some Phoenicians were bothered by the presence of Latino-owned restaurants and stores. They were equally disturbed by corn vendors stationed on empty parking lots or men riding bicycles towing coolers stuffed with Mexican popsicles.

Part of the anxiety was due to an increasingly popular restrictionist narrative that many Arizonans bought into. In October 2005, pollsters for the Phoenix-based Behavior Research Center poll surveyed six hundred Maricopa County residents. The respondents wildly overestimated the number of undocumented immigrants working in the state, and also underestimated the number of Latinos in the state who were American citizens and spoke English. In a news release explaining their findings, the pollsters wrote "the public debate and coverage of that debate up to this point in time appears to have done more to obscure the realities of the Latino population in Arizona than to clarify it and in the process runs the very real risk of branding all Latinos as illegal aliens."

II Battles

2006–2016

The Movement Rises Up

2006

Lydia Guzman had once considered Joe Arpaio a decent, fair man. He'd shown the army reservist Patrick Haab no mercy for holding migrants at gunpoint and had helped Isabel Acosta, the undocumented mother, recover her kidnapped kids in Mexico. But by 2006 she felt Arpaio was part of the evil she sensed hovering over Arizona. Her premonitions—the anxieties and fears that had eaten away at her ever since she'd moved from California—were based on what she'd seen and heard. The Chandler raids, Patrick Haab's hero status, the Minutemen, Russell Pearce and his bills in the Arizona legislature, and now Joe Arpaio and his interceptions and arrests of Mexican migrants. It sent fear rolling through Latino communities she cared about.

She'd long hoped Congress would give undocumented immigrants a path to citizenship. But momentum to pass such legislation had weakened after the terrorist attacks of September 11, 2001. Instead, the momentum shifted to restricting immigration and securing borders. Restrictionist Republicans in Congress sought to increasingly criminalize unauthorized immigrants and thus bar them from ever returning to the United States.

James Sensenbrenner, a Republican congressman from Wisconsin, proposed a law that would make it a federal felony to be in the United

States without papers. Under the Sensenbrenner bill, anyone who assisted or encouraged unauthorized immigrants to stay in the United States could be sent to prison for up to five years. This included clergy and social workers.

To Guzman's disappointment, the House passed the Sensenbrenner bill in December 2005. Just like Proposition 187 in California, she took it as a personal insult. So did many others. The Sensenbrenner bill galvanized Latino immigrants and their allies throughout the United States.

The Sensenbrenner bill sparked an immigrant rights movement that would become especially strong in Arizona. And it started organically, with protest marches throughout the country. In Phoenix, twenty thousand people took to the streets to protest the Sensenbrenner bill. *The Arizona Republic* called it the "city's biggest demonstration ever."

Nonprofits in Washington, D.C., such as the National Council of La Raza and the Center for Community Change, along with labor unions quickly jumped in to steer the anti-Sensenbrenner-bill energy on the ground into a national movement. They called their coalition "We Are America/Somos America." The coalition coordinated a separate national day of marches to protest the Sensenbrenner bill and call for immigration reform that included a pathway to citizenship for most of the country's 11.6 million unauthorized immigrants. Some had crossed the border without papers, others had entered the country legally but had allowed their visas to expire.

At the time, some senators from both parties were interested in crafting a bill that would offer unauthorized immigrants who had committed no serious crimes a path to citizenship. It also sought to curtail unauthorized immigration with border security and workplace enforcement provisions.

The April 10, 2006 marches were to take place throughout the United States and were all titled: "Somos America: Today we march, tomorrow we vote." They were designed to show the nation that immigrants and Latinos were a powerful force and would not put up with more discrimination.

Danny Ortega, who'd debated Kris Kobach, the restrictionist lawyer, just a few months earlier, knew from that experience that the opposition was powerful, well funded, and well organized.

He knew, too, that the resistance was, by comparison, young, under-resourced, and fragmented. He served on the board of the National Council of La Raza, and fretted about the upcoming Somos America march in Phoenix. Activist groups were competing with each other instead of collaborating. Different Latino organizations planned independent marches. Ortega knew the groups couldn't splinter. He believed this moment was bigger than any individual organization. He felt activists needed to gather in one room to plan a unified march.

They met in an auditorium next to a union office in downtown Phoenix. Over one hundred people representing different community groups gathered there one evening in late March. Immigrants, teachers, Democratic elected officials, union organizers, high schoolers, university students, law students, day labor organizers, and church members sat on folding chairs arranged in a large circle. Lydia Guzman was there too, representing a nonprofit group helping Latino candidates run for office.

"We sat in a big circle because we didn't want anyone to be at the head of any table," Guzman told us. "Everyone was equal."

Guzman hadn't witnessed so much collaborative energy since Proposition 187 passed in 1994, galvanizing Los Angeles-area Latinos into launching massive citizenship and voter registration campaigns. On that day in the Phoenix auditorium, she told us, she sensed she was watching more "history in the making."

Not everyone at the meeting shared the same values. One activist, in particular, worried Guzman. Elias Bermudez, she later told other activists, was "a sandwich short of a picnic." Bermudez, a silver-haired leader of an immigrant advocacy group, had been invited because he had successfully led about five thousand immigrants on a protest march to the Arizona capitol and was now planning another. Originally from Mexico, Bermudez had a large following in the immigrant community—an already organized group of possible marchers and volunteers. But Bermudez himself had unseemly aspects; he had been convicted ten years earlier for money laundering and had served time in federal prison. He was a notary public who filed immigration paperwork and drew criticism for recruiting business clients from immigrants who'd joined the civil rights groups he organized. Later, many would come to regret allowing Bermudez to join their new coalition.

Almost everyone in the room seemed impressed with Carlos Garcia, a Mexican-born MEChA activist enrolled in Arizona State University. In his early twenties, Garcia was a quiet man with a soft voice who stood five feet ten inches tall, weighed a little over two hundred pounds, and wore his long black hair in a ponytail. He had a talent for organizing students, and had led a student door-to-door campaign to register voters to fight Proposition 200.

Garcia told us years later he had started feeling like a statistical anomaly early in his life. As a young undocumented immigrant living in Arizona, he could have been deported, but instead, as a teenager, he lucked into a green card through his mother's American husband. He told us he could have dropped out of his high school and joined his friends' gang, but instead he wound up studying history at Arizona State University.

Looking back on it, he'd battled institutional bias most of his life. At his Tucson high school, he was discouraged from taking more than the two-year requisite of a subject he excelled in—math. But his Latina advisor put him on a vocational track instead of college prep classes. He came to think no one in the public high school expected him to go to college because he was a Mexican immigrant.

He wasn't thrilled about attending the activist meeting, because it was tied to a mainstream national Latino organization he didn't view as particularly effective. He understood, though, that in a time of peril "we needed to come together and do something to support our people."

Alfredo Gutierrez, who had grown up in an Arizona mining town and hadn't forgotten how unions had helped Latino workers get equal pay and rights in the mines, was among the activists who welcomed local unions into the nascent movement. The powerful Service Employees International Union, known as the SEIU, and the United Food and Commercial Workers International Union, known as the UFCW, were particularly eager to help the activists and contribute desperately needed money and organizing know-how.

Some attendees grumbled the unions would kidnap the fledgling resistance to meet their own needs. But the group forged on that night, creating consensus. They chose to give themselves the same name as the national group: Somos America. They agreed on bylaws and voted in officers—

Guzman as secretary, Garcia as vice president, and longtime activist Roberto Reveles as founding president.

Reveles, a Korean War veteran and Georgetown University graduate, had served first as a congressional staffer and then in government relations for Homestake Mining. The son of a Mexican immigrant, he told us American citizen members of his family had been barred from voting by Arizona laws intended to disenfranchise Mexican Americans. As a child growing up in Miami, Arizona, Reveles, like Alfredo Gutierrez, lived with the fear of deportation.

"If we saw a gringo approaching our neighborhood we would run home, close the door, lock it, pull the shades and if somebody knocked on the door we would not answer," he told us.

"I experienced a lot of stuff that could have been very hurtful to a young person," he said. And now, many decades later, those memories motivated him to help lead a wobbly, new, disorganized coalition that had risen up to advocate for immigrants and Latino civil rights in Phoenix.

Within days, Somos America raised more than sixty thousand dollars to pay for T-shirts, water bottles, venue rentals, banners, signs and U-Haul trucks to transport the sound system. But it wasn't enough. When organizers learned just days before the march they needed a fifty-thousand-dollar insurance policy, SEIU paid for it, proving its worth as a Somos America member.

On Monday, April 10, Guzman helped lead the march with other Latino activists and was astonished by the size of the crowd. And its courage. Undocumented immigrants once reluctant to draw attention to themselves marched with their families, in step with other immigrants, children of immigrants, whites, and people of color. Construction workers, dishwashers, hotel maids, and car wash attendants took time off to march. They carried American flags, pushed children in strollers, and wore white shirts signaling unity and peace. The massive white serpentine wound for two miles through the streets, all the way from the Arizona State Fairgrounds to the capitol. No one knew how big the crowd was. Maybe one hundred thousand people. Or maybe two hundred thousand. Certainly many times larger than the record-breaking march against the Sensenbrenner bill in Phoenix three weeks earlier.

Tens of thousands joined the We Are America/Somos America march in Phoenix on April 10, 2006. (Photo by José L. Muñoz)

This is pushback, Guzman thought. We are part of this nation and you can't do anything about it. We're here. We're not leaving.

She knew in cities across America other marchers were also holding signs and chanting "Sí, se puede"—the famed United Farm Workers cheer that translates to "Yes, we can." She felt fired up. This, she thought, is the birth of a political movement.

Gutierrez, the orator, spoke to the marchers who'd reached their destination—the green lawns and concrete terraces of the Arizona State Capitol complex. "Will we submit? Or will we resist?" Gutierrez bellowed to the crowd. "Will we allow our families to be humiliated and their rights trampled upon, or will we take up arms to defend ourselves? We shall arm ourselves, and in America the only arm that counts is the vote . . . Today we commit ourselves to create an electoral earthquake in America!"

Shortly after the march, the activists experienced a surprising earth-quake of a different kind. The marches across the nation spooked many Americans who did not identify with the message. The visuals reminded them of the demographic changes sweeping the nation.

Some Americans were taken aback by the sheer numbers of demonstrators, by the sea of white, by the gall of anyone who believed people who crossed the border without papers had civil rights, too. In Arizona, 52 percent of voters in one poll believed the recent marches hurt the cause of comprehensive immigration reform. Only 31 percent said they helped.

In the hours after the Phoenix march, Jim Williams, a production manager for a steel fabrication company, was driving home from work in a twenty-four-year-old white Ford pickup when he encountered a crowd of people. In his memory, "All you could see was a sea of T-shirts with the Mexican flag on it, people carrying the Mexican flag. Their deal was, 'Today we march, tomorrow we vote, Sí se puede,' and all of this stuff."

Latino marchers were "not getting out of the way" and were "impeding traffic," he told us. He almost got in an accident because someone walked in front of his truck. Williams, a gray-haired, bearded white man who stood six feet two inches tall and weighed about three hundred pounds, remembered his truck stalling in the middle of an intersection, people making obscene gestures and insulting him in Spanish. He thought: Oh boy, here we are in the middle of a foreign country, I'm outnumbered here.

Then he wondered: Why do I feel this way in my own country? This is my home. Who are these people? What are they doing here?

The incident marked a turning point for Williams, the son of an Arizona highway patrolman. Born in rural Arizona, Williams recalled a childhood hiking, hunting, and fishing in big, clean country. "As you grow up, you want your kids to be able to enjoy the country just like you did, not have to be worried about who's out there, who's going to bother them," he told us.

"It's getting to the point where it feels like we're in a completely different country. It feels like there's something at work trying to stop what made America great."

The marchers bothered him because he didn't feel unauthorized immigrants had a right to complain or protest deportation when they had come to the United States without documents. "I'm not interested in turning in illegals," he told us. "But I don't think I need to hear anybody whine and cry about getting busted when you knew you were breaking the law."

Williams was so upset by the marchers that he became an activist. A longtime motorcyclist and Harley enthusiast, he joined RidersUSA, a controversial motorcycle club that would ally itself with Joe Arpaio and other restrictionists.

But some Latinos were outraged by the marches, too, because they believed the campaign had unleashed an unwelcome white backlash in Arizona. Danny Ortega would not forget how his friend Pepe Acosta, who owned a taco shop in west Phoenix, chastised him for organizing the 2006 marches.

As long as nobody sees us, Acosta told Ortega, the less attention they pay us.

Those concerns were justified. In the years following the 2006 marches, Arizona lawmakers and voters would pass a spate of immigration laws that many American citizens of Latino descent would take as a personal attack. Arizona "actually got worse," Ortega told us.

Still, he would always insist the Somos America marches were a necessary first step for the resistance.

But there would be many more steps. And missteps. From that point forward in Maricopa County, the new local coalition would fight frustrating civil rights battles in the courts, on the streets, on the front porches of new and undecided voters, and in the media.

And Somos America would eventually try to take down Arizona's most famous immigrant chaser, Sheriff Joe Arpaio.

7 Hopes and Letdowns
2006–2007

In a way, blowback in Phoenix from the massive Somos America march in April 2006 couldn't have come at a better time for Sheriff Joe Arpaio, then grappling with a difficult public relations problem stemming from inmate deaths in his jails. Just a month before the local Somos America march, a jury had awarded nine million dollars to the family of Charles Agster, who lived with mental illness and severe intellectual disabilities. Agster died, his parents alleged, after staffers "killed" him by failing to properly monitor him after he was shackled into a restraint chair in Arpaio's Madison Street jail. Arpaio and the county denied wrongdoing.

Michael Manning, the lawyer for the Agster family, had first come to Phoenix to join the legal team that successfully brought down the notorious Charles Keating. As a player in the savings and loan crisis of the 1980s, Keating, through his companies, sold worthless junk bonds to thousands of trusting elderly clients.

Manning told us nothing in his legal career was as difficult as battling Joe Arpaio in court. By the time the Agster case came around, Manning had already represented the family of Scott Norberg, another inmate with mental illness who also perished in Arpaio's jailhouse restraint chair. His family alleged staffers severely beat Norberg and did not properly check him as he died in the restraint chair. The county, jail medical personnel, and Arpaio all denied wrongdoing. That case resulted in a settlement of over eight million dollars. Manning told us he'd taken on Joe Arpaio because no other "good lawyers" in Phoenix would do so. Arpaio was just too "intimidating and so powerful." At the time, he said, politicians and judges feared the sheriff. Arpaio, in Manning's view, was feared because he could go after those who crossed him and not suffer any consequences.

Manning himself recalled feeling uneasy when, on occasion, he was sure Arpaio's deputies were tailing him. It was, to Manning, a form of retaliation for all the inmate wrongful death lawsuits he'd shepherded through the courts.

Arpaio and his agency repeatedly used "dirty tricks" in court, Manning told us. He dreaded litigating a case against Arpaio and his office, because, he told us, "You know the evidence is going to get destroyed . . . You know they're going to lock arms together. They're going to hide everything they can hide. They're going to ensure there's no such thing as an honest internal affairs investigation. They're going to intimidate witnesses . . . So there is no more difficult job for a litigator than going up against that collage of dirty tricks."

Sometimes, Mike Manning would depose Arpaio or question him on the witness stand. At the beginning of his testimony, Manning recalled, Arpaio would often say he had a cold or the flu and was under the weather. Manning believed Arpaio feigned illness as an excuse for not getting the facts quite right.

We asked Arpaio to respond to Manning's allegations—feigning illness on the stand, the deputies tailing critics as a form of retaliation, the courtroom dirty tricks. Not true, Arpaio said, it was all "garbage." He viewed Manning as an opportunistic lawyer who preyed on the sheriff's department to make money. Publicly, he dismissed Manning as an ambulance chaser. In court, he always professed his innocence.

Manning told us through the years he successfully took Arpaio to court sixteen times. He secured large cash settlements or jury verdicts totaling more than forty million dollars for his clients. Nine of the cases involved inmates who died in Arpaio's jails. The other cases involved "abuse of power and constitutional violations," Manning told us. He represented county employees, members of the board of supervisors, judges, and others wrongfully charged or arrested. "He [Arpaio] was retaliating—using his office and his ability to arrest and charge perceived enemies," Manning told us.

Manning talked to us in his downtown Phoenix office, which was crammed with memorabilia from his battles with Arpaio—plaques commemorating legal victories and framed newspaper cartoons critical of the sheriff. Manning was fascinated with Arpaio's character. He viewed the sheriff as a "very insecure man" who appealed to the "darker side of human nature." He was perplexed when Arpaio chummed up to him at charitable social events, all smiles, wanting to shake his hand, saying something to the effect of no hard feelings.

After Manning scored the 2006 Agster verdict, Arpaio countered the humiliating publicity by drawing attention to a newly established squad of deputies that would come to be known as the "Human Smuggling Unit." It was set up exclusively to hunt migrants in transit from the border to their destinations. The deputies stopped carloads of migrants on rural county roads and raided drophouses.

The Human Smuggling Unit was viewed as a prestigious post. Yet Steve Bailey, a lieutenant in the special investigations division at the time, told us he had a bad feeling about the new unit and turned down an invitation to join. He wound up feeling sorry for deputies who had joined because the unit did not receive proper guidance, but was pressured from the top of the organization to make a high number of migrant arrests day in and day out. "They didn't really know what they were doing, they were never trained properly," Bailey told us years later. "They were kind of left to their own devices." Most of the deputies recruited into the unit were Latino and bilingual. Some would later say they felt conflicted about their assignments.

To gain even more attention, Arpaio dispatched volunteer posse members to join the deputies scouring the desert for migrants and their coyote guides.

Lisa Allen, Arpaio's publicist, sent out a "national media advisory" about the migrant-hunting posse. It worked—reporters from *The New York Times* and *The Washington Post* both covered the migrant hunts. A poll showed the majority of Arizona voters "supported" the effort. "My office has received thousands of letters, calls and emails from around the country about what I'm doing regarding illegal immigration and all were positive," Arpaio announced at the time. "Someone even sent me flowers."

Arpaio's best opportunity to show off his new tough-on-immigrants persona happened on a sweltering morning in the summer of 2006, on the sidewalk beneath his office. By then, Arpaio had moved his headquarters far away from the jail, to the elegant Wells Fargo Plaza in the downtown Phoenix business district.

Elias Bermudez, the immigrant-rights activist who had served time in prison for money laundering, led a protest of about three hundred immigrant demonstrators to Arpaio's doorstep. Some had sealed their mouths with blue tape, symbolizing a silenced, criminalized immigrant community. Some brought their children, dressed in black-and-white-striped jail costumes.

Arpaio strolled out of the building, uncharacteristically dressed in his photogenic beige-brown sheriff uniform instead of his usual baggy suit. Then, unexpectedly, as local television news cameras rolled, Bermudez fell to his knees at Arpaio's feet and begged him to stop arresting migrants.

As if speaking directly to his fans, Arpaio looked down at Bermudez. "You can't change my mind on this," he growled into the mics. "I will continue to lock up illegals who conspire with smugglers."

Arpaio couldn't have dreamed up a better visual metaphor depicting his efficiency as an immigration enforcer. The image of a Mexican immigrant supplicant kneeling at Arpaio's feet sent a strong message to voters watching television news that night.

Years later, Arpaio and Ava chatted about that moment as we sat with them at the round table in their sunny breakfast nook at their home in Fountain Hills. Motifs of flowers and birds danced across the white tablecloth, which was set with silverware, plates, and matching cloth napkins. Ava wore a sleeveless flower print dress and two diamond rings. Her husband drank coffee from a paper cup and munched on a jelly doughnut.

"It was nice," Arpaio told us of the made-for-TV moment when Bermudez kneeled in front of him. "It was great. Good media attention . . . sent messages out."

Asked if it felt surprising to have someone kneel at his feet, Arpaio said, "People pray. They get on their knees."

"But not to you," countered Ava.

"Well, this is his, this is what he wanted to do," Arpaio told his wife.

"It's a plead, it's more like you'd call it a plead," Ava said.

Years later Bermudez told us he'd once socialized with Arpaio in Republican circles and "at one time considered him a friend." Then Bermudez shared with us his odd take on the kneeling episode. When he knelt at Arpaio's feet, Bermudez claimed it was a transformative moment. It caused Arpaio to feel "torn" between his duty to enforce the law and the human consequences of doing so, he told us.

That vision didn't pan out.

By July 2006, Arpaio had enforced the Human Smuggling Law for four months and had arrested some 245 unauthorized immigrants, most of them on conspiracy charges.

Arpaio and Andrew Thomas were now steadfast allies. Arpaio's department was the only law enforcement agency in Arizona enforcing the Human Smuggling Law. And Thomas was the only county attorney in Arizona who believed migrants could be prosecuted for conspiring with the smuggler to smuggle themselves. Other law enforcement agencies claimed they either didn't have the resources to enforce the law or thought the law was bad policy.

Once Arpaio started using the state's Human Smuggling Law to lock up migrants, ICE (U.S. Immigration and Customs Enforcement) agents in Phoenix stopped cooperating with the sheriff. Until then, these federal immigration agents had visited Arpaio's jails to pick up deportable immigrants. But now they balked at collecting inmates who had been arrested for conspiring to smuggle themselves.

Arpaio announced he had come up with his own alternative solution. "I have decided to transport these illegal aliens 155 miles to the US-Mexican border in lieu of releasing convicted felons to the streets of Phoenix, Arizona," Arpaio wrote in a letter to Julie Myers, assistant secretary of the Department of Homeland Security for ICE.

By mid-August, Arpaio's deputies had shuttled fifty-three immigrants to faraway Border Patrol stations to ensure their swift deportation.

The American Civil Liberties Union questioned whether Arpaio, a local lawman, had the authority to transport immigrants across county lines to facilitate their deportation. But Thomas jumped in with a legal opinion endorsing the practice. The county attorney leaned heavily on Kris Kobach's contention that local cops could enforce civil violations of federal immigration law. In the months that followed, the Arpaio-ICE relationship would improve and the shuttles would no longer be necessary. But Arpaio would never forget the tactic. Years later, he would once again resort to shuttling immigrants to Border Patrol stations to ensure their deportation.

And the second time around, it would turn out differently.

Lydia Guzman had given up on her dream of becoming a journalist long ago, but she discovered in her role at Somos America that she enjoyed speaking with reporters, and could do so fluently and effectively in both English and Spanish. She was strategic when she spoke to the cameras. Hoping to communicate unity, she didn't disclose how disgusted she'd felt when Elias Bermudez knelt at Arpaio's feet.

She focused instead on helping Somos America find its sea legs. The coalition scored its first major post-march victory by defeating a local effort by restrictionist activists to force Phoenix police to enforce federal immigration laws.

The coalition turned its attention to jailed migrants arrested for conspiring with a smuggler to smuggle themselves into Arizona. Somos America raised money for the migrants' jailhouse accounts. This cash enabled the migrants to buy phone cards, toothpaste, shampoo, and packets of salt and pepper from the sheriff's expensive commissary.

Next, Somos America joined a lawsuit against Arpaio and Thomas, alleging their interpretation of the Human Smuggling Law was unconstitutional. Antonio Bustamante, who now lived in Phoenix, signed onto the legal team. In an effort to recruit migrants as plaintiffs, Guzman visited Arpaio's Estrella jail. During one visit, she met two young Mexican women in the musty-smelling waiting room. Their wrists were shackled to the table. Two weeks earlier, the women had crossed into Arizona, escaped the notice of the border patrol, spent a short time in a Phoenix drophouse, then crammed themselves with sixteen other migrants into a van headed to Las Vegas. Less than an hour into the trip, a police officer pulled the van over for speeding and called Arpaio's office.

Now the two women shackled to the jail table faced state felony charges for conspiring to smuggle themselves into Arizona. One of the women told Guzman, "I'm not a criminal, I didn't conspire. I didn't know anybody else in the group. I just wanted to be with my family." A detention officer prevented Guzman from reaching across the table to dry the woman's eyes.

The indignity of that moment would stay with Guzman for years. To her, the women seemed powerless and confused. It was the first time she had directly witnessed the human impact of Arpaio's crackdown on migrants.

"I knew that this was happening," she told us of Arpaio's human smuggling arrests. "But it wasn't until that moment that we got it."

Guzman signed the two women up as plaintiffs to join the federal lawsuit, *We Are America/Somos America v. Maricopa County Board of Supervisors*. It was the first time the coalition took on Arpaio in the courts. Seven years later, a federal judge would finally rule that the sheriff and county attorney must stop arresting and prosecuting migrants for conspiring to smuggle themselves into Arizona. In those seven intervening years, sheriff and court records show, deputies arrested more than 2,300 people on smuggling-related felony charges.

Arpaio had transformed himself from a jailer accused of mistreating inmates to a local immigration enforcer accused of terrorizing migrants. It was as if the nation's last two waves of immigration, and the restrictionist backlash they had engendered, had bookended Arpaio's life. As a young boy, he'd felt the sting of anti-immigrant vitriol because his father Ciro was an unwanted Italian immigrant. As a grown man, Arpaio harnessed that same type of animus, aimed this time at unwanted immigrants from Mexico and Latin America. Once targeted as a child, Joe Arpaio now targeted others.

As Joe Arpaio arrested immigrants for conspiring with smugglers to smuggle themselves, Lydia Guzman tried to convert her Republican boyfriend into seeing things her way. She'd met Tony Wesley on match.com, a popular online dating site, because she didn't like to date men in her activist circle. She hadn't ruled out conservative men—in fact she was often drawn to them—as long as they were open-minded and willing to listen.

Wesley was a construction supervisor, tall, slim, sandy-haired. His understanding of immigration issues was informed by Fox News and those who repeated restrictionist talking points from organizations like FAIR, he told us. "I'd heard things like [immigrants] came across the Mexican border to pick up the welfare checks at the border," Wesley said. He was grateful Guzman showed him how to find reliable information online. "I learned that by researching and by listening to her that most of my preconceived ideas were just ridiculous," he told us. Wesley wanted to help immigrants, too, and began accompanying Guzman to events. Soon, the two lived together, along with Wesley's son and Guzman's kids, in Guzman's Glendale home. The blended family had its difficulties, but it seemed to Guzman it worked well enough.

Little else seemed to be working, though. Despite the hope, promise, and show of force fostered by the giant April marches in cities throughout the nation, the prospect of reforming federal immigration law now seemed remote. In desperation, the union-backed national immigrant rights movement urged Somos America to organize a Labor Day rally in Phoenix as part of a coordinated effort to pressure Congress to pass immigration reform.

The rally fizzled. Five months after Somos America had assembled the largest march in Arizona history, the same coalition attracted only a smattering of supporters. Fifteen thousand demonstrators were expected, but only two thousand showed up. Clipboard-toting volunteers signed up only a few new voters. Guzman wondered if the movement was getting "march burnout."

About fifty hecklers stood on the sidelines. Russell Pearce dropped by to shake their hands. One heckler compared Mexican children to dogs. A man wrapped a Mexican flag around his crotch like a diaper.

Somos America was still young, battling established national and local anti-immigrant forces. The coalition was unprepared to fight well-muscled nonprofits like FAIR, and in the looming 2006 congressional midterm elections, immigration was a central issue. Governor Janet Napolitano, a moderate Democrat, was challenged by a Republican who wanted to spend state funds securing the border and creating an Arizona Border Patrol. Napolitano tiptoed on a treacherous political path. She'd signed the

Human Smuggling Law but had slapped down several restrictionist bills. Pearce called Napolitano "the best friend illegal aliens have."

Pearce too was running for re-election. He called for increased immigration enforcement and spoke favorably about Eisenhower's mass deportation program, Operation Wetback. The activists worried if Pearce stayed in power, he would pile on even more restrictionist measures. Arizona would feel even more hostile to them.

The restrictionists had been tenacious that legislative session. After Napolitano vetoed several of their bills, they reincarnated them as stand-alone ballot initiatives to be decided by voters.

One proposition sought to deny pretrial bail to unauthorized immigrants accused of felonies, including conspiring to smuggle oneself into Arizona. Another initiative proposed English as the official state language, aping the 1988 effort that had been struck down eight years earlier. Still another sought to deny unauthorized immigrants damages in civil lawsuits.

And a fourth, Proposition 300, banned unauthorized immigrants from qualifying for in-state tuition at Arizona colleges and universities. The measure sparked a new wing of the Latino civil rights movement in Arizona. Young undocumented immigrant students brought to Arizona as children, known as Dreamers, became activists because without access to in-state tuition rates, most wouldn't be able to afford college.

The risks were so high that the union SEIU, through the nonprofit Mi Familia Vota, launched an energetic effort to mobilize the Latino vote that summer. The union office in central Phoenix became a frenzied hub of voter outreach.

Nearly 44 percent of eligible Latino voters were unregistered at the time, and 5,800 who were on the rolls didn't vote in the 2004 election. This had to be changed, Guzman knew. It had taken several election cycles to mobilize Latino voters in California in the wake of Proposition 187. Common sense and experience told her it would take years of hard work to turn the tide in Arizona. She was an optimist but also a realist.

Guzman turned thirty-nine on election day. It wasn't a great birthday. That evening, she attended a Democratic watch party in downtown Phoenix. As the returns rolled over a giant screen, Guzman trained her eyes on the four anti-migrant ballot initiatives. These ballot measures were immune from gubernatorial vetoes. Each passed with more than 70 percent support. And most of the state's voters lived in Maricopa County.

"My gosh, Maricopa County really hates Mexicans," Guzman told us she remembered thinking. The SEIU drive had succeeded in signing up thousands of Latino voters, but it hadn't been nearly enough. Although Napolitano remained governor, Russell Pearce kept his house seat. Guzman hoped Napolitano would continue vetoing Pearce's bills. "We felt that sense of comfort knowing that things weren't going to get past her . . . that were going to be harmful to our community," Guzman told us.

Janet Napolitano had stumped for Guzman back when she ran for the state senate in 2004, and Guzman considered the governor a friend. So when she and Tony Wesley decided to marry a few months after the election, she invited the governor to the simple, small ceremony in the garden of an immigration law office.

It was the spring of 2007. Guzman had found a job organizing municipal workers for SEIU, but she didn't particularly like organizing workers. She stuck with it, though, because Tony feared he might soon lose his construction job. The Phoenix housing market was slumping on the cusp of the Great Recession.

Alfredo Gutierrez showed up with wine. He also signed the wedding certificate. The guests—a mix of activists, family, and friends—enjoyed carne asada. Guzman's daughter, Ashley, snapped the photos, while James and his new stepbrother played beneath the citrus trees. As a joke, Guzman chose a bride dragging a groom to the altar as the topper for the banana angel food wedding cake. .

Napolitano couldn't attend but sent an official letter of congratulations. A few months later, Guzman emailed Napolitano begging her not to sign a bill she felt would deeply harm the Latino community and the Arizona economy.

The Legal Arizona Workers Act, sponsored by Russell Pearce and reviewed by Kobach, required Arizona employers to check the immigration status of employees via a federal database before they could be hired. Employers who didn't check the database, known as E-Verify, were vulnerable to fines and losing their business licenses.

In nervous Somos America meetings, Guzman and her colleagues correctly guessed the new bill would punish immigrants and Latino workers rather than employers.

Pearce's bill was rooted in an immigration restrictionist strategy called "attrition through enforcement." If life in the United States became unpleasant for undocumented immigrants, the reasoning went, they would "self-deport." Pearce asserted once the Legal Arizona Workers Act took effect at the beginning of 2008, unauthorized immigrants in Arizona would self-deport because they would no longer have jobs. He insisted all that self-deporting would reduce Arizona's crime rate. Guzman and her fellow activists failed to persuade Napolitano to veto Pearce's bill.

The governor claimed she signed the bill because the federal government's inaction on immigration reform left her no choice. Pearce told us the governor signed the Legal Arizona Workers Act because she knew if she didn't, he would put an even more severe version of the proposed law on the ballot for voters to decide.

Eventually, Arpaio would rely on the Legal Arizona Workers Act to escalate his immigration crackdowns by raiding workplaces and jailing immigrant workers on felony charges.

"It was a way," Lydia Guzman told us, "for him to torment us."

8 Cave Creek

2007

For some residents of Cave Creek, Arizona, Sheriff Joe Arpaio's new passion for apprehending migrants was long overdue. In the early 2000s, many who lived in this remote town of several thousand residents on the northern stretch of Maricopa County had resented the sheriff for ignoring what they viewed as a scourge of immigrant day laborers ruining their cowboy-themed desert hideaway.

Cave Creek sat some thirty miles northeast of central Phoenix. The road into town looped through boulder-strewn hills spiked with green-trunked, yellow-flowering palo verde trees and saguaro cactuses with sturdy arms pointing at the sky, as if angling for a fight. Cave Creek merchants exploited the cowboy theme, selling armchairs upholstered in cowhide, tables made of saguaro cactus skeletons, and spiky metal yard ornaments shaped like agave plants. Cave Creek was a place where visitors could lose themselves in Old West cowboy mythology, if only for a day.

But hidden beneath the cowboy kitsch, some Cave Creek residents resented an influx of Latino immigrant day laborers and their advocates. They especially resented the day laborer program at Good Shepherd of the Hills Episcopal Church, a Spanish Mission-style stucco church with a bell tower and iron cross, that sat just off a busy stretch of Cave Creek Road.

Every morning except Sunday, about sixty Mexican and Central American immigrant day laborers waited on the church patio fueling up on donated day-old Starbucks pastries. They wore sturdy jeans, laced boots, long-sleeved shirts and sun-shielding baseball caps—the uniform of hard work. Eager and fit, they waited for employers in pickup trucks to ferry them to nearby construction and landscaping gigs.

Father Glenn Jenks, the church rector, was a short, round man with blue eyes and gray hair who wore a priestly white starched collar and black shirt, and occasionally shaded his delicate skin with a wide-brimmed cowboy hat. A former criminal defense and personal injury lawyer, Jenks viewed immigration as a critical civil rights issue. He called the day laborer program, which opened in 2001, "justice work." Jenks enforced strict rules to avoid worker exploitation. Employers had to agree to pay the laborers a ten-dollar hourly wage, and provide lunch and water.

The church didn't require day laborers to show immigration papers, but practically everyone in town assumed the immigrant workers were undocumented. When some parishioners griped about helping the "illegals," Jenks said the Bible instructed Christians to welcome foreigners. He lost a few parishioners, gained a few others, and made many others uncomfortable.

The day laborers at the church center abided by agreed upon rules. They donated to a communal medical fund. They couldn't use drugs or slack off. They agreed to reside in Cave Creek, and many lived in an apartment complex adjacent to the church.

Some men who didn't want to follow the rules camped out in the desert, building campfires, littering. The vagrants irked locals who treasured their unspoiled desert landscape. One local, Don Sorchych, the editor and publisher of the town paper, was particularly outraged. Sorchych had named his paper *Sonoran News* after the pristine desert and had given it a tagline, "The Conservative Voice of Arizona." In scathing editorials he railed against illegal immigration and the church program. He called the church "a magnet, drawing illegal invading aliens like manure attracts flies."

Linda Bentley, Sorchych's like-minded reporter, wrote articles noting crimes committed by local unauthorized immigrants—including driving without a license or insurance. A tall, thin woman with brown hair and large eyes, Bentley told us her unease over unauthorized immigrants traced to the 1970s, when she was in her late teens and early twenties. Back then, she was single and lived in a rough Los Angeles neighborhood. She feared the Spanish-speaking men who catcalled her when she walked home alone from the bus stop at night. Before taking a job with the *Sonoran News,* she had managed a small masonry outfit and blamed unauthorized immigrants for driving down construction wages for citizens.

In Cave Creek, Bentley fretted when immigrant day laborers gathered at the Circle K convenience store near the *Sonoran News* office. Years later, she would remember the times she drove to work and several day laborers jumped right into the back of her truck. She assumed they thought she wanted to hire them.

And even though the church day labor program was designed to prevent immigrants from seeking work on town streets, Bentley viewed the program as a magnet that drew more immigrants to the little town. "You'd have illegals that would stand on Cave Creek Road like garden gnomes," she would recall years later.

In her memory, the town never had problems with break-ins until the "illegals" showed up. She worried their campfires put nearby homes at risk. And she resented the empty Bud Light cans they left behind at what she viewed as their filthy campsites. She wondered how they could afford Bud Light, while she and her taxpaying citizen friends drank cheaper Keystone, she told us.

Even though "unlawful presence" in the United States, or being in the country without proper documents, was a federal civil violation, Bentley, like others in the restrictionist movement, viewed it as a crime. As far as she was concerned, the "illegals" were causing a crime wave in her town, and the church was their enabler.

Bentley didn't initially see Arpaio as an ally. From her perspective, Arpaio got publicity for arresting migrants elsewhere but neglected Cave Creek. The sheriff's office provided contracted law enforcement services to Cave Creek, and Bentley didn't think deputies were adequately investigating the break-ins she attributed to day laborers. Nor did she appreciate it when Arpaio jailed Patrick Haab, who had held six migrants and their driver at gunpoint at the rest stop in 2005. She viewed Haab as an American hero. After he was sprung from jail, she had hired him for handyman gigs.

Sonoran News reflected the town's growing restrictionist movement and likely helped build it.

Buffalo Rick Galeener, a retired producer of Wild West shows, visited Cave Creek often with his motorcycle group, American Freedom Riders. At the time, he told us, he often dressed in his leathers "because it intimidates everyone" and "scares the hell out of" unauthorized immigrants. Galeener told us several Cave Creek residents pointed him to a wash that paralleled Cave Creek Road. Here, hidden by thorny desert bushes and trees, was an empty migrant camp. Galeener called it a "filth hole." In his memory, he and several others who were disgusted with "illegal immigrants" and their messes shoveled up tin, tarps, cardboard, Styrofoam coolers, clothes, and feces, then hurled it all into pickups headed for the town dump.

He was a small thin man who had grown up in Phoenix, and he waxed nostalgic to us about a boyhood spent hiking, biking, and catching crawdads in irrigation canals. But as the years passed and "illegal immigrants" became increasingly more visible in the county, he became embittered. In Galeener's eyes, American citizens, including Vietnam veterans like him, got less governmental support than unauthorized immigrants. Once, the Southern Poverty Law Center, a left-leaning nonprofit that tracks alleged hate groups in the United States, called him out as a xenophobe and nativist. He told us he considered it a badge of honor.

In late 2006, Galeener and the American Freedom Riders began picketing the Good Shepherd of the Hills Episcopal Church, joined by a few Cave Creek residents and *Sonoran News* readers. The bikers returned every Saturday morning for almost a year, Galeener told us, shouting into bullhorns, while the publisher of the *Sonoran News* snapped photos of employers who picked up workers. Tim Rafferty, a member of American Freedom Riders, told us the church was targeted because it "facilitated" the hiring of unauthorized immigrants.

The restrictionist protesters carried signs. One read: "Where's the Fence?" and another read: "Rev Jenks and this church are blatantly breaking federal law."

Cave Creek was a harbinger of a widening cultural divide in Maricopa County, an ugly schism that would soon capture the attention of the nation and the world. Cave Creek would become a proving ground for Joe Arpaio's immigration enforcement, and foreshadow the immigration tensions that would one day divide the nation and define the presidency of Donald Trump.

As a drug enforcement agent, Joe Arpaio had encountered addicts who couldn't get enough heroin and kept increasing their doses to get high. Arpaio, it seemed, had developed his own cravings—for praise and publicity. Thanks in part to his busy publicists, who had in recent months issued dozens of press releases trumpeting Arpaio's successes in Human Smuggling Law enforcement, the sheriff had managed to recover from arresting Haab and helping the unauthorized Mexican immigrant mother. Polls showed him to be the most popular politician in the sprawling county. He didn't seem satisfied. He seemed to crave more.

And in early 2007, the sheriff found a way to get more approval through a new partnership with the federal government. That agreement would allow Arpaio to blaze a new trail in the local enforcement of immigration laws. He would terrify immigrants, violate the constitutional rights of Latino Americans, ramp up Arizona's restrictionist movement, and further galvanize the Latino resistance.

The agreement was a local-federal immigration enforcement partnership with a clunky bureaucratic name: 287(g)—a reference to a section of the U.S. Immigration and Nationality Act that allows federal immigration agents to certify local and state police officers to enforce certain parts of the federal immigration law. ICE signed its first agreement (with the Florida Department of Law Enforcement) in the wake of the September 11, 2001 terrorist attacks, but the program was slow to catch on. Governor Janet Napolitano had responded to illegal immigration anxiety in Arizona by negotiating some of the earliest 287(g) partnership agreements in the country for state prisons and state police.

In 2007, the George W. Bush administration ramped up 287(g) agreements as it tried to persuade Congress to pass a comprehensive immigration reform deal—one that would include increased enforcement along with legalizing millions of unauthorized immigrants.

The plan failed. But dozens of new 287(g) partnerships took effect.

In February 2007, ICE granted Arpaio the largest 287(g) partnership in the nation. The federal agency agreed to train and certify 160 Maricopa County Sheriff's Office detention officers and deputies as immigration enforcers.

Arpaio told us he'd wanted more authority "to do my job on illegal immigration."

And the 287(g) partnerships would give him that authority.

"'Hey,' I said, 'Why not? . . . Wow, this would be great,'" he told us. "I loved it and signed it."

With 287(g), Arpaio's arrests of unauthorized immigrants skyrocketed from the hundreds to the thousands. He would no longer be confined to enforcing the state Human Smuggling Law. With 287(g) powers, his deputies could interrogate and arrest anyone they suspected of being in the country illegally. And he could flag immigrants booked into his jails so they would be turned over to federal authorities for deportation upon their release.

Just a year earlier, Arpaio had clashed with his future federal partner, ICE, when its agents had flat out refused to pick up the migrants arrested by Arpaio's deputies under the Human Smuggling Law. Arpaio and Napolitano had both complained about the recalcitrant agents. Now a much more amenable special agent in charge, Alonzo Peña, had taken over the Phoenix ICE office.

According to ICE, Arpaio was supposed to use 287(g) to question criminal suspects or arrestees about their immigration status. But Arpaio had a more grandiose interpretation. He planned on hunting down any immigrant unlawfully present in the county—regardless of their criminal history. Arpaio proudly announced at a press conference that his immigration program would be "pure."

"You go after illegals," Arpaio told reporters. "I'm not afraid to say that. And you go after 'em, and you lock 'em up."

Peña, the friendly ICE agent in charge, stood politely next to Arpaio. After the press conference ended, reporters cornered Peña with additional questions. He acknowledged the sheriff's comments had not aligned with the language in their agreement. Under Peña and his successors, the local ICE office would conduct little oversight of its new partnership with

Arpaio. Unfettered by supervision, Arpaio would test the limits of his newfound power.

Arpaio's transformation, from pink underwear jailer to ruthless immigration enforcer, was widely viewed by critics as a calculated political pivot. By attaching himself to the growing restrictionist movement, Arpaio stood to gain even more celebrity, campaign donations, adulation from his constituents, and power.

But Arpaio insisted otherwise.

He often told us he started arresting immigrants simply because the state passed the Human Smuggling Law and it was his duty to enforce it. "It's in my character that I will enforce the laws," he told us. "I go very aggressive no matter what the law is."

Many wondered at the time how he could cause so much pain to people who just wanted to work and join relatives in the United States. And later, as he intensified his immigration enforcement, many would wonder how he could justify ripping apart families that included American citizens. He would respond by saying if people wanted him to stop arresting immigrants, they should get the state and federal laws changed. That was his standard line. But occasionally he mentioned his views on immigration enforcement were shaped by the injustice that befell his father's brother.

Arpaio couldn't remember his uncle's name, he told us. He never met his uncle, and now the uncle was long dead. But in the 1920s, right around the time his father came to the United States, his father's brother was blocked from entering the United States from Italy because of restrictive immigration quotas. "He ended up in Canada because he couldn't get in here," Arpaio told us. In his retelling of family lore, the uncle waited years and years to come into the United States but never got in.

The family story didn't comport with immigration policy at the time. While the uncle was likely blocked from entering the United States when he crossed the ocean from Italy, immigration laws at the time did not restrict Italian migrants from entering the United States if they'd lived in Canada for five years.

But the importance of the uncle's story, in Arpaio's view, was that good people try to immigrate legally into the United States every day, and wait and wait, and spend a lot of money trying to come in, but are rebuffed. "So all these people wait legally, and then you got people coming illegally and you take care of 'em?" Arpaio told us. "That's not fair." That's why he felt so deeply about unauthorized immigration, he told us.

After we fact-checked the history and sought his response, Arpaio acknowledged that his family mythology about his uncle, which he had used to explain his passion for immigration enforcement, was likely not accurate. We were "probably" correct about the laws, he said. "Maybe he [the uncle] got to like Canada and he did not want to come in," he offered.

During Arpaio's first decade in office, he and Lisa Allen had expertly created new story angles—coffee bans, pink underwear, chain gangs—to entice reporters to keep covering Arpaio as a tough-on-crime lawman. Now they focused on getting reporters to cover Arpaio as a tough immigration enforcer.

In the summer of 2007, as Arpaio's 287(g) squad finished federal training, Arpaio wanted the press to cover yet another immigration enforcement idea. He unveiled it on a sweltering July afternoon, after summoning reporters to Tent City. He and Allen couldn't resist the Tent City setting—the chain link fence topped with razor wire, the torn green tents, the rickety bunk beds, the perspiring inmates in their black-and-white stripes. Tent City, with its excellent optics, never failed to draw a crowd of journalists, even on hot days.

The seventy-five-year-old sheriff tolerated the brutal Phoenix heat better than most of the journalists half his age and announced his latest idea with brio.

He'd set up an illegal immigration hotline!

Anyone could now dial up the sheriff's office, and report identities and locations of suspected unauthorized immigrants. Then he, Joe Arpaio, would investigate and arrest the "illegals."

"We're not going to go on a street corner and round up a group of people because they look like they're from a foreign country," Arpaio promised when he announced the hotline. Within months, though, his deputies would do just that, by targeting Mexican day laborers.

Eventually, Arpaio painted the hotline number on sheriff's vans and trucks as a constant reminder in the community about his immigration enforcement. The hotline galvanized both sides of the growing divide in Maricopa County. Restrictionists lauded it as a way to restore law and order. Somos America and sympathetic religious leaders denounced it for encouraging discrimination.

"It was like a slap in the face," Lydia Guzman told us. "I knew that when you give this responsibility to the public, it opened a door for racial profiling."

She worried her own neighbors would become suspicious of Mexican Americans on their block. They might even report her family to Arpaio "because they wouldn't know what an immigrant looks like." Immediately, she and other Somos America activists drew parallels to the way Jews were treated in Nazi Germany.

Guzman recalled her thoughts: "Do we need to find out who needs to wear the Star of David or something? I mean, how are we going to be safe and who's going to verify who's who, right? Are we going back to that Gestapo era?"

The sheriff's office told reporters the hotline received more than 150 messages within the first four days, including missives from forty-five people reporting on members of their own families.

The sheriff got fan letters. One woman complained about Mexicans living next door. She didn't like the dead grass in their yard. She didn't like the cars parked out front. "Every week," she wrote, "the illegals fill two trash cans to overflowing. Do they pay taxes? No! Who is paying for keeping them here? Legal taxpayers!" Arpaio tucked the letter into a file folder dedicated to immigration that he kept in his office closet.

He meticulously tabulated his media coverage. On a sheet of blank paper, he scribbled the words "Hot Line." Underneath, in messy, angular script, he recorded names and dates of interviews. NPR, Lars Larson, *Fox and Friends* . . . the list went on and on.

In response, Somos America leaders announced they would start their own rival hotlines to document cases of civil rights violations and discrimination by the Maricopa County Sheriff's Office. They vowed to forward the information to the FBI and the Arizona attorney general's office.

Arpaio bristled when he heard Latino leaders had likened his illegal immigration hotline to the Third Reich's efforts to encourage German citizens to inform on Jews.

He insisted he used the hotline responsibly. Law enforcement often set up hotlines, he said. And Alonzo Peña, the local ICE head, had no problem with the hotline.

Arpaio kept notes in his immigration file about his Latino critics. He noticed that his longtime friend, county supervisor Mary Rose Wilcox, was among them.

The Latino blowback had an unintended consequence—it increased Arpaio's media exposure. After Latino leaders announced they would set up rival hotlines, Arpaio supporters called the sheriff's hotline simply to offer their praise and support. One man called to say he slept well at night because Arpaio was his sheriff. A woman in Beaverton, Oregon said she wanted to move to Arizona just to be near Arpaio. A man from California said he had already moved to Maricopa County just for the sheriff. Arpaio's staff printed out the compliments in a transcript so he could read them.

Despite all the fan support, Arpaio worried about his perceived enemies and insisted they were plotting against him. Arpaio's staff had gotten a tip that Elias Bermudez, who had once kneeled at the sheriff's feet, plotted with a violent Mexican drug cartel and the Minutemen to assassinate Arpaio. It was a preposterous conspiracy theory based on a single informant who failed a lie detector test. Nevertheless, Arpaio had spent Easter hiding in a local hotel.

A few months later Bermudez forwarded a widely circulated email showing a crudely photoshopped image of Arpaio, decked out in Ku Klux Klan couture, holding a noose before a Mexican wearing a sombrero and poncho. "Just the plain truth from the eyes of the Hispanic Community," Bermudez wrote in the email. When Arpaio got his hands on a printout of the email, he wrote in his file: "Once again he is placing me and my family in danger."

"All these people . . . comparing me to Nazi and Hitler. Put me in a KKK uniform . . . No one has said anything about what these people do to me," he recalled bitterly. "I guess I'm human like everybody else but nobody cares about all the racist remarks they make."

A new round of sympathetic calls flooded the sheriff's hotline.

One caller left a disturbing message: "I would shoot Bermudez if I could get away with it. Don't give in."

The vitriol spreading through Maricopa County had already been established in Cave Creek, and Arpaio's hotline intensified it. Father Glenn Jenks, the rector of the Good Shepherd of the Hills Episcopal Church in Cave Creek, was pressured by town officials to shut down the day labor program. Jenks told us the officials seemed pressured by citizens who complained about the immigrant day laborers. Jenks refused to shutter the program.

Next, town leaders proposed an ordinance cracking down on day laborers who strayed from the church parking lot. This pleased *Sonoran News* and its expanding cadre of restrictionist readers. Arpaio showed up to a town council meeting to endorse the proposal and talk about his newly 287(g) ICE-trained deputies. The ordinance passed easily. But a federal judge would eventually rule it unconstitutional.

Outside of the Maricopa County Sheriff's Office substation on Cave Creek Road, Arpaio's staff converted the side of a large truck into a billboard advertising the hotline in bright red letters:

HELP SHERIFF JOE ARPAIO STOP ILLEGAL IMMIGRATION AND TRAFFICKING.

The truck sign urged the public to call the hotline "with any info tips on illegal aliens."

It didn't take long for the hotline to ring with complaints about the church day labor program. Unbeknownst to Jenks, the sheriff's office sent undercover Latino 287(g) deputies disguised as day laborers to visit the church parking lot to investigate.

Early in the morning on September 27, 2007, a sheriff's deputy parked his unmarked vehicle near the Dairy Queen next door to the church. From behind a sun visor, the deputy spied three men jump into a white pickup truck in the church parking lot.

Two men sat in the back seat. Manuel de Jesus Ortega Melendres settled into the passenger seat. At fifty-three, Melendres was sturdily built, of medium height, barrel-chested with broad shoulders—as a young man he'd dabbled in amateur Lucha Libre wrestling. Melendres wore a black

T-shirt and black pants, and carried a small travel bag with a toothbrush, soap, and lotion. He was an organized, disciplined man who'd spent thirty years as a teacher and school principal in his native Sonora, Mexico before retiring a few years earlier with a modest pension. Some of his friends called him "El Profe," short for *el profesor*.

Three weeks earlier, he'd legally crossed into Arizona from Sonora. He had a valid Mexican tourist visa, and an arrival form he'd gotten at the border that documented his date of entry and his required exit date to Mexico in six months.

Melendres told us he'd had a tourist visa for fifteen years, ever since he taught in schools in Agua Prieta, a Mexican border town across the line from Douglas, Arizona. Back then, he crossed into the United States to buy groceries or sightsee in southern Arizona. After he retired, he would spend months at a time in Phoenix, staying with immigrant relatives and childhood friends.

Melendres knew his tourist visa did not permit him to work in the United States. Years later, when asked about the morning he climbed into the truck, he would insist he had no intentions of working as a day laborer. He would claim he had jumped in the truck because he wanted to go sightseeing and was seeking a ride to a nearby cluster of scenic boulders.

But minutes after the pickup drove out of the church parking lot, a Maricopa County sheriff's deputy pulled it over. Melendres knew about Arpaio's amped-up immigration enforcement and Cave Creek's efforts to crack down on day laborers, but he figured he was safe. He made it a habit of always carrying his documents in his wallet. "I thought they would not bother me because I was here legally," Melendres told us. "And in this country they respect the law." He worried though, for the two Mexican day laborers in the backseat.

One deputy told the white driver he'd been speeding. But as more deputies in marked and unmarked vehicles approached, Melendres understood the stop was about more than a driver going nine miles over the speed limit. A Spanish-speaking Latino deputy asked the three passengers for identification. When Melendres offered his tourist visa, the deputy accused Melendres of violating his visa by working.

Next, deputies patted down Melendres. They emptied his pockets. They put his wallet and visa in a plastic bag. In his memory, a deputy inspected the toiletries in Melendres's travel bag. The deputy pulled out a container of lotion, made sexual pantomimes with his hands, and asked Melendres: "How many times a week do you jack off?"

The deputies did not ticket the driver, who drove off. Melendres and his companions weren't so lucky. They were under arrest. Melendres told us his handcuffs bit into an old wrestling injury in his wrist. He wondered, as he climbed into a patrol car, what would happen to him. If these cops disregarded his legal visa, if they were willing to humiliate and dehumanize him, what else were they capable of?

Melendres and his fellow passengers were locked in a holding cell at the sheriff's substation, and soon they were joined by six more day laborers who had been arrested the same way. Eventually, the arrested men were transported to the ICE office on Central Avenue in downtown Phoenix. Melendres's ICE cell was full of Spanish-speaking men. His mouth was dry. His stomach growled. He thought he would lose his visa and be deported. "I felt I was treated like the most dangerous criminal," Melendres told us. "It was traumatic."

A Latino ICE supervisor summoned Melendres into his office and spoke to him respectfully in Spanish. The supervisor confirmed Melendres's tourist visa was valid. Melendres was free to go. By his count, he had been detained nearly nine hours. That night, and for many nights following, he couldn't sleep.

Tensions at a Phoenix
Furniture Store

2007

Joe Arpaio continued rounding up day laborers as his constituents voiced alarm about Spanish-speaking workers standing on street corners in Maricopa County. One woman claimed the day laborers ogled schoolchildren in Queen Creek, a Phoenix suburb. A chiropractor with an office in a central Phoenix strip mall complained day laborers showed "their bellies to everyone" and were "harassing school children, women and the elderly."

Throughout the fall of 2007, the sheriff responded to such citizen tips by sending out his federally trained 287(g) deputies—often to the exact intersections tipsters had just complained about. As with Melendres's arrest in Cave Creek, undercover deputies stopped drivers for minor traffic violations after the drivers had picked up day laborers. Next, the deputies arrested the day laborers in the vehicles for federal civil immigration violations. The day laborers weren't accused of committing actual crimes that would justify their arrests, but they were almost always deported because they were turned over to federal immigration authorities.

John Kleinheinz, who ran the sheriff's office Fountain Hills district, told us Arpaio and local politicians pressured him to round up day laborers who congregated near a gas station just a mile south of the town's iconic fountain. Kleinheinz ramped up patrols near the gas station, but the day laborers hanging around it were not committing crimes. Kleinheinz sincerely opposed unauthorized immigration, but he felt he had no legal justification to round up the men. "Just based on the fact that they're Mexican doesn't mean that they're illegal immigrants," he tried to explain to Arpaio.

Arpaio's commanders took matters into their own hands. Without telling Kleinheinz, they dispatched undercover 287(g) trained deputies to Fountain Hills. The deputies pulled over drivers who picked up day laborers and arrested a few men who appeared to be undocumented. These arrests would be dwarfed by what would happen next in central Phoenix.

In the 1970s, M. D. Pruitt's Home Furnishings, which billed itself as "Arizona's Pioneer Discount Furniture Store," sold velvet-upholstered couches and maple dining room sets to families living in apartments and housing developments surrounding Thomas Road in east central Phoenix. But as the years passed, the neighborhoods surrounding Pruitt's changed. Mexican and Central American immigrants, including day laborers, moved into the tired apartment buildings and homes once owned by mostly non-Latino families.

In late 2007, Pruitt's became the focus of the tensions building over day laborers that were spreading throughout Maricopa County. Two years before, in 2005, a Minuteman group began complaining to the sheriff's office about day laborers in the east central Phoenix neighborhood. Sometimes, the laborers approached cars and trucks, seeking work near Home Depot just a few blocks east of Pruitt's on Thomas Road, a noisy street with fast-moving traffic. Business owners complained the day laborers littered, urinated, defecated, and trespassed on their property, driving away customers.

For a while, off-duty Phoenix cops moonlighting as Pruitt's security guards shooed away the day laborers. But the Phoenix police chief had ordered his officers to stop.

That's when Arpaio had stepped in, allowing his off-duty deputies to act as replacements at the furniture store. And he assigned deputies to patrol the nearby streets, on the hunt for day laborers. And in so doing, the sheriff increased racial tensions on Thomas Road to a level that attracted the nation's attention. "Want to see America unraveling? Come here, to

Thomas Road and 35th Street, to M. D. Pruitt's furniture store," *The New York Times* proclaimed.

Carlos Garcia felt the spit hit his cheek. He brushed it off with the palm of his hand. He wasn't sure who'd spit on him, but he knew the culprit was among a group of perhaps a hundred pro-Arpaio restrictionist activists— mostly white, mostly middle-aged or older—facing him on the sidewalk on the north side of Thomas Road, across the street from Pruitt's. In Garcia's memory, quite a few were armed, and some wore leather motor-cycle vests. Some carried American flags. Others held signs supporting Joe Arpaio. Still others waved signs claiming unauthorized immigrants carried disease or slaughtered American citizens or stole jobs.

Garcia's group had gathered about a block to the east, at the Lutheran church, where Arpaio's deputies routinely unloaded crowd-control horses from trailers. The pro-Arpaio group, many of them bikers, had assembled by a trophy shop in a strip mall about a block to the west. The bikers had marched east, Garcia's group had marched west, until they'd practically collided in front of the Red Wok Buffet. They were inches apart from each other, close enough to spit.

The pro-immigrant group was of a similar size as the restrictionist group, but mostly brown and mostly young. They were a mix of day labor-ers, other immigrants, students, clergy members, and activists. They pro-tested Joe Arpaio, his 287(g) immigration partnership with the feds, and his detention and deportation of day laborers. The protesters on Garcia's side brandished signs too. "No human being is illegal!" one sign read. "Working people are not criminals!" read another.

"Illegals go home!" yelled the restrictionists.

"Racists!" shouted the pro-immigrant group.

Cars and trucks passed by, honking in support of one side or the other. Garcia looked across the street at M. D. Pruitt's Home Furnishings, a two-story, 80,000 square foot, rust-colored store laced with ornate white iron-work. The tall columned entryway evoked antebellum architecture. An ample asphalt parking lot fronted the store. Several of Joe Arpaio's armed deputies stood on the furniture store roof, peering at the protesters across Thomas Road. Other deputies paced Pruitt's parking lot, which was some-times blockaded by furniture trucks.

It was late 2007. Garcia, a university student, vice president of Somos America, and a union organizer, was helping his mentor, Salvador Reza, a seasoned activist. Reza had spent the last several years organizing day laborers and ran a work center for them. Reza told us he and the day laborers had designed the protests at Pruitt's to discourage its clientele from buying there in order to punish the store for coordinating with Arpaio. In response, Joe Arpaio's supporters counterdemonstrated in solidarity with the sheriff, Pruitt's furniture store management, and the day-laborer crackdown.

The dueling protests took place each week from October to the end of December. They marked a turning point in Arizona's immigration wars.

Garcia had not seen such a high level of animus and angry rhetoric. Looking into the eyes of the people on the other side, Garcia sensed he was hated for the color of his skin, for his Mexicanness.

He was born in 1983 in Cananea, Sonora, Mexico, a mining town about forty miles south of Naco, Arizona. Garcia's parents split up when he was young, and he grew up with his mother, Ciria. The two moved back and forth between the United States and Mexico. In Arizona, Ciria worked two and three jobs at a time, and learned English on television. She sent money home to her parents, while supporting herself, her son, and a nephew. They lived anxious lives. They didn't have papers. They knew they could be deported.

When Garcia was in grammar school, Ciria married Robert Hays, an American citizen who ran a used tire business in Tucson; Hays died two and a half years later. "He was awesome. He was great. I had a dad for two and a half years," Garcia would remember. Ciria, grieving, moved with her son from Tucson to Nogales, Sonora, Mexico. Garcia stopped going to his eighth-grade classes for a few months and wandered around Nogales with his friends. Americans frequently crossed the border from Arizona to buy affordable medications, and Garcia earned a few pesos from certain pharmacy owners each time he directed Americans to their establishments.

When he was fourteen, thanks to his mother's marriage to Hays, Garcia finally obtained his green card for legal permanent residency in the United States. He worried, though, about cousins, aunts, and uncles who lived every day in fear of deportation.

By the time Garcia protested at Pruitt's furniture store, he was twenty-four years old. As he scanned the aging pro-Arpaio crowd facing him, he figured he could wallop anyone there. He wasn't put off by the fact that some were armed. He'd grown up in tough neighborhoods, he wasn't afraid. But he also knew he had to control himself, he couldn't clock anyone. His mentor Salvador Reza had warned him, coached him, explained again and again that the other side *wanted* him to fight back, *wanted* arrests and perp walks and images of handcuffed brown ne'er-do-wells on television news. Garcia couldn't let that happen.

Instead, he turned his large body into a T-shaped shield, arms spread, ponytail dangling down his back.

Be calm, he told the men and women behind him.

Be calm.

Kathryn Kobor was in her sixties, a grandmother, and one of Joe Arpaio's most loyal supporters when she debuted as an activist at Pruitt's in the fall of 2007. Kobor showed up almost every week until the demonstrations ended in December, because finally she felt she could do something besides sit at home and worry about illegal immigration. She'd watched reports with her husband for years about "illegal aliens coming over en masse," she told us.

She believed the restrictionist narrative she sought out and read on her computer. And she'd gotten very worried.

"We felt that they were taking veterans' jobs, Black Americans' jobs. We had to educate them [unauthorized immigrants], feed them, clothe them, teach them to speak English, and it's okay if you have some coming in, of course. But it was a mass invasion into Maricopa County and I just got more and more irritated thinking, 'My gosh, we can't take in the whole world, there's a billion out there.'"

She had written a letter to the editor in support of Patrick Haab, taking a stand that way. But it wasn't until she struck up a conversation with a like-minded clerk at her local PetSmart store that she heard about United for a Sovereign America, or USA. The group had just been formed by a Kia car dealership owner named Rusty Childress, who hosted weekly meetings in the showroom of his dealership. On meeting nights, in the showroom, a circle of chairs replaced shiny Kias.

Kobor had blue eyes, white hair, and delicate white sun-sensitive skin. She showed up at the meetings in the car dealership dressed in three-quarter-length sleeved blouses and slacks. She munched coffee cake and chatted with bikers like Valerie Roller and her husband, George Sprankle, who had joined the Minuteman Project.

Rusty Childress declined our request for an interview. But in a 2008 report, the Southern Poverty Law Center flagged Childress as a prominent American nativist. According to the center, the speakers at his weekly USA meetings at his KIA dealership included a leader of an anti-immigrant hate group, a neo-Nazi, a white supremacist, and Russell Pearce.

Kobor didn't see Pearce and Childress as evil men or racists. She viewed them as men of integrity who wanted to save the country from the ravages of illegal immigration. "I feel like I got informed there," Kobor recalled. She told us the USA meetings "cemented my position." She wanted to stand up for American citizens, regardless of ethnicity, in the fight against what she viewed as an invasion of immigrants who would destroy the United States.

"I don't want this country to turn into a country like India with sewage running in the street, people living in cardboard boxes," she told us. "I know that's not happening in my lifetime, but I have a granddaughter and she's going to have children hopefully one day." Some branded Kobor a racist during her later years as an activist, but she told us she never viewed herself as one. All blood runs red, she often said.

Kobor told us she attended elementary school with a few Mexican American kids. They were citizens, she recalled, not "illegals." Although most Latino families were barred from many white neighborhoods by restrictive covenants, in Kobor's memory Phoenix was not racially segregated.

But through the years, she saw her beloved Phoenix change as it became, in her mind, overrun with unauthorized immigrants. At Pruitt's, week after week, she gave voice to that concern.

Sometimes, Joe Arpaio stopped by, dressed in a shiny dark brown jacket, to say hello. "He represented," she told us, "what we believed in."

Salvador Reza, widely regarded as the mastermind behind the Pruitt's protests, held a different view of Joe Arpaio. He saw the sheriff as an "opportunistic, cunning megalomaniac."

Reza, who was born in Mexico and became an American citizen at age eighteen, was now in his mid fifties and disenchanted with what it meant to be American. Bespectacled, with a white ponytail and a matching unruly mustache, Reza had served in the United States Air Force as a young man. He later graduated with bachelor's degrees in political science and Spanish literature from the University of California San Diego, where he was influenced by progressive thinkers. He told us he dropped out of his doctoral program at UCSD while he was writing his thesis in the 1980s because he became disillusioned with academia.

His professors seemed reluctant to take on injustices in the university system because they feared for their jobs, he later recalled. He worked as a civil rights organizer and English as a Second Language teacher in California but felt empty inside. He drank heavily and took drugs.

Reza's brother introduced him to the indigenous-rights movement and invited him to jog for a short stretch on a run promoting transcontinental indigenous-rights in 1992. "I started running straight from the bars, basically," he told us. He was thirty-nine at the time. He began to self-identify as an indigenous person. He was no longer Mexican, Mexican American, Hispanic, Latino. His new identity as an indigenous Chicano helped him get sober. He found solace in Native American ceremonies and moved to Phoenix to be closer to indigenous communities.

He settled into his new home in Maricopa County in January 1993, the same month newly elected Joe Arpaio moved into the sheriff's office. But it wasn't until 2006, when Arpaio paired up with Maricopa County attorney Andrew Thomas to arrest migrants for conspiring to smuggle themselves into Arizona that Reza really began noticing Arpaio.

There were troubling signs that Arpaio was expanding his authority by trying to silence critics. In October, the same month the protests at Pruitt's were getting underway, Arpaio's deputies arrested and jailed two owners of the local alternative weekly, *Phoenix New Times*. The newspaper had long been critical of Arpaio, and the arrests were widely interpreted as an abuse of power, a vengeful attack on the press. *Phoenix New Times* had outraged Arpaio by publishing the contents of a bogus subpoena issued by the sheriff's lawyer. The subpoena demanded information about the newspaper's readers. The *Phoenix New Times* owners were released after a few hours in jail, charges were dropped, and years later, Maricopa County would pay the owners 3.75 million dollars for the wrongful arrest.

Two weeks later, Arpaio's deputies arrested the new legal director of the American Civil Liberties Union of Arizona during a Pruitt's demonstration. The lawyer, Dan Pochoda, told us he'd gone to Pruitt's to observe the demonstration and meet Reza. He'd made the mistake of parking on the Pruitt's parking lot. He was arrested for trespassing by Arpaio's deputies, whom he dubbed "jack booted thugs." Pochoda was jailed and released in less than a day. At a subsequent trial, he was acquitted of trespassing.

Arpaio timed his visits to Pruitt's for maximum press attention. As journalists followed him, he would often shake hands with his supporters, then would walk over to Reza's side. Reza told us the sheriff often attempted to strike up a conversation, but Reza ignored him. "I never engaged too long in conversation with him because, I mean, he loves to do that, because then he gets you into his little realm, and then he'll try to charm you," Reza told us.

Reza's boycott of Pruitt's was intended to hurt the store during the holiday season. "Economic pressure, economic pressure," was how Reza summed up his strategy for us. If corporations like Pruitt's lost money, he reasoned, then the corporations themselves would address injustice.

"Don't buy racism!" Reza and his allies yelled at passing cars.

In keeping with her Native American tradition, Reza's wife, Dr. Sylvia Herrera, burned sage to purify and bless the area. The anti-Pruitt's side would often have live music—*banda* or mariachi or a trio of guitars—and demonstrators would belt out the lyrics in Spanish and English. Veteran activists, including Danny Ortega, Alfredo Gutierrez, Lydia Guzman, and Antonio Bustamante stood in solidarity.

Bustamante had tried to swear off activism so he could focus on building his law practice and better support his family. But the protests at Pruitt's pulled him right back into it. He told us he was "disgusted" by the "level of racism" on the restrictionist side, and he felt the bikers and others treated the Latino protesters like "vermin."

He started a chant meant to shame the mostly working class pro-Pruitt's, pro-Arpaio crowd: *What college did you go to? What college did you go to?* He knew it was the wrong thing to do—it didn't soften the hearts of people, instead it probably hardened them, and they weren't going to listen anyway. But it felt good. "I yelled at these ignoramuses," he told us. "That was not the way to do it and Cesar [Chavez] would be very upset with me."

People who turned out to support Arpaio told us they often felt threatened by the insults hurled at them. They reported being pelted with rocks and bottles by pro-immigrant activists. They believed the protesters were paid leftists. And they believed they had to stand their ground, because they were on the side of good. This was America, several participants told us, and their government seemed to be treating "illegals" better than its own citizens. And if they didn't support people like Joe Arpaio, their country would be so overrun with immigrants it would fall into ruin.

They were anxious about their changing nation. In the United States, the undocumented population had climbed from about 8.5 million in 2000 to about 11.6 million in 2006. Arizona's share of unauthorized immigrants had increased by roughly 50 percent—from 330,000 to about 500,000. Many of the undocumented immigrants in Arizona lived in the state's population center, Maricopa County, at the very time the county plunged into the Great Recession. From the first half of 2006 to the second half of 2007, about 150,000 nonfarm jobs had disappeared in Maricopa County.

Tim Rafferty, who sharpened knives and sold cutlery to meat cutters, demonstrated in favor of Arpaio and Pruitt's because the sight of underpaid day laborers jumping into expensive pickups outraged him. "It's just infuriating that our country, both Democrats and Republicans, have let this go on," he told us. "The illegals and Sal Reza were pulling this economic hostage on Pruitt's," he remembered. He stood on the sidewalk each week to show Pruitt's and Arpaio he was glad they were taking a stand. Once, a protester on the other side spit on his shoulder. He wanted to fight but controlled himself.

Rafferty's friend, Valerie Roller, the grandmother, Minuteman, and RidersUSA motorcycle club member, told us she stood on the sidewalk and shouted into her bullhorn. "Word of the day: Assimilate!" and "What part of illegal don't you understand?"

Jim Williams told us bikers like him made people who lived in the area feel safe. "They were afraid of the illegals," he told us, "They wouldn't even come out of their house, or they were afraid to get out there and confront them because they didn't know what was going to happen."

"When we finally started getting out there, I think everybody in town decided, 'Hey, there's safety in numbers, let's get out there and let them know how we feel.'"

By early January 2008, Reza and Pruitt's management reached detente. Store management fired Arpaio's off-duty deputies. The day-laborer demonstrations on Thomas Road wound down.

Valerie Roller and her fellow bikers and likeminded protesters now had a new law on their side, the Legal Arizona Workers Act. The law promised to punish employers who hired undocumented workers. The law was slated to take effect January 1, 2008. Around that time Roller and other restrictionist protesters moved to north Phoenix. There, they set up a shade umbrella, a table, and coolers on a sidewalk in front of the Macehualli Work Center, the day labor center managed by Reza. The work center sat on a large sunbaked lot in a stretch of north Phoenix punctuated with strip malls, apartments, and working class homes. Prospective employers pulled into a u-shaped driveway and picked up day laborers who waited for them beneath shade structures.

The restrictionists vowed to pay Reza back for the economic damage he'd leveled on Pruitt's. For months, they positioned themselves on the sidewalk and wrote down the license plate numbers of every employer who picked up day laborers. "The strategy was to educate people that hiring someone who was illegal—even if it was at a day labor center—was still illegal," Roller told us. The protesters wanted to scare off prospective employers so Reza's work center would go out of business.

Buffalo Rick Galeener, the former Wild West Show promoter who'd helped "clean up the wash" where migrants had camped in Cave Creek, demonstrated against the Good Shepherd of the Hills Episcopal Church day labor center, and protested at Pruitt's, now often sat on the sidewalk fronting Macehualli, jotting down the plate numbers "to put Sal Reza out of business." Galeener told us white laborers couldn't get work at Macehualli. Only "illegals." He resented this. Because all the while, he told us, he struggled to make ends meet, surviving on Social Security and sixty-five dollars a month from the Department of Veterans Affairs.

Manuel de Jesus Ortega Melendres, the Mexican tourist, suffered flash-backs and unnerving bouts of fear after he was arrested by Arpaio's deputies in the September 2007 roundup of day laborers in Cave Creek. He told us he felt hunted after his arrest. Once, he said, a sheriff's vehicle drove alongside his car for a mile as he drove to a friend's house. They are going to stop me, they are going to jail me, Melendres worried. The deputy eventually drove off. But Melendres, shaken, remained convinced sheriff's deputies were surveilling him. He was tense, out of sorts.

Father Glenn Jenks, the pastor of Good Shepherd of the Hills Church in Cave Creek, told some local lawyers about Melendres's arrest. Word got to Julie Pace, the clearheaded Phoenix attorney who had been a spokesperson for the coalition that sought to stop Proposition 200 back in 2004. A Phoenix lawyer, Pace was a Republican who opposed the party's increasingly extreme measures against unauthorized immigrants. She advised businesses on immigration issues and was working on a legal challenge against the Legal Arizona Workers Act. That case would become a federal lawsuit, *U.S. Chamber of Commerce v. Whiting*. At the time, some business owners complained about their Latino workers getting ensnared in Arpaio's traffic stops. Pace figured Melendres might be a good plaintiff in a second lawsuit designed to curb Arpaio's immigration crackdowns, which were negatively impacting some businesses. Such a lawsuit would be expensive, but she knew a businessman who would secretly bankroll it. Still, she'd have to convince her law partners to take on a case against the politically powerful and popular sheriff.

Her husband, an attorney named David Selden, interviewed Melendres at the church in Cave Creek. Soon, Pace and a colleague filed a federal lawsuit on Melendres's behalf in December 2007, two and a half months after the Cave Creek traffic stop. The case, *Melendres v. Arpaio*, would become one of the most high-profile immigration-themed civil rights lawsuits in the nation.

But at the time, few knew about the *Melendres* case.

In court papers, Melendres contended Arpaio's deputies had violated his Fourteenth Amendment rights by stopping and detaining him simply because of his race and national origin. He argued the deputies had also violated his Fourth Amendment rights by holding him for questioning when they did not have probable cause or reasonable suspicion of a crime.

Melendres alleged Arpaio and his deputies "grossly exceeded the limits of their lawful authority" and "egregiously trampled . . . the constitutional and civil rights" of Melendres and "countless other Hispanic and Latino members of the Maricopa County community."

In his lawsuit, Melendres asked the court to prevent Arpaio from racial profiling, disband Arpaio's specialized immigration squad, shut down his illegal immigration hotline, and award Melendres monetary damages.

He acknowledged in the lawsuit Arpaio had a 287(g) agreement with ICE to enforce federal immigration law, but he argued Arpaio had violated that agreement. Melendres pointed to ICE's own fact sheet, published on the agency's website days before his arrest, stating local police officers in the 287(g) program "cannot randomly ask for a person's immigration status or conduct immigration raids." According to ICE's own rules, 287(g) partnerships were not designed to impact "day laborer activities" or "to perform random street operations."

Arpaio's 287(g) agreement allowed local police only to question criminal suspects about their immigration status. Hapless passengers ensnared in traffic stops, like Melendres, were not supposed to be targets.

When Joe Arpaio learned Melendres had sued him, he pounded down his thoughts on his Smith Corona typewriter. "Frivouus law suits," Arpaio typed, sputtering out typos. "I have complete confidence in my trained deputies enforceming all aspects of the State and federal immigra tion laws, and I will continue to do my job as sheriff."

Arpaio had every reason to be confident. He was empowered to enforce immigration laws at both the state and federal level. His theatrical immigration arrests helped cement his image as the nation's toughest immigration enforcer, and he enjoyed widespread popularity in Arizona. Arpaio viewed the *Melendres* case as inconsequential—"frivouus." He denied wrongdoing and his lawyers filed a motion to dismiss the case. It would take years for the sheriff to take real notice of the *Melendres* lawsuit.

10 Mayonnaise Tacos and Easter Baskets

2008

Lydia Guzman opened the refrigerator door and peered inside. The fridge was empty. She closed the door and turned to look at the three teenagers in the small kitchen. *"Mi'jo,* have you eaten anything?" she asked the eldest, who was about sixteen.

"Mayonnaise tacos," the boy answered.

They'd been surviving on tortillas slathered with mayonnaise. There was no other food. The three boys' only caregiver, their father, an immigrant from Mexico, hadn't come home one night. Their father had always told them not to worry if he didn't make it home. He'd always come back. But the boys waited for days and grew hungry. They knocked on neighbors' doors, hoping to sell their puppy to buy food.

The boys learned their dad was arrested by police on an outstanding warrant stemming from a misdemeanor DUI on Christmas Eve. Once he was booked into jail, Arpaio's 287(g) officers turned him over to ICE for deportation.

Guzman didn't want to see the boys turned over to state child protective services authorities. She suspected deported parents might never get their kids back if the kids were under the care of the state. Instead, she helped gather donations for the boys and tracked down their grandmother in another state.

"It just broke my heart," Guzman told us.

It was early 2008, and Guzman had finally found an immigrant advocacy job that paid. Her new boss was Jason LeVecke, the owner of more than fifty fast food restaurants, mostly Carl's Jr. and Hardee's eateries. Guzman quickly learned Julie Pace had recruited LeVecke to secretly fund the *Melendres* lawsuit against Joe Arpaio.

"We wanted to see the sheriff stopped," LeVecke told us in 2016. This was the first time he'd revealed to journalists that he was the incognito benefactor of the *Melendres* case. He said he chose to fund the lawsuit anonymously because it was "too frightening" to go public, "particularly with the sheriff having very real power and seeming to use that power against political opponents—we felt it was just too great a risk at the time." In an effort to counter the anti-immigrant climate in Arizona, he had hired Julie Pace and joined other concerned business people to develop a strategy to counter it.

One element of that strategy was to create a bilingual hotline for immigrants who needed help but were too afraid to call the police or the sheriff's office. The hotline, Respect-Respeto, would double as a way to find potential plaintiffs who might join the *Melendres* lawsuit.

LeVecke paid Guzman sixty thousand dollars and benefits annually to run the Respect-Respeto hotline. He set up a toll-free number and hired a part-time assistant to help Guzman field calls on a clunky black flip phone.

Guzman drove her red Dodge Durango, plastered with Betty Boop decals, to visit desperate hotline callers throughout Maricopa County, like the three brothers surviving on mayonnaise tacos. She also helped immigrants cheated out of paychecks, facing eviction, and coping with domestic violence.

LeVecke had created a way for immigrants to reach out for help.

LeVecke was the grandson of Carl Karcher, who founded the Carl's Jr. fast food restaurant chain. LeVecke, a muscular man who'd served in the Marine Corps, recalled for us the Horatio Alger-like story of his grandfather's success. Karcher, the son of a German immigrant, had a seventh-grade education. He built a multi-million-dollar company by first selling tamales and hot dogs on the streets of Southern California.

As a teenager, LeVecke worked the cash register at a Carl's Jr. in Orange County alongside Mexican immigrants, who reminded him of his industrious grandfather. He believed the country benefited from immigrants.

His workforce of eleven hundred included many Latino and immigrant employees. In his own restaurants, he witnessed mounting anti-immigrant animus fanned by Arpaio and the state's new laws. His employees complained they were harassed by customers who chastised them for speaking Spanish and threatened to get them deported. LeVecke found himself in the curious position of speaking out against his own patrons when he told *The Arizona Republic,* "There is a general lack of understanding that just because you don't speak English doesn't mean you are illegal."

He attributed some of the backlash at his restaurants to restrictionist activists who wanted to punish LeVecke for his opposition to the Legal Arizona Workers Act. He felt the new law was unfair to business owners because it penalized them for unknowingly hiring unauthorized immigrants presenting borrowed or stolen documents.

A libertarian-leaning Republican, LeVecke disliked "onerous" government regulation. "I think there can be no greater affront to freedom than a government that tells people where they can be," LeVecke told us.

Guzman was thrilled about her collaboration with LeVecke, and she expected her Somos America colleagues to be thrilled too. With LeVecke's permission, she eagerly told her Somos colleagues about their new allies in the business community, the Respect-Respeto hotline, and how it could advance the *Melendres* lawsuit.

But her colleagues weren't enthused, at least not at first. "Something doesn't smell right," one activist emailed Guzman. The activists blitzed Guzman with questions. Were LeVecke's restaurants unionized? How come they were hearing from LeVecke now? Didn't fast food restaurant owners prioritize cheap labor over immigrant rights?

"I see this as a golden opportunity to help us—he's got something that we need," Guzman emailed the other activists. "Let's make this work for us." She set up meetings between LeVecke and the activists, and many came to view LeVecke as an ally.

Antonio Bustamante enjoyed having lunch with LeVecke, who shared ideas "from a conservative bent that make me think, that made sense, and that are not based in hysteria or hatred or prejudice or injustice but are based on a completely different way of looking at the world."

"I really love him because he had the courage and the immense generosity to get the *Melendres* litigation going," Bustamante told us.

"He's never been really recognized for that. He's never been honored for that . . . In terms of the civil rights history of Arizona, he's an important figure."

The hotline rang and rang.

It helped that a Spanish language TV station let Guzman participate in live telethons in which she repeated the hotline number and invited victims of racial profiling and employment discrimination to call in. Callers reported problematic run-ins with Maricopa County Sheriff's Office deputies, as well as other law enforcement agencies, including the Phoenix Police Department. They also reported bosses who had ripped them off. Guzman understood most callers were vulnerable to exploitation because they dared not contact authorities to intercede on their behalf in anti-immigrant Maricopa County. "These people have no recourse," she told us. "So they become the perfect victims."

It angered her that Joe Arpaio successfully painted these same immigrants as criminals who were over-represented in his jails. *The Arizona Republic* contrasted Arpaio's narrative when it showed the unauthorized immigrant population in Arpaio's jails was proportionate to the undocumented population in the county. Arpaio responded to the article by insisting "serious" felonies "are committed substantially by illegal aliens."

Guzman knew that many of those "serious" felonies were actually violations of state immigration crimes, like conspiring to smuggle oneself into Arizona. And she knew Arpaio's statistics were skewed by a new voter-approved law that prevented unauthorized immigrants from posting bail, thus forcing them to stay in jail. From what she heard on her hotline, it seemed to her, undocumented immigrants were disproportionately crime *victims*.

Over the Martin Luther King Jr. weekend in 2008, Arpaio once again targeted neighborhoods surrounding M. D. Pruitt's Home Furnishings—

the site of the earlier protests and counterprotests—to pilot a new shock and awe immigration enforcement strategy.

Arpaio told reporters the two-day crackdown was a response to a request from local businesses to "reduce the ongoing property crimes occurring there, including the illegal immigration problem." He dispatched an army of uniformed deputies and posse members, some dressed in the agency's regulation black "raid shirts," to stop cars for minor traffic violations, like cracked windshields, broken tail lights, or failing to signal. If immigrant drivers or passengers had no valid identification, a 287(g) officer could arrest them on suspicion of being undocumented. Those without documents eventually wound up in ICE custody.

Arpaio called this a "saturation patrol" or "crime suppression operation." His critics called it a "community raid."

Salvador Reza, who'd taken to carefully observing Arpaio's behaviors, saw the sweep as ugly retaliation for the day laborers' victory in the Pruitt's protest—getting the furniture store to stop contracting with off-duty sheriff's deputies to scare off day laborers. "Arpaio felt like he could not admit to a defeat," Reza told us. "So he raised the ante."

Two months later, the Maricopa County Sheriff's Office once again returned to the area surrounding the Pruitt's furniture store, apprehending immigrants during a time that was sacred to many of them—the holy days leading up to Easter.

On the Saturday before Easter, Lydia Guzman watched Joe Arpaio's deputies handcuff a Mexican immigrant who'd been pulled over for driving with a cracked windshield. As the man was led away after being arrested on a warrant for an earlier traffic violation, his thirteen-year-old son stood on the pavement alone, clutching a bag containing brightly colored plastic Easter eggs.

The boy caught Guzman's eye. She felt he asked her, silently, "Are you going to help me get my dad back?" Guzman later learned from the boy's mother that deputies had placed the boy in a patrol car, questioned him about his father's immigration status, and had driven him home. His father was eventually turned over to ICE for deportation.

"That was the first time that I actually saw what it did, psychologically, to children and the traumatization that it did to kids," she told us. Guzman would recognize that same look again and again as she tried to help children ensnared in Arpaio's uncompromising immigration enforcement.

Arpaio's staff had erected a makeshift mobile command center in the parking lot of a run-down partially vacant strip mall dotted with palm trees just a few blocks west of Pruitt's. Sheriff's vehicles cluttered the asphalt—patrol SUVs, buses, vans, and a portable trailer—most of them emblazoned with Arpaio's name. After sunset, portable lights illuminated the command center like a stage. Deputies marched handcuffed men and women to the trailer for processing.

The sheriff had alerted the media a day in advance to ensure optimal coverage.

As TV cameras rolled, handcuffed men and women were loaded into vans advertising Arpaio's illegal immigration hotline number and adorned with the words "Do Not Enter Illegally." The vans transported immigrants to either the Fourth Avenue jail or straight to ICE headquarters.

The sheriff greeted supporters who turned out for the spectacle—bikers in leather vests, T-shirted men with bandannas wrapped around their foreheads, people waving American flags. Minutemen who'd previously protested at Pruitt's, and now picketed Salvador Reza's day labor center, showed up to applaud Arpaio's show of force.

Members of the Latino resistance would remember those two days in mid-March 2008 as the "Good Friday" raids, marking an uptick in the sheriff's abuse of his 287(g) federal immigration authority to gain political advantage and ingratiate himself with his followers. Immigrants and their American citizen relatives paid the price, while activists scrambled to help them and witnessed their terror.

For Lydia Guzman, Good Friday 2008 marked a turning point in her role in the fight against Arpaio. Her new job with Respect-Respeto and her participation in Somos America positioned her to become a key organizer of a team of volunteers responding to Arpaio's neighborhood sweeps.

After Arpaio announced the Good Friday–Holy Saturday sweep, Guzman helped recruit Los Abogados, a well-respected group of Latino attorneys, to show up at Arpaio's command center to offer pro bono legal services. Sympathizers held posters advising those impacted to seek the help of the lawyers.

Guzman urged Somos America activists, in an email, to help document Arpaio's racial profiling. "We have all you need, cameras, log sheets, water. But we need bodies—this is a great way for you to invite a friend and be a part of protecting justice and civil rights."

Filming deputies required courage. Volunteers had to assert their First Amendment rights while risking arrest. Dennis Gilman, a white, self-described "hell raiser" who had recently come to activism by leaving water on desert trails for thirsty migrants, followed deputies tenaciously with a new video camera. He created an archive on YouTube.

Meanwhile, Danny Ortega and Alfredo Gutierrez took turns yelling into a bullhorn, hoping their shouts were within earshot of the handcuffed men and women marching into Arpaio's command center: *¡No digan nada!* ("Don't say anything!"), *¡Pidan hablar con un abogado!* ("Ask to speak to a lawyer!").

If just one person could be spared deportation, Ortega thought, it would be worth it. He told us he'd never imagined his legal training would take him "outside a raid trailer yelling at people to try to help them protect their rights."

On Spanish-language television, Guzman warned immigrant viewers to stay away: *Está saturado* ("It's saturated"), *Permanezca adentro* ("Stay inside").

Some saw Guzman on live television and raced over to tell her their stories about being stopped or harassed by deputies. She scrawled their names and numbers on the backs of protest signs. She learned deputies interrogated drivers and passengers about their citizenship if they had no appropriate identification. Many American citizens of Latino descent were stopped for "some BS reason" as Guzman called it, only to be questioned and released once they proved their citizenship.

Guzman figured Latino American citizens would make excellent plaintiffs in the *Melendres* case. They were Americans, after all. And she believed they'd been wrongfully stopped and questioned by deputies hunting for unauthorized immigrants. To Guzman, their stories proved Arpaio was engaging in unconstitutional racial profiling.

Alfredo Gutierrez didn't like the way in which the sweeps were being covered by the mainstream English-language news outlets. "They were reporting a horse race," he told us. "They were reporting a car wreck. They were reporting that Arpaio was there, that he was arresting people, that they were taken away, that he did this, he did that."

"The real context is, it was Good Friday, God damn it. . . . He was after Mexicans."

At the end of the two-day sweep, sheriff's records indicated deputies had arrested forty-three people. All but one had a Hispanic surname. Thirty-nine were suspected undocumented immigrants.

Lydia Guzman would call the weekend "Arpaio's Easter Egg Hunt" in which "only the brown eggs were picked up."

The next sweep came after restrictionist activist Buffalo Rick Galeener and others encouraged a handful of businesses to sign onto a letter urging Arpaio to police the area around Salvador Reza's Macehualli Work Center for day laborers.

The sheriff responded with gusto just five days after the Good Friday sweep. Arpaio's deputies set up their massive command center just a block away from Macehualli, in the parking lot of a strip mall near a Checker Auto Parts store.

"This is just terrible and we seem to be losing this battle with Arpaio," Guzman emailed other activists.

Guzman knew her own family was increasingly annoyed when she dashed off to help immigrants. Sometimes she found sticky notes from her daughter, Ashley. The notes would be plastered on the table or mirror. "Mom, we need to go grocery shopping are you trying to starve me?" one read. And another said "Mom, you don't love me. You are never here."

The new raid would take place on a Thursday, and Guzman knew some volunteers had already called in sick to attend the Good Friday raid the week before. They couldn't keep going at this pace.

Nevertheless, she pulled out her Nokia flip phone and started texting. She'd created a text tree system to quickly mobilize the resistance and warn immigrants of the sheriff's plans. Guzman could only text ten coalition leaders at a time. She immediately texted cameraman Dennis Gilman, Danny Ortega, Antonio Bustamante, Sal Reza, Carlos Garcia, Alfredo Gutierrez, CopWatch leaders, and a Mexican consulate lawyer who had special access to Mexican arrestees. They, in turn, texted their contacts and the text tree branched out.

This saturation patrol was particularly tense. Pro-Arpaio and anti-Arpaio protesters were separated by orange and white traffic barriers and yellow police tape. There was a strong possibility of violence. Bikers waved signs praising the sheriff and yelled "Illegals go home!" By evening, several hundred pro-Arpaio and anti-Arpaio protesters had gathered near the command center. Arpaio's detractors were mostly Latino, including local teens and neighborhood families. They chanted, booed, shook their fists, called Arpaio "KKK Approved." Occasionally someone blew a shrill stadium horn.

The next day, the Democratic Phoenix mayor condemned Arpaio's actions. It was the first time a non-Latino elected official had publicly taken on the popular, powerful sheriff. "They locked up brown people with broken tail lights," said Phil Gordon, the mayor, speaking to a sympathetic audience at an annual luncheon honoring Cesar Chavez, the deceased leader of the United Farm Workers of America who had mentored Antonio Bustamante, Alfredo Gutierrez, and other Phoenix activists. "[Arpaio] calls this being tough. He calls it crime suppression. It is neither." The mayor criticized the sheriff for inciting potentially violent confrontations.

Guzman, who attended the luncheon, jumped to her feet to applaud the mayor. "I'm thinking to myself, 'Phil Gordon for President!' He was like our hero," Guzman told us.

With two powerful white supporters—Jason LeVecke secretly funding the *Melendres* lawsuit and Phil Gordon publicly speaking out against the sheriff—she didn't feel Latino activists were alone in the battle against the powerful sheriff.

There was hope.

But then after the luncheon, Guzman returned to the sweep that was now in its second day near the Macehualli Work Center for day laborers. There, she saw another child victim—a four-year-old girl with a dark ponytail sitting alone, cheeks flushed, in a hot car watching deputies lead her handcuffed mother away.

The child's mother, Maria Aracely Reyes, was a passenger in a car pulled over for a broken brake light. Deputies arrested Reyes after she was unable to prove she was in the country legally. Her husband picked up the child. Reyes, whose visa had expired, was deported to Nogales, Mexico within a few days.

When Antonio Bustamante learned about the little girl, he was deeply upset. Bustamante, who was outside the command center volunteering legal services, began shouting through the bullhorn at Arpaio.

"You are the toughest sheriff in America? You are nothing! How dare you victimize children!" he bellowed. "Come here, apologize to this little girl. Your thugs just took her mother away."

Bustamante years later told us Arpaio looked at him and said nothing. Bustamante knew he had to curb his own temper, because some protesters were about to explode. One anti-Arpaio demonstrator showed up with a gun. The man backed off after Latino leaders begged him to leave. Violence seemed imminent. At one point, a man who was not clearly affiliated with either side showed up with a rifle strapped on his back. A monster pickup truck brandishing large American flags drove up to the Latino protesters. As people scattered, the pro-Arpaio side erupted into "USA! USA! USA!" cheers.

Alfredo Gutierrez and Carlos Garcia stood in front and stretched their arms wide to prevent the truck, driven by a man in a white cowboy hat, from running over protesters. Garcia would remember that night as the closest he ever got to a physical fight. He would remember asking deputies to help keep the crowd under control. "'Can you do something, are you going to do something?" he remembered asking a deputy.

In his memory, the deputy laughed at him.

After Arpaio's officers drove the jail vans full of arrestees away, and the protest was winding down, the bikers launched into a favorite deportation chant: "Nah nah nah nah, nah nah nah nah, hey, hey, hey, goodbye."

Guzman drove home shaking.

Six days later, Arpaio launched his next sweep.

This time he chose Guadalupe, the tiny township tucked in the Phoenix metro area that had been settled by Yaqui Indians and Mexicans. Arpaio announced to the press that Guadalupe town leaders concerned about illegal immigration had invited him to conduct this "crime suppression operation." The town mayor denied this and asked Arpaio to leave.

He didn't.

In Guadalupe, parents kept seventy kids home on the day Arpaio launched the raid, according to the principal of the elementary school. Deputies and posse members on horseback, in unmarked cars, patrol vehicles, and even in a helicopter frightened other parents from picking the children up from school. Teachers volunteered as chauffeurs to drive their students home.

Businesses closed early in the town, which covered less than a square mile. Residents drew their blinds. At night, protesters gathered at the command center. Drivers honked their horns in solidarity, only to be pulled over, questioned, and cited by deputies. American citizens complained that deputies demanded the citizens show identification simply because they walked on the sidewalk.

When Phoenix mayor Phil Gordon heard about Guadalupe, he asked United States Attorney General Michael Mukasey, a George W. Bush appointee, to investigate Joe Arpaio for civil rights abuses. He mentioned in the letter that a Latina aide in the mayor's office had been stopped by sheriff's deputies and was asked to show her Social Security card.

A few weeks later, Mayor Gordon called Guzman because he'd heard she was collecting evidence for the *Melendres* lawsuit. Gordon asked Guzman to share her notes with the Federal Bureau of Investigation. He wanted her to document a pattern of civil rights abuses that could be investigated by the United States Department of Justice.

"I'm on it," Guzman replied.

Around the same time, Ron Wakabayashi, regional director of the justice department's community relations service in Los Angeles, also reached out to Guzman. He was not an investigator, but a specialist in community conflict resolution. As such, he wanted more information about racial profiling in Maricopa County.

Guzman transcribed the scribbled names, phone numbers, and license plate numbers of potential Latino racial profiling victims that filled her notebooks. She emailed the most egregious cases to the special agent in charge at the Phoenix FBI office. And she arranged a meeting with Wakabayashi.

She felt something had to happen, fast.

11 Payback
2008-2009

Lydia Guzman joined hundreds of people angered by Joe Arpaio's immigration agenda on a hot Thursday morning in June 2008. It was an odd setting for a protest—a budget hearing held by the Maricopa County board of supervisors. There were old people, young people. Black, brown, and white people. They crowded into the county auditorium and an overflow room, wearing red T-shirts that said: *Stop wasting OUR money. No more lawsuits. No more media circus. No more money for Arpaio.*

A new Somos America spin-off group, Maricopa Citizens for Safety and Accountability, had convened the protest to try to pressure county supervisors to hit Arpaio where it hurt—his budget. The protesters aimed to turn the routine budget meeting into a referendum on Arpaio's policing and his poor financial management skills. They came armed with economic arguments about Arpaio's misuse of taxpayer dollars, citing among other things his expensive immigration sweeps and the costly, wrongful inmate death lawsuits.

The way activists saw it, if Maricopa County residents and the conservative board of supervisors weren't outraged by the crying children victimized by Arpaio's sweeps, maybe his financial record would convince them to turn on the sheriff.

Mary Rose Wilcox, the lone Democratic county supervisor, had already proven herself to be a key ally to the movement. She had quietly lobbied Governor Janet Napolitano to withdraw 1.6 million dollars in funding, which Arpaio relied on to help support his Human Smuggling Unit. And Wilcox had encouraged activists to come to this budget meeting, a strategic venue for a rowdy protest that would earn media attention.

The county was grappling with financial fallout from the Great Recession. Foreclosures had driven down property tax revenues, and supervisors were poised to slash nearly 100 million dollars in spending. The county was hurting. Guzman had recruited Jason LeVecke to speak to the board. He liked to keep a low profile, but he walked up to the podium in his usual suit and tie, and stood before the supervisors who were seated on a raised platform. "I may be the last person you expect to be here," LeVecke told the board. "I came from a very conservative family, very conservative roots, and consider myself to be a very conservative Republican." But he believed in good stewardship over tax dollars, and he criticized Arpaio's expensive "crime sweeps on intersections where we don't have high crime."

"Business volume at those intersections is still down," LeVecke said. "Because nobody, and I mean nobody, goes to an intersection where there's two hundred police officers."

Next, an animated Latino activist named Randy Parraz asked the supervisors to make Arpaio account for his monthly spending of public funds. (Only Mary Rose Wilcox agreed.) When Parraz's allotted three minutes ran out, five uniformed sheriff's deputies inched closer to Parraz until he left the podium. At that point, many anti-Arpaio protesters followed Parraz out to the courtyard for a rally.

A couple dozen restrictionist activists stayed behind to defend the sheriff, including Barb Heller. Her thick blond hair gathered in a ponytail, sunglasses on her head, reading glasses low on her nose, and an American Flag bow wrapped around one spaghetti strap of her white tank top, Heller was an energetic advocate for law enforcement officers and veterans.

As a teenager in the early 1970s, Heller groomed horses and cleaned stalls at a Phoenix race track. She began living on her own and supporting herself at age sixteen, for reasons she declined to discuss. In her memory, unauthorized Mexican immigrants worked for less money, so she routinely lost jobs to them. And someone told her the immigrants discussed taking over the country in Spanish. This offended Heller, the daughter of a World War II veteran.

She notified federal immigration authorities, who she said sent buses to the racetrack and rounded up undocumented workers. She said her anger deepened over illegal immigration when someone told her an undocumented immigrant who worked at the race track had gotten drunk, killed someone in a car accident, and fled to Mexico. "We've got enough crazies and lawbreakers in this country," she said. "We don't need to import people that are going to break our laws and take lives."

Heller was among Arpaio's most devoted supporters. She warned the supervisors, without evidence, that some people came into the country illegally because they could not pass health screenings, thereby causing an uptick in "drug resistant tuberculosis, leprosy, AIDS, measles, hepatitis, STDs." She believed complaints about Arpaio and racial discrimination were unfounded. Arpaio deserved support, not criticism. "Where's the compassion for our country and our people? This is about law enforcement," Heller told the board. "It's not about profiling."

Heller asked Arpaio's supporters to stand up, and her allies, who now made up the majority of those left in the auditorium, stood.

The four Republican supervisors signaled their loyalty to the sheriff by taking turns standing, too. It was politically perilous for county Republicans to oppose the sheriff. Especially on this day, when he addressed the supervisors in a no-nonsense tone. Wearing a gray suit accented with his pistol-shaped gold tie clip, Arpaio thanked the Republican supervisors for their support and reminded them their authority over him was limited. "I am the elected sheriff. I make the decisions on how to run my office. You know that you don't do that."

The sheriff turned on his former friend, Supervisor Mary Rose Wilcox, the woman he once said he "could never get mad at." Arpaio seemed now to despise Wilcox. And his tone served as a warning to the other supervisors not to cross him. He accused Wilcox of conspiring with Mayor Phil Gordon and Governor Janet Napolitano to deprive him of funds he used for immigration enforcement.

Still, Guzman felt encouraged. *The Arizona Republic* later reported on the disorderly meeting, detailing the concerns about Arpaio's financial mismanagement of his office. The activists would continue showing up at county meetings for at least two years to point out over and over that the Maricopa County Sheriff's Office was mismanaged by a fiscally irresponsible leader—Joe Arpaio.

Arpaio punched back in what the activists viewed as blatant retaliation. Sometimes, his deputies arrested activists at meetings, claiming trespass or disorderly conduct violations. Once, deputies marched critics out of a county meeting and jailed them for applauding an anti-Arpaio public comment. Seven protesters eventually sued the sheriff for wrongful arrest and won close to half a million dollars in a taxpayer-funded settlement.

Which drove home the protester's key message—Arpaio was a financial drain on taxpayers.

While the sheriff's office diverted resources and manpower to immigration enforcement, deputies neglected other policing duties in towns that contracted with the office for policing services. Serious felonies, including sex crimes against children, went uninvestigated in the town of El Mirage. At the same time, the sheriff's office had exceeded its budget by paying overtime to deputies, particularly those tasked with nabbing immigrants in Arpaio's Human Smuggling Unit.

These stories were reported in the *East Valley Tribune*, a suburban daily newspaper, just weeks after the protests at the county budget hearing. The newspaper series detailed how Arpaio's immigration enforcement violated federal racial profiling guidelines.

For years, Arpaio's carefully crafted media image of a lawman on the right side of the law had overpowered concerns about cruelty in the jails, agency mismanagement, and constitutional violations in sweeps and traffic stops. Many Arpaio critics felt the *East Valley Tribune*, a mainstream news outlet, had now validated their perspective—that Arpaio was not only cruel but an incompetent manager whose obsession with immigration enforcement resulted in inadequate policing and civil rights violations. Latino activists emailed story links to congressional leaders and senators. Guzman sent the series to Ron Wakabayashi at the justice department's community relations service.

Arpaio discounted the series as "garbage."

Inside the sheriff's office, deputies continued to feel pressure to keep up immigration arrests. "That's what Arpaio was living on—how many immigrants were taken into custody," Steve Bailey later told us. As a lieutenant in the special investigations division, he recalled that he had conducted operations that were unrelated to the Human Smuggling Unit, only to be asked how many "illegals" had been arrested so it could go into a press release.

Joe Sousa, a lieutenant in the Human Smuggling Unit, later told an independent investigator that as his team was busy filling out paperwork pertaining to their most recent sweep, Arpaio and his command staff would pressure them to do another one. "They wanted it now, now, now, and they didn't care," Sousa said.

That summer, Arpaio ratcheted up a new immigration enforcement tactic—dispatching deputies to raid businesses to arrest undocumented immigrant workers. He relied on a provision in the state's new Legal Arizona Workers Act that made it easier to slap an identity theft felony charge on immigrants who used stolen or fake documents to get a job. Even immigrants who used a fictitious Social Security number were vulnerable to felony charges.

The sheriff dispatched his deputies to water parks, restaurants, landscaping firms, a candle manufacturer, a paper company, and other businesses around the county.

Panicked workers who spotted sheriff vehicles approaching texted their loved ones, who notified Guzman via her hotline. By the time Guzman showed up, notebook in hand, anxious relatives of workers often already stood on nearby sidewalks. This might be their last chance to catch a glimpse of a loved one before a deportation would separate a family for years—or a lifetime. Guzman watched as some raged in anger, while others seemed numb as the moment they dreaded the most became real. Once arrests were underway, Arpaio's office invited media to film ski-masked deputies leading frightened, zip-tied employees out of the workplaces to the jail vans waiting outside. Sometimes, the deputies relied on business records to track down and arrest off-duty workers at their homes.

The felony charges ensured most arrested immigrants would be ineligible for any kind of immigration relief and would be deported. After the immigrants served their sentences in Arpaio's jail, his 287(g) detention officers turned them over to ICE for deportation. Over the next six years, Arpaio's deputies would arrest more than four thousand immigrants in these worksite raids.

Guzman did her best to respond. She tried to find attorneys for arrested immigrants. She located kids waiting alone at home for parents who did not return. She scribbled down names, phone numbers, and key details to forward to the justice department in the hope it would take action.

Immigrant families began fleeing the state. The likely reasons included fewer jobs during the recession, Arpaio's focus on immigration enforcement, and the Legal Arizona Workers Act. One estimate found that about 92,000 unauthorized immigrants of working age—about 17 percent of that cohort—left Arizona between 2008 and 2009.

The restrictionist goal of "attrition through enforcement" seemed to be working.

Lydia Guzman's cell phone rang as she was observing a worksite raid at a car wash in Peoria, Arizona, a Phoenix suburb.

"Señora Lydia," whispered a man's voice on the other end of the call. "I'm inside the car wash." Guzman was confused. Where was the guy? Deputies had already led all the arrested workers onto a jail transport van. Then she realized the caller was hiding inside a car wash water tank.

He had kept his head and cell phone above water and was calling the Respect-Respeto hotline. At that moment, Guzman saw a deputy approaching the water tank where the caller was hiding.

"Don't move," she warned.

He sobbed into the phone.

Callese, she urged. "Be quiet."

Once it was safe for the man to whisper again he gave Guzman his wife's name and phone number. "Please tell her I love her in case they don't hear from me."

That wasn't necessary. Hours later, after the deputies left, the man jumped out of the water tank and escaped.

Sometimes when Guzman stood outside of the worksite raids taking notes, deputies let her know they knew who she was. She shivered when they greeted her by name. Once, one of Arpaio's public information officers told

A man in an ICE vest ushers arrested immigrant workers into a van during a Maricopa County Sheriff's Office worksite raid at On Your Way Carwash in Peoria, Arizona on October 17, 2009. (Photo by José L. Muñoz)

her the sheriff wanted to have coffee with her. Guzman politely declined. She told us there was no way she was going to let the sheriff spin a coffee meeting into some kind of photo opportunity that implied he had her support.

"I ask everybody to come in and let's talk," Arpaio told us. "All they wanted to do is screaming and I'm trying to talk to them. It's very difficult to talk in demonstrations, unless you're going to sit down face to face."

Guzman often wondered if the sheriff might try to arrest her. He seemed to be lashing out at his detractors with more ferocity as the Latino-led movement against him began to gain traction.

"I was on my best behavior," Guzman told us.

She begged her daughter, son, and stepson, now all teenagers, to stay away from the neighborhood park where some of their peers hung out. She worried sheriff's deputies might be waiting for a chance to bust her kids for something trivial.

Jason LeVecke worried too. He knew he was taking a risk by secretly bankrolling the Respect-Respeto hotline and the *Melendres* lawsuit. He worried that if the sheriff ever found out, Arpaio might push back, perhaps by sending deputies to conduct a worksite raid of one of LeVecke's fast food restaurants.

Arpaio had already conducted a worksite raid after a public feud with George Gascón, the Latino police chief in Mesa, a Phoenix suburb. Gascón had scoffed at Arpaio's "three-ring circus" neighborhood sweeps and had gone so far as to undermine one in Mesa by swarming the area with city police officers. Arpaio responded by sending deputies and posse members to raid Mesa's city hall and main library in the middle of the night, where they arrested unauthorized immigrant janitors cleaning the city buildings.

"I don't think illegals looking at wastebaskets of sensitive material should be working there as janitors, so I did it," Arpaio told us in 2020, denying that he retaliated against Gascón or any other elected official, judge, or public figure he perceived as a foe.

But in 2008, Phoenix mayor Phil Gordon felt the sheriff used the power of his office to punish him for requesting a justice department civil rights investigation of Arpaio. Two weeks after Gordon had written the justice department, he learned he was being investigated by the sheriff's office.

The probe centered on a tip from an informant, Rev. Jarrett Maupin, who had falsely alleged to Arpaio that Gordon had molested an underage teenage boy.

"Supposedly they had proof of me with a kid—a tape," Gordon recalled. There was no such tape. Gordon knew it was the kind of smear that if made public would ruin his reputation even though it wasn't true. "At that point I was terrified," he told us.

Around the same time, the sheriff's office publicly demanded Gordon and his staff turn over more than six months of emails, cell phone records, and calendars.

The sheriff's tipster for the criminal investigation, Maupin, was a political rival of the mayor. Maupin had been active in the Somos America coalition but—counterintuitively—was also friendly with Arpaio. Maupin heard the unsubstantiated rumor about the mayor from a city aide and personally reported it to the sheriff. Arpaio responded with vigor—five sheriff's office staffers investigated Arpaio's political foe. Maupin later falsely claimed to sheriff's deputies that he had seen evidence of the alleged crime.

Mayor Gordon sought help from Paul Charlton, a former United States attorney for Arizona and prominent local Republican. Charlton told us he had once considered the sheriff a "legitimate law enforcement official" but felt Arpaio "became a different person" after pivoting to immigration enforcement. Charlton knew few lawyers wanted to risk opposing the sheriff, but he told us he decided it was the right thing to do. At Gordon's request, Charlton persuaded the FBI to take over the sheriff's criminal investigation into Gordon.

The FBI interviewed Maupin and found he had lied. Maupin pleaded guilty to a felony—making a false statement to a federal agency. Once again the Maricopa County Sheriff's Office had funneled resources and manpower into what appeared to be a baseless politically motivated investigation that benefitted Arpaio.

"When you cross this guy [Arpaio], for legitimate reasons," Charlton later said, "You are going to find yourself under investigation for illegitimate reasons."

Maricopa County voters still supported the sheriff despite the protests at county meetings, the pending *Melendres* racial profiling lawsuit, and the *East Valley Tribune* newspaper exposé.

To Lydia Guzman, Arpaio felt unstoppable, and she was not surprised when the sheriff won his fifth election in November 2008. That same day, though, Barack Obama was elected president. Which meant the Latino resistance now had a shot at gaining powerful allies in Washington, D.C.

Obama seemed sympathetic to the nation's immigrants. His father had come to the United States on a student visa from Kenya. The newly elected president had promised an immigration reform bill—including legal status for most of the nation's undocumented immigrants—in the first year. Latino and minority voters were key to his victory. Democrats also strengthened their majorities in Congress, making immigration reform viable once again.

By then, Guzman had been elected president of Somos America, which now focused on pressuring the Obama administration to investigate Arpaio for civil rights violations, revoke his 287(g) partnership, and disband the federal-local partnership immigration enforcement program altogether.

In an unexpected twist, the fate of the 287(g) program in the new administration would be determined by Janet Napolitano. The Arizona governor had become the new administration's Secretary of Homeland Security, a position that oversaw ICE.

This wasn't exactly good news as far as Somos America was concerned. Napolitano's constitutionally appointed successor was the conservative Republican Arizona secretary of state Jan Brewer. Now it was entirely possible that Governor Brewer would sign Russell Pearce's restrictionist bills. And it wasn't clear how much of an ally Napolitano would be in her new role. She had a history of supporting the 287(g) program.

Somos America needed to build national momentum to reach its goals. The coalition would have to pump out the narrative of Arpaio's civil rights abuses and agency mismanagement to win over the hearts and souls of Americans. This would have to become a national story. Arpaio's hunger for national media attention played right into the movement's strategy. Weeks after Obama's inauguration, the sheriff opened a separate section of Tent City just for "illegal aliens." They would serve their time bunking outdoors before their deportations.

And what Arpaio did next provoked international outrage. He paraded some two hundred undocumented immigrant inmates from the indoor jail to their new Tent City quarters. It was a humiliating forced march of mostly Latino inmates in striped chinos, pink socks, and shower sandals. The inmates' wrists were shackled together. They clutched plastic bags holding their personal belongings. TV cameras captured their misery.

Lydia Guzman and other activists protested from outside the jail's fence.

The sheriff couldn't have handed the Latino resistance a better opportunity to launch its national agenda. At a press conference, Mary Rose Wilcox promised to pressure the justice department to investigate. "Things have changed in Washington," Wilcox told the crowd. "We will put a stop to this."

National immigrant rights organizations, including the Los Angeles-based National Day Laborer Organizing Network, jumped in to help organize a response to Arpaio's latest move. The National Council of La Raza called it "yet another stunt to distract people from his [Arpaio's] incompetent, lawsuit-riddled folly of a department." The nonprofit circulated a petition asking the justice department to investigate Arpaio, urging: "Send a clear message to Arpaio and his thugs that we will not stand for these kinds of abuses in our nation."

Immigrant inmates are paraded in front of news cameras as they march to Joe Arpaio's Tent City jail on February 4, 2009. Their uniforms incorrectly say they were unsentenced. (Photo by José L. Muñoz)

Joe Arpaio speaks to reporters at the Tent City jail in Phoenix on February 4, 2009. (Photo by José L. Muñoz)

One of Carlos Garcia's photos of shackled immigrant inmates marching to Tent City wound up in *The New York Times,* thanks to a sympathetic contact on the editorial board. The newspaper had already furthered the movement's narrative with several editorials criticizing the sheriff. And after Sal Reza filmed deputies arresting an undocumented mother in front of her crying children during a sweep, he sent the video to the editorial board. The newspaper posted the video link to its website, along with a note from Reza: "The 'hell' we are living here in Arizona . . . is getting worse instead of better."

Now the newspaper's editorial about the Tent City march condemned both the "degrading spectacle" and the 287(g) program.

It was the exact message the activists had hoped to get out.

Four Democratic members of the House Judiciary Committee, led by a former civil rights activist, Representative John Conyers of Michigan, endorsed the activists' calls for a justice department investigation and asked the Department of Homeland Security to review Arpaio's 287(g) agreement.

Arpaio faced a serious challenge. In a February 24, 2009 letter to Conyers, he rationalized the televised march of shackled immigrants to Tent City by saying it was multi-ethnic—the marching inmates weren't just Latino immigrants. They "included people from Korea, Vietnam, Central Africa, Mexico and Jamaica," he wrote, adding: "We do not racially profile people nor do we scour Latino neighborhoods looking for undocumented immigrants."

The letter didn't hold much sway. Less than three weeks later, the justice department notified Arpaio that it was launching a civil rights investigation into "alleged patterns or practices of discriminatory police practices" and "allegations of national origin discrimination."

"I wanted to run around in circles and do jumping jacks," Guzman told us. Instead, she called everyone in Somos America to share the good news. The information she had funneled to federal investigators had paid off. She imagined the federal government would quickly force Arpaio to stop tormenting her community.

For years, Guzman, with the help of Somos America members, would forward evidence of civil rights abuses both to the *Melendres* attorneys and federal investigators. In her mind, the lawsuit and the federal investigation were the movement's best hopes for battling restrictionism and taking down Arpaio. And if one tactic failed, she told us, surely the other would succeed.

That spring, Somos America focused on pressuring the Obama administration to revoke Arpaio's 287(g) authority in order to rein in the sheriff's immigration enforcement. The coalition organized a march led by the Latino front man of the rap-rock band Rage Against the Machine. They dispatched a young Latino American citizen who was wrongfully detained in a worksite raid, along with Arpaio rival George Gascón, to testify before Congress about what they viewed as civil rights violations generated by the federal-local partnership.

And they got the attention of many Americans with the story of Katherine Figueroa, a nine-year-old daughter of undocumented immigrant parents jailed by Arpaio's deputies after a carwash raid. The child had seen her parents led away in zip ties on TV, because she had been watching the news at her aunt's house. "Mr. President I need you to help me," the little girl said in a viral video that Guzman and Dennis Gilman recorded. "My family and my parents, I want them back with me again. And I don't want Sheriff Joe Arpaio getting other people and my parents again. Please."

Guzman realized she had the business card of a White House immigration advisor she had met when he visited Phoenix. She asked the advisor to show Obama the video.

The campaign to shed light nationally on Arpaio's civil rights abuses may have been one reason Janet Napolitano revisited Arpaio's 287(g) agreement in October 2009. She revoked the part of the agreement that allowed deputies to enforce federal immigration law on the streets of Maricopa County. But Arpaio still had 287(g) authority in his jails, which meant his detention officers continued to turn over undocumented immigrant inmates to ICE. The sheriff insisted "nothing has changed."

Joe Arpaio liked a good fight. He remained defiant. He made his resistance to the Obama administration part of his brand.

As for the justice department investigation, Arpaio dubbed it a "a badge of honor." He publicly insisted he would not stop his immigration enforcement.

At a restrictionist fundraiser in Texas, the sheriff told a crowd that after the justice department launched its probe he arrested five hundred more unauthorized immigrants "just for spite."

At the same time, Arpaio grumbled about how his relationship with Latino constituents had deteriorated. "I was a hero. Now I'm the worst enemy of the Hispanic group because I am enforcing the illegal immigration laws," he told us in May 2009.

He was a hero, though, to the burgeoning Tea Party movement, a new fringe wing of the Republican Party formed to oppose the new president and his administration. Deporting unauthorized immigrants was central to the Tea Party brand.

Arpaio's staff created his Twitter account—@RealSheriffJoe, and then managed it because the sheriff refused to learn how to use a computer or a smartphone. Social media enabled Arpaio to communicate with an even broader audience around the country—just like a future president, Donald Trump.

Now that Arpaio had lost his 287(g) field authority, he told reporters the federal program was just extra bureaucracy he didn't need. He could continue arresting immigrants even without it. He could still enforce state immigration laws and bust migrants for smuggling themselves and pick up immigrant workers in worksite raids. And he insisted, incorrectly, that there was a federal statute from 1996 that allowed local police to detain undocumented immigrants even when they had not committed a crime.

In a Fox News interview with conservative pundit Glenn Beck, Arpaio stumbled as he tried to explain. "If local law enforcement comes across some people that have an erratic or scared or whatever, uh, they're worried . . . if they have their speech, what they look like—if they just look like they came from another country, we can take care of that situation."

Beck seemed puzzled.

"That sounds like profiling," Beck said. Later he asked, "I mean are they wearing sombreros?"

A few days later Arpaio's press team issued a correction. Arpaio had quoted a federal statute that never existed. A sergeant, who had no legal training, had mistakenly copied and pasted the bogus citation from a restrictionist website and passed it on.

After the debacle with the fake statute, the sheriff's office hired Kris Kobach, the restrictionist lawyer who had masterminded the legal theory that local police have the authority to enforce federal immigration law.

Kobach had just finished a stint as chairman of the Kansas Republican Party, and was running for Kansas secretary of state. Still, he visited Phoenix and made a series of training videos that became mandatory viewing for deputies. On the videos Kobach insisted that Arpaio's deputies while on patrol could continue to detain suspected unauthorized immigrants who had committed no crimes and transfer them to federal immigration authorities.

This rationale was based on Kobach's controversial theory that local cops had "inherent authority" to enforce federal immigration law. Once deputies established "reasonable suspicion" that someone was undocumented, Kobach said on the video, deputies could question the individual about their immigration status and contact ICE or Border Patrol. If these authorities indicated an interest in picking up the immigrant, deputies could arrest and transfer the immigrant to federal custody.

In the video, Kobach cautioned deputies not to consider ethnicity as a factor when establishing "reasonable suspicion." He then listed twenty factors deputies could consider. Some seemed to invite racial profiling—"the individual's appearance is unusual or out of place in a particular locale" or "indications from the dress or appearance of the individual that he has been, has recently, that he is an illegal alien and perhaps that he has just entered without inspection." (Kobach defended these factors, telling us legal precedent allowed immigration authorities to consider whether someone looked like they had just traveled through the desert.)

Armed with this legal advice from Kobach, Arpaio's deputies now had even more justification to round up immigrants.

"Washington obviously did not like my deputies enforcing all immigration laws," Arpaio said in a press release. "But I refused to roll over and play dead. Now, just as I knew all along, a nationally recognized immigration expert opines that local law enforcement can, in fact, enforce federal immigration laws."

A federal judge would later rule Kobach's advice was incorrect, at least in Arizona and other western states, given the 1983 *Gonzales v. City of Peoria* decision by the Ninth Circuit.

By late 2009, Mary Rose Wilcox knew Joe Arpaio was coming after her.

All that year, she had used her perch on the board of supervisors to speak out against Arpaio's immigration enforcement. She had traveled to Washington, D.C. to tell Congress about his civil rights violations. And she had offered guidance to the activists who protested Arpaio at county meetings.

"I was on the inside and had access to the budgets and what the sheriff was trying to do behind the scenes," Wilcox told us. She turned around and tipped off activists, and figured the sheriff suspected as much.

Arpaio started calling Wilcox his "nemesis."

It seemed to Wilcox that the more the Obama administration clamped down on the sheriff, the more Arpaio demonstrated his policing muscle. He'd formed an "anti-corruption" task force with Andrew Thomas, the young county attorney who partnered with him in prosecuting immigrants for conspiring with their smugglers. The duo used their task force to go after their shared political enemies including, it would turn out, Mary Rose Wilcox.

As Wilcox saw it, tensions mounted after she and other county supervisors were forced to cut Arpaio's and Thomas's budgets due to the recession.

Arpaio and Thomas complained the county should instead scrap a long-standing plan to construct a new 330-million-dollar court facility, known as the Court Tower Project. When the supervisors refused, the "anti-corruption task force" investigated the court tower construction project. And alleged they had found a corrupt county conspiracy.

Arpaio's chief deputy David Hendershott, a man some underlings would describe as vindictive and abusive, was the face of the anti-corruption task force. Under Hendershott's leadership, deputies knocked on the doors of county employees late at night and grilled them about the court tower plans. Soon the task force threw more than one hundred felony charges against Don Stapley, a Republican county supervisor who had been closely examining the sheriff's spending. The task force claimed Stapley failed to include some real estate holdings on disclosure forms. When the case began to fall apart, the sheriff's office and county attorney slapped him with another one, this time ninety-three felony charges. Hendershott ordered deputies to cuff Stapley and take him to jail.

Wilcox was terrified, but not surprised, when she read in *The Arizona Republic* that Arpaio had begun investigating her. She tried to put on a brave face when she gave a comment to the newspaper. "The sheriff has a vendetta, and he's just throwing a big net out, and he's doing it to scare me," she said.

When she peered out the windows of her high-rise condo in downtown Phoenix, she often noticed sheriff's squad cars parked in front.

But things only got worse. In early December 2009, a grand jury indicted Wilcox on thirty-six felony counts in what was widely viewed as a retaliatory abuse of power by the sheriff and the county attorney. Wilcox's criminal case followed an earlier publication of a *Phoenix Magazine* story that reported Wilcox had failed to disclose on her financial form that she and her husband had borrowed money from a for-profit subsidiary of Chicanos Por La Causa, the Latino nonprofit. At the time the loans were outstanding, Wilcox voted to award county contracts totaling about one million dollars to Chicanos Por La Causa. The magazine did not accuse Wilcox of any crimes but did raise questions about the ethics of not disclosing the loans.

Thomas and Arpaio and the "task force" had tried to pin dozens of felonies on Wilcox because she had not disclosed the loans.

Wilcox maintained her innocence. "I might not be the most organized person in the world, and I like, move fast and stuff," she told us. "I knew I wasn't crooked, I knew I never took bribes. I am a politician because I want to help people."

Her life changed immediately as word spread she was an accused felon. People she had known for decades suddenly shunned her. An interfaith council withdrew an award. Even her grandsons wondered if she had done something wrong.

El Portal, the restaurant, lost loyal customers. It was no longer the place to see and be seen. "People were so very afraid to come to it," Wilcox told us. "Everybody was afraid of the sheriff." Within a year, she and Earl made the painful decision to shutter the restaurant.

Wilcox feared all she had accomplished fighting for her community as the county's highest-ranking Latina official might be erased.

The same month Wilcox was indicted, Arpaio and Thomas brought a federal lawsuit against her and other county officials—senior county administrators, supervisors, judges, and lawyers—accusing them of "racketeering" and acting as a "criminal enterprise" by trying to thwart the task force's earlier corruption investigations.

After a Maricopa County superior court judge disqualified Thomas from investigating the court tower project due to a conflict of interest, Thomas criminally charged the bewildered judge with accepting a bribe and obstructing justice.

Gary Donahoe, the judge, had ruled against Thomas several times. He had also scolded Arpaio and his agency for backing up the court calendars by not providing transport officers to move inmates from the jail to the courthouse for scheduled hearings, and then back to the jail again.

In the busy county courtrooms, judges and lawyers waited and waited for jail inmates. The inmates either didn't show up at all or came in late, thanks to a shortage of transport officers at the sheriff's office.

Donahoe told us he was targeted by Arpaio and Thomas because he had ruled against Thomas, and he had questioned whether Arpaio was diverting resources intended for crucial court transportation into immigration enforcement. The judge had also charged a sheriff's detention officer with contempt of court for removing documents from a defense lawyer's table.

Once Thomas filed criminal charges against Donahoe, the judge was "conflicted out." He had to bow out of all criminal cases brought by Thomas and Arpaio, which ended his career as the court's presiding criminal judge.

Under normal circumstances, Arizona Attorney General Terry Goddard might have tried to stop Arpaio and Thomas. But Goddard was also under investigation by the Arpaio-Thomas anticorruption task force. The investigation of Goddard went on and on, and would never lead to a criminal charge, but it ensured the state's highest law enforcement officer could not use his legal authority against either Arpaio or Thomas.

"I couldn't bring a grand jury proceeding against somebody who I had a conflict on," Goddard told us. "That's the real objective here," he added.

In the end, none of the criminal charges stuck against any of the targets. The case against Wilcox was dismissed by a Tucson-based judge, John Leonardo. The judge also ruled Arpaio had "misused the power of his office" by targeting county supervisors for criminal investigation.

Wilcox and ten other county officials who were wrongfully investigated or indicted by Arpaio and Thomas won settlements totaling more than fourteen million dollars for damages and legal bills.

Since the county was self-insured, county taxpayers shouldered the bill for what many viewed as Arpaio and Thomas's retaliatory actions against perceived foes. The baseless criminal prosecutions later led the State Bar of Arizona to disbar Andrew Thomas. David Hendershott resigned from the sheriff's office amid multiple scandals. Arpaio himself never faced any consequences for the alleged retaliations. Years later, he told us: "I'm not going to comment on those cases. But let me just say this, there's a lot of smoke out there. Maybe it wasn't done properly, you know."

12 Drowning in a Glass of Water

2010

Lydia Guzman was about to lose her home. She'd just gotten a foreclosure notice.

She no longer had a paying job, and neither did her husband, Tony Wesley.

"I just feel like I'm drowning in a glass of water," she emailed three fellow activists in February 2010, just a few weeks after Jason LeVecke could no longer afford to pay her to run the Respect-Respeto hotline.

LeVecke felt terrible about it. But he'd lost customers at his fast food restaurants as thousands of immigrants fled Arizona due to the recession and strict immigration enforcement. Business was down. He had to make cuts.

Guzman vowed to keep the hotline open, even if she had to pay for it herself. But she didn't know where she'd find the money. Wesley's construction work had dried up. Now he was training to get a commercial driver's license, hoping to become a truck driver.

In the meantime, Guzman had siphoned money from unemployment checks and a tax refund to pay for hotline expenses and gasoline so she could carry on with her immigrant-rights work. She did this even as she sensed her husband and kids resented her prioritizing immigrants over the family.

She'd applied for a grant. If she could only get grant money, she could carry on with the hotline and pay her bills. She knew the grant was a long shot, and there was no Plan B.

"I'm getting pretty desperate here," she confessed to friends.

Guzman considered getting temp jobs, but then decided against it because she'd have to abandon the hotline. She still believed the courts could deliver justice. She wanted to continue fielding calls from Arpaio victims who might qualify as plaintiffs in the *Melendres* racial profiling case.

But that wasn't the only reason Guzman was anxious to keep the hotline open. She felt it was one of the only safe places immigrants could rely on when they needed help. She couldn't turn away from children searching for missing parents. She couldn't ignore pleas for help with evictions, spousal abuse, hunger, arrests, or confinement in Joe Arpaio's jails.

It seemed to her sometimes that Arpaio's brutality would never end. Nor was there ever enough money for groceries or gas. She dealt with a nagging guilt for neglecting her family, especially when her mother pointed it out. But still, she couldn't brush off the hotline calls.

"How were these people going to win?" she recalled. "Were they going to win at the end? There weren't any happy endings sometimes—most of the time."

Daniel Magos had jotted the Respect-Respeto hotline number on a yellow sheet of legal paper that he kept in his weathered green Ford pickup truck. The sixty-four-year-old contractor sometimes shared the number with undocumented workers he met at construction jobs if he heard they had an immigration problem. Magos, a small man with neat, closely cropped gray-brown hair and dark intelligent eyes, had gained his American citizenship more than forty years earlier, after immigrating from Mexico legally as a child, so he didn't expect to use the hotline himself.

But that changed one morning in December 2009, when Magos and his wife, Eva, who had come along to keep him company, headed from their home to a job at an apartment building in south Phoenix. Magos had loaded landscaping tools in the back of the truck, and had hitched a trailer to it. He explained to Eva that he had to trim sage brushes and mesquite trees in addition to doing some remodeling, so the trailer would be useful for hauling debris.

Out of the corner of his eye, Magos could see the tall watchtower hovering over the Tent City jail, a landmark of sorts that signaled to locals that a sprawl of Maricopa County Sheriff's Office jails and administration buildings were nearby. Magos turned left, onto a straight, wide lane of Durango Road. There wasn't a lot of traffic, just landscaping trucks pulling trailers laden with grass clippings and tree branches. The trucks were likely driven by Latino landscapers heading to a nearby landfill, Magos knew. He'd driven this road many times, but on this day he would come to realize that the abundance of landscaping trucks en route to the dump and the proximity to the jails made this area an excellent hunting ground for deputies in search of unauthorized Latino immigrants.

He had rolled down his window before making the turn onto Durango Road, only to lock eyes with a sheriff's deputy driving past him in the opposite lane. The deputy, Dan Russell, turned around and flashed his police lights.

Magos soon realized he was the target. He drove past a cornfield and some industrial buildings, and pulled over to the side of the road near an abandoned farmhouse with a rickety chicken coop.

The details of what happened next come from Magos's memory and sheriff's records. The Maricopa County Sheriff's Office declined our three requests to interview Deputy Dan Russell, who we had identified from sheriff's office records of the Magos traffic stop. The sheriff's office did not respond to our request to confirm Russell's identity from its own records.

Magos would not forget the traffic stop, which had started so innocently. He wondered why the deputy wasn't getting out of his vehicle. He and Eva, who had no reason to mistrust police, got out of their truck to see what he wanted. The deputy jumped out, shouting and gripping his holstered gun. Magos and Eva scrambled back into their truck, and Magos feared that if he questioned the deputy's authority, he might get shot. He tried to follow the deputy's commands. Still, Magos felt he had to point out the absurdity of the deputy's demand to see his wife's driver's license. "I told him I was the driver, she was not driving," he would remember. The deputy insisted, and they both turned over their licenses.

It's not all that unusual for Arizonans, who live in a gun-friendly state, to pack handguns or rifles in their vehicles. Magos felt he needed to keep a handgun in his truck for self-protection, because he often worked in crime-ridden neighborhoods. When Magos told Russell about the handgun in his truck, Russell ordered Magos to step out of the vehicle, and splayed him against the truck bed panel on the driver's side. Magos was wearing sneakers, and when the deputy kicked his feet apart, pain shot through his ankles. He smelled soap, as though Russell had recently had his morning shower and had just driven out of the sheriff's compound for the start of the shift. Russell patted down Magos's entire body, including his groin. Magos could see Eva watching through the back window, her frightened dark eyes framed by her glasses. He hated that his wife, the daughter of Mexican immigrants, had to witness this. "I could not defend myself and I could not protect her either," Magos later told us.

Magos didn't believe Russell when he explained he'd stopped him because his trailer had no license plate. Magos felt certain this was untrue; he believed he was stopped because Russell had suspected he and Eva were undocumented Mexican immigrants. Magos would always believe, though he also knew he could not prove it, that the license plate had been affixed to his trailer at the start of the stop and the deputy himself had removed it to invent an excuse for having pulled them over.

After Russell verified the couples' driver's licenses, he let the two go without a citation.

"I'm a proud American," Magos later wrote in his journal. "And yet they detained us on the side of the road because of Our Brown Skin." The traffic stop had taken less than sixteen minutes. In that short time, Magos lost his sense that he had the same civil rights as other Americans.

When Magos reached Guzman through the hotline, he wept.

Guzman told us she knew right away Magos was exactly the kind of plaintiff she had been hoping to recruit. He was a law-abiding American citizen pulled over for something so minor the deputy didn't bother to issue a citation. The traffic stop had ended once he and his wife could prove they were lawfully present. Magos's story, like so many others she had heard for years, suggested the sheriff's office was still targeting Latino drivers even after losing 287(g) authority.

She doubled down on her resolve to keep the hotline open.

Even as Guzman kept running the hotline without a paycheck, not everyone appreciated her labor. She told us a local Spanish-language radio host criticized her and her Somos America colleagues, calling them self-serving leaders who cared more about themselves than the immigrant community. On the air, in Guzman's memory, the talk show host suggested Guzman was in the immigrant-rights game simply to make money. And this made some listeners distrust Guzman.

She learned that firsthand one day when she tried to talk to a potential *Melendres* case plaintiff who listened to the radio show. The woman, a Spanish speaker, had recently been stopped by Arpaio's deputies during one of his massive sweeps. Activists with cameras had written down the woman's license plate number, and a private investigator who worked with the movement had found the woman's address. Guzman decided to go see her.

As the woman unloaded groceries from her car, Guzman caught up with her, volunteered to carry a grocery bag, introduced herself, explained the *Melendres* case, and asked the woman if she'd be willing to testify. Instead of answering politely, the woman repeated the talk show host's words, calling Guzman a "pseudo leader." The woman asked Guzman if there would be any financial recompense for her participation in the case. Guzman tried to explain the *Melendres* lawsuit didn't seek monetary damages. Instead, it aimed to stop Arpaio's racial profiling and reform the sheriff's office.

The angry woman jerked the grocery bag from Guzman's arms. A package of dry beans fell onto the sidewalk and ripped open. Beans scattered on the concrete.

Guzman climbed back in her old Dodge Durango. It hadn't been a great day. Wesley had given her money to buy groceries for dinner and she'd spent it on gas instead so she could drive to meet the woman who'd just insulted her. Now she had no money to buy groceries. So later that day, she returned to the angry woman's house. Brushing sweat and tears from her face, she bent down and gathered the spilled beans off the dirty, cracked sidewalk.

She would never forget boiling those beans and serving them with tortillas for dinner that night.

By April 2010, the Latino civil rights movement in Maricopa County seemed to be cycling into another low point. Republican governor Jan Brewer was hinting that soon she would be signing Arizona's most severe immigration bill into law. The Support Our Law Enforcement and Safe Neighborhoods Act was Senate Bill 1070. Heartily supported by Arpaio and coauthored by Kris Kobach and Arizona senate president Russell Pearce, it had attracted a lot of national attention.

Senate Bill 1070 focused on criminalizing undocumented immigrants and encouraged police to collaborate with federal immigration officials. The proposed law, among other things, commanded all Arizona law enforcement officers, regardless of whether they worked for small towns or the state itself, to check the immigration status of those they suspected might be in the country unlawfully. This part of the law, Section 2(B), was derisively nicknamed by Guzman and other activists as "Show me your papers."

The bill sought to criminalize legal immigrants in Arizona who did not carry their papers with them. It criminalized unauthorized immigrants who worked or sought work. It criminalized seeking work on the street, the way day laborers do, if traffic was being impeded. It criminalized drivers who picked these workers up. It criminalized Arizonans for "harboring" unauthorized immigrants by simply driving them in a car.

The proposed law also enabled police to arrest legal immigrants without a warrant if the officers suspected these immigrants had previously committed "any public offense that makes the person removable from the United States." And it allowed residents to sue officials or agencies for inadequate immigration enforcement and allowed judges to impose fines on those officials or agencies as punishment.

Once again, the longtime restrictionist tenet "attrition through enforcement" sought to drive unauthorized immigrants out of Arizona. The purpose of Senate Bill 1070, legal scholar Jack Chin wrote in *The New York Times,* "is essentially to induce self-deportation, a federal responsibility, and to override decisions assigned by Congress to federal agencies."

But many Americans of Latino descent and immigrants alike feared that this new bill, were it to become law, would give the police power to unconstitutionally hunt them all.

The bill felt dangerous to Guzman. She told reporters Senate Bill 1070 would hurt every Arizonan. It would shutter businesses that relied on immigrant labor, economically damage working families, and drive off tourists.

She sensed Senate Bill 1070 would turn all of Arizona into Maricopa County. Dozens of Joe Arpaio clones might harass American citizens and immigrants alike by racially profiling them during traffic stops.

The bill was particularly popular in Maricopa County, which was still suffering the effects of the Great Recession. Jobs were still scarce. Citizen activists associated with FAIR and its network of related nonprofits blamed "illegals" for taking jobs from Arizonans. At the time, however, illegal immigration had slowed to levels not seen since the 1970s.

After a cattle rancher, Robert Krentz, was gunned down on his family ranch abutting the Mexican border, the bill gained even more support. The murder occurred in late March, just weeks before the Arizona Senate would vote on Senate Bill 1070. Some senators had been wavering over how they would vote, but public outcry over the Krentz murder gave them a reason to vote yes on the hardline immigration bill. If Janet Napolitano had stayed in the governor's office, she likely would have vetoed Senate Bill 1070.

Jan Brewer was finishing out Napolitano's term in 2010, and wanted to be governor in her own right, by winning that year's election. But at the time she was an unexciting candidate who lagged behind in the Republican primary. Signing the increasingly popular Senate Bill 1070 into law could assure Brewer a primary victory and pave her way to a full term in the governor's office. She announced she would either sign or veto the bill by April 24.

As that day approached, a long line of portable blue toilets appeared on the capitol grounds. The plastic outhouses were meant to accommodate thousands of protesters congregating on the patchwork of concrete sidewalks and lawns connecting the capitol complex, a cluster of state buildings fanning out from the historic capitol building. A weathervane of a winged white angel atop the copper-domed capitol swung around in different directions with changing winds.

Cars and vans crowded into the visitor parking lot, which fronted the Wesley Bolin Memorial Plaza, a public park populated with dozens of concrete and granite tributes to pioneers, fallen peace officers, World War II heroes, Martin Luther King, Jr., and Arizona's Confederate troops.

Carlos Garcia organized a protest in which nine college students chained themselves to the doors of the most iconic structure in the sprawling

Indigenous and day laborer rights activist Salvador Reza speaks during a protest of Senate Bill 1070 at the Arizona State Capitol in Phoenix on April 20, 2010. Mary Rose Wilcox and Danny Ortega stand together in the middle row on the far right side. (Photo by José L. Muñoz)

complex—the historic state capitol building. Antonio Bustamante and a team of lawyers representing the students stood near them as police cut the chains. The students were led away and briefly jailed, but were not prosecuted.

Near the site of the protesting students, a group recited the rosary as they stood around a statue of the Virgin of Guadalupe, the patron saint of Mexico. Petra Falcón, a longtime Latina activist and a devout Catholic, had organized the vigil. Falcón's group would maintain the capitol prayer vigil for several months. Many of the men, women, and children in her group were undocumented, risking personal safety to oppose Senate Bill 1070.

Salvador Reza, the indigenous activist, drowned out the soft chorus of Hail Marys by beating an enormous drum with a red stick. He viewed Senate Bill 1070 as just one more oppressive law in a chain of cruelties suffered by native people in the five-century span since Spaniards "invaded Mexico" with a "hunger for gold and power," Reza told us.

Members of Promise Arizona walk to a prayer vigil at the Arizona State Capitol in Phoenix in July 2010. The group was protesting Senate Bill 1070. (Photo by José L. Muñoz)

Governor Brewer's office sat on the ninth floor of the capitol's executive tower building. She could look down on the protesters. She would later single out Reza's ear-shattering drum beats as part of the "waterboarding" she endured from opponents of Senate Bill 1070. "They were there every day, marching, chanting, and beating drums. Always beating drums," she wrote in her 2011 book, *Scorpions for Breakfast*.

Soon, RidersUSA bikers, some wearing their leathers, arrived at the capitol to support Brewer. Valerie Roller told us Latino protesters screamed "racist" at her. This hurt, "because a racist is someone who's bigoted, who's hateful, who's uneducated, who's just nasty with a black heart." And Roller didn't feel she was a racist. Nor did she acknowledge any discomfort over the state's browning demographics. But she heartily endorsed Senate Bill 1070 because she thought it would restore law and order in Arizona. Crossing the border without papers was neither lawful or orderly, and it outraged her.

Kathryn Kobor demonstrated in favor of the bill, too. She marched right alongside the bikers because she wanted the world to know regular

Arizonans—people who looked like her, people who wore sensible clothes and tennis shoes—didn't want the United States to turn into a third world country like Mexico, she told us. In Kobor's memory, several Latino protesters screamed she was a racist and Nazi. And once, she told us, someone spit on her cheek.

Kobor's friend Pam Pearson, a short, amiable grandmother with tidy bobbed blond hair, told us she endured immigrants pushing, squeezing, and pressing against her as she demonstrated her support for Senate Bill 1070.

"I've had them get around me and squeeze on me, men, illegal men," she told us.

"They all took their bodies, they didn't really use their hands, they just started squeezing in on me and said, 'Is it worth it to you?' and I said, 'Yes. Yes it is.'"

Amid the disappointments fed by the near certainty that Senate Bill 1070 would become law, Lydia Guzman looked forward to receiving an award from the Latino nonprofit Chicanos Por La Causa. The award recognized Guzman for documenting civil rights abuses in Maricopa County and for advocating for immigrants who called the Respect-Respeto hotline.

Wesley was out of town attending truck-driving school. But Guzman invited other relatives to sit at her table at the awards ceremony at the Sheraton Hotel in downtown Phoenix. The gala would take place on April 22, two days before Brewer's deadline to sign or veto Senate Bill 1070. The Latino nonprofit had invited Brewer to give the keynote speech months before.

Given the worries over Senate Bill 1070 and the concern that Brewer would sign it to get elected, Carlos Garcia was outraged that Arizona's most famous Latino nonprofit had not rescinded their invitation to Brewer. He expected the governor "to sign the worst law we'd ever seen." The nonprofit's actions amounted to "spit in our face," Garcia told us. He hoped to shame and embarrass the dinner guests into not going into the hotel, to show they were "on our side."

"We had to do that protest," he told us.

As the dinner was about to get underway, Garcia, Salvador Reza, and other irate protesters stood on the sidewalk fronting the Sheraton Grand

Hotel in downtown Phoenix. It was a warm evening. Date palm trees shimmered silver in the setting sun. Dressed in jeans and T-shirts, sandals and boots, the protesters waved signs saying things like *End the Fourth Reich.*

Dinner guests in cocktail attire made their way into the hotel, looking down when they passed by Antonio Bustamante, who was so outraged by "that joke-of-a-human-being governor" that he pounded as hard as he could on a drum. "People asked me, 'How come you're not going in?' and I said, 'Why would I go in? *This* is where it's at,'" Bustamante told us.

Garcia hoped Guzman would change her mind, too, and not go inside. He had mixed feelings about her. He thought of her as an activist "who's able to kind of play both sides" and yet admired "her great work." Still, he felt that Guzman and others who were true to the cause shouldn't dignify the governor with their presence. Ideally, Garcia told us, Guzman "would have never shown up" at the dinner.

Guzman, dressed in her best black jacket and black pants, had no intention of staying outside with the protesters. She marched in high heels toward the Sheraton, toward Garcia and Reza and Bustamante beating the drum, and she thought the activists would insult her for going into a dinner in which Brewer had been asked to speak.

As she passed Garcia and Reza, she forced a smile. "Hey, guys, how are you doing," she managed. She knew they weren't happy with her decision to go inside but was relieved they didn't insult her.

Then she was in the building, inside the walls where she could make a difference, following the advice she'd gotten from her father so many years before. She knew, everyone knew, Brewer was going to sign Senate Bill 1070. And Guzman had planned on giving the governor a piece of her mind when she got her award. But Brewer was ushered out of the Sheraton before Guzman had a chance to confront her.

It was an excruciating evening for the governor. She could hear the drum thunder outside. Chicanos Por La Causa's board chairwoman had hardly given her a warm welcome. "The eyes of our state and the eyes of our nation are upon you," Erica Gonzalez-Melendez had told Brewer, adding that Senate Bill 1070 was the "most hateful piece of legislation directed at Latinos in the recent history of our state." She demanded Brewer veto the bill. "There were screams of applause. There was a standing ovation,"

Brewer wrote in her book. "Every word of this speech was insulting, even slanderous."

In her brief speech, Brewer promised she would do the best thing for the state.

"Veto the bill! Veto the bill! Veto the bill!" the dinner guests chanted as Brewer's aides whisked her out of the ballroom.

"Outside, there was a huge group with signs of me dressed in Nazi attire alongside Joe Arpaio, our famously tough sheriff—and a supporter of the bill—sporting a Hitler mustache," Brewer recalled in her book.

Inside, Guzman's mother, Rafaela Avila, her siblings, and other dinner guests watched a video featuring Danny Ortega and Alfredo Gutierrez paying tribute to Guzman's advocacy work with the Respect-Respeto hotline. Avila was moved. She told us she had not known the extent to which her daughter was helping the Latino community.

Guzman felt affirmed by her family and a rip-roaring ovation from the audience. She had followed her heart and become an advocate. Now, despite all the financial and personal struggles, she knew it had been worth it. It was a brief moment in which she felt content.

A few days after Jan Brewer signed Senate Bill 1070 into law, Lydia Guzman's mailbox was filled with sticky green relish, the kind that goes on hot dogs. She never figured out who did it, or why.

And then a few days after that, burglars broke into her house. They dumped the contents of dresser drawers, closets, and cabinets on the floors. Guzman's makeshift office—the kitchen table—was in disarray and her laptop containing her notes on hotline calls was missing. Her daughter's cameras and two other computers were stolen. So were boxes containing notebooks detailing immigrant contacts in worksite raids. The family's other valuables were untouched, which made Guzman believe the culprit was after the evidence she was collecting. Police never found the burglar.

She felt close to a meltdown anyway. The family was on food stamps. The cable company had disconnected the internet. Then her son, James, got a concussion and split his chin open in a skateboard accident. The state picked up the emergency room bill because Guzman and her family lived below the poverty line. But she didn't have the money to pay for James's medicine.

A friend paid for her internet service and lent her a computer so she could carry on with the hotline. The volume of calls had doubled now that Senate Bill 1070 loomed. Immigrants were confused and terrified.

Guzman got her first break in early July 2010. She received part of a fifty-thousand-dollar Four Freedoms Fund grant. Now she could run the hotline. Now she could pay her mortgage. Now she could reimburse friends who had lent her money.

That same month, she felt relieved when the United States Department of Justice sued the state of Arizona in federal court in Phoenix. The justice department contended Senate Bill 1070 was unconstitutional because immigration is the exclusive domain of the federal government, therefore Arizona was preempted from writing its own immigration laws. The justice department argued the law should be immediately blocked before it took effect on July 29, 2010.

On July 28, United States District Court Judge Susan Bolton sided with the justice department and temporarily blocked four key sections of the law. These included the so-called "Show me your papers" requirement that police officers check immigration status, the provision that criminalized unauthorized immigrants for working, the provision that criminalized legal immigrants who failed to carry around their papers, and the provision that gave police the authority to make warrantless arrests of immigrants suspected of a deportable offense.

Activists had already planned acts of civil disobedience for July 28, and decided to go ahead with them. Salvador Reza was arrested with others for protesting in front of Arpaio's downtown Phoenix jail. The United States marshal for Arizona, who was a friend of Alfredo Gutierrez, arrested Gutierrez after the two had coffee. Dozens of others, including faith leaders, were charged with misdemeanors and released, thanks to Antonio Bustamante and a battalion of volunteer defense attorneys who worked all night.

Arpaio's deputies arrested Reza again the next day, wrongfully, for standing across the street watching other activists protesting the sheriff. Reza thought of his arrest as a retaliation. He sued the sheriff for the wrongful arrest, and years later settled with the county for ninety-five thousand dollars.

The signing of Senate Bill 1070, the most extreme state immigration law thus far, signaled to many that Arizona had been taken over by restrictionists. Brewer later justified her signing of the law with fabricated examples of border violence, including non-existent "beheadings" in the Arizona desert. The controversy over Senate Bill 1070 magnified the racial divisions that had plagued Arizona for generations. Arizona's historic scorn for "Mexicans," now modernized in online restrictionist sound bites and memes, manifested itself in widespread animosity toward people who spoke Spanish in public. And it showed up in places like Russell Pearce's email inbox and outbox.

The American Civil Liberties Union of Arizona eventually obtained three thousand pages of Pearce's sent emails and used several in federal court filings intended to show Senate Bill 1070 was a racist law. One email sent by Pearce said: "Tough, nasty illegals and their advocates grow in such numbers that law and order will not subdue them. They run us out of our cities and states. They conquer our language and our schools. They render havoc and chaos in our schools." Another, with the subject line "What's a Racist?" read, "I'm a racist because I don't want to be taxed to pay for a prison population comprised of mainly Hispanics, Latinos, Mexicans or whatever else you wish to call them . . . I'm a racist because I want to deny citizenship to all anchor babies born in this country pre 2006 and here after."

When asked about the emails, Pearce didn't deny their existence, but claimed he "never name called, I've never demeaned the people as a whole." He said opponents who accuse him and Senate Bill 1070 of being racist, "can't win on the issue, so they do the character assassination stuff."

Nevertheless, the rhetoric in the emails descended from the early twentieth-century anti-immigrant eugenics movement and still carried its message. It appealed to people like J. T. Ready. The troubled former precinct committeeman for the Arizona Republican Party marched with neo-Nazis and white supremacists in Phoenix and conducted paramilitary migrant-hunting patrols in the desert. Ready claimed Russell Pearce had been his "mentor and family friend" and "a surrogate father" who told "Mexican jokes" on his front porch. The two had a falling out several years before Ready went on a killing spree. The victims included a sixteen-month-old toddler named Lilly. Then Ready killed himself.

Pearce had publicly distanced himself from Ready long before the tragedy. He later told us Ready was a "Judas Iscariot." Pearce told us when he met Ready, he was fresh out of the Marines and seemed to "say the right things" to Republicans in his district. "Sometimes you just don't know people as well as you think," Pearce told us. When Ready began showing extremist views, Pearce said, he led the charge to successfully remove him from the local Republican party.

Like Ready, Shawna Forde linked herself to the far-right wing of the Republican party. The hairdresser-turned-Minuteman from Washington State came to Arizona on a mission to keep America safe from unauthorized immigrants. To fund her own border militia, Forde and two others burglarized a home in Arivaca, Arizona and ended up murdering nine-year-old Brisenia Flores and her father, Raul Flores Jr., a Pima County Superior Court jury in Tucson found. The jury imposed the death penalty on Forde in 2011.

Forde always said she was innocent. In a rambling letter that she penned from death row in 2012, she painted a vivid picture of Arizona's restrictionist underground. She self-identified as "very active in the GOP, a right-winger, as some say." The "conservative party," to which she belonged, she wrote, was "full of anger, Hate, non compromise but are passionately patriotic and lovers of the Constitution, rule of law, God, Freedom, liberty. So there are many asspects that are very attractive and easy to embrace." She had endured severe child abuse, often at the hands of those entrusted with her care. In the letter, she wrote "my true love for my nation is in place for the parents I never had."

Forde networked with other extremist border militia aficionados in and out of Arizona. She wrote in her letter that Arpaio was held in high regard in that world. "Many across America love Joe and view him as their last chance to stop the 'takeover,'" she wrote.

Forde worked briefly with Chris Simcox when he wanted to set up militia groups on the northern border with Canada. A former schoolteacher who'd sold all his belongings and moved to Arizona to protect the border, Simcox was a cofounder of the Minuteman Project that had attracted Valerie Roller, George Sprankle, and so many others to the Arizona-Mexico border around the time Patrick Haab held the migrants at gunpoint at a highway rest stop in the spring of 2005.

Minutemen were often given credibility in the media. Forde was featured in a Belgian documentary, while Simcox was celebrated on Fox News. Simcox developed political ambitions and appeared with Joe Arpaio at an immigration-themed rally in Sun City in 2009. Simcox was later arrested, convicted of child molestation, and sent to prison.

The Minuteman movement lasted about seven years, roughly, and accomplished "nil" the author David Neiwart wrote in his book on extremism on the Arizona border, *And Hell Followed with Her*. "The movement crumbled under the weight of the extremists it attracted, despite numerous warnings—not merely from its critics—that because of its agenda and its politics, it ran a nearly ineluctable risk of becoming a haven for violent racists," Neiwart wrote.

The Minutemen heyday coincided with the years during which Arizona's elected officials passed the Human Smuggling Law, the Legal Arizona Workers Act, and Senate Bill 1070. At the time, many progressives felt Arizona had dropped out of the United States of America. The far-right wing of the Republican Party controlled all branches of state government. Some Latino activists, like Lydia Guzman, hinged their hope on the fact that three state immigration laws, and the sheriff's alleged racial profiling in Maricopa County, were being challenged in federal court.

And in the meantime, in the wake of Senate Bill 1070's passage, activists called for a boycott of their own state. Within weeks after Arizona governor Brewer signed the law, more than fifteen cities—from Austin, Texas to St. Paul, Minnesota—passed resolutions to halt business dealings with Arizona. Musicians cancelled Arizona shows. Upcoming conventions were cancelled. Mexican universities yanked their study abroad programs in Arizona schools.

Near the end of 2010, the liberal Center for American Progress estimated Arizona had lost more than 140 million dollars as a consequence of cancelled conventions.

During the March 2011 legislative session, sixty business leaders wrote a letter to Senator Russell Pearce urging him to stay away from immigration matters. "It is an undeniable fact that each of our companies and our employees were impacted by the boycotts and the coincident negative image," the business leaders wrote. Pearce told us he was not swayed. But the Arizona legislature soured on passing immigration bills.

13 Licking Their Chops

2009–2012

Each time Lydia Guzman walked into the federal courthouse in down-town Phoenix, she showed the guards her driver's license, passed through a security scanner, then stepped onto the shiny gray floor of a seven-story atrium that was often muggy and smelled faintly of human perspiration.

Constructed of steel beams and glass walls, the atrium of the Sandra Day O'Connor courthouse lacked air conditioning, and relied instead on a dysfunctional air misting system that made the walls sweat. Sometimes only the statue of the building's native Arizonan namesake, Supreme Court Justice Sandra Day O'Connor, seemed oblivious to the cloying heat. An inscription near the statue read: *Be independent. Be fair. Venture to be wise.*

Guzman had faith the *Melendres* case would be adjudicated independently, fairly, and wisely. Still, she was tense. Much was at stake. Redemption for the Latino-led resistance. The civil rights of tens of thousands of county residents. The community's trust in an American institution—the courts. The battle over whether local cops could enforce federal immigration law. The defeat of the nation's most notorious restrictionist, Joe Arpaio.

After Manuel de Jesus Ortega Melendres sued Joe Arpaio and his deputies for racially profiling and wrongfully arresting him during the 2007 traffic stop near the church in Cave Creek, Guzman had poured her energies into advancing the *Melendres* case. She respected the court as an institution and viewed it as a last hope for those targeted by Joe Arpaio. The court could cut off Arpaio's power and get justice for the Latino community, she felt. For this reason, she'd worked tirelessly to find Latino drivers or passengers who had been wrongfully detained by the sheriff's deputies in traffic stops and thus might qualify as co-plaintiffs in the case. She faithfully attended court hearings, too.

But people impacted by Arpaio's sweeps had little faith that anything was getting accomplished in the courthouse. Sometimes, they asked Guzman why she even bothered spending time on the hopeless lawsuit.

And it was true that Arpaio's power, popularity, and alleged retaliations against those who opposed him had nearly monkey-wrenched the *Melendres* case in its early years. Few local attorneys wanted to oppose the sheriff. Julie Pace, who'd originally filed the *Melendres* lawsuit with Jason LeVecke's secret backing, told us she withdrew from the case in 2008 because her law firm partners didn't want to take on Arpaio.

After activists scrambled to find another lawyer to represent Melendres, David Bodney, a well-respected Phoenix media and constitutional law attorney, signed on to replace Pace.

LeVecke quietly paid Bodney's legal bills, and three nonprofits—the Mexican American Legal Defense and Educational Fund, the American Civil Liberties Union of Arizona, and the American Civil Liberties Union Immigrants' Rights Project—also joined the case. The nonprofits specialized in civil rights litigation and wouldn't charge a dime, hoping instead to collect lawyers' fees from Maricopa County.

The new legal team wanted to convert the case into a class action lawsuit. In addition to Melendres, the named plaintiffs included Jessika Rodriguez (who was Phil Gordon's aide), three other American citizens, and Somos America—as an "organizational plaintiff." Together they would represent a "class," or group, of people who alleged their constitutional rights were violated by Arpaio's deputies during prolonged traffic stops. Instead of seeking monetary damages, the plaintiffs wanted to reform the sheriff's office, and force Arpaio and his deputies to stop violating the constitutional rights of Latino drivers and passengers.

Soon after, the plaintiffs asked the sheriff's office to preserve and turn over printed and electronic records—including videos—pertaining to the traffic stops.

"At that time ... I didn't pay much attention to all this legal stuff," Arpaio told us. As the sheriff of the nation's fourth largest county, he was sued often by inmates and their families, mostly for alleged constitutional violations. He won some of these cases, and lost others.

But from the onset, the *Melendres* case hadn't gone well for Arpaio. In 2009, the *Melendres* judge, Mary Murguia, denied Arpaio's motion to dismiss the *Melendres* case.

By then, Arpaio had already gotten an email from supporters who claimed Mary Murguia, "the 'token' Hispanic female judge," was biased. "We plan to get her in trouble for not recusing herself from this case, given that we have solid evidence that she's an ally of Salvador Reza and Somos America. Quite uncool of Murguia to sit, or shit on this case. How did Reza, Somos, Gordon [Phoenix mayor Phil Gordon] and others influence her? Dinero? Favors? Human smuggling money?"

The sheriff forwarded the conspiracy-tinged email to members of his command staff and the media relations department.

A few weeks later, Arpaio's lawyers noted in court filings that Mary Murguia had a twin sister—Janet Murguia, who was the president of the National Council of La Raza. Included in the court filing was a copy of a recent National Council of La Raza online post that referred to Arpaio's deputies as "thugs" and encouraged people to request a justice department investigation. Arguing Janet Murguia's organization had made statements that are "biased and prejudiced against Defendant Arpaio," the sheriff's attorneys called for Judge Mary Murguia to recuse herself because she could not be fair and impartial.

"The idea that an Hispanic judge should never preside over a controversial case concerning alleged acts of racial profiling purportedly committed against Hispanics is repugnant," Murguia wrote in court documents. But she recognized the National Council of la Raza statements "greatly disparage MCSO deputies and personally attack Sheriff Arpaio" and asserted Arpaio's deputies had engaged in racial profiling—which was central to the lawsuit. She concluded "even the slightest chance" the public might question the fairness of the case outcome was too great a risk to take. Murguia recused herself from the *Melendres* case in July 2009.

For Guzman, Murguia's recusal was devastating. In the *Melendres* lawsuit, the judge, not a jury, would decide the outcome. Guzman felt Murguia would have understood the constitutional issues surrounding Arpaio's traffic stops.

But now a new judge, Grant Murray Snow, a Republican white man who'd been nominated to the federal bench by President George W. Bush, would replace Murguia.

Oh my gosh, Guzman thought, we're screwed.

Snow was born in 1959 and grew up in Boulder City, Nevada, a small orderly town near Las Vegas, in a neighborhood with ranch houses and green lawns. A tall, stocky teenager with protruding ears and a shy smile, he attended Brigham Young University, where he played on the offensive line for the football team. He was, by all reports, a fearless football player. After graduating, he went on to BYU's J. Reuben Clark Law School, which, like BYU itself, is funded by the Church of Jesus Christ of Latter-day Saints. The law school emphasized "the development of moral character and enlightened devotion to the rule of law."

Snow moved to Phoenix and joined a law firm, Osborn Maledon. He and his wife settled into a simple house in a Phoenix suburb and started raising a family. When he wasn't working or attending his kids' sports events and birthday parties, Snow donated his time to the Church of Jesus Christ of Latter-day Saints, where he served as a bishop. Here, he counseled everyday people struggling with loss, shame, fear, and uncertainty. These men and women, who were soldiering quietly through their troubles, became his heroes.

By the spring of 2010, amid the nerve-wracking tensions surrounding Senate Bill 1070, the legal team for the Latino plaintiffs in the *Melendres* case was once again in danger of collapsing. The sheriff's office had withheld documents. And deputies, who had never been ordered by their superiors to preserve records, had destroyed traffic stop records and emails that should have been turned over to the plaintiffs' lawyers. The Phoenix attorney Michael Manning told us Arpaio's agency had used a

similar tactic in courtroom battles Manning had fought on behalf of grieving families whose loved ones had died in Arpaio's jails.

When they discovered the evidence destruction, the plaintiffs' attorneys
wanted to ask the court to sanction the defendants and force Maricopa
County—the financially responsible party for the sheriff's department—to
pay plaintiffs' legal fees. But to do so, David Bodney would likely have to
reveal that Jason LeVecke had been secretly paying him.

LeVecke had hoped the *Melendres* case would be about much more
than stopping Arpaio. He'd always viewed Arpaio as a symptom of "the
hardening across America" against immigrants. "The goal," he told us,
"was always to stop the attitude, not just Sheriff Joe."

But LeVecke's restaurants were still struggling in the Great Recession
and the case had already cost him about four hundred thousand dollars.
He could not afford to keep supporting the case. Nor did he feel he could
afford possible retaliation from Arpaio if LeVecke's role in the case was
revealed. He felt he had no choice but to stop funding the *Melendres* case.
He never got his legal fees reimbursed.

"It was too risky," LeVecke told us.

Bodney and his law firm withdrew. The remaining plaintiffs' lawyers
from the nonprofits knew they couldn't fund the expensive case alone.
They needed a well-resourced firm, or a rich benefactor, to step in.

Dan Pochoda, the legal director of American Civil Liberties Union
Arizona, failed, after a vigorous months-long search, to convince any
Arizona law firm to join the case. Pochoda told us firms either had conflicts because they represented the county in another matter or "politically
[they] were not interested—most of the people they represent were voting
for the sheriff."

Then, at the last minute, Covington and Burling, an American law firm
with global reach that had previously joined the ACLU on pro bono civil
rights cases, agreed to join the case for free.

Game on, Guzman thought.

After Judge Snow issued stern, no-nonsense orders about providing
requested documents to the plaintiffs, the sheriff's office eventually produced tens of thousands of documents. They included a mishmash of
records prepared by deputies, internal agency emails, memos, directives,

and everything in Arpaio's immigration file, which he'd kept locked in his closet. That file turned out to be a treasure for the Latino plaintiffs. Stanley Young, a California-based Covington and Burling lawyer who'd signed on to the case, immediately recognized what he called "explicitly racist" content in the sheriff's file.

For Stanley Young and his colleagues, the drive to dismantle institutionalized racism through the lawsuit was a personal mission as well as a legal one. Young and fellow plaintiffs' attorney Cecillia Wang were both children of Chinese immigrants (Wang's Chinese parents grew up in Taiwan before immigrating to the United States). Another lawyer, Annie Lai, who'd shepherded the *Melendres* lawsuit through key stages of its early development, was the daughter of Chinese-Indonesian and Taiwanese immigrants.

Wang had confronted Arpaio before, in a legal challenge to an Arizona law denying bail to immigrants. Despite her role as opposing counsel, the sheriff had insisted on giving her an autographed pair of pink boxer shorts. Through that experience, she viewed the sheriff as a man "who craves adulation, who craves attention."

She told us Arpaio was "extremely dangerous" because he was "motivated entirely by political dynamics and catering to a very narrow band of the community . . . people who sent him letters demanding raids because people were speaking Spanish at McDonald's."

She knew about those letters because Arpaio had tucked them into his immigration file. And she hoped the letters, along with other contents in the file, could help prove in court that Arpaio conducted sweeps motivated by racial animus to please constituents.

As the plaintiffs' lawyers meticulously prepared the *Melendres* case for a looming but as yet unscheduled trial, Joe Arpaio and his deputies paused their dramatic neighborhood sweeps in the fall of 2011. But deputies still continued raiding workplaces to bust immigrants working with fake papers and continued to enforce the state Human Smuggling Law, nailing immigrants for conspiring with the smuggler to smuggle themselves into Arizona. In accordance with Kris Kobach's training video, if deputies could not pin state criminal charges on undocumented immigrants, they detained the immigrants anyway and called a local ICE hotline. Frequently, ICE agents instructed the sheriff's office to deliver these immigrants to the ICE office in downtown Phoenix. ICE referred to this program as "Law

Enforcement Agency Response," and sheriff's deputies called it the "LEAR protocol."

By 2011, five states had passed laws similar to Arizona's Senate Bill 1070. And just like Senate Bill 1070, most of these laws were stayed by the courts.

The culture of ICE was slowly shifting, or at least showed signs of it, under the Obama administration. In the summer of 2011, Barack Obama's ICE director, John Morton, advised federal immigration prosecutors to focus on prosecuting and deporting criminal immigrants instead of law-abiding unauthorized immigrants with strong ties to the United States, like veterans or parents of young children.

What's more, the sheriff's restrictionist allies in Arizona were being stripped of their power. Russell Pearce, the Arizona senate majority leader who had pushed through the state's immigration laws, was recalled in 2011 after extensive neighborhood canvassing by mostly Latino volunteers. The next year, Pearce ran again for his old post but lost the Republican primary.

Arpaio was facing scrutiny, too. His agency stood accused of misspending upwards of one hundred million dollars over the preceding six years. County officials had discovered the sheriff's office improperly used funds from a jail tax to pay salaries of non-jail employees, including Human Smuggling Unit deputies focused on immigration enforcement and deputies in the anti-corruption unit. The sheriff's office had previously hidden this misspending with two sets of books.

The way Guzman saw it, the Latino-led movement, the press, and the courts were unmasking Sheriff Joe Arpaio, and sooner or later Maricopa County, and the nation, would tire of him. Her only disappointment centered on the slow progress of two federal investigations.

It was difficult for locals to keep track of the two federal investigations of the sheriff and his office. One probe was the justice department inquiry into alleged civil rights abuses of Latinos by the Maricopa County Sheriff's Office. This was the investigation Somos America and national allies had pushed the Obama administration to pursue after Phil Gordon had first requested it in April 2008. By late 2011, this civil rights investigation, based in Washington, D.C., had dragged on for more than two and a half years with little sign of progress.

The other investigation was a criminal probe led by the United States Attorney's Office in Phoenix into whether the sheriff and the county attorney abused their power by retaliating against perceived foes and critics. Around Phoenix, the probe was called the "abuse of power investigation." The public first found out about the probe in early 2010 when county officials revealed they had been summoned to testify against Arpaio before a grand jury. The FBI and United States Attorney's Office in Phoenix had quietly begun investigating in 2008.

Federal authorities never disclosed what triggered their criminal investigation of Arpaio, but Phil Gordon, Paul Charlton, George Gascón, Terry Goddard, and a former county attorney, Rick Romley, had prodded the FBI to take action on the abuse of power allegations. The investigation broadened after county officials discovered the sheriff's misspending in late 2010.

Both the justice department's civil rights investigation and the United States Attorney's criminal probe in Phoenix had once been a source of excitement and anticipation for the Latino resistance. Latino activists followed news about the local abuse of power investigation closely, wondering if the sheriff would soon be criminally indicted. For years, they shared information with the justice department in Washington, D.C. hoping to strengthen the case against the sheriff's office.

Carlos Garcia told us he and other Somos America members had shared three terabytes of information with federal investigators, including videos, interviews, and affidavits of Latino residents who alleged their civil rights had been violated by the sheriff. But as time passed with no sign of progress, Garcia dismissed the justice department as a feckless bureaucracy.

"We were imagining the cavalry coming and taking Arpaio out," Garcia recalled. "We didn't realize there was a couple of folks with polo shirts that were actually going to ask us to do all the work for them."

Garcia was one of several Latino activists who became disenchanted with the federal governments' slow pace on both investigations. Guzman and a few others still held out hope that the justice department would come through.

The civil rights investigation did come through, finally. It was headed by Tom Perez, the son of immigrants from the Dominican Republic, who directed the Washington-based civil rights division of the justice department. Perez later told us that when his team talked to deputies during the investigation, some deputies complained Arpaio's immigration crusade thwarted their efforts to build public trust. "He made their jobs harder by having this unrelenting, unconstitutional focus on whether *abuelita* [granny] has papers," Perez told us.

Perez detailed key investigation findings in a press conference at a federal office in downtown Phoenix on December 15, 2011. "We find reasonable cause," he said, "to believe that MCSO [Maricopa County Sheriff's Office] engages in a pattern or a practice of unconstitutional policing."

The agency's expert who analyzed the sheriff's traffic stops concluded, according to Perez, that "this case involved the most egregious racial profiling in the United States that he had ever personally observed."

The justice department investigators found the sheriff's office racially profiled the county's Latino residents and unlawfully stopped, detained, and arrested them. Deputies targeted and harassed Latino drivers. And jail staffers discriminated against Latino jail inmates with limited English skills, forcing them to sign papers they didn't understand, ignoring their grievances and pleas for assistance, and baiting them with racial slurs.

And even as the other abuse of power investigation inched along in Phoenix, the Washington-based civil rights division found that Arpaio and his department unlawfully retaliated against critics.

Arpaio had refused to cooperate with the justice department for two years and three months, the justice department report said. It was only after the justice department successfully filed a court action to win access to the sheriff's records that the investigation made headway.

And the report referenced uninvestigated sex crimes, first brought to the attention of the justice department by the *East Valley Tribune* and then further investigated by The Associated Press, which reported that Arpaio's department, famous for immigration enforcement, neglected to properly investigate more than four hundred sex abuse cases.

Perez, who would later go on to direct the United States Department of Labor and, after that, chair the Democratic National Committee, hoped Arpaio would consent to reforming his agency under the supervision of a federal judge. He didn't want to sue Arpaio again, he said, although he would if Arpaio refused reforms.

Guzman listened, gobsmacked. She recognized in the justice department's findings many of the cases she and other activists had turned over to the federal agency.

It had been worth it after all, she thought.

That same day, the Obama administration's Department of Homeland Security revoked Arpaio's 287(g) partnership in his jails. The federal agency had already revoked Arpaio's 287(g) partnership that allowed some deputies on patrol to enforce federal immigration law. That meant Arpaio now had no 287(g) partnership with the federal government to enforce federal immigration law.

By then, Arpaio's jail detention officers had already conducted immigration checks on nearly 500,000 inmates, and had flagged 44,000 immigrant inmates for eventual deportation, according to a sheriff's office press release. The end of the 287(g) partnership in the jails sounded like a victory for the Latino resistance, but it wasn't. Even though Arpaio's jailhouse detention officers could no longer act as immigration law enforcers, ICE replaced them with its own agents, who continued to identify undocumented immigrant inmates. That meant anyone who was undocumented and wound up in Arpaio's jail was still in a likely pipeline to deportation.

Eight days after the justice department issued the results of the civil rights investigation, and Arpaio's 287(g) powers were revoked, the sheriff faced his third setback, which would cause him to view the *Melendres* case as not just another lawsuit and Judge G. Murray Snow as not just another judge.

Snow filed two powerful rulings that curtailed Arpaio's immigration enforcement. In a "preliminary injunction" that would cause problems for the sheriff's office for years, Snow prohibited Arpaio and his agency from detaining immigrants who had committed no crimes and turning them over to ICE.

The sheriff's office no longer had 287(g) authority, the judge noted. Without that, local cops did not have "inherent authority" to conduct civil immigration arrests, Snow ruled. The judge cited the 1983 ruling in the *Gonzales* Peoria farmworker case, among others, to make his point.

In short, the judge said, Arpaio and his deputies were prohibited from "detaining any person based solely on knowledge, without more, that the person is in the country without lawful authority."

The sheriff's office could only investigate immigrants for violations of federal criminal laws or state laws, the judge said.

At that point, Snow officially turned the *Melendres* case into a class action lawsuit by certifying a huge "class" of plaintiffs: "All Latino persons who, since January 2007, have been or will be in the future, stopped, detained, questioned or searched by MCSO [Maricopa County Sheriff's Office] agents while driving or sitting in a vehicle on a public roadway or parking area in Maricopa County, Arizona."

In a separate order, the judge sanctioned Arpaio and his agency. He ruled that in the upcoming trial, he might make unfavorable assumptions about what was in the destroyed evidence.

On the day after Christmas in 2011, Lydia Guzman, Alfredo Gutierrez, Salvador Reza, Mary Rose Wilcox, Danny Ortega, and Antonio Bustamante, among others, met at the shuttered El Portal restaurant to celebrate and talk to reporters. It was a time, Antonio Bustamante told us, "to trumpet to the world we had been vindicated." Snow's ruling, he felt, not only stopped the sheriff from conducting more sweeps, it predicted a good outcome for the next step in the *Melendres* case: an upcoming trial that would determine whether Arpaio's deputies had racially profiled Latino motorists.

In light of Snow's ruling and with a racial profiling trial on the horizon, the sheriff's office no longer flooded neighborhoods to pull over cars in search of undocumented immigrants. Gone were the neighborhood sweeps with horses, SUVs, helicopters, and command centers with stadium lights. Then something fell onto Arpaio's lap. Something to counteract the loss of his sweeps, the bad publicity from the incriminating justice department civil rights investigation, the lawsuits alleging retaliation, and the publicity about the many millions Arpaio had cost county taxpayers.

It had started in Trump Tower in New York in April 2011, when, unbeknownst to Arpaio, two Tea Party Republicans and a state representative from Arizona met with Donald Trump, then the star of the television show *The Apprentice*. The Arizonans sought Trump's endorsement of a proposed Arizona "birther bill," which took aim at Barack Obama, who would run for a second presidential term in 2012. The stale, debunked conspiracy theory upon which the proposed state law was premised posited Obama was born in Kenya, had a fake American birth certificate, and was ineligible for the presidency.

Just a day before he'd met with the Arizonans, Trump insisted to NBC and MSNBC journalists that Obama's grandmother had witnessed his birth in Kenya. Trump based his claim on an edited YouTube video and the writings of Jerome Corsi, the conspiracy theorist and author.

Trump backed the Arizona birther bill, which was vetoed by Governor Brewer. A few months later, Corsi, along with some Arizona birthers who were affiliated with a Tea Party group in Surprise, a Phoenix suburb, asked Arpaio to launch an investigation of Obama's birth certificate. One Surprise Tea Party member, Brian Reilly, told us Arpaio was interested, but he needed a letter to rationalize the investigation. Reilly remembered Arpaio explaining: "Write me a letter in such a way that it puts me in a box."

"I'm in a box," Arpaio told us five years later in 2016, when he was still investigating Obama's birth certificate with no credible results and no end in sight. He told us he started the investigation because he just couldn't ignore the Tea Party group that sought his help. Plus, it was entirely within his duty as sheriff to investigate identity theft and forged government documents. And his investigation showed, he falsely claimed, Obama's birth certificate was a "phony document."

Why, exactly, Arpaio embraced the birth certificate conspiracy theory for years depends on who you ask. And when. His 2012 campaign director, Chad Willems, and Lisa Allen, the media relations director, warned Arpaio that a birther investigation would make him look foolish. Arpaio dug in, saying it would bring in campaign donations. But when we talked to him a few years later, he denied he'd launched the investigation to get campaign contributions. He believed the birther conspiracy theory had merit. As a former fed, he told us, "I'm a conspiracy guy." He was not a kook, he told us. But there were conspiracies everywhere, including the coverup "by the press and by the politicians" who refused to give credibility to his investigation of President Barack Obama's birth certificate.

Just two days before the racial profiling trial in Snow's courtroom was set to begin in July 2012, Arpaio held a press conference. He claimed without credible evidence that an "exhaustive inquiry" by his "cold case posse" revealed Obama's birth certificate was "undoubtedly a fraud."

Arpaio had caught the attention of restrictionists all over the country, including fellow birther Donald Trump, who tweeted from his @realDonaldTrump handle: "Thanks to @RealSheriffJoe @BarackObama can't hide anymore."

It was a distraction from so many things. For years, Arpaio had policed Maricopa County with little accountability. But soon, the Latino plaintiffs in the *Melendres* case hoped to prove in court that Arpaio and his deputies racially profiled Latino drivers and thus violated their constitutional rights.

Arpaio seemed confident he could prove in court that neither he nor his deputies engaged in racial profiling. In his drug enforcement career, he'd always managed to come out on top. He thought of himself as a fighter. And he relished defending himself in the upcoming trial at the federal courthouse in Phoenix.

"We are licking our chops," one of Arpaio's lead lawyers said on the eve of the trial.

14

Driving While Brown

2012

Joe Arpaio slumped in the witness box. He seemed to have shrunk in his baggy dark brown suit and maroon tie. Dark lines encircled his eyes. He looked old and timid and confused. His voice sounded weak. Under questioning from plaintiffs' attorney Stanley Young, Arpaio explained he had a touch of the flu.

The courtroom was filled to capacity. After years, the *Melendres* case had finally progressed to the trial stage. Lydia Guzman, watching from a crowded wooden bench in the stuffy gallery, wondered how Arpaio, who normally projected so much vigor and power, could appear so diminished on the witness stand.

Stanley Young knew not to underestimate the sheriff. The silver-haired, tall lawyer had deposed Arpaio before the trial, and viewed him as a careful and well-trained witness. Young, an intellectual property lawyer from California, chose to be a calm interrogator. In his deep monotone, he began questioning Arpaio about seemingly incriminating evidence from the sheriff's own files and statements to the press.

Judge Snow, poker-faced in his black robe, sat at a large desk and looked down at Arpaio. A forelock of graying hair dangled onto Snow's wide forehead.

Guzman felt the press of other activists' bodies on either side of her. She heard local and national reporters typing quickly on their laptops in the back of the room. Her clothes were damp with sweat after walking from the parking garage to the courthouse in the sweltering July heat earlier that morning. There had been a line to get inside the courtroom to hear Arpaio testify. The opening days of the trial took place in a circular courtroom on the second floor with a mezzanine for overflow seating. This was a sentimental space for Guzman. Nine years earlier, the same room had hosted Rafaela Avila's citizenship ceremony where Guzman had been the surprise speaker.

Mary Rose Wilcox, Salvador Reza, Alfredo Gutierrez, Roberto Reveles, and other activists sat near her. This trial was a culmination of years of hard work by Guzman and Somos America activists. They had filmed traffic stops and searched for prospective plaintiffs in the hopes that one day they could sit in this very courtroom and hold Arpaio accountable. Yet now that the trial was finally underway, Lydia Guzman felt more anxious than triumphant.

In the months leading up to the trial, she had contacted the prospective plaintiffs she had found over the past four years to get them on the schedule to testify. To her disappointment, several had refused. She hadn't been able to persuade some with the most egregious stories, like the Mexico-born naturalized American citizen who had been pulled over and questioned by deputies multiple times for no clear reason. Many potential plaintiffs told her they feared retaliation by the sheriff. She couldn't blame them. She knew Manuel de Jesus Ortega Melendres, the Mexican tourist who the case was named for, would not testify either. The stress from his arrest and the lawsuit had caused patches of his thick hair to temporarily fall out. He feared Arpaio. He wanted nothing to do with the trial he had set into motion.

Guzman wondered if she'd done her part to ensure a legal victory. She dreaded the idea of a vindicated Arpaio winning the *Melendres* case, pounding his chest for the cameras. If Arpaio triumphed in court, she feared, he would be even more emboldened to interrogate Latino drivers, terrorize immigrants, and separate families. And she worried other local police departments would mimic Arpaio's racial profiling tactics if he got away with it now.

Less than a month before Arpaio testified in his racial profiling trial in the *Melendres* case, part of Senate Bill 1070 had been revived by the United

States Supreme Court. The high court's decision renewed anxiety in the Latino community, and fears that Arpaio-style policing would soon spread. On June 25, 2012, the court permanently struck down three of the four most controversial provisions in Senate Bill 1070 but paved the way for Section 2(B), the "Show me your papers" provision, to eventually take effect. The justices found local police could check immigration status if they have reason to suspect someone they stop, detain, or arrest is in the country illegally. Still, Justice Anthony Kennedy's opinion warned Section 2(B) would have to be implemented carefully, because detaining people "solely to verify their immigration status would raise constitutional concerns."

Kennedy's opinion had included a sympathetic nod to Arizona's mission to stop illegal immigration and had given credence to a misleading report from the restrictionist think tank, the Center for Immigration Studies. That report claimed unauthorized immigrants made up only about 9 percent of the Maricopa County population but committed about 22 percent of the felonies in the county. The problem was that the report had failed to note that the high numbers of immigrant felonies were attributable to Arpaio's arrests—and Andrew Thomas's prosecutions—of immigrants who'd broken state laws by working with fake papers or conspiring to smuggle themselves.

The Supreme Court's mixed ruling on Senate Bill 1070 confused many Arizonans. Guzman worried it gave immigrants more reason to fear the police. And she predicted brown-skinned drivers and passengers on Arizona roadways would get stopped for minor traffic infractions, like going a mile over the speed limit, just so police could interrogate them about their immigration status. The best way to fight that dangerous possibility, Guzman believed, was to squash Arpaio in the *Melendres* case. Should Snow rule Arpaio had racially profiled Latino motorists, it would likely scare other Arizona police departments away from overzealous enforcement of the "Show me your papers" provision of Senate Bill 1070. So, a victory in the *Melendres* case, Guzman told us, was "the key to what could stop all the other madness."

The two lead attorneys tasked with defending Joe Arpaio were Tim Casey, a private lawyer hired by the county, and Tom Liddy, a deputy county attorney. Liddy happened to be the son of G. Gordon Liddy, Arpaio's friend from the Nixon administration who had gone to prison for

Watergate crimes. Both attorneys had ties to Arizona Republican politics—Casey had previously worked for the state party, and Liddy, who'd once dabbled in talk radio, had served as a Maricopa County Republican chairman and had lost a congressional bid. Both were affiliated with Senator John McCain's moderate wing of the GOP, rather than the faction focused on restrictionism.

The nine attorneys crammed behind and near the plaintiffs' table were diverse in gender, age, and ethnicity. Most were children of immigrants. Together, they reflected the nation's shifting demographics and the multicultural, changing America they championed.

Most of the plaintiffs' attorneys lived in California or New York, and several had already started making regular trips to Phoenix to participate in various immigration-themed lawsuits. Arizona's experiments with restrictionist policies in recent years had given the attorneys plenty to litigate.

Cecillia Wang and her ACLU and Mexican American Legal Defense and Education Fund colleagues, as well as other allies including Danny Ortega, were waging their own legal war against Arizona's Senate Bill 1070 at the time. This lawsuit was separate from the Obama justice department challenge to Senate Bill 1070, which had just been decided by the Supreme Court. Using different legal arguments that focused on the potential for civil rights abuses, Ortega, Wang, and their colleagues sought to get Senate Bill 1070 struck down entirely. They argued the law was unconstitutional because former Senator Russell Pearce and other bill sponsors had been motivated by racial animus against Latinos. Arpaio was also a defendant in this legal challenge to Senate Bill 1070, and Tim Casey represented him in that case, too. Several attorneys on the plaintiffs' legal team in the *Melendres* case had also previously squared off against Casey and Arpaio while challenging Arizona's law that denied undocumented immigrant arrestees the right to pre-trial release from jail on a bond.

The two legal teams in *Melendres* had sparred in multiple venues over the role of local police in immigration enforcement and equal protection under the law. To some courtroom observers, the *Melendres* trial was a key test of which vision for America would prevail.

Attorney Stanley Young stood calmly at his podium, questioning Arpaio about dozens of neatly filed exhibits—including a stack of the sheriff's old press releases trumpeting his immigration sweeps, anti-Mexican emails that were forwarded around his agency, and restrictionist fan mail. To help prove his case, Young needed to establish the sheriff's policies were intentionally discriminatory.

But on the stand, Arpaio was presenting as a bewildered old man. Sometimes, he would remove his glasses, peer down at the black three-ring binder with tabbed exhibits in front of him and pucker into a frown, as though he couldn't quite understand Young's questions.

Young confronted the sheriff with seemingly biased past comments about Mexican immigrants. He turned to the 2008 memoir Arpaio coauthored with Len Sherman, *Joe's Law: America's Toughest Sheriff Takes on Illegal Immigration, Drugs, and Everything Else That Threatens America*. At a book signing, Arpaio had once told his fans, "I was very careful writing this book. I wrote it like I was testifying in court." But under questioning from Young, Arpaio distanced himself from *Joe's Law*. He now said he hadn't read it all. When Young read aloud inflammatory passages, such as "second and third generations of Mexican immigrants" in the Southwest do not assimilate like other immigrants and instead "maintain identities" that are "separate from the American mainstream," Arpaio blamed his coauthor. Arpaio also distanced himself from the language in press releases, despite an earlier deposition in which he had acknowledged reviewing releases written by his public relations staff.

"We should never racial profile," Arpaio testified. He called the practice "immoral" and "illegal."

Arpaio testified with skill, but the evidence from Arpaio's own files gave Young the upper hand. Young read a series of racially charged letters to Arpaio. The letters dated to the time Arpaio was still conducting sweeps, and begged the sheriff to target particular neighborhoods where day laborers stood on street corners seeking work. The sheriff had forwarded these letters to staff, including one from someone named Jack who urged Arpaio to conduct a number of sweeps around the county, including one in Mesa. "Do the Mesa, AZ sweep!!! It needs it terribly!!!" Jack wrote. Those "illegals" seemed to be everywhere. Arpaio had his secretary send Jack a thank you note that said, "I will be going into Mesa." Within two months, the sheriff's office conducted two sweeps in Mesa.

Arpaio defended the Jack letter by insisting he sent thank you notes to everyone who wrote him. And the sheriff testified he didn't think it significant that he forwarded letters from restrictionist tipsters to his staff. Under Young's persistent questioning, the sheriff acknowledged he could not recall arresting a single Caucasian immigrant for illegal immigration violations when his office had 287(g) authority.

The sheriff also admitted under oath that he was not aware if his office had ever created a written policy banning racial profiling—even after the *Melendres* lawsuit was filed and the justice department had initiated its civil rights investigation.

One critically important bit of Arpaio's testimony went by too quickly for most courtroom observers to notice. It happened when Arpaio was questioned by his own lawyers. He wasn't nearly as feeble a witness then, and his bravado showed through when he testified his deputies had arrested forty "illegal aliens" in the last two weeks. The deputies, Arpaio testified, had turned all the immigrants over to ICE without incident— including those who had not committed any state crimes. This testimony would turn out to be a costly blunder—it showed that Arpaio had continued to violate Snow's 2011 order, which had prohibited the sheriff's office from arresting unauthorized noncriminal immigrants for civil immigration violations.

Judge Snow did not call attention to Arpaio's testimony at that moment. But he listened intently. So did the astonished plaintiffs' lawyers, who nudged each other and exchanged scribbled notes.

"Arrest Arpaio! Not the people!" Carlos Garcia chanted with other young Latino protesters outside the courthouse as Arpaio testified inside. Earlier that morning, his group had hung a giant banner from a parking structure that was visible from the courthouse's eastern facing windows. It said: *Arpaio, Your Time is Up. Game Over.*

Garcia was gaining national recognition for his vibrant, in-your-face activism. And he didn't want the media covering the *Melendres* trial to report only on "attorneys coming to save the day" in the courtroom. As a leader of the Puente Human Rights Movement, he helped train many unauthorized immigrants to "come out" and oppose Arpaio and the restrictionist attitudes that kept him in power. The public needed to see

Puente activist Carlos Garcia, who launched creative campaigns seeking to remove Joe Arpaio from office, speaks to reporters in downtown Phoenix on January 13, 2012. (Photo by José L. Muñoz)

"communities standing up to Arpaio, fighting back, and resisting what he was doing to us," he told us.

About a year before the trial, Garcia and his mentor, Salvador Reza, had a falling out. It was painful for Garcia. But for Reza, it was "better to let it go." The two had disagreed on grant funding and organizational matters. Garcia had retained control of Puente and pointed it in a creative new direction. Under Garcia's leadership, Puente's youthful volunteers organized colorful and daring street protests that aimed to keep the pressure on both Arpaio and the Obama administration, which so far had failed to deliver immigration reform during the president's first term.

The split between Garcia and Reza was just one of the fissures emerging in the six-year-old Somos America coalition. Some members, like Guzman, trusted the justice department, had faith in the federal courts, and believed Democrats would one day deliver immigration reform. But at twenty-nine, Garcia saw the limits of those institutions. He believed people vulnerable to deportation should have tools to defend themselves.

His model of activism focused on impacted people—immigrants like him-self—leading the resistance by engaging in civil disobedience and framing human stories for maximum media impact. Years later, in the Trump era, Garcia would teach this model to advocates in other states.

The fact that the high court had just allowed the "Show me your papers" provision of Senate Bill 1070 to take effect cemented Garcia's reluctance to place his trust in the judiciary. Nor did he trust Democrats. Deportations under Obama far outpaced the deportations of the Bush administration. In the immigrant community, Obama was known as the "Deporter in Chief."

Garcia had already felt the sting of the Obama deportations. One cousin had been deported. A different cousin, who Garcia viewed as a brother, was sitting in a federal detention center awaiting an immigration court hearing. Under Garcia's leadership, Puente launched publicity campaigns about people in immigration detention. The point was to pressure federal authorities to not follow through with the immigrants' deportations.

Obama was "speaking out of both sides of his mouth" on immigration, Garcia told us, and deserved to be targeted with protests, just like Arpaio.

The Obama administration had publicly sided with immigrant rights advocates by instructing its justice department to conduct a civil rights investigation of Arpaio, by challenging Arizona's Senate Bill 1070 in the Supreme Court, by suggesting ICE use discretion when deciding which deportation cases to pursue, and by revoking Arpaio's 287(g) authority on the streets and in his jails.

But Garcia knew that ICE officials still were scooping up undocumented people who had landed in Arpaio's jails. And he knew the Obama admin-istration was quietly replacing the controversial 287(g) program nation-wide with a jail fingerprint program—Secure Communities—meant to identify deportable immigrants who had been arrested and booked into jail.

Garcia and other Puente activists wanted to show the world that the Obama administration still collaborated with Arpaio, albeit quietly. So, when the *Melendres* trial broke for lunch, Puente launched the group's boldest action to date. Standing in the searing July sun, four Puente mem-bers outed themselves to the media as undocumented immigrants and then sat down at the intersection of Fourth Avenue and Washington just east of the federal courthouse. Each protester sat on one corner of an enormous poster carpeting the hot asphalt. The poster read: *No Papers No Fear: Sin Papeles y Sin Miedo.* The unauthorized immigrants stayed put even after Phoenix police ordered them to disperse. One activist, a thick-set Mexican man with glasses named Miguel Guerra, told reporters in Spanish, "We are not the criminals. We are coming out to say we are not scared, and the real criminal is inside testifying." The protesters were doing exactly what most undocumented people feared: putting themselves in the dangerous position of getting booked into Arpaio's Fourth Avenue jail where ICE agents might choose to deport them.

By going public with their arrests, the activists sought to prove that the federal government was still coordinating with Arpaio. They wanted to highlight what they viewed as Obama's complicity in Arpaio's out of control immigration crackdown.

One of the undocumented activists hugged her young daughter before her imminent arrest. "Give a kiss to your brother and your papi, OK?" she told her child in Spanish. Minutes later, Phoenix police took her and the other three immigrants into custody.

The action was extremely risky, and Garcia knew it. The four Puente members could wind up in deportation proceedings. But he had planned carefully. All four immigrant protesters had clean records. Garcia hoped ICE would use its "prosecutorial discretion" to not deport the immigrants if Puente kept the pressure on and media amplified the story. The Puente activists were following a playbook established by young Dreamers who had been arrested in protests as a way to pressure Congress to pass the DREAM Act. Such high-stakes acts of civil disobedience had paid off— just a month earlier Obama had responded to the pressure by granting work permits and temporary protection from deportation to young unauthorized immigrants who came to the country as children. He called the program Deferred Action for Childhood Arrivals, or DACA.

Garcia accepted the fact that many older, more moderate activists sitting in the *Melendres* courtroom disapproved of his criticisms of Obama and thought it risky and irresponsible for undocumented immigrants to engage in civil disobedience. As it turned out, though, his strategy was on target. Three of the immigrant protesters were released from jail that afternoon. The fourth protester, Miguel Guerra, was transferred from the jail to ICE custody. It was a harrowing night. Garcia stayed up consoling

Guerra's family. Puente blasted the news to the media and successfully pressured ICE eventually to release Guerra.

Being bold had paid off.

In the days that followed, Garcia and Puente members piled onto a vintage 1972 school bus they had painted with migrating Monarch butterflies and *No Papers No Fear*. They drove their "Undocubus" through the South to protest Senate Bill 1070 copycat laws. They were arrested in civil disobedience actions along the way, including at a hearing over Alabama's strict immigration law where they interrupted Kris Kobach.

Then they traveled to North Carolina to protest outside of the Democratic National Convention.

They would keep shaming Obama for his deportation record.

Sometimes, after court business wrapped up for the day, Judge Snow played darts in his chambers. He invited his clerks to join him while they discussed legal matters. Once, a clerk assigned to the *Melendres* case named Andrew Case missed the dartboard altogether and hit the wall instead. "Shit!" Case blurted. Snow called him "Mr. Potty Mouth" for a week.

"You could see with Judge Snow that there is an appropriateness of formality, and dignity, and doing the right thing by the book or even going beyond the book to make sure you're doing the right thing," Case told us.

But to Lydia Guzman sitting in the courtroom as the trial continued, the judge was as inscrutable as a sphynx. By then, the crowds had thinned and the trial had moved into Snow's smaller sixth-floor courtroom, where the round United States District Court's emblem of an eagle hung on the wall above Snow's chair, framing the judge's head in a halo.

Guzman stared at Snow's expressionless face and looked for clues that would help her figure out how the case was going.

She watched Snow listen noncommittally to an expert's analysis of the sheriff's traffic stop data, which found that sheriff's deputies disproportionately targeted people with Hispanic surnames during saturation patrols and detained them longer.

She sometimes wondered if Snow, who often listened with his chin on his hand, was bored. "I don't think that the judge believes any of this," she once told her brother Eddie, who sat by her side at the trial whenever his work schedule allowed it. "He must think it's all bullshit."

Daniel Magos stands with his wife, Eva, near the federal courthouse in Phoenix before testifying in the *Melendres* racial profiling trial in July 2012. (Courtesy Daniel Magos)

When Daniel Magos testified about the traffic stop with his wife, Eva, he described feeling "Humiliated. Worthless. Defenseless."

The entire courtroom was silent as Magos fought back tears.

Another plaintiff, Diona Solis, testified she'd been a passenger in a minivan with her son's Boy Scout troop when a sheriff's deputy pulled them over on a highway for alleged speeding. Solis said the deputy quizzed her and the driver about their immigration status, and asked everyone in the car to show identification, even the Boy Scouts, who were all under the age of twelve.

Victor David Vasquez, an information technology specialist, testified he and his wife were pulled over for a minor windshield crack during a sweep. The deputy asked him if he spoke English, Vasquez said. Once he was back on the road, Vasquez said he told his wife: "I believe I was pulled over for driving while brown."

Guzman herself testified on the fifth day of the trial. On her way into the courthouse that morning, she'd seen immigrant women from Promise Arizona, a group led by the longtime civil rights activist Petra Falcón.

Many in the group had stood vigil outside of the state capitol after Brewer signed Senate Bill 1070. Now they gathered under the shade of the skinny trees near the courtyard with their rosary beads and travelling Virgin of Guadalupe statue. They held Guzman's hands, bowed their heads, and prayed for God to help her find the words she needed for her testimony. Guzman felt duty-bound not to let these women down when she testified. This is not for me, God, this is for them, she thought.

In the courtroom, Guzman testified in her capacity as Somos America president and court rules forbade her from saying anything beyond her own experience. She couldn't talk about all the immigrants she'd met with, or their problems, or their broken families. Instead, she described being tailed by a deputy during a sweep and told the court that Somos America had been harmed by Arpaio's tactics because the organization had to divert resources from citizenship fairs and immigration reform events to help the sheriff's victims.

Soon after she stepped down from the witness box, Arpaio's lawyers made their case.

Arpaio's attorneys had found an expert witness, a retired law enforcement expert, who praised Arpaio's policies as "race neutral." Defendants also called on Stephen Camarota, a researcher from the restrictionist Center for Immigration Studies, to poke holes in the plaintiffs' data analysis.

Deputies, some of whom stood personally accused of racial profiling, testified that race and ethnicity had no bearing on their traffic stops. Under questioning from plaintiffs' attorneys, though, some deputies who had been 287(g) certified said ICE had taught them they could consider Mexican appearance as one factor among many when investigating immigration status.

The most confounding defense testimony came from Ramon Charley Armendariz, a burly bilingual Human Smuggling Unit detective who self-identified as "Mexican" but apprehended an unusually high number of Mexican immigrants and Latino Americans. He testified he wasn't concerned that most of the motorists he arrested were Latinos because he believed "we're a Latino state . . . we're the majority, and so it's not uncommon that there would be more Latinos, you know, arrested." There was a collective murmur in the courtroom gallery—everyone knew Latinos made up not quite 30 percent of the Maricopa County population. Even

Snow seemed visibly surprised. The judge asked the deputy to repeat himself.

Armendariz had grown up in El Paso, Texas and had been hired by the Maricopa County Sheriff's Office in 2005. "Sheriff Joe had a very good reputation," Armendariz explained to Snow. The deputy had admired Arpaio for his management style, like allowing "his law enforcement personnel to enforce laws and so I wanted to be a part of that." He got his wish after he worked his way up from a jail detention officer to a deputy certified to enforce immigration law during Arpaio's short-lived 287(g) partnership with ICE.

Earlier in the trial, siblings Manuel Nieto Jr. and Velia Meraz, both American citizen plaintiffs, had testified about the trauma they experienced when they encountered Armendariz during a sweep. It happened when the two were driving up to a Quick Stop convenience store for Gatorade and cigarettes in March 2008. The radio in their Suburban was blasting cumbia music when they saw Armendariz cuffing a Latino driver and passenger. At one point, Meraz had shouted in Spanish to the two detained men in Spanish, "Don't sign anything you don't understand!"

Each sibling remembered Armendariz rushing over to their car and ordering them to leave right away. He then called for backup over the radio. His voice was so agitated, one of his colleagues thought someone was trying to run him over.

Other deputies, lights flashing, chased the siblings in their vehicle to their dad's auto mechanic shop. The deputies pointed a gun at Nieto, who was frantically dialing 911, and pulled him out of the car and handcuffed him. Meraz's father came out of the shop and shouted to the deputies that his children were citizens, and the deputies backed off. Nieto showed his valid driver's license, and the siblings were released without a citation.

On the stand, Armendariz insisted he had feared for his safety, and that is why he had called for backup. He also testified he did not racially profile Latino motorists. He pulled cars over for traffic violations and said he couldn't go down the street without seeing one.

In his testimony, Armendariz unwittingly admitted he'd often engaged in a practice of unconstitutional policing. He said during traffic stops he routinely asked all passengers for identification. He detained those passengers whose identity he could not verify.

The defense team had chosen a witness who hurt their side and helped the plaintiffs.

As Alfredo Gutierrez took in the seven days of *Melendres* trial testimony, it seemed to him that the human pain and misery the Latino community had experienced at the hands of Arpaio and his deputies had been reduced to clinical legalese in the courtroom. To him, the trial had not felt like a true airing of the "horrendous acts of discrimination and hurting others." The "clinical nature of the courtroom process," he told us, had washed that all away.

That pain was palpable outside the courtroom, though. When court let out one day, dozens of Latino teenagers stood outside the courthouse with clipboards and voter registration forms. Most were years away from being eligible to vote, but they wanted to register others. Several had family members who had been deported. The teenagers, who were part of a union-backed voter registration drive, wore matching T-shirts that advertised their mission: *Adiós Arpaio*. The kids reminded Guzman of herself at their age. But more importantly, they gave her hope that engaged young Latinos would eventually reshape Arizona's political landscape.

It would take several months for Snow to issue a ruling in the *Melendres* racial profiling trial. In the meantime, the teens were determined to knock on doors and register new voters who could boot the sheriff out of office that November.

15

Why Are You Trembling?
2012–2013

Joe Arpaio pinned a large badge, shaped like the state of Arizona, to his lapel. He attached his gold pistol-shaped tie clip to his necktie. Decked out in a dark brown blazer, a pressed shirt, striped tie, and slacks, he no longer presented as the faltering old man in rumpled clothes, frail with the flu, who couldn't recall much of anything when he testified in his racial profiling trial in the *Melendres* case. Now, one month later, in August 2012, Arpaio presented himself as a vigorous elder statesman for twenty-first century American immigration restrictionism when he attended the Republican National Convention in Tampa, Florida.

Arpaio backed the Republican presidential nominee, former Massachusetts governor Mitt Romney, who'd suggested unauthorized immigrants would all "self-deport" once they realized life was better for them in their home countries.

Kris Kobach, the restrictionist lawyer who had coauthored Senate Bill 1070 with Russell Pearce and had controversially trained Arpaio's deputies on their "inherent authority" to enforce immigration law, had advised Romney's campaign on immigration. That year the GOP's platform on immigration echoed Kobach's hardline stance. "Granting amnesty [to unauthorized immigrants] only rewards and encourages more law breaking."

During a Fox News Latino interview on a perch overlooking the convention floor, a reporter asked Arpaio if he and Kobach, and their rhetoric, drove Latino voters away from the Republican Party. The sheriff didn't really answer, pivoting instead to his popularity among the (mostly white) Republican conventioneers.

"Everywhere I go all these delegates come up to me and thank me," he replied.

"They like me because I am enforcing the illegal immigration laws."

Judge Snow still hadn't issued a final ruling on Arpaio's racial profiling trial. And Arpaio had seemingly forgotten, or didn't understand, or didn't care, that Snow had already forbidden Arpaio from detaining unauthorized immigrants simply for civil violations of federal immigration law. It had all been spelled out clearly in Snow's December 2011 "preliminary injunction."

Again and again, Arpaio expressed his intention to continue arresting immigrants. And that meant, in some cases, his deputies disobeyed Snow's December 2011 preliminary injunction.

To be fair, Arpaio focused on immigration enforcement amid a landscape of changing state and federal immigration laws, policies, and agreements that were being tested in the courts. Still, the sheriff's office failed to issue new training to rank and file deputies in the wake of Snow's 2011 preliminary injunction. Most deputies weren't informed by the sheriff's office of Snow's 2011 ruling. What the deputies did know is that they worked for an agency led by a man who was hyper-focused on arresting immigrants. The deputies knew they would be rewarded with praise and advancement if they apprehended unauthorized immigrants. The sheriff's office continued to ignore Judge Snow's 2011 preliminary injunction even after the Ninth Circuit Court of Appeals sided with Snow in September 2012. "We have long made clear that, unlike illegal entry, mere unauthorized presence in the United States is not a crime," the appellate court wrote, affirming that local police could not make immigration arrests.

The appellate court decision mattered for two reasons. Importantly, it upheld Snow's 2011 preliminary injunction forbidding the sheriff's office from detaining noncriminal immigrants and turning them over for deportation. It also marked yet another instance in which Snow's ruling was brought to the attention of the sheriff's office and its leader.

Arpaio's lawyer, Tim Casey, later testified that he had explained Snow's orders to Arpaio and his high-level staffers in December 2011, right after it was issued, and multiple times in 2012. He said he had clearly communicated that the sheriff couldn't detain immigrants who were not suspected of committing state crimes. He had explained the sheriff could not enforce federal immigration law. Sometimes the sheriff had seemed resigned to his situation. Sometimes it had angered him.

Snow's 2011 orders were detailed in a prominent story in *The Arizona Republic*, which Arpaio read every morning. His media relations team also monitored news coverage of the sheriff's office. Yet his media relations director Lisa Allen told us no one had told her about the judge's orders.

Jerry Sheridan, who had replaced David Hendershott as chief deputy in 2010, claimed he did not know about Snow's 2011 order until 2014, despite being in meetings where the order was discussed and receiving emails about the orders from Casey. Sheridan, blue-eyed, with silver hair shorn into a tidy crew cut, had worked at the sheriff's office for decades and had run the controversial jails. He told us he wasn't assigned to *Melendres* and was dealing with other major challenges within the agency, such as allegations of financial mismanagement, another inmate death, the justice department's litigation, and repairing the fractured relationship with the county caused by Arpaio and Thomas's anti-corruption unit. He told us Arpaio was checked out and more interested in his own celebrity than the crises facing the agency. "He cared more about getting his media attention and putting his press releases out every morning," Sheridan told us.

An independent, court-ordered investigation later found Sheridan was not truthful in his assertions that he did not know about the 2011 order. Sheridan would deny the allegation.

Five years later, we asked the sheriff to explain why Snow's 2011 order was disregarded. He pivoted to a standard sound bite.

"I kind of delegated that to my lawyers and all my people," Arpaio told us.

"Maybe I should have taken more attention but I believed in the lawyers at that time and our guys doing the best they can to abide by the judge's order ... and nobody could understand [the preliminary

injunction] anyway . . . we kept enforcing the illegal immigration laws
which I feel wasn't a violation against the judge's order."

Later that fall, a white Chevy truck rumbled along a highway on the fringes
of southeastern Maricopa County. The driver, Francisco, and the passenger, his brother Samuel, had just put in a long day laying floor tiles in a
housing development about thirty-seven miles southeast of Phoenix. They
were headed home to a Phoenix suburb.

The brothers, whose names we changed upon their request, were
undocumented immigrants from Mexico. Twenty-five-year-old Samuel
had lived in Arizona for a decade. Francisco, twenty-three, had lived in
Arizona almost that long.

Like most other members of the unauthorized immigrant community
in Maricopa County, they'd heard about Joe Arpaio. Samuel knew what
most unauthorized immigrants in Maricopa County knew—Arpaio's deputies had torn parents away from their American-born kids, and had targeted Latinos with a variety of sweeps and workplace raids. A churchgoing
Christian, Samuel often prayed for Arpaio, asking God to bless the sheriff
with newfound tolerance and love.

Samuel and Francisco knew that as Mexican immigrants, they risked
getting pulled over by Arpaio's deputies in traffic stops. But they'd heard
on the news that the Obama administration now focused on deporting
only criminal unauthorized immigrants. Because they hadn't committed
any crime, they figured they were safe.

As the white truck trundled along, Samuel sagged into the passenger
seat. He would always remember he had two hundred dollars in his
pocket. He was exhausted from the day's work, eager to eat dinner with his
wife and two kids waiting for him at their home in the outskirts of Phoenix.

But that wasn't going to happen.

The brothers were pulled over by Charley Armendariz, the deputy
who'd unwittingly delivered testimony that damaged Arpaio's case just a
few months before. Armendariz approached Francisco's window. Over the
roar of the traffic behind him, the deputy asked in a loud voice to see
Francisco's license and vehicle registration. When the brothers did not
respond, Armendariz switched to Spanish.

"Why are you trembling? Are you scared?" Armendariz asked the brothers.

Francisco didn't have a license and handed over his Mexican passport. Then the deputy turned to Samuel. "Do you have a license, *mi'jo?*" Armendariz asked, addressing Samuel with the familiar word for "son." Armendariz was doing exactly what he'd testified about—demanding identification from a passenger in a traffic stop. Samuel handed over his Mexican passport.

The deputy soon figured out the brothers were undocumented. Armendariz told Francisco and Samuel their license plate light was out. Armendariz and another deputy did not give Miranda warnings when they questioned the brothers.

Armendariz arrested Francisco for failing to provide identification, even though Francisco had handed over his Mexican passport. The deputy had no cause to arrest Samuel for a crime since he was just a passenger. Still, Armendariz tried to get ICE to pick up Samuel. The agency refused. Soon, two of Armendariz's colleagues showed up in a sheriff's van to shuttle Samuel to a Border Patrol station in the next county. It was the same take-them-to-the-Border-Patrol strategy Arpaio's deputies had used years earlier when ICE wouldn't pick up immigrants.

En route to the Border Patrol station, Samuel thought he'd been kidnapped. It seemed to him the sheriff's detention officers were deliberately driving in circles. He would later remember his two hundred dollars went missing after he let one of the officers look at his wallet. At the border patrol station, Samuel was caged in a cold room with migrants shawled in silver mylar blankets. They had just been caught crossing the border and were about to be deported. Samuel was told he, too, was about to be deported. He shoved aside the voluntary deportation papers the immigration authorities urged him to sign. He said he'd lived in Arizona for a decade, had worked for the same company for years, had a wife and two American kids, and had not committed any crime. He demanded to see a judge.

Samuel was shuttled from the Border Patrol station to the ICE detention center in Eloy, Arizona. It took him days to get word to his wife about his whereabouts. In the meantime, Francisco had been released from the county jail. He put together three thousand dollars for Samuel's bond. By the time his brother bailed him out of the detention center, Samuel had been detained for nine days. The ordeal ended up costing Samuel about thirteen thousand dollars in lost wages and legal expenses. Samuel's boss lost money, too. With the brothers missing, jobs could not be completed.

Years later, an immigration judge closed Samuel's case, but Samuel's immigration status hadn't changed. He was still an undocumented immigrant and now the authorities knew where he lived.

"I never imagined," Samuel told us, "that a traffic stop, just for being seated in a car, would result in what occurred."

Samuel was detained after the Ninth Circuit Court of Appeals had upheld Snow's 2011 order forbidding such actions. Yet Arpaio trumpeted Samuel's detention in a press release. "Detectives transported the illegal alien to the Border Patrol in Casa Grande where he was processed for deportation. This is the 82nd arrest made over the last month."

Andre Segura, an ACLU lawyer for the Latino plaintiffs in the *Melendres* case, and his colleagues had been monitoring Arpaio's tweets. When Arpaio's office tweeted a press release about Samuel's arrest, Segura notified the sheriff's lawyer that Arpaio might be violating Snow's 2011 preliminary injunction. Years later, Casey acknowledged in court testimony that he'd been alarmed by Segura's note. He said his "preliminary view" was that there had "likely" been a violation of Snow's 2011 order. Casey said in court he had participated in "not a pleasant conversation" with the sheriff about how Snow's 2011 preliminary injunction prohibited the sheriff's office from detaining noncriminal immigrants and turning them over for deportation. Arpaio replied other agencies detained immigrants and turned them over for deportation. Casey told his client that he was under judicial orders not to do it. Arpaio finally agreed it would not happen again.

But the sheriff's office continued violating the judge's order.

Joe Arpaio's 2012 sheriff's race was the toughest he'd ever gone through. He was eighty years old and saddled with well-publicized legal troubles. His forty-five-year-old Democratic opponent, a former Phoenix police sergeant named Paul Penzone, was an enthusiastic campaigner. Some pre-election polls showed Penzone within striking distance.

Often that election year, when Arpaio read his morning *The Arizona Republic*, he'd come across a story about the *Melendres* case or his ongoing clashes with the justice department.

In the spring of 2012, the Washington-based civil rights division of the justice department had sued Arpaio in federal court, alleging civil rights violations of Latinos in the jails and on the streets. This same lawsuit alleged the sheriff had retaliated against critics—including judges, lawyers, activists, and community leaders—with baseless investigations and arrests. And the justice department emphasized a culture of racism in the sheriff's office: "The Defendants' violations of the Constitution and laws of the United States are the product of a culture of disregard in MCSO [Maricopa County Sheriff's Office] for Latinos that starts at the top and pervades the organization. MCSO jail employees frequently refer to Latinos as 'wetbacks,' 'Mexican bitches,' and 'stupid Mexicans.' MCSO supervisors involved in immigration enforcement have expressed anti-Latino bias, in one instance widely distributing an email that included a photograph of a Chihuahua dog dressed in swimming gear with the caption 'A Rare Photo of a Mexican Navy Seal.' MCSO and Arpaio's words and actions set the tone and create a culture of bias that contributes to unlawful actions."

Tom Perez, the head of the civil rights division of the justice department, claimed his agency had tried and failed to get the sheriff to cooperate in an out-of-court effort to reform the Maricopa County Sheriff's Office. Among other things, the justice department had wanted to embed a "monitor" in the agency. The monitor would report back to the justice department on progress of policing reforms, or lack thereof.

"I am the constitutionally and legitimately elected Sheriff and I absolutely refuse to surrender my responsibility to the federal government," Arpaio had thundered in a press release a month before he was sued. "And so to the Obama administration, who is attempting to strong arm me into submission only for its political gain, I say, 'This will not happen, not on my watch!'"

Despite Arpaio's bluster, Lydia Guzman and many others felt that any day Arpaio would be hit with a criminal indictment. It would stem from the other justice department investigation—the Phoenix-based United States Attorney's criminal abuse of power probe that reportedly was investigating Arpaio and Thomas's retaliation against judges and county officials.

On a Friday in August, the United States Attorney's Office in Phoenix dashed those hopes. A top prosecutor announced the office was "closing its investigation into allegations of criminal conduct by current and former members of the Maricopa County Sheriff's Office and the Maricopa County Attorney's Office." Guzman, her fellow activists, and many members of the legal community were crestfallen.

Michael Manning, the lawyer who'd successfully sued Arpaio for a string of wrongful jailhouse deaths and political retaliations, told us the closure of the criminal abuse of power investigation was "one of the most heartbreaking episodes in my legal career."

"I think there was too much anxiety about going after a man as powerful as he was at the time," Manning told us.

Some abuse of power allegations against the sheriff—including arresting activist critics—had ended up in the federal civil rights case overseen by Tom Perez in Washington. But that was little consolation to Guzman and others in the resistance who had long hoped to see Arpaio charged criminally.

In the sheriff's race, Penzone tried mightily to convince white Maricopa County voters that Arpaio's missteps had caused a serious economic burden to county taxpayers. In one campaign ad, Penzone accused Arpaio of costing county taxpayers 182 million dollars during his twenty years in office. Those costs were tied to lawsuits and agency mismanagement.

By late October, Penzone had managed to raise more than five hundred thousand dollars for his campaign. Unions kicked in another five hundred thousand dollars to a PAC opposing Arpaio. By comparison, Arpaio had raised about eight and a half million dollars, mostly from donors living outside Arizona. He spent almost all of it on campaign advisors and television ads portraying him as a kind grandfatherly cop. One ad featured Ava looking into the camera and assuring people her husband was a great guy, and, well, she ought to know.

In the end, Arpaio was elected to a sixth term with his tightest margin ever—five points.

On election night, November 6, 2012, at the Republican watch party in a downtown Phoenix hotel, Arpaio showed up with a small entourage. Ava was with him, of course. The fading movie star Steven Seagal, who'd starred in the film *Above the Law*, also tagged along, and so did a videographer filming footage for a revelatory documentary film that would come out in 2014, called *The Joe Show*.

Arpaio and Ava climbed onto the stage alone. A single forlorn bouquet of red, white, and blue balloons clung to the ceiling. Behind the Arpaios, a life-size cardboard cutout of Mitt Romney, hands in pockets, grinning, was propped against the curtain. Romney would be walloped that night by the incumbent president, Barack Obama.

"I'm not going to express my emotions in public but when I get home with my wife, just between her and I, I'll vent," Arpaio said.

Then he started venting. Instead of celebrating his victory, Arpaio seemed bitterly angry. At Obama. At the endorsement of his opponent by *The Arizona Republic*. At journalists. He scolded reporters for favoring Penzone "just because they wanted to get rid of me."

Ava stood quietly, dressed in a black dress, red blazer. The diamonds in her gold sheriff's star pendant winked.

"I have a message for the president of the United States of America," the sheriff told the reporters. "He's gone after me . . . But you know what, I'm still the sheriff. I don't report to the president. I report to the people."

Before he stepped off the stage, he vowed to reach out to Latinos.

That same evening, as Arpaio's media relations director Lisa Allen shepherded the sheriff through a gaggle of television reporters pleading for live one-on-one interviews, Arpaio stopped to answer questions from a Spanish-language Univision reporter.

Allen tried to steer Arpaio to English-language, high profile channels.

"Why Telemundo?" she exclaimed, getting the channel's name wrong. "This is not that important."

On the night Joe Arpaio won his sixth term in office, Lydia Guzman turned forty-five. As she thought about it, this last decade of her activism had caused serious personal consequences—angry kids, a troubled marriage, financial problems, and her own lingering sadness over the human suffering she'd witnessed. When she looked in the mirror each morning, she felt the stress and work and sadness had changed her. She saw strands of gray in her hair and worried she was developing jowls.

She'd campaigned hard in 2012 for Joe Arpaio's opponent, Paul Penzone, only to see him lose. The Latino teenagers she had found so inspiring had managed to register thirty thousand new Latino voters for the Adiós Arpaio campaign, but it hadn't been nearly enough.

Not only was Arpaio still in power, but his deputies were still detaining unauthorized immigrants and turning them over to ICE in violation of Snow's order. On one level, Arpaio seemed to be challenging the authority of the federal judiciary. And on another level, his apparent defiance of the court undermined the battle to get Snow to rein him in. Now the Latino community itself was calling the *Melendres* case into question.

"What was all this for?" people would ask Guzman.

"You see," they would tell her. "I told you. Nothing has changed. Business as usual."

She'd been asked to step down from her leadership role in Somos America.

It was time for younger activists to take over, the thinking went. Many of the activists who'd driven the early Somos America momentum—Sal Reza, Alfredo Gutierrez, Danny Ortega, Carlos Garcia—had moved on. Reza was organizing immigrant neighborhoods and helping people reconnect with their indigenous roots via a local nonprofit called Tonatierra. Gutierrez was mentoring younger activists and was about to publish his memoir, *To Sin Against Hope*. Ortega was practicing law and lending his talents to Latino civil rights groups. Garcia was taking Puente onto the streets of Phoenix and was becoming a nationally known civil rights leader.

But for Guzman, distancing herself from Somos America was difficult. The coalition had anchored her activism, from the early civil rights marches to the hotline to the *Melendres* case.

She was increasingly worried about her teenage son, too. James was seventeen, angry, and rebellious. Guzman feared he would drop out of high school and join a gang. She was full of guilt and deeply loved James. And he loved her too, despite his anger. After Guzman's gray cat died, James brought her a black kitten.

There were more tears, though, when Guzman's house on Sanna Street was finally foreclosed on in April 2013. She'd purchased the house back in 2002 to prove to herself and her mother that she could take care of herself and her kids. What a happy house it had been, at first. Almost as soon as she'd bought the house, she'd taken the kids to the Humane Society because they finally had a place to keep a dog. They'd chosen an arthritic, aging chow named Sue. The dog had watched over James and Ashley and the neighborhood kids when they played on the front lawn, shaded by a tall Aleppo pine tree.

And when Guzman and Tony Wesley had fallen in love, back in 2005, they'd planted a mesquite tree in the back yard. It was a spindly sapling then, but Wesley had promised it would grow into a sturdy desert tree. And it had. Weather permitting, she'd often settled behind a little table on the back porch near the mesquite tree, phone in hand, firing up the text tree so thousands would know the whereabouts of Arpaio's latest worksite raid or neighborhood sweep. She sometimes manned the Respect-Respeto hotline in this spot or gave interviews to journalists there. She wondered now what the mesquite tree would say if it could talk.

On her last day in the house on Sanna Street, after the furniture and cardboard boxes were all loaded onto the extra-large U-Haul truck, she'd walked down the hallway for the last time, remembering moments with her children. Then she said goodbye to the mesquite tree, now sturdy and fifteen feet tall, budding a generous canopy of vivid green, feathery leaves.

She picked up the black kitten and drove away.

Her life in the house she'd loved was over.

So, too, was her marriage. Not long after they moved out of the Sanna Street house, Guzman and Wesley decided to split up. They held no anger toward each other, but her activism had taken its emotional and financial toll on the blended family. She would always remember the time she and Wesley took her son to the mall to buy school supplies, only to realize they didn't have the money. She remembered Wesley announcing to the family he was sick of being poor. So sick of it. And another time, she remembered, Wesley didn't have the money to buy a battery for his truck. She'd sensed he was miserable.

By then Wesley had gotten a job at a building supply store, selling to contractors. He still had good credit. They agreed Wesley would buy another house solo, then Wesley would sign it over to Guzman when he and his son moved out. Guzman, in the meantime, would make all the house payments.

"I will never know anyone in my life that I respect more than that woman," Wesley told us. "She was absolutely fierce and . . . she dedicated her life to people and I will always respect her for that."

Still, he couldn't stay with her. "I knew that being able to provide for my family and my son and, you know, was desperately important to me," he told us, "but I was so conflicted at the time as well, because I respected so much what she did but also had to find a future for my son and myself."

"It was really tough, really tough."

16 "Ganamos!"

2013–2014

Lydia Guzman tried to pull herself out of her financial problems by earning a little money running three hotlines.

The Respect-Respeto hotline now fielded calls for the ACLU, which was interested in hearing from community members who were illegally detained, racially profiled, or otherwise impacted by the "Show me your papers" provision of Senate Bill 1070. The provision, which allowed Arizona police to contact federal officials to check immigration status of people they'd detained, had gone into effect in Arizona a few months after the Supreme Court had ruled on it. The decision only served to heighten anxiety for many in the Arizona Latino community.

Julie Pace, the Phoenix business lawyer, counted among her clients many employers of immigrant workers. After ICE audited two grocery store chains in Arizona and California, these businesses had to abruptly fire some immigrant workers. Pace recommended the grocery store chains hire Guzman as a contractor to answer phone calls in Spanish from these workers. Guzman was tasked with linking the callers up with churches and other service providers that might be able to help them. In addition, she screened callers who might make good plaintiffs in a potential legal challenge.

Guzman was working this temporary job in May 2013 when Judge Snow finally issued his long-awaited verdict on Arpaio's racial profiling trial held the previous summer. The judge found Arpaio and his agency had racially profiled Latino drivers and passengers in Maricopa County.

She jumped up and down, she was so happy. She tapped her joy out on a Facebook post:

OMG . . . OMG . . . WE WON . . . WE WON! GANAMOS . . . GANAMOS!!

Judge Snow's painstakingly detailed, carefully thought out, 142-page ruling traveled through history. It chronicled Arpaio's hunts for day laborers in Cave Creek, the detention of immigrants near Pruitt's furniture store, and the large scale "saturation patrols" in places like the little town of Guadalupe. The ruling revisited Arpaio's failed 287(g) partnerships with ICE. The judge delved into Arpaio's policies, state immigration laws, and trial testimony from expert witnesses, deputies, commanders, victims, and Arpaio himself.

The judge noted Kris Kobach, who was "apparently legally trained," had erroneously told deputies they had the "inherent authority" to continue enforcing federal immigration law.

Snow found the sheriff's department was "aggressively responsive to the wishes of a significant portion of the Maricopa County electorate that desires vigorous law enforcement operations against unauthorized residents by state and local law enforcement authorities," and had continued immigration enforcement after it no longer had the legal basis to do so.

And in the end, Judge Snow concluded the Maricopa County Sheriff's Office, and Joe Arpaio, had repeatedly and rampantly violated the constitutional rights of Latino motorists in Maricopa County.

He noted that during day laborer sweeps, deputies targeted vehicles that picked up Latinos and that many sweeps took place in heavily Latino areas or places where day laborers gathered. In these operations, the judge found, the sheriff and his department had racially profiled Latino motorists, subjecting them to unlawful searches and seizures, in violation of the Fourth Amendment, and depriving them of their rights to equal protection under the law, in violation of the Fourteenth Amendment.

During the trial, the plaintiffs had proven the sheriff's 287(g) deputies had incorrectly learned they could consider "apparent Mexican appearance" as one factor when deciding whether to investigate immigration violations. The training, which had come from ICE, was in conflict with Ninth Circuit precedent, which forbade the consideration of Hispanic appearance for immigration investigations.

Snow acknowledged the faulty training had come from ICE but held the sheriff's office responsible. By improperly considering race, Snow found the sheriff's office had not only violated the Fourth and Fourteenth Amendments, but also the Civil Rights Act of 1964. He found, too, that sheriff's deputies unconstitutionally prolonged traffic stops to inquire about immigration status.

After analyzing records from several saturation patrols, Snow concluded at least four deputies, including Charley Armendariz, had considered race in these sweeps—despite testimony to the contrary. The judge's analysis showed over the course of nine large-scale saturation patrols, Armendariz had arrested ninety-seven people. Of these, 77 percent had Hispanic surnames. Snow pointed out that despite Armendariz's "simply wrong" trial testimony that Maricopa County is majority Latino, in fact, Latinos only make up 30 percent of the population.

Finally, Snow noted the sheriff's office "violated and continues to violate" his 2011 preliminary injunction by continuing to detain immigrants for civil immigration violations and turn them over to ICE. (The sheriff's deputies had arrested noncriminal immigrants and turned them over to immigration authorities under the so-called LEAR protocol, which Snow ruled violated his 2011 order and the constitutional rights of immigrants.)

Snow cemented his 2011 preliminary injunction by permanently enjoining the sheriff's department from making civil immigration detentions. He also forbade deputies from using Latino ancestry or race as a factor to unconstitutionally lengthen traffic stops or determine a person's immigration status.

Later, Snow would, in open court, reflect on the " blood and tears" that he had put into the case. "I spent a long time on that order, and I'd reviewed—what I think, I reviewed the evidence quite extensively." He said he worked hard on the order because, regardless of whether the Maricopa County Sheriff's Office agreed with him, he wanted them to understand why, exactly, he found the sheriff's office was "violating the constitutional rights of the plaintiff class."

Arpaio responded to Snow's blistering findings a few days later on YouTube.

Wearing a green shirt, a tan jacket, and a blue patterned tie, the sheriff sat with his hands clasped on his desk. His nightstick was mounted on the wall behind him. Flanked by a state flag and an American flag, Arpaio said: "We will appeal this ruling. You know, as sheriff I uphold the law. The court's order is now clear. We will no longer detain persons believed to be in the country without authorization whom we cannot arrest on state charges. I have already instructed my deputies." He didn't mention that the judge had already ordered him to stop such arrests seventeen months earlier.

For years after the May 2013 ruling came down, Arpaio and his commanders would incorrectly insist Judge Snow had not ruled that the agency "racially profiled" Latinos because the judge hadn't used those precise words in his order. Their denials persisted even after the judge responded by clarifying in court that "the Maricopa County Sheriff's Office has used race—has illegitimately used race as a factor—and to the extent that constitutes racial profiling, that's what it is, and that's what I found. . . ."

Within the agency, many deputies disagreed with the judge's finding. Captain John Kleinheinz told us he found it "unfathomable" that his colleagues had engaged in systemic racial profiling, which he, like many in the sheriff's office, defined as pulling over drivers solely because of the color of their skin. Kleinheinz didn't discount Snow's ruling entirely, though. He was angered and disturbed to learn that an immigrant being in the country without papers has only committed a federal civil violation, not a criminal offense, because that meant the sheriff's office had long performed improper and unlawful immigration arrests. "You don't do things unless you know that you are on solid legal ground," Kleinheinz told us. But, he said, it seemed the sheriff's office had not performed its due diligence in researching immigration laws.

A few months later, the Latino resistance triumphed in court again when a federal judge struck down the Thomas-Arpaio interpretation of the Human Smuggling Law. The victory stemmed from the *We Are America/Somos America v. Maricopa County Board of Supervisors* lawsuit filed seven years earlier. The ruling cited the United States Supreme Court's opinion on Senate Bill 1070 and *Melendres* opinions from Snow and the Ninth Circuit Court of Appeals. This meant Arpaio could no longer arrest people for conspiring with a smuggler to smuggle themselves into Arizona. Arpaio had relied on this conspiracy charge to make immigration arrests and investigate immigration status ever since he'd lost his 287(g) partnership.

When Guzman read the ruling, she remembered the bewildered unauthorized immigrant women shackled to the table in Arpaio's jail trying to figure out why they were charged with conspiracies. "Was very emotional . . . but worth it," she wrote reporters. "Like the attorney says, 'Another win for the good guys and gals.'"

Three weeks later, in October 2013, Snow issued a fifty-nine-page order that everyone had been waiting for—a roadmap to reforming the sheriff's office. Snow ordered what Arpaio had energetically opposed—a court monitor installed in the sheriff's office. The monitor would report back to the judge on progress of court-ordered agency-wide reforms. And the judge ordered, among other things, the creation of court-approved policies focused on preventing two problems—biased policing and enforcement of federal immigration law. He also ordered Arpaio's agency to hold regular community meetings and heed the concerns of a community advisory board. The sheriff's staff was required to reach out in good faith to many in the Latino community who feared them.

In his closing pages, Snow brought up the possibility of contempt of court. If Arpaio and his agency resisted reforms Snow had ordered, and the two sides couldn't resolve the problem informally, the Latino plaintiffs could "apply to the Court for appropriate relief, up to and including the imposition of contempt sanctions."

Joe Arpaio by then had started marketing himself as a humanitarian, an altruistic sheriff whose deputies rescued "people here illegally in the desert." But since the judge wouldn't let his deputies call ICE anymore, he said, he was in a "Catch-22" about what to do with apprehended migrants.

"Everybody is after the sheriff. Which is interesting," he told us. "I haven't heard one activist call me, thank you, you rescued thirty people. They don't call. If I arrested thirty people I would be in a headline. It is all politics."

The very idea of a court-appointed monitor had long rankled him. He didn't want an outsider nosing around his department. He'd fought installing a monitor when the justice department suggested it. And he'd fought it in the *Melendres* case. But despite Arpaio's energetic efforts, the dreaded monitor would soon be appointed.

"I have received a copy of the court order and I am in the process of discussing it with our attorneys," Arpaio announced on October 2, 2013, the day Snow issued the ruling. "We are identifying areas that are ripe for appeal. To be clear, the appointed monitor will have no veto authority over my duties or operations. As the constitutionally elected Sheriff of Maricopa County, I serve the people and I will continue to perform my duties and enforce all laws."

Two weeks later, the sheriff announced a "crime suppression operation" in a four-square-mile westside neighborhood where a detention officer was allegedly murdered. Arpaio claimed the operation, which was similar in format to his discontinued neighborhood sweeps, would focus on gangs, guns, and drugs. It wouldn't be about immigration. He wanted to make that clear. Prior to the sweep, the assigned deputies had met in a classroom in the sheriff's office for training. There were new protocols to learn due to Snow's latest order. Now, as soon as deputies made a traffic stop, they were required to radio in the reason. They were also required to note the perceived ethnicity of the drivers they had pulled over. As Arpaio's chief deputy, Jerry Sheridan, discussed the new protocols with the deputies, he called Snow's reform order "absurd."

Sheridan also minimized and mischaracterized Snow's earlier findings that the sheriff's office had violated the rights of Latino drivers.

Years later, Sheridan shared his state of mind with us. "I'm emotional, I love the sheriff's office. I've never seen anybody do anything harmful against a Hispanic, or Black, or anybody else. And now I've got to send out a hundred people with guns into a gang-ridden neighborhood. And what they're concerned with is, 'We have to worry about this, we have to worry about that.' They're demoralized. They're looking for a leader to step up and say something to them." He said he "had to be George Patton" that day.

Judge Snow, Sheridan told us, had meted out the same punishment and reform orders that other law enforcement agencies got for "murdering people of color, they were shooting them down in the streets, they were sticking broomsticks up their rectums."

That day in the classroom, Sheridan referred to Snow's reform order as "ludicrous" and "crap," and said Snow "violated the United States constitution."

Deputies had to follow the ruling, he said, but it would be appealed.

Then it was Arpaio's turn to speak to the deputies: "What the chief deputy said is what I've been saying . . . We don't racially profile. I don't care what everybody says. We're just doing our job. We had the authority to arrest illegal aliens under the federal programs."

On October 18, 2013, the sweep launched. Arpaio, wearing his tan sheriff's uniform, stood against a backdrop inscribed with gold Maricopa County Sheriff's Office stars. "Some courts want community outreach. I just started," he told a television reporter, mocking the court orders.

The sheriff's office's next steps—allowing court-ordered community meetings to take place outdoors without chairs on cold days and appointing a Human Smuggling Unit deputy as the community liaison to preside over these chairless meetings—seemed intended to undermine Snow's order, too.

In early 2014, Judge Snow chose Robert Warshaw as the court-appointed monitor. Warshaw was a white-haired man, tall, prone to dress for court and public meetings in pinstripe suits accented with bold patterned ties and matching silk pocket handkerchiefs. He had been a deputy drug czar for President Bill Clinton. He now served as an independent court-appointed monitor for several law enforcement agencies around the country, including the Detroit and Oakland police departments.

He assembled a team of former cops of different ethnicities to help him monitor the Maricopa County Sheriff's Department. What Team Warshaw reported about the sheriff's office would kickstart the last chapter in the mano-a-mano between the local sheriff and the federal judge. This last clash would test the strength of the federal judiciary in a time when American restrictionism was reviving itself nationally. And eventually, it would capture the attention of the nation, and a new president.

Almost immediately, Warshaw discovered and handed over to Judge Snow a video copy of the training session in which Sheridan called the judge's ruling "crap." The judge was not pleased. Court hearings followed. As he learned the extent of Arpaio's resistance to his orders for reform, Snow became visibly, increasingly, exasperated with the sheriff and his office. "I'm concerned about sending mixed messages to those deputies about whose orders they have to comply with," he said at one hearing. "'Crap' is not a very decorous word. But it's not my word, it's Deputy Chief Sheridan's word. He called the order ludicrous. He called it crap. What kind of message is he sending to his own deputies? Whose order, then, do they follow? And what kind of protection does that make for them?"

Sheridan showed up in court in his uniform and badge. Snow wanted to know why Sheridan had mischaracterized and insulted his orders. Sheridan hung his head. He apologized. He'd been frustrated. He'd been stressed. He'd been wrong.

The angry judge ordered the sheriff's office to distribute an eight-page summary of his orders to all personnel. All staffers and posse members would be required to sign a statement attesting they had read and understood the summary of the court's order.

Joe Arpaio seemed removed from his chief deputy's struggles with Snow. Sheridan at the time was loyal to Arpaio and didn't publicly complain. But years later he told us that Arpaio had been so consumed with his own image he "wasn't involved in fixing, or complying with the judge's order. He didn't care about that stuff."

Arpaio claimed the whole *Melendres* mess was not his fault, or his department's. He blamed ICE. And he sent a letter saying just that to Obama's attorney general, Eric Holder, who oversaw the justice department, and to ICE's head lawyer. Because he claimed ICE had misguided his deputies during 287(g) training by saying race could be a factor in determining immigration status, he demanded ICE pay the past, present, and future costs of the *Melendres* case. That amounted, by his calculations, to about thirty-eight million dollars. The Obama administration did not agree to pay the money.

And then filmmaker Randy Murray came out with *The Joe Show*—a documentary film that had been ten years in the making. The documentary focused on Arpaio's addiction to the media, and the media's role in enabling Arpaio to brand himself as America's Toughest Sheriff and chief immigration enforcer. Murray began filming in 2003, and followed Arpaio through his different stages—pink underwear and the America's Toughest Sheriff moniker, immigration sweeps, political campaigns, the birth certificate "investigation." The film delighted Latino civil rights advocates, who saw it as confirmation of Arpaio's intention to use immigration sweeps to get attention and build his brand.

Murray told us Arpaio viewed the film and didn't like it. But after the film captured the attention of local and national media, Arpaio took an interest in the publicity, Murray told us.

"What are you doing on TV without me?" Murray remembered Arpaio asking. "You are using my fame to get on TV."

Within days, Murray and Arpaio hopped a Southwest Airlines plane bound for California. *The Joe Show* would be screened at a Beverly Hills film festival, and Arpaio wanted to be part of it. He didn't seem concerned about the *Melendres* case. He was more concerned with the warm reception he got on the plane. The flight attendant made a heart sign when she saw the sheriff sitting in the front row. She announced him as a celebrity guest over the intercom. Passengers clapped. And when Arpaio disembarked at the airport in Burbank, strangers asked Arpaio to pose for selfies.

At the iconic former Grauman's Chinese Theatre, Arpaio met up with Kathryn Kobor and Pam Pearson. The two friends, who had known each other since they'd demonstrated on Arpaio's behalf near Pruitt's furniture store so many years ago, still supported Arpaio. Kobor thought Judge Snow was punishing the sheriff for political reasons—she had long believed the sheriff had done nothing wrong, had only done his job, conscientiously, in enforcing immigration law. Kobor told us she and Pearson wanted to protect Arpaio from liberal attacks in Hollywood, and show their solidarity as he sat through the film. They stationed themselves behind the sheriff when the screening began in the nearly empty theater.

Arpaio sat with a reporter on each side in an otherwise vacant row of seats, and stared at himself on the big screen from beginning to end. Once or twice, he shook his head. When it was over, he struggled to get out of his seat. The film was "garbage." And he was disappointed in the poor turnout. Only about thirty-five people had attended the screening.

He wondered aloud why he'd wasted his time coming to California when he had work to do. His deputies had just arrested a man who'd allegedly had sex with animals and that was bound to get a lot of publicity back in Maricopa County.

And there were other things he was working on, he hinted on the return flight to Phoenix, things that he couldn't talk about just yet.

17 Conspiracy Theories and Videos

2013–2015

When Lydia Guzman first started getting the text messages in the summer of 2013, she wasn't sure who was sending them. They were from an anonymous sender with a Google Voice number. "Now is the time to start asking questions about the Human Smuggling Unit," one cryptic text read. "They are still a unit and working. It's business as usual."

She soon realized the mysterious texter was Charley Armendariz, the burly deputy on the sheriff's Human Smuggling Unit, who self-identified as "Mexican" and had testified on Arpaio's behalf at the *Melendres* 2012 racial profiling trial. She remembered how she and her brother, Eddie, had nudged each other as they listened to the deputy's testimony—Armendariz had sounded like a cruel fool.

She had first met the deputy several months after the trial, in February 2013. Guzman at the time had just finished a TV interview in front of a Maricopa County jail and was pulling out of the parking lot when Armendariz unexpectedly called out her name from his SUV: "Lydia! I need to talk to you! Latino to Latino."

She followed him to a nearby Jack in the Box, where Armendariz began crying. He hinted he knew about illegal activity inside the sheriff's office. He insisted he wanted to share information with the justice department and the FBI. Guzman sensed Armendariz was repentant for his activities in the Human Smuggling Unit. She suspected whatever this immigrant-hunting deputy had to say might help the justice department with its civil rights case. The two exchanged cell phone numbers and Guzman notified her justice department contacts about Armendariz. But she ran into a snag—the justice department couldn't ethically interview Armendariz because he worked for the sheriff's office, the very agency the justice department was suing. If Armendariz were to resign from the sheriff's office, he would be able to talk to the justice department, so Guzman and Armendariz swapped texts that summer about other job opportunities.

Then, in late April 2014 Guzman saw a news story about Armendariz barricading himself in his home and threatening suicide. A few days later, Armendariz called Guzman. Weeping, he said he had been arrested and had just gotten out of jail. "They are trying to make me like I'm crazy, and I'm not," he told her.

The deputy resigned from the sheriff's office days after he had heard voices coming from the inside of his couch and had suffered a nervous breakdown.

Guzman told a justice department contact he was finally free to talk. But it would be too late.

Charley Armendariz should never have been a law enforcement officer. His behavioral problems were evident in his first law enforcement job with the Austin Police Department. Back then, his superiors disciplined him for pointing a gun at someone for no reason. He resigned from the police department, briefly became an emergency medical technician, then moved to Phoenix.

Steve Bailey, who had been promoted to captain overseeing internal affairs investigations in the sheriff's professional standards bureau, later told an outside investigator Armendariz's "pre-employment paperwork" indicated that Armendariz should never have been hired in the first place.

Armendariz ramped up his aggressive policing techniques once he became a sheriff's office deputy. And he likely engaged in criminal behavior. One woman he'd stopped accused him of stealing three hundred dollars, and a Latino man he'd pulled over claimed Armendariz had pocketed his two thousand dollars. And Armendariz wrongfully arrested immigrants like Samuel, who'd been driving home with his brother in 2012. In the last three years of Armendariz's career at the sheriff's office, at least seventeen people who had been stopped by Armendariz had formally complained about his aggressive policing.

There were signs Armendariz was struggling with mental illness. In 2012, Armendariz received treatment at a residential behavioral health center following a domestic dispute with his boyfriend. He later told colleagues he was considering suicide. Toward the end of Armendariz's tenure, sheriff's office staffers suspected the deputy repeatedly urinated and threw soiled toilet paper on the bathroom floor. Armendariz's boss requested the deputy be transferred out of the Human Smuggling Unit, but the request was not honored. Bailey figured higher ups in Arpaio's command team protected Armendariz and allowed him to remain in the Human Smuggling Unit because they wanted to produce "high stats"— meaning immigration arrests. Armendariz seemed to deliver. But the deputy was taking shortcuts. "He just stopped a lot of people and he didn't have probable cause," Bailey told us. Still, Armendariz was getting talking-tos from supervisors as more and more people complained to the department about him. Finally, he was transferred out of the Human Smuggling Unit and into regular patrol duty in August 2013. But the sheriff's office continued to receive complaints about him.

When Armendariz called Phoenix police in late April 2014, he insisted an intruder was lurking in his garage. When the police arrived, Armendariz, wearing only boxer shorts, was blasting pepper balls at an imaginary burglar. At some point, Phoenix police had summoned a sheriff's department sergeant. Armendariz told the sergeant a man was hiding in a Christmas tree box in his garage. Soon, the sergeant spied official evidence bags from the sheriff's department stashed on a shelf. A woman's purse peeked out of one bag.

The next day, sheriff officials searched Armendariz's house. They found more than 1,600 items, including 540 compact discs storing videos documenting nine hundred hours of Armendariz's on-the-job policing, hundreds of drivers' licenses and vehicle license plates, Mexican consular cards, Mexican voting cards, money including pesos and dollars, credit and debit cards, weapons, methamphetamine, marijuana, LSD, heroin, oxycodone, cell phones, wallets, a scale, drug paraphernalia, thumb drives, and memory cards. Some of the items in Armendariz's house would later be traced to traffic stops involving other members of the Human Smuggling Unit.

No one knew why all of this evidence, which should have been logged and stored at the sheriff's department, was stashed in Armendariz's house. Perhaps the items had been stolen from the victims during traffic stops and Armendariz was hiding them. Or perhaps some of the items had been retrieved from the sheriff's office property lockers at some point for some reason. In either case, it was illegally stored in Armendariz's house and was a clear signal that Arpaio's premier immigration enforcement unit was in a state of chaos and was either corrupt or mismanaged.

Armendariz insisted, when he was questioned by a sheriff's department investigator, that many of his colleagues in the Human Smuggling Unit possessed evidence that hadn't been processed and a coworker had gathered it all up to store at his place.

He was admitted into and later released from a mental health facility. He was slapped with drug possession charges, arrested, jailed, and released from jail. In the days that followed he spoke of suicide, summoned Phoenix police to check on even more imagined dangers, and apologized to neighbors for the police presence. He announced an upcoming press conference to expose the sheriff's office (it never happened). He vowed to go to rehab, ignored an appointment to get an ankle bracelet, gave his friends jewelry, ingested methamphetamine, antihistamine, and antipsychotics, and recorded a video telling his estranged boyfriend he loved him.

Then he hung himself.

Sheriff's deputies discovered his body after knocking on the door of his west Phoenix tract home on May 8, 2014. No one answered. They dispatched a robot into the house to do reconnaissance. The robot found what appeared to be a body. Officers entered through the backyard, which was in a state of uncharacteristic neglect. The kidney-shaped swimming pool was tinted green with algae, and a string of lit party lights sagged from the covered patio. Inside the house, the purple-faced corpse of Charley Armendariz, clad in a black T-shirt, red underwear, and ankle socks, slumped from the pool table. Armendariz had tied a blue-and-white rope around one leg of the table, stretched the rope across the table top, wrapped it around his neck four times, knotted it, and asphyxiated himself. He was forty years old.

Lydia Guzman would always wonder what secrets Armendariz had taken with him. She knew Armendariz had been a bad cop. But still, she told us, "Charley had something to say . . . He had something he needed to get off his chest, and he was very remorseful . . . what did he have to say that was so important that caused him so much crying and so much grief? I'd like to know."

The suicide of Charley Armendariz, and what happened in the days leading up to it, would open a window into the hidden costs of Joe Arpaio's political ambitions. And it would reveal how police misconduct can arise when a local law enforcement agency focuses on immigration enforcement to satisfy the political needs of an elected sheriff.

After the sheriff's lawyers alerted Judge Snow about the contents of the evidence bags found in Armendariz's garage, Arpaio and his legal team were summoned to the courtroom. Two lawyers for the plaintiffs—Cecillia Wang from the American Civil Liberties Union Immigrants' Rights Project and Dan Pochoda from the Arizona branch of the American Civil Liberties Union—were also present. So was the court-appointed monitor, Robert Warshaw, and a colleague. It soon became clear this was no ordinary court hearing, which is why Judge Snow had closed it to the public.

During the course of inventorying Armendariz's illegally stored evidence, the sheriff's investigators had found compact discs that stored videos of thousands of hours of traffic stops made by Armendariz. He'd worn an eyeglass camera. He had another camera mounted on his dashboard. And he wasn't the only deputy with such equipment, Judge Snow learned. Armendariz was among several deputies who had video cameras and audio equipment, which they sometimes used to record traffic stops.

Yet in the seven years the *Melendres* case had rumbled through the court system, the Maricopa County Sheriff's Office had never once alerted its attorneys, the plaintiffs, or the judge, to its collection of audio or video recordings. Which was a big deal, because those audios and videos of traffic stops should have been turned over to the plaintiffs' lawyers during the pretrial discovery period.

Snow was not pleased. Because the judge and practically everyone else in the room knew this hidden evidence might reveal misconduct in the sheriff's office that extended far beyond Charley Armendariz.

The Maricopa County Sheriff's Office hadn't come up with a plan quite yet on how, exactly, to collect the audio and video evidence. Arpaio told the judge he figured his chief deputy could handle it. "I have delegated . . . this situation to the chief deputy, and I'm sure, with all his experience, that he knows how to carry it out and put the resources to accomplish that mission," Arpaio told the judge.

"I don't want this to sound like a threat," Snow warily replied. He said Arpaio certainly had the right to delegate, but he was responsible for what went on in his agency and he needed to supervise it, and lead his employees to understand "no matter who the truth hurts or how it hurts, it's coming out."

Arpaio agreed.

And so did Jerry Sheridan.

The judge wanted the video and audio tapes collected quietly, without warning, so errant deputies would not get a chance to destroy them first. Sheridan agreed with the plan.

A day later, Sheridan did the opposite. He ordered an underling to email deputies alerting them to the fact that the video and audio material would be collected. Sheridan blamed his behavior on a migraine headache, fatigue, and confusion.

In June, the alternative weekly *Phoenix New Times* quoted sources who claimed Arpaio dispatched two agency detectives to the suburbs of Seattle, Washington to assist a controversial "confidential informant." The informant, Dennis Montgomery, a former contractor for the Central Intelligence Agency, had surfaced in newspaper and magazine articles as a guy who'd conned the federal government out of millions of dollars with a conspiracy theory about terrorists plots and false promises that he could uncover terrorist schemes with his own software program that would later be discredited. Now, *Phoenix New Times* reported, some members of the sheriff's office believed Montgomery was scamming Arpaio. The newspaper's headline read: "Joe Arpaio's Investigating Federal Judge G. Murray Snow, DOJ, Sources Say, and Using a Seattle Scammer to Do It."

The story had a ring of truth to it. It fit Arpaio's character. Ever since he became sheriff, he'd investigated and relied on implausible conspiracy theories. Sometimes he used them for political gain—like his never-ending investigation of Barack Obama's birth certificate. Other times, he used them to retaliate against his critics. And still other times he used them as a means to get media attention. Arpaio periodically told reporters someone was conspiring to assassinate him or hurt his family—like the time he alleged a coalition of drug lords, Minutemen, and the activist Elias Bermudez were conspiring to kill him. Arpaio wrote about the alleged murder plot in his second memoir. Bermudez told us he was too frightened to sue the sheriff for defamation. Instead, he moved out of the county for a time.

Now, the *Phoenix New Times* reported, a new conspiracy theory had captured the sheriff's imagination. The informant, Montgomery, had convinced the sheriff that Snow, a conservative Republican judge, was conspiring with Obama's liberal justice department to bring down Arpaio.

The sheriff might have grounds to get Snow kicked off the *Melendres* case if the allegation turned out to be true. The sheriff's office began paying Montgomery as a "confidential informant," which meant his name and his investigation were hidden from the public. Montgomery, two deputies, and a posse member secretly collaborated on the so-called "Seattle Investigation."

The newspaper also reported that a deputy discovered Montgomery was conning the sheriff with fake data. The sheriff reportedly was furious with the deputy.

But the *Phoenix New Times* story didn't get much traction.

At least not at first.

Throughout what was left of 2014, Warshaw, the court appointed monitor, and his team tracked additional bits and pieces of mishandled evidence in the Maricopa County Sheriff's Office. More Mexican identification cards. More auto license plates. More women's purses. More stashes of cash. More proof money was taken from arrested immigrants. Much of it was tied to the sheriff's prized Human Smuggling Unit.

Lydia Guzman figured Charley Armendariz, troubled as he was, had told the truth when he said there was something sinister going on inside the agency. She'd long heard immigrants on the hotline alleging some sheriff's staffers had stolen their money. Judge Snow wondered aloud in court one day if deputies were shaking down arrested immigrants.

Snow didn't know at the time, but there were other signs that Human Smuggling Unit deputies were wrongfully seizing property, and in some cases stealing it, in the course of their duties.

One former Human Smuggling Unit deputy, Cisco Perez, said during an unemployment hearing that he and his colleagues "pocketed statues, flags, shirts, drug paraphernalia . . . a big 62-screen-inch TV" from drop houses where migrants were held and "used them in our offices as training items." Perez had lost his job after a wiretap revealed he had asked another deputy to sell a gun for him without regard to whether the buyer was a legal purchaser. On one recorded call, Perez had said, "Hopefully, I'll be able to pocket some shit," in reference to raiding a drop house.

Yet instead of vigorously responding to allegations about misconduct, the court monitor later told Snow, the internal affairs division of the sheriff's office didn't seem to want to get to the bottom of it. Investigators questioned deputies as though they had already concluded there was no misconduct, according to the court monitor. Sheriff's office investigators also "displayed a cavalier, if not a contemptuous attitude" to the monitoring team while conducting internal investigations, the court monitor reported.

Judge Snow subsequently called the sheriff's internal affairs investigations a "joke."

After years of presiding over the *Melendres* case, the judge had dealt with multiple violations of his orders. Early on, evidence was destroyed. Then came the revelations about misconduct kick-started by the Armendariz suicide. And now the whitewashed internal affairs investigations. The case was cannibalizing court time, because the monitor kept finding unpleasant surprises that had to be dealt with.

On November 20, 2014, Snow got yet another unpleasant surprise. It came in a court hearing, after Arpaio's lawyers indicated they had something confidential to share just with other lawyers and the judge. Snow cleared the courtroom. Then Tom Liddy, the son of the Watergate conspirator and the lawyer who represented Arpaio on behalf of the Maricopa County attorney's office, broke the news. He said the traffic stop videos found in Charley Armendariz's garage showed the deputy detained immigrants without criminal charges in November 2012—almost a year after Snow had issued his 2011 order forbidding the sheriff's office from doing so. Arpaio's lawyers were apparently unaware that Snow's 2011 order had never been implemented. But after Liddy saw the Armendariz video, he interviewed lieutenants in the Human Smuggling Unit. "And those interviews have revealed, and the MCSO [Maricopa County Sheriff's Office] has concluded, that this Court's order was not communicated to the line troops," Liddy told the judge.

Snow had known there had been scattered violations of his 2011 preliminary injunction. But after he learned Arpaio's deputies had never been informed of it in the first place, he seemed outraged and exasperated. Two weeks later, he made this clear in open court: "The very unit that did most of the immigration patrol[s] never received any indication that they shouldn't continue doing them, and in fact did continue doing them. And that is a serious violation in direct contradiction to this Court's authority that apparently lasted for months and months, more than a year at the minimum, it appears."

The judge wondered aloud how authorities could find the unauthorized immigrants who had been wrongfully detained. Could they be located and compensated for this violation of their constitutional rights? And would they be willing to step forward, after all they'd been through?

The court's authority was at stake.

So, too, was the sheriff's future.

To determine the scope of the violations of his order, and whether they were intentional, Judge Snow planned a contempt-of-court hearing. If the judge were to find the violations were intentional, Snow could refer Arpaio to the United States Attorney for possible prosecution for criminal contempt of court. And should America's Toughest Sheriff ever be convicted of this crime, it was unlikely, but possible, that he might spend time in a federal prison.

Court watchers wondered if Arpaio had unwittingly neglected Judge Snow's orders because he'd abdicated oversight of his agency to focus on feeding his addiction for media coverage. Or perhaps he had intentionally disobeyed the orders and presided over his agency's culture of disrespect for the federal judiciary. And then there was the question of Arpaio's state of mind. At times Arpaio seemed cagey and controlling. Other times, he appeared to be a vulnerable old man who'd fallen prey to his vanities.

"I'm not going to talk about it," he told us at the time when we asked him to characterize the legal battle in Judge Snow's courtroom.

"The only thing I will say is this: I run this office."

For years, Joe Arpaio had presented himself in the media as the nation's most famous local immigration enforcer. He'd cemented his restrictionist brand by marching jailed immigrants before the television cameras, or by inviting reporters to sweeps, or by shouting at jail inmates as journalists stood by. Such practices not only reinforced his image as a tough immigration law enforcer, but also helped distract voters from widespread reports of misconduct in his agency.

But by 2015, he couldn't promote himself as the nation's toughest immigration cop any more. The federal courts, in stripping away Arpaio's immigration law enforcement powers, also stripped away his photo ops and weakened his brand reinforcement.

Arizona's experiment with local immigration enforcement was largely over. Federal courts had struck down Arizona's Human Smuggling Law and much of Senate Bill 1070. Even the law preventing unauthorized immigrants from posting bail to get out of jail had been struck down. And thanks to a 2014 federal lawsuit—waged by Carlos Garcia, immigrant Puente members, attorneys Annie Lai and Ray Ybarra Maldonado, and others—Arpaio had reluctantly halted his prodigious worksite raids.

All of this dismantling of Arizona's immigration policies had been orchestrated by the same players—Latino grassroots activists, their supporters, and their legal allies, including private lawyers, the ACLU, the Mexican American Legal Defense and Educational Fund, and other immigrant-rights groups. Many hoped to bring down Joe Arpaio in the *Melendres* case.

Arpaio and his chief deputy Sheridan had tried hard to avoid a contempt-of-court hearing in Judge Snow's courtroom. In hopes of doing this, they admitted to Snow they'd committed civil contempt of court by violating his orders. The key, they said, was they hadn't done it intentionally. They expressed remorse. They wanted to make amends. They sought a settlement hearing. They wanted to donate a total of one hundred thousand dollars to a civil rights organization.

But the Latino plaintiffs wouldn't settle with Arpaio and his chief deputy, so Snow scheduled a civil contempt of court hearing for late April, 2015. Television news vans sprouting antennae parked across the street from the federal courthouse. Protesters waved signs that said things like: *Contempt of Court, Tip of the Iceberg.* Inside the building, people lined up like passengers at an airport gate, hoping to get a spot in Snow's sixth floor courtroom. Father Glenn Jenks, the former rector of the Good Shepherd of the Hills Episcopal Church, waited in a wheelchair. He'd retired but hadn't forgotten Arpaio's roundups targeting the Cave Creek day laborers he'd tried to protect. And he would not forget how he'd found a lawyer for Melendres, the Mexican tourist who'd been unconstitutionally detained by sheriff's deputies.

Lydia Guzman settled in the courtroom with Mary Rose Wilcox, who had left her county office to run in a failed bid for Congress. Roberto Reveles, the first Somos America president, sat near the scholar-activist Dr. Angeles Maldonado, who'd helped organize the protests outside Pruitt's furniture store so many years before. At those protests, she'd met her husband, Phoenix civil rights lawyer Ray Ybarra Maldonado. The two had become prominent voices in the Latino resistance.

Kathryn Kobor and Barb Heller sat stiffly in the courtroom. They wanted Arpaio to know he was not alone. "He's a human being," Kobor told us. "He's a very nice person. He's an animal rights advocate ... anybody that's an animal rights advocate cannot hate other people because of their color."

"Gee," said Heller, "I'd like to see if there'll be any contempt held against the federal government for not ... enforcing the laws of this country and stopping the surge across the border. And we wouldn't be here if that was being done. "

The courtroom felt stuffy. The close air was redolent of aftershave and perfume. There were so many people crammed inside—members of the monitor team, lawyers, uniformed sheriff's officials, plaintiffs, and Arpaio himself. Local reporters sat in their usual places in the back, near the electrical outlet where they could charge their laptops. Spectators who couldn't get in waited in the hallway. The activists inside the courtroom didn't dare go to the bathroom lest the marshal guarding the door give away their seats.

Arpaio was already down one lawyer. Tim Casey had announced he was "ethically required to withdraw" around the time he learned the sheriff's office never implemented Snow's 2011 order. Now it was Tom Liddy's turn to withdraw. He said that as a deputy county attorney he now had a conflict of interest due to a recent appellate court ruling that made Maricopa County a party to the case. This meant he was prohibited from representing Arpaio. That left one grim-faced civil lawyer, Michele Iafrate, and Melvin McDonald, a criminal defense lawyer who Arpaio had hired in case he would later be charged with criminal contempt of court.

At that same hearing, Sergeant Brett Palmer, who had once been a supervisor in the Human Smuggling Unit, testified he was one of the few in his unit who had learned about Snow's 2011 order early on. He thought deputies agency-wide should be trained about the judicial order since it represented a "180-degree shift" in how they handled immigration arrests. Palmer had tried to develop materials for training, but his commanders never implemented them. When Cecillia Wang asked Palmer why he believed the training never happened, he said, "It was contrary to the goals and objectives of the sheriff."

Palmer testified he and the sheriff once clashed when Arpaio had ordered him to detain a group of unauthorized immigrants who had committed no crimes, just long enough to march them in front of reporters during a press conference. When Palmer told Arpaio this would violate Snow's orders, Arpaio "became argumentative."

During the hearing, Arpaio sat at the defense table with folded hands. He seemed not to hear well. During courtroom breaks, his attorneys huddled close to him, appearing to explain what had just taken place.

For the next two days, Arpaio squared off against plaintiffs' attorney Stanley Young, who once again methodically questioned the sheriff. Arpaio answered Young's questions in his usual way. He couldn't recall, he didn't remember, he delegated, he didn't understand.

Young showed TV clips of Arpaio bragging about activities that blatantly violated Snow's 2011 order. Young played a video in which Arpaio boasted about sending noncriminal immigrants to ICE for deportation.

He told Fox News host Neil Cavuto that ICE takes "these illegal aliens off our hands when we have no state charge against them."

Responding to Young's queries about the Cavuto video, Arpaio testified he "didn't know all the facts of this court order, and it really hurts me to have after fifty-five years, fifty-five years, to be in this position." He turned to Snow and added, "So I want to apologize to the judge that I should have known more of his court orders. It slipped through the cracks."

Snow, expressionless, did not respond.

Later that same day, Snow unexpectedly initiated the strangest moment in seven years of *Melendres* litigation.

"Are you aware that I have ever been investigated?" the judge asked Arpaio.

"You investigated?" Arpaio answered. "No, no."

Judge Snow handed Arpaio a copy of the *Phoenix New Times* article, now nearly a year old, which detailed how Arpaio had hired Dennis Montgomery to investigate whether Judge Snow had conspired with the justice department to bring down Arpaio. "Did you ever—you see that the article says that what Montgomery was actually doing was investigating me. You see that that's what the article says?" Judge Snow asked.

"It's not true," Arpaio sputtered.

In convoluted testimony, Arpaio said he'd hired Montgomery to investigate "computer tampering" and "bank fraud." He claimed he didn't hire Montgomery to investigate Snow. But then he cryptically noted that Montgomery was looking into "information about many judges being infiltrated or wiretaps."

The courtroom was unusually quiet. Lydia Guzman felt almost numb. Was this really happening?

"The shit hit the fan," she later told us. "The shit finally hit the fan."

But there was even more.

Arpaio admitted on the stand there was a sheriff's office investigation that did involve Snow, and, indirectly, his wife. Arpaio testified someone named Grissom claimed in an email to him that "Judge Snow wanted to do everything to make sure I'm not elected."

"Okay. And how did this person purport to know that?" the judge asked.

Sheriff Joe Arpaio testifies in the *Melendres* civil contempt of court hearing at the federal courthouse in Phoenix in 2015. (Court sketch by Maggie Keane)

"The person met your wife in a restaurant, and she's the one that made those comments," Arpaio replied. He said his lawyer had hired a private investigator to look into the matter.

The judge remained calm. He ordered Arpaio and his agency to save all materials related to the investigation involving his wife. He also ordered the sheriff to secure and preserve everything related to Montgomery and the Seattle Investigation including communications, documents, cell phones, computers, and funding records.

It would later be revealed that in 2013, someone named Karen Grissom had alleged to Arpaio in a private message on Facebook that she had run into Snow's wife, a childhood acquaintance. "She told me that her husband hates u and will do anything to get u out of office," Grissom had written.

U.S. District Court Judge G. Murray Snow addresses Sheriff Joe Arpaio during the *Melendres* civil contempt of court hearing at the federal courthouse in Phoenix in 2015. (Court sketch by Maggie Keane)

Arpaio had seized on this tip. His lawyer Tim Casey had dispatched a private investigator to interview the Facebook tipster. Nothing conclusive had come out of the interview. Casey had told the sheriff to drop the matter because "the Grissom information is, in my judgment, so fundamentally flawed in its substance that it likely cannot be used."

Some court observers wondered if Arpaio's inquiry into the Facebook tip could be a criminal attempt to intimidate and retaliate against a federal judge. But the sheriff didn't see it that way. Instead, he felt Snow had embarrassed himself by asking questions in his own courtroom that forced Arpaio to reveal that Snow's wife had let it slip that the judge was biased. Arpaio would always believe the Facebook tip had been true. Judge Snow "never came back to deny it," Arpaio told us.

When court adjourned on April 24, 2015, Guzman fought the crazy urge to start a football-stadium-like wave for Judge Snow, right there in the courtroom. Arpaio was going down, she just knew it. He'd crossed the line one too many times. She wanted to leap up from her bench and yell: "Awright Judge Snow!"

A few weeks later, in May 2015, Snow announced that his preliminary review of Seattle Investigation documents suggested that Arpaio's office had paid Dennis Montgomery to investigate a sham conspiracy theory involving Snow. The judge rebuked Arpaio for "attempting to construct some bogus conspiracy theory to discredit this court" at the exact time the sheriff's office should have been investing resources into reaching compliance with the court's orders for reforming the agency.

Court records would later unravel the odd story of how Arpaio met Montgomery through a prominent birther. Montgomery had first presented himself to Arpaio as a whistleblower who could prove the Obama administration was snooping into private cell phone records and bank accounts of everyday Americans, including Maricopa County residents. Early on, Montgomery added the "bogus conspiracy theory" about Judge Snow to his so-called whistleblowing services. Montgomery gave the sheriff convoluted timelines and graphics that suggested an anti-Arpaio scheme perpetrated by Snow, the justice department, Stanley Young's law firm, and others.

Experts hired by the sheriff's office at one point analyzed Montgomery's "data" and found it was either fabricated or a jumble of readily available records. Sheridan, the chief deputy, didn't believe Montgomery was credible. "This is fiction," Sheridan told Arpaio. "Montgomery just did this just so we continue to pay him—so you continue to pay. Your confidential informant is broke on the balls of his ass. He wants to give you something that's going to get you excited . . . Come on. This is ridiculous. You know, do you really think that there's a conspiracy out there with Covington and Burling and Murray Snow and all this stuff? This is crazy, Sheriff. This is crazy."

But Arpaio clung to the conspiracy theory. "Sometimes maybe he [Montgomery] wasn't always telling the truth," Arpaio conceded to us.

"But I always had a little confidence in that flowchart that he put out, all the connections."

The Seattle Investigation cost at least a quarter million dollars. The sheriff's office paid Montgomery in part with federal grant money that was supposed to be used to combat drug trafficking.

In May 2015, as the strange story began unraveling, Snow wanted to get to the bottom of Arpaio's motives for hiring Montgomery. But the civil contempt hearing had already swallowed up four full court days. Now it was clear it would take many more court days to discover what was truly going on with the Seattle Investigation and other unexplained mismanagement and misconduct inside the sheriff's office. The contempt hearing would take place in fits and starts, and drag on for months.

It would benefit Arpaio if Snow no longer presided over the *Melendres* case. And there had been a precedent—Arpaio had been successful, years before, in getting rid of the first *Melendres* judge, Mary Murguia, due to a perceived conflict.

Now Arpaio attempted a similar conflict strategy with Snow in June 2015. It all had to do with the "hates u" Facebook tip by Grissom, who had alleged she heard Snow's wife say the judge wanted Arpaio out of office. Since Snow had asked Arpaio about the Grissom tip in court, Arpaio's lawyers argued Snow was too conflicted to preside over the *Melendres* case and should recuse himself. "No reasonable person with knowledge of the facts can deny that Judge Snow is now investigating and presiding over issues involving his own family," the lawyers wrote. A similar motion had already been filed by Dennis Montgomery, who had attempted to intervene in the case, and was represented by the right-wing attorney Larry Klayman.

Snow would not recuse himself. But Arpaio's attempt to get rid of Snow delayed the second round of contempt hearings for months. Shortly after Snow announced he would stay on the case in July 2015, he found out from the court monitor that the sheriff's office had apparently disobeyed his judicial orders yet again. Members of the court monitor's staff had met with attorney Michele Iafrate, along with Captain Steve Bailey and others on the sheriff's department professional standards bureau, and had asked pointedly if anyone in the sheriff's office was investigating additional identification documents that had been improperly stashed in the office. Bailey and Iafrate had stayed mum about the fact that they had discovered and were investigating more than 1,400 new identifications. The monitor also discovered fifty Seattle Investigation hard drives the sheriff's office had failed to turn over to the court. This time, the judge had no patience. He ordered federal marshals to race down to the sheriff's office and retrieve the IDs and hard drives.

The fact that a federal judge was forced to dispatch marshals to seize evidence made for yet another round of bad *Melendres*-related publicity for Joe Arpaio. In late May, Arpaio's approval ratings had dropped again. Now, only 38 percent of respondents said the sheriff was doing an "excellent" job.

As the feud between the sheriff and the judge intensified in federal court, Lisa Allen, Arpaio's media relations director, organized a party for her boss at the sheriff's office. Arpaio wanted to "get it out to the whole world" that he was the "longest serving sheriff" in Maricopa County history, Allen told us. Arpaio had by then been in office for twenty-two and a half years.

There was an air of forced frivolity at the western-themed event held on a sweltering June afternoon. Attendees were mostly the sheriff's employees, along with a few local journalists, and Ava. "This is a happy day for us," Allen told us pointedly before the speeches began. We took it as her way of saying she didn't want reporters mucking up the happy day with tough questions.

"If you want to break it down, it is one hundred and ninety-seven thousand hours and ten million minutes," Arpaio informed his guests, referring to his tenure as sheriff.

The sheriff was presented with a brown cowboy hat, which was too big, and almost rested on his glasses. Outside on the shaded patio, a deputy held the reins of an old, gentle bay gelding named Max. Arpaio, who was days away from his eighty-third birthday, didn't attempt to get on the horse. Instead, the sheriff gamely held Max's reins and posed for the TV cameras, grinning from beneath the ill-fitting hat.

He removed the cowboy hat and stepped away from the horse. He would run again for sheriff in 2016, he said. "I am not going to surrender. I am going to keep fighting," he told us. He was back to his old sound bites. But everyone knew that in a matter of months Snow might refer him for possible criminal prosecution for disobeying court orders.

18 "Build the Wall!"

2015-2016

Ava Arpaio was in her early eighties when she was diagnosed with abdominal cancer in the fall of 2015. She didn't want to worry her husband, she told us, because he was "getting things done at the sheriff's office."

The sheriff was in the middle of on-again, off-again civil contempt of court hearings in Snow's courtroom. These were the hearings in which Snow was gathering evidence to help him understand the scope of misconduct in the sheriff's office, identify necessary reforms, and decide whether he'd refer Arpaio to the United States Attorney for the District of Arizona, in Phoenix, for possible criminal prosecution. The possibility of a criminal referral was the topic of media speculation and a stream of news stories that didn't help Arpaio's declining popularity with Maricopa County voters.

Things kept getting worse for Arpaio in court, though he was pleased by one slightly positive legal development. The justice department lawsuit filed by the civil rights division in Washington, D.C., the case championed by Tom Perez, was finally settled. It had alleged racial profiling of Latinos on the streets and in worksite raids, civil rights abuses of non-English speaking Latinos in Arpaio's jails, and retaliations by Arpaio's office against the sheriff's critics. Roslyn Silver, the federal judge in Phoenix who was adjudicating *United States v. Maricopa County*, ruled she agreed with

Snow—the sheriff and his deputies had racially profiled Latino motorists, so that piece of the justice department civil rights case was put to rest first. By then, Arpaio had already stopped his worksite raids due to the 2014 Puente federal lawsuit, but he agreed to conduct them lawfully and let the justice department weigh in on his policies should he ever start them up again. By that point, the sheriff's office had already convinced the justice department that discrimination against non-English speaking jail inmates had stopped, and so that part of the lawsuit was resolved. Arpaio settled the retaliation charges by signing a document promising to institute an agency-wide policy to not "take action against any individual in retaliation for any individual's lawful expression of opinions in the exercise of the First Amendment right to the freedom of speech."

After the justice department attorneys settled the case in Silver's courtroom, they started showing up in Judge Snow's courtroom because they joined the *Melendres* case to help ensure Arpaio followed Snow's orders for reforming the sheriff's office.

With so much going on, Ava didn't tell her husband about her tumor until additional tests diagnosed it as a virulent cancer, and she'd scheduled a round of exhausting chemotherapy and radiation.

The sheriff insisted his wife would get better. And Ava told us with some pride that her husband "never had to do any waiting on me" during her illness. Their adult children, Sherry and Rocco, became Ava's caregivers. They took turns cooking, running errands, driving their mother to appointments. Then they went home to their families and jobs. Rocco was running what was left of Starworld Travel, and Sherry, a writer, had a houseful of kids.

When Lydia Guzman learned of Ava's illness, she wished Ava a speedy recovery in a Facebook post decorated with three red roses in a white vase. That post earned 570 "likes" and mostly positive comments from the Latino community. This touched Guzman. The very people Arpaio had tormented expressed compassion for his wife.

As Ava recuperated, she watched Fox News. She especially enjoyed it when Donald Trump, the reality television star, real-estate billionaire, and Republican presidential primary candidate, popped onto her screen for a Fox News interview.

In June 2015, Trump and his wife, Melania, a Slovenian immigrant and former lingerie model, had famously floated down an escalator to the atrium of Trump Tower in New York, where Trump announced his intent to run in the 2016 Republican presidential primary election. In so doing, he set the tone for his candidacy by trumpeting nationalism and disparaging Latino immigrants. Without proof, he accused Mexico of intentionally sending "people that have lots of problems" into the United States. "They're bringing drugs. They're bringing crime. They're rapists. And some, I assume, are good people," he said.

Trump's rhetoric traced back to the early twentieth century American eugenics movement that influenced the nation's immigration policies. By the time Trump decided to run for president, various restrictionist nonprofits had weaponized anti-immigrant data in their studies, and Trump liked to quote them in his speeches. This message resonated with his twenty-first century followers: inferior immigrants had invaded and infested the nation, endangering and preying on American citizens, and the United States needed to clamp down on immigration to preserve its national character—which to some Americans meant preserving the white majority.

Shortly after announcing his candidacy, Trump held one of his first rallies at the Phoenix Convention Center. The night before, Barb Heller hung "Stolen Lives Quilt" banners in the ballroom where Trump spoke. The banners honored dozens of victims of crimes committed or allegedly committed by unauthorized immigrants.

Many of the four thousand or so rallygoers who'd braved the 106-degree heat to hear Trump didn't need Heller's banners to remind them of what they perceived as the menace of unauthorized immigrants. They were already upset and angry. And to get in the convention hall doors, they had to pass a group of perhaps a hundred demonstrators standing on the sidewalk. One protester carried a sign that branded Trump and Arpaio as twin racists. Another waved a placard that brought attention to Trump's casting Mexican immigrants as criminals and rapists. The sign said: *Trump, the only criminals here are ICE and Arpaio.*

Joe Arpaio was proud to introduce Trump at the Phoenix rally. His fondness for the candidate signaled to the nation that Trump was the real restrictionist deal, just like him. "We love you Sheriff Joe!" some people sang out after Arpaio walked on the stage with the American flag backdrop. He told the crowd he and Trump had much in common—investigating "the birth certificate," getting tough on "the illegal immigration problem" and the fact that the two shared a birthday, June 14, Flag Day, though of course "not the same year."

Before he stepped down from the stage at that first Trump rally in Phoenix, the sheriff saluted the crowd by telling them he would always serve "the people," they were his "secret weapon," they were the "silent majority."

"The silent majority is back!" Trump proclaimed during his seventy-minute speech. Trump spoke as he always did, loudly, as though there were no mic available. Like Arpaio, he had created his brand in the media. On the television show *The Apprentice*, Trump had presented himself as a successful billionaire, overpowering concerns about his failed businesses and lawsuits alleging swindles. Now Trump wanted to add restrictionism to his brand. During this particular speech, he first said he loved Mexicans, then disparaged Mexican immigrants by insisting once again, and without proof, that the Mexican government was intentionally sending its ne'er-do-wells across the line. "Every time Mexico really intelligently sends people over," he boomed, "we charge Mexico one hundred thousand dollars for every person they send over!" Wild applause. Trump "fired up the crazies," Arizona's Senator John McCain, a moderate Republican, later summed up.

This first Phoenix rally was pivotal for Trump, and the nation. Ten days before, Trump had placed seventh in a field of presidential primary contenders, according to *The Washington Post*. Ten days after the event, Trump had soared to first place.

The sheriff attached himself to Trump immediately and fiercely. Now Arpaio had a distraction from legal problems, his wife's illness, his eroding brand, declining poll numbers, and the near certainty that an army of Latino volunteers would again sign up voters who wanted him out of office.

But the sheriff, by becoming a key Trump surrogate, did more than just distract himself from his problems and try to spruce up his brand. He helped facilitate the migration of divisive Arizona-style restrictionism into the rest of the nation. And as it began to envelop the country, many of

Arizona's Latino activists would become role models for others seeking to resist nativism in their states.

From Phoenix, Arizona Highway 87 snakes through volcanic hills, black boulders, and desert shrubs with twisted thorny branches. Right before the turnoff to Fountain Hills, three people chained themselves to vehicles blocking the road. Standing in front of the human roadblock, a battalion of perhaps two dozen activists held banners, drummed, and chanted.

WHAT DO WE WANT?
DUMP TRUMP!
GET THIS CLOWN OUT OF OUR TOWN!

A coalition of local grassroots Latino-led organizations, including Puente, planned and carried out the blockade. It was a March afternoon in 2016, three days before Arizona's presidential primary election. Trump had come to Arizona once again. He was scheduled to give a speech in Fountain Hills, where his biggest booster, Joe Arpaio, lived.

Trump and Arpaio planned on driving to Fountain Hills together after taping a Fox News interview in Phoenix. But when the blockade began snarling traffic on the main road into the town, no one knew if the two friends would make it to the rally.

Dozens of Trump supporters jumped out of their paralyzed vans, trucks, SUVs, and sedans and approached the activists. Carlos Garcia waited. He feared that some of the Trump supporters, who were mostly white, had guns. It was, he told us, "enemy territory" for the brown demonstrators. He walked through the crowd, trying to "de-escalate" tensions to make sure no one got hurt. "Go back to Mexico!" some Trump supporters yelled. "Go back to Europe," the activists retorted.

The blockade typified Puente's civil disobedience actions, and the new style of Latino civil rights activism in Arizona, which was gaining national attention. It was fearless, young, theatrical, street-smart, organized, and designed for maximum social media reach and press coverage. It provided a clean visual metaphor sending out the intended message. In this case, Garcia told us, the message was "stopping" hate.

Since the Maricopa County Sheriff's Office was contracted as the police agency for Fountain Hills, Arpaio's commanders dispatched deputies to

Joe Arpaio (left, seated with hands folded) watches presidential candidate Donald Trump speak after introducing him at a campaign rally in Fountain Hills, Arizona on March 19, 2016. (Photo by Gage Skidmore Licensed under Creative Commons)

dismantle the blockade. They cut the three demonstrators loose from the vehicles. Then they arrested them.

Which impressed Donald Trump.

Trump and Arpaio arrived at the rally late, looking a little wilted in the spring heat. Arpaio introduced Trump, shook his hand, then stood back with Jan Brewer and other local Republican luminaries.

"You have some sheriff!" Trump exclaimed.

"There are no games with this sheriff, that's for sure!"

Trump assured the rallygoers he was the only serious Republican candidate, and he'd take action on illegal immigration. He'd build a "beautiful wall that nobody is crossing." The crowd chanted "USA, USA, USA" and "Build the Wall! Build the Wall!" and waved signs that said things like *The silent majority stands with Trump!*

"We have a silent majority that is no longer silent," Trump shouted. "And *we* are going to be heard!"

After he won the Arizona presidential primary three days later, Trump tweeted: "I want to thank @RealSheriffJoe for all of his help in our historic Arizona win. Could not have done it without you Joe!"

Sheriff Joe Arpaio sat at his desk in his large office decorated with framed tributes to himself—newspaper and magazine profiles, badges, photographs of himself posing with famous people. It was Friday, May 13, 2016. He still hadn't read Judge Snow's Findings of Facts issued earlier that day. He didn't want to talk about the findings, he told us. His lawyers would do the talking, and that was that. He wouldn't even read the document, 162 pages of white paper stacked neatly on his otherwise uncluttered desk.

The papers on his desk did not bode well for the eighty-three-year-old sheriff. After twenty-one days of civil contempt of court hearings that spanned four months in 2015, Snow found that Arpaio and his second-in-command, Chief Deputy Jerry Sheridan, had "knowingly and intentionally" and repeatedly committed civil contempt of court by disobeying his orders.

Snow ruled Sheridan and Arpaio had violated his 2011 order prohibiting the sheriff's office from detaining immigrants simply for being in the country without papers. The judge found at least 157 noncriminal immigrants had been detained by the Human Smuggling Unit in violation of his order, and these people needed to be found and compensated. (Later, the number of wrongfully detained immigrants would be revised to at least 189). And Arpaio, the judge ruled, had intentionally disobeyed him as part of a political strategy to win the 2012 election.

What's more, the judge ruled, Arpaio and Sheridan had not told the truth when testifying in court about Dennis Montgomery's activities, which had included an investigation targeting Snow. Beyond that, Snow ruled, Arpaio and Sheridan were at the helm of an agency that had withheld evidence from plaintiffs and had whitewashed internal investigations into misconduct by deputies and others who'd violated the judge's orders.

"[T]he Court finds that the Defendants have engaged in multiple acts of misconduct, dishonesty, and bad faith with respect to the Plaintiff class and the protection of its rights," Snow wrote.

"They have demonstrated a persistent disregard for the orders of this Court, as well as an intention to violate and manipulate the laws and policies regulating their conduct. . . ."

The judge also found Brian Sands, a former executive chief for the Maricopa County Sheriff's Office, and Lieutenant Joe Sousa, who led the Human Smuggling Unit for a time, in civil contempt of court for violating the preliminary injunction. But nothing in the ruling said Sands and Sousa *willingly* violated his orders. So that meant only Arpaio and Sheridan, who "knowingly and intentionally" violated his orders, faced the very real possibility that the judge would soon refer them to the United States Attorney's Office for criminal prosecution.

Sousa would later say he felt his bosses had "set me up for failure" in the Human Smuggling Unit, and the civil contempt of court hearings had shifted his own understanding of what went wrong. "I've been giving my bosses the benefit of the doubt that none of this was intentional," he told a court-appointed independent investigator in 2017. "But . . . I just can't say that with 100 percent certainty anymore after listening to the totality of everything that went on during that civil hearing."

By the time Snow issued his 2016 Findings of Facts, Joe Arpaio had lost two key aides. After twenty-three years as Arpaio's media relations director, Lisa Allen had moved to faraway Idaho with her husband. "As a media person, many inside the agency saw me as a wolf among sheep," she wrote in her farewell press release. "It took years to earn a semblance of trust. But I succeeded only because of the unfettered support of Sheriff Arpaio . . . I am here to say that he is a good man, a great boss, and will continue to be a fine sheriff for years to come." After Allen moved to Idaho, the *Phoenix New Times* reported Allen had contracted with the sheriff's office to update its website and write press releases. She worked under her own limited liability company tag, "Wizard of Paws and Prose."

Not long after Allen left her full time job at the sheriff's office, so did Len Sherman, who coauthored two books with Arpaio and had joined the sheriff's public information office. Sherman became disillusioned, and wrote a bitter opinion piece in *The Arizona Republic* explaining his departure. "To understand what has happened, start by understanding that illegal immigration and the 'birther' business have one fascinating thing in common: Both began as crass ploys to appeal to voters, with Arpaio's tone hardening as he somehow, over time, convinced himself that what he was peddling was actually so," Sherman wrote. "And it worked. Millions of dollars needed for his increasingly difficult re-election campaigns rolled in, along with the media attention he so desperately craves."

The sheriff appointed a new media relations director, Chris Hegstrom. And on the day in May 2016 when Snow issued his Findings of Facts, Hegstrom sat with Arpaio, who voiced more interest in this book than Snow's orders. How many chapters, Arpaio asked us, would include him? Would he be on the cover?

Or would we put a sombrero on the cover?

"Whoa!" Hegstrom exclaimed. He darted out of the room to procure pretzels for his boss, who had been in no mood to eat lunch.

Then CBS rang up Arpaio, seeking comment on Snow's ruling. Arpaio uncharacteristically refused comment. Downstairs, a reporter for the local NBC affiliate sought an interview. The station never had a spare reporter for a positive story, Arpaio muttered, but always had a spare reporter for a negative story, like today. The sheriff turned his attention to a large framed photograph of Donald Trump. It was a reminder of happier days—the rallies, the supportive crowds, and the ride he had once taken in Trump's private jet with the gold sink in the bathroom.

He had positioned Trump's photo so he could always see it when he looked up from his desk. It hung on the north wall of his office, guarding the window facing the nearby federal courthouse, where Snow had his courtroom and chambers.

That spring, Lydia Guzman's life had taken an unexpected, happy turn. She had met Tom Black on an online dating site in December 2015. The two had a first date at La Barquita, a little Mexican restaurant in central Phoenix. Black was a widower and Guzman hadn't dated in years. They began seeing each other often, and she soon told him about the ups and downs of her activism in Arizona—fighting Arpaio, the sweeps, the worksite raids, the financial and marital struggles, the hotline, the work of finding plaintiffs for the *Melendres* case, and how she still carried the weight of it all. Black was captivated. He'd never met anyone like Guzman. A tall white guy with a crew cut, graying goatee, and kind brown eyes, Black was a respiratory

Lydia Guzman and Tom Black outside the federal courthouse in Phoenix on May 31, 2016. (Authors' photo)

therapist at the Carl T. Hayden Veterans' Administration Medical Center in Phoenix. He loved cooking and carpentry and was in the middle of remodeling his suburban home, where soon, Guzman would move in with him.

Guzman was financially secure again and had a good job doing community outreach at Chicanos Por La Causa. Everything seemed to be working out. Her kids had grown up and now respected her activism. Once, Ashley came across a cardboard box full of Guzman's awards from civic groups. "These are amazing," she said, "you need to display these." Ashley liked Tom Black, too. He joshed with her mother and fit in with the family in a way no others had.

Dressed in purple scrubs, Black accompanied Guzman to court on May 31, 2016, a couple of weeks after Snow found Arpaio in contempt of court. Members of Tonatierra, the indigenous rights group, and Puente stood on the sidewalk strumming guitars and carried signs that said *Arpaio Guilty*.

Guzman expected Snow to refer Arpaio and Sheridan for criminal prosecution on that day. She wondered if her heart would stop, just hearing it, after all these years of trying to get to this moment. She looked over at Alfredo Gutierrez, inscrutable, arms folded, shades atop his gray crew cut. Everyone rose when Snow walked in, his red tie and white shirt peeking out of his black robes. Snow did not sit at his desk but instead stood before a podium, looking stern. Snow said he now had no confidence in the Maricopa County Sheriff's Office. There was still possible misconduct by the command staff and deputies that should be probed by an independent authority—including the whitewashed internal investigations and agency personnel who'd violated his order.

I love this judge, Guzman thought.

This is ridiculous, Kathryn Kobor thought as she sat in the courtroom to support the sheriff. The whole case seemed to be spiraling out of control, she felt. And it was so expensive to taxpayers. She hoped once Trump got elected, the nonsense would stop. Arpaio didn't deserve this political vendetta. He was a dedicated, devoted, and responsible person and she would support him until she was six feet under. Joe Arpaio didn't go down easy, even if he had a liberal judge, and neither did she.

She adored the sheriff, she told us. This was a bogus witch hunt from the beginning. "This judge has no authority to go after the sheriff of Maricopa County," she said.

Outside, Puente activists introduced their latest visual metaphor—a twenty-foot-high balloon, or inflatable, depicting Joe Arpaio in handcuffs and jailhouse stripes. The message, Carlos Garcia told us, was "to mock and ridicule" the sheriff in exactly the same way as the sheriff had mocked and ridiculed Latinos.

It took three volunteers to maneuver the unwieldy inflatable, tethered to a wheeled cart. They moved slowly up and down the sidewalk. The inflatable was an immediate hit with photo journalists, whose pictures would appear for months in local and national media. They also captured the image of Mary Rose Wilcox, laughing as she pretended to pull the inflatable.

Guzman had so many press interviews, she'd skipped lunch. So she and Black climbed the stairs from the lobby to the second floor, hoping to find a Snickers at the vending machine. When she rounded the corner, she found Arpaio sitting alone in an alcove, out of sight.

With the iconic Arpaio inflatable in the background, protesters gather at the federal courthouse in Phoenix on October 11, 2016. (Photo by José L. Muñoz)

"Hi Sheriff," she said, surprised.

"Thanks for your Facebook post," Arpaio responded. "You're a nice lady." He told Guzman Ava was doing ok. She was a fighter. She read the Bible. "How come you don't come visit me," Arpaio said. "You never come visit me." Then he turned to Black, and repeated, "She's a nice lady."

Joe Arpaio entertains fans at a Trump rally at the Veterans Memorial Coliseum in Phoenix on June 18, 2016. (Photo by Gage Skidmore Licensed under Creative Commons)

Guzman sent good wishes to Ava, then the couple set off to buy the Snickers.

A few minutes later, they hurried back to the courtroom.

Snow addressed the possibility of referring Arpaio for criminal prosecution. It seemed to be the only way to hold the sheriff accountable.

Agency staffers, like Sheridan, who willfully disobeyed Snow's orders, could get fired, the judge said. But no one could fire Arpaio. He was an elected official. A criminal contempt of court referral seemed to be the only way to hold the sheriff accountable.

But at the end of the day, the careful judge made no criminal referral. Guzman tried not to be disappointed. Snow was careful, and these things took time. They always took time.

Throughout much of the 2016 Republican National Convention in Cleveland, Ohio, Joe Arpaio, a delegate from Arizona, tried to figure out how to get on the convention speaking schedule. He'd made the trip from

Arizona alone, without Ava. She'd lost a lot of weight. She was weak. She encouraged him to go without her.

He felt out of sorts without his wife. The volunteers who shepherded him from the Doubletree Hotel to the Quicken Loans Arena for convention events, seemed to sometimes not know where to take him, and when. Sometimes, Arpaio was shuttled around so much, he missed meals. It didn't help that he'd fallen on the first night when visiting with the New York delegation, hurting his leg. And even though he limped, his minders sometimes asked him to walk long distances. During one of these walks, Code Pink demonstrators approached him on the sidewalk, shouting about his brutal treatment of inmates in Tent City jails. "It had nothing to do with illegal immigration," he told us, dismayed. "They weren't Hispanic."

Still, despite his well-publicized legal problems, he was a celebrity among Republican conventioneers. He posed for selfies, addressed the Arizona delegation at breakfast, met with Mike Pence, attended a meeting with GOP strategist Frank Luntz, and batted balloons on the convention floor with a fellow Arizona delegate he'd once criminally investigated.

He began to wonder if Trump's handlers were keeping the two apart, perhaps because of the case in Snow's court. He sensed Trump wouldn't be concerned about the case or any bad press related to it. And if he hadn't bumped into one of Trump's bodyguards he knew from the campaign trail, he might never have seen Trump. The bodyguard took him to a "small room" someplace in the convention center, where Trump and his campaign chairman Paul Manafort waited.

"So I go into the room . . . And Trump sees me, he walks up, runs over, hugs me and you know, I get all excited . . . I said, 'Don't you ever ever think that I turn you down to speak at the convention.' He went bananas. 'You mean you're not?' He couldn't believe it. He tells Manafort 'You get him on that stage,'" Arpaio told us. "So here's the point . . . They blocked me from him. I'll never forget that."

Trump made sure his friend had air time. On Thursday night, during television prime time, the sheriff addressed the applauding conventioneers. The Arizona delegation jumped to its feet. "Joe, Joe, Joe," they yelled. Dressed in a black suit, white shirt, a dark tie and his pistol tie clip, standing against a border wall background, the sheriff announced his most important mission in his law enforcement career was to help Donald

Trump get elected. He struggled with the teleprompter, but he soldiered on, insisting without evidence terrorists were crossing the southern border, infiltrating communities, and causing destruction and mayhem. Trump, he said, would stand with him. They'd secure the border. They'd restore law and order.

After about five minutes, the speech was over. Everything had worked out, after all. And he'd found it exciting, like Hollywood. Not the grim Hollywood of *The Joe Show* screening, where few noticed him, but glamorous Hollywood, where he was somebody, ushered through passageways with all the other luminaries. And he'd gotten to use the Cleveland Cavaliers' bathroom, which wasn't all that elegant, but still.

That night, he celebrated until one o'clock in the morning and didn't have a chance to sleep before his three o'clock wake-up call.

19 Bazta Arpaio
2016

Joe Arpaio needed a shave, and his leg still bothered him from his tumble during his visit with the New York delegation. He made it down to the hotel lobby in Cleveland by three thirty the next morning, boarded the shuttle, and once at the airport, caught the first flight to Phoenix. He had to rush back for yet another hearing that afternoon in Snow's courtroom. Although exhausted, he arrived at the courthouse in good spirits, still reminiscing about the Republican National Convention, his prime-time speech, and Donald Trump.

It was close to 112 degrees that day and so stiflingly breezeless the American flag wilted on its pole. Even so, about twenty men and women had gathered on the sidewalk outside the courthouse. They chanted "Arrest Arpaio, not the people," drummed, and played guitars.

By the time the sheriff settled into his chair at the defense table, the activists in the gallery waited apprehensively. Snow was in no mood for nonsense. Throughout much of the hearing, he stood behind his desk, a tall, broad-shouldered, serious jurist towering over the litigants. He had called this hearing to help determine whether he would refer Arpaio and Sheridan, along with Captain Steve Bailey and defense attorney Michele

Iafrate, to the United States Attorney's Office for criminal contempt of court prosecution.

The previous year, in an attempt to stop the civil contempt hearings from moving forward, Arpaio and his second-in-command, Jerry Sheridan, had admitted they'd committed civil contempt of court. Now, criminal defense lawyers for Arpaio and Sheridan scrambled to persuade Snow not to move forward with a criminal contempt of court referral. Their clients were good men, the lawyers said. They'd devoted their lives to law enforcement. They'd mistakenly disobeyed Snow's orders. They were sorry.

"They lied to my face," Snow shot back from his standing desk.

His jaw trembled.

"They lied not only to me, but they lied to internal investigators."

Alfredo Gutierrez leaned forward. This was a stunning moment. He was confident the movement would have another legal victory soon. The judge saw right through Arpaio and what Gutierrez viewed as his "army of lying deputies."

One by one, lawyers for the four asked the judge not to refer their clients to a criminal prosecutor. The judge listened carefully, typing away on his laptop on the standing desk. But by the end of the hearing, he still hadn't revealed his next steps. The sheriff's lawyers huddled around him. Arpaio nodded over and over. He wasn't worried, he told us a few minutes later. If the judge did anything, it would only be a referral for a prosecution, not a conviction. He wouldn't surrender. He'd fight. He hobbled down the tropically hot hallway toward the elevator, still talking about Donald Trump and the Republican National Convention.

Guzman left the courtroom feeling jubilant. Once again, she'd expected the judge to make criminal referrals that day, but he hadn't. But if she'd read the judge right, Joe Arpaio would soon face a criminal trial. It would be a symbolic victory for the movement. Because to Lydia Guzman and so many in the community, Arpaio was a symbol. Of racism. Of white supremacy. She couldn't forget the terror and sadness she'd witnessed. If only she could see him in a federal prison jumpsuit, even for one day, suffering some of the humiliations he'd meted out for so many years, she'd be happy.

"Felicidades! Felicidades!" she crowed, high-fiving and shaking hands with activists and plaintiffs' lawyers. "Congratulations! Congratulations!"

The day Lydia Guzman had hoped for finally happened on August 19, 2016. In a detailed thirty-two-page ruling Snow referred Maricopa County Sheriff Joe Arpaio to the United States Attorney for prosecution of criminal contempt of court. He also referred Chief Deputy Jerry Sheridan, Steve Bailey, and Michele Iafrate, who by that point had withdrawn from the case. Should the United States Attorney decide to go ahead with the prosecution, there would be a criminal trial presided over by a different judge in a different federal courtroom.

In his ruling, Snow once again detailed a litany of deliberate and repeated acts of disobedience committed by Sheridan and Arpaio. They'd disregarded his 2011 preliminary injunction orders. They'd mischaracterized the judge's orders to others in the sheriff's office. They'd manipulated internal investigations pertaining, among other things, to the illegal stash of identification cards, drugs, weapons, cash, and women's purses in Charley Armendariz's garage. They'd made "multiple intentional false statements" to the court.

And they'd withheld evidence—including the Seattle Investigation hard drives—from the judge and Latino plaintiffs. Further, in violation of court orders, Sheridan, Bailey, and attorney Iafrate had failed to disclose more than 1,400 stashed identification cards, the judge ruled.

The court's authority had been undermined. "Criminal contempt serves to vindicate the Court's authority by punishing the intentional disregard of that authority," the judge wrote.

When Guzman found out about the ruling, she and Black raced over to the reopened El Portal restaurant to speak to reporters. She sat at the familiar long table with her activist colleagues—including Mary Rose Wilcox, Danny Ortega, Antonio Bustamante, Alfredo Gutierrez, Roberto Reveles, Martín Quezada (an Arizona state senator), and others. Behind the table, immigrant activists flanked by American and Arizona flags stood in front of the oversized portrait of Martin Luther King, Jr.

Anti-Arpaio activists speak to the press at El Portal on August 19, 2016. Seated from left: Antonio Bustamante, Arizona state senator Martín Quezada, Alfredo Gutierrez, Danny Ortega, Mary Rose Wilcox, Lydia Guzman, Roberto Reveles, Tony Navarrete, Jason Odhner, and Joanne Scott Woods. Standing from left: Rob McElwain, Maria Meza, and Angelina Rodriguez. (Authors' photo)

"Wow, wow, this has been a long time coming," Guzman said. She recalled her dismay when Arpaio had "thumbed his nose at the justice system and continued to violate people's rights." She'd felt so discouraged. "But then the judge took matters into his hands . . . When someone violates a court order there is going to be consequences, and Arpaio is going to face these consequences."

"This is a moment of celebration," Alfredo Gutierrez said. "It is a moment of extraordinary relief. It is a moment of redemption for all of those people who were dragged out in the middle of the night, for mothers who were forced to give birth shackled in one of Arpaio's jails. It is a moment of redemption of all those children . . . left in the street . . . while they took their mothers and fathers away. There are videos of that. He celebrated those moments, Arpaio did."

"And I think it is only fair we should celebrate this one moment."

A week later, nothing had been decided. The United States Attorney in Phoenix declined to take on Arpaio's case, citing a conflict of interest and referring it instead to the agency Arpaio had long said was out to get him—the justice department in Washington, D.C.

In the Arizona Republican Party headquarters in central Phoenix, a large portrait of Ronald Reagan hung on the wall above a table holding a printer, a stack of clipboards, and a small, framed autographed photo of Sheriff Joe Arpaio, which leaned awkwardly against a cardboard box, like an afterthought. It was August 30, 2016.

Arpaio walked stiffly into the building. He seemed to be getting frail. In the last three years, he'd tripped and tumbled on a downtown Phoenix sidewalk, he couldn't climb the stairs at the Chinese theater during the Hollywood screening of *The Joe Show*, and he'd hurt his leg in a fall at the Republican National Convention. Now staffers (he called them body-guards) drove him around Maricopa County in what he called a "soccer mom van," which was easy to climb into.

Kathy Hedges, a sixty-seven-year-old retired high school teacher and lifelong Republican, led Arpaio into the kitchen and gave him a cheese-burger. She hadn't been swayed by Arpaio's criminal contempt of court referral. "A man who speaks to people's hearts is not going to get beaten," she told us. Arpaio was in good spirits, and hungry. He bit into the cheese-burger. He'd just won the primary race for sheriff, easily beating a former small-town police chief, a retired deputy, and a former posse member. If only his father, Ciro, could see him now, "I'm sure he'd be very proud," Arpaio told us. After maybe five minutes, he walked out to meet reporters. He wasn't worried about political fallout from the criminal referral, he said. He didn't think it would sway voters in the general election. After all, it was just a referral. It wasn't an indictment. He hadn't been charged with any crime. It hadn't hurt him at all in the primary election.

"So I think the voters are smart, they read through all this, and they understand me, they understand my character and personality, they understand I work hard, and they understand I come from a good family," he told a scrum of reporters.

He seemed to look forward to the upcoming election, where he'd face off against Democrat Paul Penzone again. He spoke of Ava, how he loved her, and how she'd be at his side when he celebrated his victory in November at the Hyatt Hotel in downtown Phoenix.

The next night, Arpaio opened once again for his friend Donald Trump at the Phoenix Convention Center, where Trump had delivered his historic restrictionist kickoff rally thirteen months before. But this time, the rallygoers looked angrier. They applauded mightily for Joe Arpaio, who stood in front of American flags and rambled on about the Republican National Convention, the new unsilent silent majority, the war on cops, Trump's love of cops, and Trump's restrictionist bonafides.

If there was any remaining doubt about those bonafides, Trump set it to rest that night when he presented his immigration policy, which sounded as though it had been trotted out by established Washington-based restrictionist think tanks. He quoted questionable FAIR data that vastly overstated the costs of unauthorized immigrants to the American taxpayer. And he portrayed unauthorized immigrants swarming into the United States as predacious criminals and promised it would only get worse if his Democratic opponent, Hillary Clinton, ascended to the presidency. "The result will be millions more illegal immigrants; thousands more violent horrible crimes; and total chaos and lawlessness," he said.

"We will begin moving them out, day one!" he exclaimed. Several people who said family members were murdered by undocumented immigrants were paraded onto the stage. Each one talked about the anguish of losing a loved one and dutifully endorsed Trump.

The candidate repeated his promise to build a border wall and have Mexico pay. He vowed to block federal funding for so-called sanctuary cities, localities that chose to limit their engagement with federal immigration authorities. He wanted to suspend visas from certain Muslim countries, revitalize federal-local immigration enforcement partnerships, and admit immigrants based on skills as opposed to family ties.

Trump did not acknowledge that illegal immigration from Mexico had declined dramatically. More Mexicans were leaving the United States than coming in, the Pew Research Center reported. Border Patrol apprehensions in Arizona had dropped more than 80 percent compared to a decade earlier, in 2006.

Outside the convention center, Aztec dancers crowned with elaborate feathered headpieces danced to drum beats in protest of Trump and his policies. The Arpaio-in-prison-stripes inflatable waddled on its tethers, near a companion inflatable of Donald Trump attired in a Ku Klux Klan robe.

From the beginning of the Trump-Arpaio alliance, Carlos Garcia was struck by how eerily similar the two were. As human beings. As politicians.

"I think they're very politically smart," he told us. "They may or may not be racist, but they realize that the constituencies have racist tendencies or easily buy into that."

He admired their talents as populists. "I remember hearing Arpaio speak," he said, "Like Trump, he would connect with people, tell them a story, take them through a range of emotions, and get them to a place where they would feel that he has their best interests [at heart] and he's going to solve their problems ... And then people walk out the room believing it." The two men shared the same vanities, Garcia believed, based on a "white male" assumption they could do anything they wanted and not pay the consequences.

But Garcia and his colleagues made sure there would be consequences, at least for Arpaio. After activists had engineered the road blockade at the Fountain Hills Trump rally in March, they launched the Bazta Arpaio campaign that summer. The coalition included community groups that would change Arizona's direction—Puente, Living United for Change in Arizona (LUCHA), Poder in Action, and Mijente. Bazta Arpaio aimed to prevent Arpaio's re-election. But it also took aim at Trump, who activists called the "national Arpaio."

What marked this streetwise coalition, backed by progressive foundations and labor unions, was that it signified a generational shift in the style of Latino resistance to civil rights abuses. And yet it descended from the Arizona Chicano movement pioneered by Alfredo Gutierrez, Danny Ortega, Antonio Bustamante, and Mary Rose Wilcox, the struggle against California's Proposition 187 waged by Lydia Guzman and others, the day-laborer rights movement led by Sal Reza, the Somos America marches, and the battle for justice in the *Melendres* case.

Bazta Arpaio welcomed unauthorized immigrant activists who were fighting deportations after being ensnared in Arpaio's raids. The campaign focused on signing up a voting bloc of eligible nonvoters that others had discounted, celebrated Mexican art and culture in theatrical and unexpected ways, communicated adeptly on social media, and welcomed a diverse group of volunteers from all cultures, gender identities, and sexual orientations.

The number of eligible Latino voters was on the rise in Maricopa County. Every month, about two thousand Latinos turned eighteen and could vote. These new voters were children when Arpaio raided the streets and workplaces of the Phoenix metro area. Yet most never forgot those raids. Some had lost relatives to deportation. Some had canvassed voters for the Adiós Arpaio movement in 2012. Now they were of voting age, and dozens volunteered for Bazta Arpaio.

Their goal was to keep the "national Arpaio" from becoming president and prevent the re-election of Joe Arpaio. They hoped outrage over the local sheriff would carry over to outrage over Trump. They canvassed tirelessly. They engaged voters in a number of ways, including YouTube videos encouraging voting and palm cards showing Trump embracing Arpaio, captioned in English and Spanish with the words: "We cannot let Trump & Arpaio win! This November their time is up!"

They paraded an ancient red school bus, with traditional Mexican ranchera music pouring out of its speakers, up and down quiet cul-de-sacs as they canvassed neighborhoods. They demonstrated in front of the United States Attorney's Office in support of Arpaio's prosecution.

Their trademarks became the ungainly inflatables depicting Arpaio in handcuffs and Trump in a Ku Klux Klan robe. They wanted to show the Latino community, activist Alejandra Gomez told us, "it was possible to remove these clown-type people from office."

One day in September 2016, a group of Republican business people gathered at the exclusive Phoenix Country Club to raise money for Democrat Paul Penzone, running for a second time against Arpaio in the upcoming sheriff's race. As guests nibbled on crudités, Penzone focused on the harm he believed Arpaio brought to the business community. He said he wanted to live in a state that wasn't known around the world as the place "where that wacky sheriff lives." He said if elected, he wouldn't send a SWAT team out to get unauthorized immigrants. He highlighted litigation costs of Arpaio lawsuits to county taxpayers—two hundred million dollars and counting.

Beau Lane, a lifelong Republican who owned a Phoenix advertising agency, told us Republicans wanted to donate to Penzone but "feared reprisals" from Arpaio "even now." As someone in the marketing and branding business, he told us, "I don't like the way that our community is portrayed through that office—either locally or nationally and internationally. I do a lot of travel and I'm really growing weary of hearing about the craziness of what's happening in our community. And, you know, I think Joe has been there long enough; it's time for him to move on."

That same fall, 54 percent of Arizonans in a statewide poll viewed Arpaio unfavorably or very unfavorably. In Maricopa County, the number jumped to 57 percent. A later poll indicated the majority of Arizonans did not want a border wall and disagreed that all unauthorized immigrants should be deported. The same poll showed Arpaio lagging behind Penzone by fifteen points.

The Arizona Republic hadn't endorsed Arpaio in years. "Arpaio's cactus-kicking version of a good old boy lawman included institutionalizing a system of racial profiling against Latinos, who make up nearly one-third of Maricopa County," the newspaper wrote when it endorsed Penzone.

Taken together, the polling and the erosion of Arpaio's Republican base evidenced at the gathering at the Phoenix Country Club indicated many Maricopa County voters had tired of restrictionism and were ready to move on. Perhaps sensing the state's Arpaio fatigue, the progressive philanthropist George Soros started a political action committee, which spent over three million dollars to defeat Arpaio.

George Soros "can spend billions to get rid of me," Arpaio told the Tea Party Patriots in Surprise, Arizona. In a meandering talk to the friendly conservative group whose representatives had once met with Donald Trump to discuss Obama's birth certificate, Arpaio emphasized his birther credentials. He said the sheriff's race was "tough" and "they're coming after the sheriff." His campaign had raised close to thirteen million dollars, much of it from out-of-state donors. Penzone had raised about one million dollars.

As the election drew near, Arpaio was shocked to learn he would indeed be prosecuted for criminal contempt of court. On October 11, 2016, John Keller, a lawyer for the justice department's Public Integrity Section in

Washington, announced in a federal court hearing that he would prosecute Arpaio for at least one criminal count for violating Snow's 2011 preliminary injunction. Keller said he'd pursue a misdemeanor charge rather than a felony, which meant a maximum sentence of six months of prison time for Arpaio.

Later the justice department would decline to prosecute three others who Snow had referred for possible criminal prosecution—Jerry Sheridan, Captain Steven Bailey, and attorney Michele Iafrate. Prosecutors said the statute of limitations had passed. For the same reason, the justice department couldn't prosecute Arpaio for two additional counts of contempt stemming from failing to disclose to the court materials related to Dennis Montgomery and the Seattle Investigation.

Arpaio believed the criminal referral, just days before early voting began in Maricopa County, amounted to political retaliation for his investigation of Obama's birth certificate. "In 2011, I started the fake birth certificate investigation," he told us. "They didn't want me around."

Shortly before the election, Bazta Arpaio threw a street-fair-like Arpaio "retirement party" outside his downtown office with food trucks, the red school bus, a disc jockey, and the Trump and Arpaio inflatables. Five hundred volunteer canvassers had knocked on thirteen thousand doors hoping to sign up voters.

Now Bazta Arpaio volunteers—including immigrant mothers who had once been jailed in Arpaio's worksite raids—joined hands and sang, *Va a caer, va a caer, el Arpaio va a caer* ("He's going down, he's going down, Arpaio's going down").

Arpaio, dressed in a tan jacket, watched from the sheriff's office lobby.

On election night, Arpaio and Ava did not show up at the Republican watch party at the Hyatt Regency Phoenix hotel, as Arpaio had promised back when he'd won the primary race. Instead, Arpaio hunkered down a few blocks away in his downtown Phoenix office, watching the results. When it was clear he'd lost his bid for his seventh term, he phoned Paul Penzone and offered his congratulations. Penzone thanked Arpaio for his service. Then Arpaio went home to Fountain Hills.

As a sad-faced uniformed posse member worked security at the Republican gala, most partygoers seemed not terribly upset by Arpaio's loss. They were, instead, elated that Donald Trump had defeated Hillary Clinton in the presidential race. They jumped, hugged, and teared up over Trump's win. One man blew a horn each time Trump scored electoral votes. "Hillary must be squealing like a stuffed pig!" another man yelled. "Lock her up!" people shouted. "USA! USA! USA!"

Kathryn Kobor and Pam Pearson settled into a sofa in the lobby of the hotel, preferring to watch the election returns away from the noisy crowd. Kobor was "thunderstruck" when Arpaio lost the election. "My first thought was 'OMG we're going to get millions of people rushing our southern border,'" Kobor wrote us in an email. "We will no longer have our 'Support Joe Arpaio' rallies,'" she wrote. "What will I do with my dozens of handmade Sheriff Joe signs??? My 'God Bless Sheriff Joe' shirt will be retired. I can no longer display the pink underwear at rallies. I will have to take my 'Sheriff Joe' posters down from my Sheriff Joe room."

That same night, Lydia Guzman stood with Tom Black on a carpet with dizzying wave motifs that covered the ballroom floor of the Renaissance Hotel in downtown Phoenix. CNN displayed election updates on a large screen at one end of the room. As the couple mingled with old friends at the Democratic watch party, they began to receive surprising news. Donald Trump unexpectedly had begun winning the presidency, electoral vote by electoral vote.

"God help us if Trump wins. If he does, it will be like Arpaio all over. But on steroids," Guzman texted us.

As soon as she got the word that Arpaio had lost, Guzman and her husband headed back home. She and her fellow activists had worked so hard for so many years to register voters even as they struggled to fight unconstitutional state immigration laws and strip Arpaio of his power in legal battles. Still, she wasn't as happy as she thought she'd be. Because even though she'd helped defeat restrictionism in Arizona, she knew it would soon go national with a Donald Trump presidency.

"I remember I was happy about the results with the sheriff losing," she told us. "But the moment that we started to see the numbers for Trump winning, I wanted to run. I don't remember how we got into the car . . . I was numb, and I just wanted to run like a war had broken out."

For the young Bazta Arpaio activists, the sheriff's defeat early in the night was a victory that was a cause for celebration. Garcia and the Bazta Arpaio volunteers gathered at a public park near Mary Rose Wilcox's restaurant. The Arpaio inflatable, now slightly deflated, served as a backdrop for a mariachi band. Many of the 150 or so partygoers danced. They then marched a few blocks to the sheriff's office, chanting: "Joe Arpaio is guilty, guilty! The whole damn system is guilty, guilty!" They posted a large banner on the front doors of the sheriff's office.

~~SHERIFF~~ JOE EVICTION NOTICE

FOR CRIMES AGAINST HUMANITY

"This is proof," Garcia told us, "that our community can move mountains."

Alfredo Gutierrez was at the Bazta Arpaio celebration, too. First he gave a speech congratulating the young volunteers. Then he talked to us. Arpaio "lost his base, and he lost his base simply because his life, his actions caught up to him. The signs of the financial losses, the lawsuits, the hundreds of millions it is costing this county and its taxpayers to keep this criminal fool a sheriff, had simply become too great a burden."

"What I look forward to now," he told us, "is the day we accompany him to jail. We will be there. Even if it's a symbolic one day."

We dialed Arpaio's cell phone several times over the course of the evening, but he didn't pick up. When we reached him the next morning, his voice faltered and he sounded exhausted. And angry. He blamed the Obama justice department and George Soros for his loss. "I don't know what the future holds for me," he told us. Then he perked up a little.

"Don't forget. I retired once before."

III Changes
2016–2019

20 The National Arpaio

2016–2017

Lydia Guzman and Tom Black married beneath an antique town clock in a city park. It was December 10, 2016, a year to the day the two had their first date at La Barquita, the Mexican restaurant. They chose to say their vows at Murphy Park in Glendale, Arizona. They timed the ceremony to coincide with the sunset, which tinged the sky lilac. The park glittered with thousands of holiday lights. Guzman wore her pearls, a black jacket, and black pants. Black bought a new charcoal gray suit for the occasion. This was her fifth marriage, his second. And they sort of eloped.

Black hadn't invited anyone. He knew some relatives privately might not approve of him marrying a Latina. This bothered him, and he didn't want any such ugliness at his wedding. Guzman hadn't invited her kids, her mother, or her friends. Her sister, Sylvia, and husband, also named Tom, were the only ones invited, and they served as witnesses. A justice of the peace, who was a friend, met the tiny wedding party at the town clock.

The couple had chosen to marry quietly in part because Guzman didn't want anyone to judge her as she said her vows. Yes, it was her fifth marriage. She didn't need any cynical guest to point that out. Or even think it.

253

The ceremony was short, dignified, romantic—exactly what the couple wanted. They celebrated with dinner at an Italian restaurant. Black felt "almost euphoric." Guzman had a strong feeling that this time, she could make it work.

Only the looming Trump presidency, and Guzman's fear that what happened in Arizona with Joe Arpaio would soon repeat itself all across the nation, ate away at her.

As Joe Arpaio's staff prepared for the transition to a new administration at the sheriff's office, there was no longer time to arrange meet-and-greets with the departing sheriff's fans. For years, admirers all over the country had called his office seeking face-to-face meetings, according to his secretary Amy Lake. She told us some people included in their bucket lists the experience of shaking Arpaio's hand. The ritual of meeting admirers in the sheriff's office, like so many others that Arpaio relished, was winding down.

Few official tasks remained for Arpaio now that he'd lost the election. A month before he moved out of his fifth-floor office with the window that looked out on the federal courthouse, Arpaio staged one of his last media events. In this one, he said goodbye to posse members who patrolled shopping mall parking lots in an effort to protect holiday shoppers from thieves.

Dressed in his tan uniform, the sheriff stood on a cracked asphalt parking lot fronting a nearly empty central Phoenix shopping mall. Staffers had parked a black bus emblazoned with the sheriff's gold insignia as a backdrop. It was likely one of the same vehicles where, years before, recently arrested immigrants had been processed as Alfredo Gutierrez and Danny Ortega yelled *¡No digan nada!* ("Don't say anything!"), *¡Pidan hablar con un abogado!* ("Ask to speak to a lawyer!") through bullhorns. But those days were over. The once-fearsome command center had turned into a television-news-friendly stage set as the lame duck sheriff spoke to the glum posse members, some with tears in their eyes. A handful of staffers stood by, as well as fourteen reporters and a fan who happened to be passing through the parking lot and stopped to listen.

Standing in front of the familiar mics on a chilly cloudy afternoon, the outgoing sheriff reminisced about his career and the department he'd headed for twenty-four years. He hinted he was available to take a job in Trump's cabinet. "If the president of the United States calls, I have to serve my country," he said.

A reporter asked Arpaio if he had a message for many in the Latino community who were happy to see him leave office. "I never had any problems with Hispanics," he answered. "Why all at once since I started the crackdown on illegal immigration ten years ago, the whole sky seems to be falling. Why? Just trying to do my job." Asked by reporters if he would apologize to Latino families separated in his raids, he refused.

As the press conference wound down, Arpaio told us he'd recently advised President-elect Trump that the 287(g) federal-local immigration partnerships were a great program. With such a like-minded president, he said he was sad to leave the sheriff's office, because with Trump in power, things could get "very interesting."

"I'm the type of guy, I will never ask Trump for anything," he said.

His criminal contempt of court trial loomed. We asked if the case didn't go his way, would he accept a pardon from the new president? He seemed to hold out hope prosecutors would drop the case before the trial. "I would like to think that no matter what there is no case to begin with, ok? So we will see how that pans out. I am a funny guy, when I think I am right I don't surrender," he told us. To Arpaio, the criminal charge for disobeying Snow's orders simply represented the tail end of the Obama administration going after him.

In mid-December, Joe Arpaio held his final press conference as sheriff. The large room at the sheriff's department training center was half empty. There were a few poker-faced staffers, along with someone wearing a T-shirt sporting the infowars.com logo, and several Tea Party members from Surprise, Arizona. The sheriff chose a favorite conspiracy theory for his theme, and said he'd solved it. After a five-year investigation, he falsely proclaimed that Barack Obama had a "fake, fake birth certificate." His associates, all devoted birthers, presented the "findings"—long-discredited allegations about mismatched fonts, along with the theory that Obama's birth certificate was forged off of a real document belonging to a woman born in Hawaii.

"All we have ever wanted, ever wanted was the truth in this matter— with the great hope that the document was indeed a valid representation of the original document," Arpaio said smugly. "Think of that. We were trying to clear the president. It didn't work out that way."

Someone in the room streamed the event on Facebook Live. The posted responses from Facebook viewers revealed how well the birther conspiracy theory resonated with some members of the sheriff's fan base. "White Power," one person wrote.

"I would love to see imposter Obama and his whole gang led away in chains," wrote another.

And someone else posted misspelled versions of the N-word, in an apparent effort to not get bumped off Facebook while still communicating the harmful slur to fellow white supremacists.

Cowboy boots hung from the ceiling of the Buffalo Chip Saloon, a barbecue joint in Cave Creek. Western-themed beer signs, a horse collar, cowboy hats, a rifle, a portrait of Wyatt Earp, and bucking bronco license plates covered the dining room walls. Two sheet cakes—decorated with *Congratulations, thank you for your service* in blue icing—sat on side tables, near a framed poster listing ten commandments for cowboys, which included corny, faux western colloquialisms like: "Honer yer Ma & Pa."

The close air in the room smelled of alcohol and smoked meat. Sheriff's office employees, fans, and political allies had packed the large restaurant to say goodbye to Arpaio and his chief deputy, Jerry Sheridan, who was retiring.

Cave Creek hadn't changed much in the nine years since Arpaio's deputies had unconstitutionally detained Manuel de Jesus Ortega Melendres, triggering the lawsuit in which Snow finally put an end to Arpaio's immigration raids and ordered him to reform the sheriff's office. And even though everyone in the room likely knew Arpaio would soon face a criminal trial, only Russell Pearce publicly besmirched Judge Snow.

Pearce, the recalled state senator who had pushed so many restrictionist bills through the Arizona legislature, including Senate Bill 1070, wore a large white cowboy hat as he toasted the sheriff. Arpaio, Pearce thundered, was "not in contempt of law, he's in contempt of a liberal judge."

"Shame on that man," Pearce said of Judge Snow, "and shame on Congress for not having the guts to remove those kinds of judges from office."

Russell Pearce pays tribute to outgoing Sheriff Joe Arpaio
and his wife, Ava, at the Buffalo Chip Saloon and Steakhouse
in Cave Creek, Arizona on December 17, 2016. (Authors'
photo)

Ava, in one of her first public appearances since her cancer treatments, did not take off her warm animal print coat. She sat next to her husband and smiled. The two picked at mounds of chicken, ribs, beans, coleslaw, corn on the cob, and cornbread that someone with a much larger appetite had plated for them.

Republican governor Doug Ducey stopped by to shake the sheriff's hand, then made a quick exit. As Barb Heller sliced up and served the cake, Arpaio reminisced as usual about his long law enforcement career and his halcyon days as Maricopa County sheriff. His outgoing chief deputy, Sheridan, teared up when he spoke about those days and about what a magnificent boss Arpaio had been. At the end of the evening, a jail detention officer who doubled as an Elvis Presley impersonator and the sheriff formed a duet and sang "My Way"—"Regrets, I've had a few, but then again, too few to mention."

Arpaio sometimes quoted from his signature song to boast about how he and Trump were so much alike. "My personality is something like Trump. We seem to be traveling the same highway," he said, borrowing from the lyrics "I traveled each and every highway."

On inauguration evening, January 20, 2017, about a month after he was feted at the Buffalo Chip Saloon, Joe Arpaio was Donald Trump's guest at the inaugural Liberty Ball at the Walter E. Washington Convention Center in the nation's capital. It turned out that along with sharing a fondness for conspiracy theories, a birthday, personality traits, and political viewpoints with Joe Arpaio, Trump also liked Arpaio's favorite song. When the band struck up "My Way" for Trump's first dance as president of the United States, Arpaio was gobsmacked as he watched the new president and his white-gowned wife box-step to the music. Arpaio was thrilled. Later, he told us how he felt at the time: "He's playing 'My Way' with the First Lady there. Hey, what is this? My own song! There's a million songs, patriotic songs, all . . . He's playing *my* song! Think of that!"

He missed Ava, who had stayed in Arizona. Chris Hegstrom, Arpaio's former media relations director, shepherded Arpaio through Trump's inaugural events.

Five days after the presidential inauguration, the former sheriff sat at the defense table in Judge Susan Bolton's courtroom at the federal court-house in Phoenix. Bolton, who had stayed Senate Bill 1070 back in 2010, was assigned to preside over Arpaio's upcoming criminal trial that stemmed from Judge Snow's findings after the long on-again, off-again civil contempt hearing.

Lawyers for the justice department had prepared to prosecute Arpaio for the last several months, painstakingly going over thousands of court records, trying to catch up with ten years of litigation in *Melendres*. But they knew their new boss Attorney General Jeff Sessions could close the case, leaving Judge Bolton to appoint a special prosecutor who would have to start over. Or President Trump could preemptively pardon his friend ahead of time, closing any possibility for a trial.

Chimal Garcia was a champion chess player and an avid Phoenix Suns basketball team fan. But the ten-year-old son of Carlos Garcia and Alexis

Aguirre was also sensitive to what it meant to be an unauthorized immigrant. He'd tagged along with his father to visit an undocumented relative in a federal immigration detention center. And, like many children, he was upset by the election of the new president because he worried about friends and family members who were undocumented.

"We had kids crying the day after the election," Chimal told us. "I was really sad when I woke up and I heard that [Trump's victory]. He's not my President but he was elected, and he was . . . I was really scared. I couldn't go to sleep for those first five days that I knew that he was elected."

He asked his parents, "What's going to happen?"

"I was just really worried," Chimal said.

Chimal told us that during that time, a close school friend, who had a parent who was a Trump supporter, told him: "You're Mexican, you're probably going to get deported by Trump, too!"

"I tried to explain it like . . . people who cross, that they're risking their lives. They're risking everything just so their kids have a fighting chance and so that they can be here and they can have more opportunities," Chimal recalled. The two boys remained friends but stopped talking about undocumented people.

The incident hurt the father as much as the son. When he looked back on the last decade, Carlos Garcia realized he'd awakened every morning and thought about how to stop Joe Arpaio. But now that Arpaio was no longer sheriff, Garcia's work had only gotten more challenging. Trump, he told us, was a "bigger enemy."

Now he wondered if he could teach others to resist Trump as he had resisted Arpaio in Arizona. Could his brand of activism be effective on a national scale? It had been informed by years of struggle—being undocumented himself for much of his childhood, working with Sal Reza and the day laborers, being spit at during the Pruitt's furniture store protests, videotaping Arpaio's traffic stops with CopWatch, being taunted by Minutemen, organizing street actions, boycotts, hunger strikes, bus trips, fighting Arpaio's worksite raids in court, going to jail, getting out the vote.

Still, ever since the election, Garcia had been called out of state to advise other activists about how to resist Trump. He hoped the lessons he'd learned in Arizona would translate. He vowed to serve his community and fight for change as long as he was useful. As long as he could be helpful. As long as he had fresh ideas.

Because now, a more ferocious conflict loomed.

Within days of moving into the White House, President Donald Trump began steering the nation into an era of Arizona-style restrictionism. He issued a series of executive actions, some of which would be challenged in the courts. The new president ordered the withholding of federal grants from cities that had chosen not to cooperate with the federal government on immigration enforcement (the so-called sanctuary cities). He ended Obama-era prosecutorial discretion by establishing more strict deportation priorities. He ordered the expansion of the 287(g) federal-local immigration partnerships that had encouraged Arpaio's unconstitutional policing. He pushed for the construction of the southern border wall. He set up an office within ICE that would later establish an Arpaio-like hotline for victims of crimes allegedly perpetrated by "removable aliens." He banned foreign nationals from seven predominantly Muslim countries from entering the United States.

Guzman and Black joined hundreds of others on a cold Sunday afternoon at the Phoenix Sky Harbor International Airport to protest the president's travel ban, which critics called a "Muslim ban."

It was Black's first protest. He carried a sign that said No H8. He'd once believed that "no Muslims are good Muslims," he told us, but then he realized his earlier feelings about Muslims were "all hogwash."

"It felt good," Guzman told us, to protest with such a large, diverse crowd. It was exactly what she needed after the bruising presidential election.

"It was a sense of, okay, there is light, we can do this, we can do this."

A few days later, a federal judge temporarily stayed Trump's travel ban. And that was in part thanks to Cecillia Wang, of the American Civil Liberties Union Immigrants' Rights Project, who was also a key plaintiffs' lawyer in Melendres. She understood Arpaio's place in the growing national restrictionist movement led by his friend Trump. "The policies that Joe Arpaio pioneered, that Arizona then implemented . . . those are the policies that President Trump and his administration are trying to implement on a nationwide basis," she told us. "They want to expand the

287(g) program, they want local agencies to do more immigration enforcement. And we of all people, who have been involved in this [*Melendres*] case, who live in this country, know where that road leads."

In her view, that road led to constitutional abuses. But to restrictionists, local immigration enforcement was a good thing. And Trump was surrounding himself with restrictionist advisors. He'd listened to Joe Arpaio during the campaign, and now one of the most vociferous restrictionists in the United States Senate, Jeff Sessions, had become Trump's attorney general. Sessions's former aide, Stephen Miller, was a devoted Trump advisor. A gifted writer, Miller penned many of Trump's nativist speeches. He and Sessions had worked together on Trump's Phoenix rally in 2016, the one in which Arpaio introduced Trump, and where Trump had laid out his immigration policy and disparaged immigrants. Miller collaborated with another key advisor, Steve Bannon, formerly of Breitbart News, to write the so-called Muslim ban. Kris Kobach, who'd authored Senate Bill 1070, was an on-again, off-again visitor to the White House. With such allies in place, restrictionist organizations such as FAIR and the Center for Immigration Studies had unprecedented access to the president.

Alfredo Gutierrez, a student of history, sensed a rebirth of the early twentieth century eugenics movement in the Trump administration. People hated Mexican Americans and other "swarthies" in the 1920s, he told us. Now another cycle of hatred was sweeping across the nation. "All of us have to accept it is a genuine and ongoing part of America," he said.

In Arizona, where one cycle of nativism was getting beaten down, newly elected Maricopa County sheriff Paul Penzone was sworn into office by Judge Mary Murguia. It had been seven years since the judge had recused herself from the *Melendres* case. Now she was a judge for the Ninth Circuit Court of Appeals. Danny Ortega, who attended the swearing in ceremony at the Heard Museum in Phoenix, viewed it as "poetic justice."

During Penzone's run for sheriff, Ortega had introduced the candidate at different events and had contributed money to his campaign. Ortega was respected by Republicans and Democrats alike for his level-headedness, his ability to listen to the other side. He'd rarely been the loudest voice in the room. He was often in the background, working on civil rights cases or advising immigrant-rights activists seeking justice.

Just a few months before the Penzone swearing-in, Ortega had helped negotiate a settlement over the enforcement of what remained of Senate Bill 1070 with Attorney General Mark Brnovich, a conservative Arizona Republican.

Snow's *Melendres* ruling, the one that said immigrants could not be detained by local law enforcement unless they were suspected of committing crimes, heavily influenced the settlement. Now Arizona law enforcement officers were not supposed to detain someone simply for being in the country without proper documents.

Senate Bill 1070 had been largely neutralized, many thought.

Still, witnessing the Penzone swearing in, Ortega told us, "was bittersweet to say the least" in the wake of Trump's election. "I mean, to see Trump get elected was shocking because I never believed that he could win," Ortega told us. "And given the way he treated our community, I couldn't believe that we would have to deal with—on a national level—what we dealt with on a local level through Sheriff Arpaio. So it was like, wait a minute, we get rid of one and get a bigger one."

Arizona was moving away from extremism, thanks to the gritty activism that had risen up against it. Ortega remained hopeful the nation would eventually follow the same path. He advised out-of-state activists resisting Trump's restrictionist agenda to "be aggressive in challenging this behavior, these laws, these regulations in the courts and on the streets."

"Don't give up because we were there once, too," Ortega told them.

Guadalupe Garcia de Rayos didn't know what to do.

She worried she'd soon be separated from her husband and two American citizen kids now that Donald Trump had taken office and issued his executive orders. She found her way to the Puente headquarters in central Phoenix. There she met with Carlos Garcia and others and explained her situation.

She'd been arrested by Arpaio's deputies several years before during a worksite raid at a local water park, where she'd worked at the time. Like so many unauthorized immigrants arrested by Arpaio, she was jailed and then placed in deportation proceedings.

She fought to remain in Phoenix. It worked, for a while. Even though an immigration judge had ordered her deportation in 2013, ICE had allowed her to stay. By then, Arizona immigration lawyers had highlighted a conflict between ICE and the justice department. Since federal immigration courts were part of the justice department, and since the justice department was arguing in *United States v. Maricopa County* that Arpaio's worksite raids violated the civil rights of Latino workers, ICE, a federal agency, should not deport immigrants arrested and charged in those same raids, the attorneys pointed out. As a result, many pending deportation cases against immigrants caught in Arpaio's raids were administratively closed starting in 2013. In the Garcia de Rayos case, ICE used its discretion not to enforce her deportation.

Things changed when Trump issued new executive orders saying that any immigrant with a deportation order, even Arpaio's worksite raid victims, were prioritized for deportation.

Garcia de Rayos had been reporting each year to the ICE office in Phoenix. Soon she would have to report again. If she showed up for her appointment, she would probably get deported. If she stayed at home, ICE knew how to find her. She decided to rely on Puente to whip up public sympathy for her case.

As Garcia de Rayos feared, she was taken into custody when she showed up to her ICE appointment. That night, Carlos Garcia and about a hundred Puente volunteers gathered at the ICE building, the same place where Melendres had been wrongfully detained ten years before. The protesters blocked the driveway, where a van carrying Garcia de Rayos and other deportees would exit. They carried posters showing Garcia de Rayos, her husband, and their two American citizen teenagers gathered around a Christmas tree.

When the white van carrying Garcia de Rayos, who was thirty-five years old, slinked down the driveway and stopped in the crowd, seven activists chained themselves to it. Garcia de Rayos looked out the window as her children knelt in front of the van.

The tactic of chaining activists to vehicles had shut down ICE maneuvers in the Obama era. But they weren't as effective in the Trump era. Phoenix police officers unchained the protesters and arrested them. The van headed to Nogales, Sonora, Mexico.

Antonio Bustamante watched the van drive away, leaving in its wake another divided immigrant family. He had seen so much hate in his life.

He'd bodyguarded Cesar Chavez, who had made enemies simply by advocating for farmworkers. He'd gone after ranchers who'd tortured Mexican immigrants. He'd yelled legal advice through a bullhorn to victims of Arpaio's sweeps. But now, he told us, the country was becoming hostile to immigrants on a scale he had never seen. "Trump and his advisors," Bustamante said, "care absolutely nothing about the lives that are being shattered by this kind of new policy."

Lydia Guzman watched the protest on Facebook Live. She'd criticized Puente in the past for parading immigrants around to get attention. That night, though, she realized the efficacy of Garcia's actions, which focused international media attention on the human cost of Trump's new immigration policies.

"Those kids," she told us, "they do great."

21 The Rescue

2017

Lydia Guzman was comforted by the familiar scene of demonstrators standing on the sidewalk of the federal courthouse in Phoenix. They'd taken to showing up with signs depicting Joe Arpaio as a cartoonish convict. It was July 6, 2017, the last day of Arpaio's criminal contempt of court trial in Judge Susan Bolton's courtroom. It was not publicly known at the time, but before the trial began, Attorney General Jeff Sessions had refused Trump's request to drop the case. The case was moving forward and soon Arpaio would either be convicted or acquitted.

In the eyes of many in the resistance, the former sheriff, now eighty-five, had been rendered powerless. He was now almost as clownish and irrelevant as his goofy likenesses on the protesters' signs. Stripped of his immigration enforcement power by Snow and voted out of office in 2016, Arpaio was, in their eyes, defanged. He no longer evoked terror.

"He's only a caricature . . . He's nothing more," Antonio Bustamante told us.

Alfredo Gutierrez told us that he now thought of Arpaio as a weakened "old racist that every so often gets to go on television and spew some hate."

But as pathetic as Arpaio seemed to them now, they still viewed him as a powerful symbol of race-based restrictionism in a state with a long and uncomfortable history of animus toward Latinos. Arpaio's conviction for criminal contempt of court, and a possible but unlikely sentence of up to six months in a federal prison, would be a symbolic victory for the movement that had battled him for so many years.

For Guzman, who clung to faith in American institutions, Arpaio's conviction and sentencing would mean all that and more. It would prove her enduring trust in the justice department and federal judiciary had not been misplaced. The justice department had disappointed many in the movement for years with sluggish investigations and tepid court settlements, but now it could redeem itself—and Guzman—by successfully prosecuting Arpaio and obtaining a conviction.

And that moment, many thought, was drawing closer in Judge Susan Bolton's courtroom. In decor and demeanor, Bolton's courtroom resembled Snow's courtroom on the sixth floor. There were long tables for the defense and prosecution, and rows of austere, pew-like benches for spectators. Bolton, a self-assured jurist with brown hair and a big diamond ring, sat at a tidy desk equipped with a canister of sharpened yellow pencils. She was attentive and calm, just as she had been seven years before, when she stayed Senate Bill 1070.

Guzman and Tom Black squeezed onto a bench. Daniel Magos, who still suffered recurring flashbacks from the time he was stopped and frisked by a deputy during a traffic stop in 2009, was already seated. So was Sal Reza, Dr. Angeles Maldonado and her husband, Ray Ybarra Maldonado, and Danny Ortega, who came in a few minutes late and had to sit on the floor.

Arpaio's family, as far as we could see, did not attend the criminal contempt of court trial, which was not unusual. We'd not seen them in court during the years we'd covered the *Melendres* case. But on this day Arpaio did have supporters—white men and women in pastel-hued polo shirts, Arpaio's campaign manager Chad Willems, and former chief deputy Jerry Sheridan. Barb Heller was there too, rocking quietly on a bench and shaking her head. She told us she didn't understand how Arpaio could be charged with a crime for enforcing the law. She insisted he would never intentionally disobey a federal judge.

Joe Arpaio slumped on his elbows at the defense table. He had energetically fundraised for his legal defense. The National Center for Police

Defense, a controversial nonprofit billing itself as "a pro-law enforcement organization," reportedly raised at least five hundred thousand dollars for Arpaio's legal defense. This was done in part by sending out a hyperbolic fundraising letter on Arpaio's behalf that claimed justice department lawyers were "hoping to put him in jail for the rest of his life!"

We asked the former sheriff how much he'd accumulated in his defense fund, which was not public record. He wouldn't tell us.

At the time of his criminal contempt of court case, Arpaio had already admitted in court that he'd committed civil contempt of court in connection with disobeying Snow's 2011 order. When Arpaio admitted to civil contempt, he claimed he had not intentionally disobeyed the judge. It was just an innocent mistake.

A few months before his criminal trial, Arpaio had tried to take back his admission of civil contempt. In court filings, Arpaio now claimed he had been led to believe he would be spared criminal contempt charges if he admitted to civil contempt. His earlier admission was "coerced," he claimed. He blamed Judge Snow for misleading him. And he said his own attorney had provided ineffective counsel. Arpaio's attorney Mel McDonald quickly withdrew from the case, which seemed to be the point of Arpaio's filing the motion in the first place. Arpaio's new legal team included Mark Goldman, a stocky lawyer with a long black curly ponytail, matching goatee, and silver earrings, along with Phoenix attorney Dennis Wilenchik and his son, Jack.

The closing arguments were the last chance for the justice department to prove beyond a reasonable doubt that Snow's order was clear, that Arpaio knew about it, and that he intentionally violated it.

John Keller, the justice department prosecutor, was dispassionate, straightforward, and organized. He cited prior testimony and Arpaio's public pronouncements to show Arpaio received, understood, and intentionally flouted Snow's order for seventeen months. (This was the time period in which Samuel, the floor tile installer who'd been a passenger in a truck stopped by Deputy Charley Armendariz, was wrongfully detained and turned over for deportation.) Keller contended Arpaio wanted to win votes in the 2012 election and thus "cast himself as an anti-federal government immigration hardliner. He wanted to raise money and he wanted to get re-elected and it worked."

"He did so at the expense of a federal judge's order, and in defying that order he committed criminal contempt."

Judge Bolton slowly twirled a pencil in her fingers and listened.

"Nobody gets to defy a federal judge's order," Keller concluded, "especially not the head law enforcement officer of an entire county. He should be found guilty."

Dennis Wilenchik, Arpaio's lawyer, wore an elegant black suit for closing arguments. Wilenchik tried to persuade Bolton that Snow's order was unclear and muddy, and that Arpaio had not intentionally violated it. "The only one who understood what Snow meant was Snow himself," he said. Wilenchik argued it was common practice in Arizona for police departments to turn over suspected undocumented immigrants to Border Patrol, just as Arpaio had done. He argued Snow's 2011 order did not make clear the sheriff's office could no longer contact and cooperate with federal immigration authorities when deputies came across suspected undocumented immigrants. He portrayed the sheriff as a dedicated career law enforcement professional who would never intentionally defy the federal judiciary.

The justice department's suggestion that Arpaio enforced immigration as a way to raise money and get votes for his 2012 campaign, Wilenchik said, was inaccurate. Arpaio never had trouble winning an election. He didn't disobey a federal judge to win this one.

"This prosecution is wrongful, it was political, it achieved its success, now it is nothing but an embarrassment to the federal government for having brought this," Wilenchik concluded. "And I ask you to find the sheriff not guilty."

After closing arguments ended, we hung back with Arpaio as he lingered in the courthouse lobby, avoiding the scrum of reporters outside on the patio. We asked him how he felt, now that the criminal trial was over. He told us he didn't feel anything. We asked whether he'd ask Trump for a presidential pardon. He said he didn't need Trump to interfere in his business. Trump was, after all, busy taking care of North Korea. (The president had been sparring with North Korean leader Kim Jong-un, who had provocatively tested missiles and nuclear weapons as a show of strength against the United States.)

When Arpaio finally exited the courthouse, he ignored the Spanish-speaking demonstrators waving placards depicting him as a clownish convict. He stepped quickly into his lawyer's Bentley, which purred down Washington Street and out of sight.

Lydia Guzman sensed Bolton could rule either way. No matter the outcome of the trial, she decided, the community had taken on a powerful tormentor. The resistance had never backed down and could be proud of that, regardless of the trial's outcome.

About three weeks after the closing arguments, Guzman was driving Tom Black to the Cheesecake Factory for lunch with friends on his day off when the first text message came through on her phone. It was from longtime activist Carmen Cornejo.

"Guilty verdict! Congratulations!"

Guzman nearly crashed her SUV. She pulled over to focus on her phone, exploding with text messages and social media alerts. The Latino community finally had its vindication. Judge Bolton's ruling showed that Joe Arpaio was the real criminal—not the Latino Americans his deputies had pulled over, not the undocumented immigrants he'd arrested and turned over for deportation in defiance of Snow's order. Guzman looked over at her husband and apologized. There would be no Cheesecake Factory lunch, and he'd be stuck watching reporters interview his wife all day. Black didn't care. "I'm proud of you," he said.

Back at her office Guzman pulled up Judge Bolton's fourteen-page ruling on her computer.

Bolton ruled Snow's 2011 order wasn't muddy and confusing, as Arpaio's defense lawyer contended. It was clear. It explicitly forbade Arpaio and his deputies from detaining immigrants and turning them over to federal immigration authorities simply because the immigrants were undocumented. And, Bolton ruled, Arpaio's lawyers explained the order to the sheriff. But despite that, at least twenty times, in press releases and public statements, Arpaio insisted he would continue enforcing immigration laws. "Not only did Defendant abdicate responsibility, he announced to the world and to his subordinates that he was going to continue business as usual no matter who said otherwise," Bolton wrote.

For years, Guzman had smarted when fellow activists had criticized her for selling out the Latino community by working with the justice department. But now, the justice department finally had delivered. Arpaio, who she thought of as the "poster boy" for white supremacy, would be remembered in history as a criminal, not as America's Toughest Sheriff. All over Maricopa County, activists celebrated.

Sal Reza hastily called a press conference in front of the federal courthouse. Wearing khakis and a black polo shirt, his white hair pulled back in a ponytail, Reza told reporters he hoped for the maximum sentence for Arpaio: six months in a federal penitentiary.

"I know a lot of people are going to say he is elderly now, and he served all his life in law enforcement and all of that. But anybody else that disobeys a federal judge has to pay a high price," Reza said. He acknowledged the possibility that Arpaio might be rescued by a presidential pardon.

Still, no one at the press conference wanted to think too much about a presidential pardon on this day. It was enough to savor the symbolic victory.

At the central Phoenix headquarters for Tonatierra, the indigenous-rights group, fifty or so people gathered for a feast. Someone had plopped a big papier mâché mask of Arpaio's scowling face on the floor. Mary Rose Wilcox carried in two sheet cakes with Arpaio's name and the Spanish word for "guilty," *culpable*, spelled out in icing.

Alfredo Gutierrez celebrated more quietly. He'd kept tabs on Arpaio's criminal contempt of court trial and had prepared himself for an acquittal. When they learned of Arpaio's conviction, Gutierrez and his partner, Sharon Zapata, sat on their front porch and sipped Italian sparkling wine.

Arpaio's guilty verdict, to Gutierrez, was eclipsed by the unabashed white supremacy permeating the Trump presidency. This danger, Gutierrez sensed, could be as bad or worse as anything Arizona had seen under Arpaio.

Cecilia Wang sensed the danger too. The ACLU lawyer, who had helped win the *Melendres* racial profiling victory, congratulated Maricopa County residents for bringing down Arpaio. She warned in a blog: "This story did not end well for Arpaio, and each chapter inflicted terrible harms on the people of Maricopa County and civil rights and civil liberties . . . Politicians who are pushing for these backward policies should heed the lesson that Joe Arpaio learned the hard way."

Daniel Magos wished he could share the long-awaited victory with his dead wife, Eva, who had been at his side the day of their 2009 traffic stop. "You won! We won, baby!" he cried out alone in his home. Now, with the racial profiling victory in the *Melendres* case and Joe Arpaio convicted of criminal contempt of court, he felt his full Americanness had been restored. He was, for the first time in years, truly happy. He told us he hoped closing this ugly cycle in Arizona history would help people see each other as equals. At the same time, Magos indulged himself with a little schadenfreude, knowing Arpaio likely felt as powerless as he had felt the day he was pulled over in 2009.

"Whatever impotence he is feeling now," Magos wrote in his journal, "that is exactly the way I felt that morning: I felt violated, humiliated, defenseless, and intimidated."

Arpaio's supporters were dismayed by his conviction. Linda Bentley, the reporter who ten years before had indignantly written articles about the day laborers in Cave Creek, told us Judge Bolton's verdict was based on politics.

Judge Snow, an "open borders dude," had started this, she told us. She penned an op-ed in the *Sonoran News*. "This will most likely go down as the only case in history where a sixty-year career lawman is found guilty of criminal contempt for enforcing the law, stemming from a complaint originally filed against him by foreign nationals who violated the law," she wrote.

Kathryn Kobor was at first angry and discouraged after she learned about the verdict from an ABC news website. If somehow Bolton sent such an old man as Arpaio to prison, she told us, it would be "an act of cruelty and inhumanity."

She and her fellow Arpaio supporters wouldn't take it sitting down. There would be protests. Rallies. Letters and emails to Washington. And she would stand out on the street again waving a sign.

But she was an optimist, and told herself Trump would pardon her hero.

Arpaio learned the judge had issued the verdict when a reporter from a Phoenix conservative talk radio station phoned him asking for a comment. The former sheriff was surprised the verdict was in because he had assumed he'd be summoned back to court and Bolton would read him the ruling there, face to face.

"What is it, not guilty?" Arpaio asked.

"Guilty," the reporter replied.

How could this be, Arpaio thought. He could not fathom he'd done anything wrong. And now that he faced a sentencing on October 5, 2017, for the first time he contemplated his age. News stories often cited his advanced years. He told us he wondered if "Father Time has caught up with me."

"So talk about my age, actually I didn't even know how old I was, seriously, until all this has come about," he told us. "You know, why are you going to put an eighty-five-year-old person in jail?"

"Holy Christ, I am eighty-five! How many more years do I have left?"

In the days that followed, he joked he would at least get better food in a federal detention center than he would in his own jails. And he repeatedly minimized his misdemeanor conviction by likening it to the penalty for having a barking dog.

Three days after President Trump had hinted to a cheering crowd at the Phoenix Convention Center that he would pardon his friend "Sheriff Joe," the president made good on his word.

It was August 25, 2017, Ava's eighty-sixth birthday. Arpaio's lawyer Mark Goldman delivered an envelope containing the presidential pardon to the Arpaios at their home.

At the time, Hurricane Harvey was racing toward Texas and Louisiana, where it would later kill nearly a hundred Americans.

After Goldman assured Arpaio the pardon was not a fake document, Arpaio and Ava joined their son and daughter-in-law for Ava's birthday dinner at Arrivederci Cucina Italiana, an Italian restaurant near the artificial lake with its enormous spouting fountain. Arpaio barely touched his linguine with clams and calamari. Instead, he spent most of his wife's birthday dinner answering congratulatory phone calls and talking to reporters.

At one point, he talked to Fox News host Sean Hannity, a close ally of the president. "You came under fire for obeying what are the laws of the land," Hannity told Arpaio. "I applaud the president for what he did tonight. It was the right thing to do."

"Well, it's great," Arpaio crooned. "I love that president. He supports law enforcement and I am very humbled."

Arpaio asked someone that night to post his gratitude to Trump on Twitter. "I am humbled and incredibly grateful to President Trump. I look fwd to putting this chapter behind me and helping to #MAGA." He then tweeted out a link to his legal defense fund.

The president later revealed at a White House press conference that he'd chosen August 25th to grant Arpaio clemency because Hurricane Harvey had amped up television ratings.

EXECUTIVE GRANT OF CLEMENCY

DONALD J. TRUMP

President of the United States of America

To All Whom These Presents Shall Come, Greeting:

BE IT KNOWN, THAT THIS DAY, I, DONALD J. TRUMP, PRESIDENT OF THE UNITED STATES, PURSUANT TO MY POWERS UNDER ARTICLE II, SECTION 2, CLAUSE 1, OF THE CONSTITUTION, HAVE GRANTED UNTO

JOSEPH M. ARPAIO

A FULL AND UNCONDITIONAL PARDON

FOR HIS CONVICTION of Section 401(3), Title 18, United States Code (Docket No 2:16-CR-01012-SRB) in the United States District Court for the District of Arizona, of which he was convicted on July 31, 2017, and for which sentencing is currently set for October 5, 2017; and

FOR ANY OTHER OFFENSES under Chapter 21 of Title 18, United States Code that might arise, or be charged, in connection with *Melendres v. Arpaio* (Docket No. 2:07-CV-02513-GMS) in the United States District Court for the District of Arizona.

IN TESTIMONY WHEREOF, I have hereunto signed my name and caused the seal of the Department of Justice to be affixed.

Done at the City of Washington this twenty-fifth day of August, in the year of our Lord two thousand and seventeen and of the Independence of the United States of America the two hundred and forty-second.

DONALD J. TRUMP
PRESIDENT

Even though it was a Friday, Trump told reporters, "I assumed the ratings would be far higher than they would be normally. You know the hurricane was just starting. And I put it out that I had pardoned, as we say, Sheriff Joe."

"He is loved in Arizona," Trump continued. "Sheriff Joe protected our borders. And Sheriff Joe was very unfairly treated by the Obama administration, especially right before an election—an election that he would have won ... So I stand by my pardon of Sheriff Joe, and I think the people of Arizona, who really know him best, would agree with me."

2017–2019

Lydia Guzman was at home, getting ready to sit down to dinner with her family, when she learned of the Arpaio pardon via text messages.

She felt physically ill, and betrayed, and outraged, but she changed into her trademark black pants and a black blouse, put on her makeup, and headed out the door. This can't be how it ends, she thought.

Tom Black had an early morning shift scheduled the next day at the hospital, but he sensed his wife was upset and refused to leave her side that night. First, the couple rushed over to the federal courthouse plaza to show solidarity with younger activists. Carlos Garcia had called a press conference and stood at the podium, his black hair gathered in a low ponytail. Other activists in their twenties and thirties stood behind Garcia in the setting sun. The giant Trump and Arpaio inflatables bookended the scene.

Guzman had grown to admire Garcia. He had become a driving force in the movement. He was organized. He collaborated with other millennial activists in a way that came naturally to him. He inspired a generation of digital natives who she couldn't always reach via her television interviews, conference panels, and PowerPoint slides.

Garcia had a knack for latching on to a news event and turning it into a savvy campaign.

Which is exactly what he did with the Arpaio pardon. Seizing the pardon as a hook, Garcia and his collaborators themed their press conference around a call for national action against white supremacy, which will "not be pardoned."

The former sheriff was inconsequential, Garcia said that day, because the community had defeated him and marginalized him. But there was something bigger, and more dangerous, happening in America, he warned. The violent Unite the Right rally in Charlottesville had happened two weeks earlier. Garcia tied Trump and Arpaio, and their immigration policies, to the consequences of white supremacy "we have lived [with] in Maricopa County."

Now, he said, Arizona activists were obligated "to let the country know what is coming to them."

Arizona activists would never forget the sting and insult of the presidential pardon, he said, but "we will use this anger to take out Donald Trump in the same way we took out Sheriff Joe Arpaio."

Next up was Viridiana Hernandez. The young Bazta Arpaio leader was a Dreamer, and had begun her activism in high school. She'd been arrested for civil disobedience for publicly opposing restrictionism in Maricopa County, and was fearless.

"We have lived under Arpaio . . . and we have kicked him out," she said.

"Trump is just one more . . . We are going to get him out. And we are going to resist every single day as we have been resisting our whole existence."

Guzman and Black slipped away. They had been the oldest people standing behind the young activists' press conference on the federal courthouse plaza. They hurried off to El Portal restaurant. Footage of Hurricane Harvey played on the restaurant's big screen television when they walked in. Danny Ortega was already there. He'd been fighting racism since he was a sophomore at Phoenix Union High School. "It never stops . . . but we will never stop," he said. He finished the sentence angrily before taking his place behind the heavy wooden table with his old friends Antonio Bustamante, Mary Rose Wilcox, Lydia Guzman, and a few others.

For years, the activists had gathered here to update reporters on the *Melendres* case, on fights over state immigration laws, and on the Arpaio contempt of court trial and his guilty verdict. But this time, the grieving

Arizona activists warned of the dangers the Trump presidency posed to the nation.

"This pardon was done for purely political reasons," Mary Rose Wilcox said. Post Charlottesville, Trump "wanted to throw red meat at his base," she said.

"It puts him in line with the KKK, with the Nazis, with white supremacists. And, this is our president. We have no choice but to resist, resist, resist."

"I feel totally betrayed," Guzman said. "This is an utter shame."

"I'm upset for so many reasons," she went on. "The community won in court. Arpaio was found guilty . . . He violated our constitutional rights and now, for a president to say, 'You're forgiven,' what a slap in the face."

Congressman Ruben Gallego, the son of immigrants, a Harvard graduate, and a veteran, spoke somberly. "Many of these people here, we were there from day one when it was very unpopular to go against sheriff Joe Arpaio," Gallego said. "We believed in the rule of law. We believed in justice. We believed that we were going to get to this man through two methods, either through the electoral process or through the justice system. And we did. We continued to campaign. Eventually we got him out, thank God."

As Gallego spoke, Guzman wondered about the families she'd talked to who'd lost a loved one to deportation. Now they might see her on television, and they might question why they'd even bothered sharing their stories with her and putting their faith in the courts. She knew she didn't have an answer for them. Because at that moment, she didn't have an answer for herself. She always tried to put on a brave face for the community when she was on camera. But now, as she sat at the table as part of the press conference, she could not hold back her tears. She dabbed furiously at her eyes with a folded-up tissue.

Antonio Bustamante, who'd heard about the pardon as he was smoking a cigar in the back patio of his law office, wasn't shocked by the news. He was confident historians would place Arpaio in the "trash bin of history."

"We have to put things in a bigger perspective," he told the reporters at El Portal, leaning forward into the mic. "After centuries of fighting for our rights, for our dignity, for our humanity, you know, you come across racists who do this kind of thing, so we've become accustomed to it . . . We have a criminal liar president who will be shown to be a criminal before his time is up in the White House. We have *that* kind of buffoon pardoning *another* buffoon who a court has already found to be a criminal. And, history will never absolve that. History will never erase that."

A reporter read aloud a statement from Arizona governor Doug Ducey, who just months before had attended Arpaio's party at the Buffalo Chip Saloon. In his statement, Ducey said he respected the Trump pardon, which "brought finality to this chapter in Arizona's history." At that point, Danny Ortega slipped out the back door. He hadn't spoken. He was deeply upset. He told us he didn't have anything to say that hadn't already been said.

Before the night ended, the Wilcoxes, Bustamante, Guzman, and Black locked arms, and, smiling bravely, posed for a photo beneath the portrait of Cesar Chavez.

In a way, the presidential pardon Joe Arpaio had wanted so much backfired on him. It became a topic of widespread national discussion and reminded Americans every day that America's Toughest Sheriff had committed a crime. And that was not how he wanted to be remembered.

Legal scholars, newspaper editors, historians, and everyday Americans penned nationally published opinion pieces deeming the pardon either an abuse of power, or an impeachable offense, or unconstitutional, or a dog whistle to white supremacists in Trump's base, or cronyism, or any combination of these.

In Arizona, the once reliably conservative editorial board at *The Arizona Republic* in Phoenix wrote that Trump's pardon of Joe Arpaio "elevated the disgraced former Maricopa County sheriff to [Confederate] monument status among the immigration hardliners and nationalists in Trump's base. This erases any doubt about whether Trump meant to empower them after the violence in Charlottesville. Arpaio is their darling. Arpaio is now back on his pedestal thanks to their president."

We called Arpaio several times and sent him text messages on the day he was pardoned, but he didn't respond. When we reached him a few days later, he was no longer the triumphant, redeemed Arpaio glowing in the media attention he'd gotten on Ava's birthday, when the pardon was delivered to him.

Instead, the national controversy left him surprised, angry, bewildered, and depressed. All these stories about him, he told us, were so unfair. So one-sided. They called him a racist. They called him a white supremacist.

A reporter years ago had heard him refer to his Tent City as a "concentra-
tion camp." Now he'd noticed the anecdote echoing in the national media.
"It's amazing how they copy. Can't someone do their own work, huh?" he
complained to us. Often reporters did not even seek a comment from him.
What had happened to America, anyway?

"I'm not a racist," he told us. "You know that. Everybody knows that."

"I've got two new titles now," he went on. "'The Disgraced Sheriff,' that's
everywhere, 'Disgraced Sheriff.' And the other one is 'Racist.' So I've got
two new titles. I lost my 'America's Toughest Sheriff' title."

He told us he'd gotten two or three death threats. "Dear Fat, Greaseball
Dago Piece of Shit," one letter writer began. "I understand your wife Ava
has cancer. I hope she dies a long, slow, excruciatingly painful death."

An emailer called him "Sicko. Sadist. Depraved vile criminal" and
wished for him to watch his family members murdered. He was shaken.

The slurs, he told us, were the same slurs hurled at him when he was a
little kid in Springfield, Massachusetts, but that was a different time and
he just took it with a grain of salt back then. But now, he told us, you can't
say anything about Hispanics but you can still go after Italians.

As sheriff, Arpaio's office had responded swiftly and seriously to anyone
who made threats against him. Now, he grumbled, the new sheriff, Paul
Penzone, wouldn't care.

Arpaio insisted he was a fighter. He was angry about the way this was
going, angry about what these judges had done to him. Can you imagine,
he asked us, what the election would have looked like without this contempt stuff?

After he'd lost the sheriff's race in 2016, he'd told Ava, "I'm finished
with this." But he changed his mind after the pardon. Now he was back
"full force" in politics. Three days after the pardon, he'd floated the possibility that he'd run for the United States Senate.

And meanwhile, Arpaio's attorneys, emboldened by the presidential
pardon, had filed a motion in federal court seeking to dismiss the entire
criminal contempt of court case. And they wanted all of Bolton's rulings
vacated, including her guilty verdict.

Danny Ortega and Antonio Bustamante joined about two hundred
attorneys—Republicans, Democrats and Independents—standing in front

of the federal courthouse to protest the pardon and show solidarity with the rule of law and the federal judges who had found Arpaio in civil and criminal contempt. The Phoenix legal community had rallied like this only once before, eight years earlier in opposition to the former county attorney Andrew Thomas's unethical court filings against Arpaio's critics.

It was hot enough that day for some mobile phones not to work. But the attorneys spent their lunch break clustered on the courthouse plaza. Most wore sunglasses, and some brought umbrellas. The rest stood in whatever shade they could find on the east side of the courthouse.

"If you are a true Republican I would wonder why you are not here if you aren't here," former Arizona attorney general Grant Woods told the crowd. Woods was in his sixties now, and had a receding hairline and furrowed brow. He was an old-fashioned Republican, on the other side of the spectrum from the extremism of the alt-right wing of the party that had gained ascendance with the Trump presidency.

Trump was a fake conservative, Woods told his fellow lawyers. True conservatives wouldn't lionize and pardon Arpaio, who systematically abused the constitutional rights of American citizens and disobeyed a federal judge's orders. True conservatives respected the courts and didn't whine that judicial orders were based on politics.

"We are the lawyers of this community, and we know these judges don't do that. They put their personal feelings and politics aside, and in the shadow of the courtroom where Arpaio was found guilty of contempt we stand here to support the judges who did the right thing in this case," he said.

"We are from Arizona, and Arizona is better than we are often portrayed."

Sheriff Paul Penzone took steps early in his tenure to publicly dismantle Arpaio's legacy. He invited Grant Woods, Lydia Guzman, and others to join a new sheriff's office advisory board, and heeded the board's advice to shut down Tent City.

The new sheriff also ended the practice of holding immigrant jail inmates for extra time to allow ICE agents a chance to pick them up. But within days, Penzone seemed to have had an about-face. He modified his plan and said his agency would alert ICE when an immigrant inmate was about to be released.

Some Latino activists who had helped elect Penzone began denouncing him for continuing to allow the jail to serve as a deportation dragnet. At court-ordered community meetings, Sal Reza and other immigrant activists protested Penzone and called on him to kick ICE out of the main Fourth Avenue jail.

As sheriff, Penzone also had to comply with Snow's orders in the *Melendres* case, which continued to drag on. *Melendres v. Arpaio* became *Melendres v. Penzone*.

In late September 2017, Snow held a hearing to discuss how the sheriff's office would implement overdue measures to curtail biased policing. Arizona State University researchers had recently published an audit of more than thirty thousand sheriff's office traffic stops between 2015 and 2016, and the results were discouraging. Latino drivers were less likely to get a warning compared to their white peers, and were nearly 65 percent more likely to be arrested. People of color were subjected to longer traffic stops than whites. The researchers determined a small number of deputies were arresting and performing searches on people of color at twice the average rate for their district.

Snow was understandably frustrated that the sheriff's office had still not carried out one of his court-ordered reforms, known as an "Early Intervention System," or EIS. The data program would alert the Maricopa County Sheriff's Office to the possibility that a deputy might be engaged in biased policing.

"It was four years ago . . . *four years ago* . . . that I first ordered that there be EIS," Snow said. "*Four years* later we are now implementing EIS. I am a little tired of this process taking that long."

Another hearing would be scheduled. Another motion would be filed. And so it would go, year after year.

Cecillia Wang remained active in the *Melendres* case. She felt reforms were painfully slow because Arpaio's culture of resistance was still embedded in the current sheriff's department. It needed to be rooted out. "Everyone here wants this agency to succeed," she told reporters after the hearing.

The last months had exhausted Wang, because the Trump administration was moving forward with its promised restrictionist immigration agenda. Wang and her colleagues were busy challenging many of these policies in court. Trump was expanding local-federal 287(g) immigration enforcement partnerships. He threatened to withhold funding from cities that limited cooperation with federal deportation efforts. What's more, to get around legal challenges, Trump had ordered multiple iterations of the so-called "Muslim ban." He was taking steps to weaken the asylum system and seeking to deprive Dreamers of DACA—the program that gave them work permits and a temporary reprieve from deportation. Plus, he had pardoned Arpaio.

Wang hoped Trump's appetite for restrictionist immigration policies would turn out to be as costly for Trump as it had been for Arpaio. She hoped Americans would look to Arizona for guidance and vote out a president who, in her view, fostered white supremacy in his policies.

On a sunny October morning in 2017, a new bunch of demonstrators appeared outside the federal courthouse in Phoenix. They were Trump/Arpaio supporters, but not the familiar longtime loyalists like Kathryn Kobor. This was a jubilant, younger, more energetic group, out to support the former sheriff on the day Judge Bolton would hold a hearing on legal ramifications of Arpaio's presidential pardon.

They clashed with the anti-Arpaio protesters, who were holding their handmade signs and chanting in Spanish. "This is America, speak English!" shouted a woman wearing a leopard print cardigan and brown boots.

Lydia Guzman was recovering from pneumonia. Even so, she showed up in court because the courts had ruled over and over in favor of the movement, and she held out hope that Bolton could somehow nix the pardon.

She knew several amicus briefs maintained the pardon was invalid. One brief, from more than thirty Democrats in Congress, argued Trump had violated the constitution. The pardon, they wrote, "is an encroachment by the Executive on the independence of the Judiciary."

Guzman sat near Daniel Magos. He, too, hoped Bolton would revoke the presidential pardon that day.

Several weeks before, Arpaio had spoken with us in his office in Fountain Hills, with the framed pardon hanging on the wall where everyone could see it. He told us he was bothered by the notion that pardons were only for people who were guilty. He said he was not guilty. Had never been guilty. That's why he wanted Judge Bolton's guilty verdict revoked, now that he had a pardon.

"I'm the victim of all this, when you look at the courts and everything that happened in eight years," he later told us.

"I'm the big victim."

The "big victim" didn't show up in Bolton's courtroom on that morning in October to hear his lawyers try to get his conviction wiped out. When Bolton marched in and took her place at her desk with the canister of sharpened pencils, the courtroom was full. She got right down to business. Most of the amici briefs, she said, argued that Trump's pardon was unconstitutional.

"I have concluded that the pardon is valid," she said, noting she was bound by a Supreme Court case that found criminal contempt of court is a federal crime that can be pardoned by the president. "This pardon in this criminal contempt has the effect of allowing Defendant Arpaio to escape punishment for his willful violation of the preliminary injunction in *Melendres*," she said.

"The court finds the pardon valid," she said again, adding "it requires this action for criminal contempt be dismissed with prejudice."

Next, Arpaio's defense attorney asked Bolton to vacate her rulings, including Arpaio's conviction for criminal contempt of court.

What happened next nearly jolted Guzman out of her seat. The justice department prosecutor, John Keller, agreed the guilty verdict he had fought for just months earlier should indeed be vacated.

Keller, a short, slender man with a controlled courtroom demeanor, appeared to wince when he turned away from the judge and walked to his seat.

On the way to the elevator, we asked Keller if he could share his emotional reaction to first prosecuting the case and then arguing to vacate Arpaio's guilty verdict he'd worked so hard to obtain. We asked him if his bosses forced him to try to throw out Arpaio's guilty verdict. He said he couldn't comment.

At the close of the thirty-minute hearing, Bolton had not yet said how she would rule.

Stunned, disappointed, Lydia Guzman stood on the courthouse plaza. She'd always thought of the justice department prosecutors as kids, about the same age as her daughter. Ashley. When they'd obtained the conviction, she'd imagined their parents' pride. Now she felt they'd abandoned their ethics because they couldn't stand up to Jeff Sessions, who ran the Trump justice department.

Then the Trump/Arpaio supporters began shouting "USA! USA!" as they marched around Guzman, other activists, lawyers, and reporters standing together on a section of the plaza where no demonstrations were allowed. "Today the constitution won!" "USA! USA! USA!" Their voices drowned out reporters' questions and muted the traffic sounds on Washington Street.

Guzman and Magos turned to each other, hugged, and wept. The demonstrators evoked all the animus against Latinos they'd seen and felt in the last decade. And once again they felt excluded—this time from the new "USA" ushered in with the Trump presidency.

Arpaio hadn't attended the hearing, but he watched the drama on the courthouse plaza on the news. "Lydia was there," he told us. "You know she's there all the time . . . But I was, I never, you know, I never saw her in tears. But I was kind of shocked when she was crying over the pardon, you know."

In that moment, Joe Arpaio did something that surprised us. He paused and pondered what Lydia Guzman and the Latino activists he'd battled for years were feeling.

"I don't know if it was hatred towards me," he told us. "Or it was just that they fought so hard, and they were just waiting for the day that their sheriff . . . the former sheriff would be put in handcuffs and put in jail."

"I think that's where a lot of emotions came from."

Joe Arpaio wanted his guilty verdict removed. But it wasn't. In mid-October 2017, Judge Bolton allowed the guilty verdict to stand when she denied Arpaio's bid to vacate her rulings. Donald Trump's first presidential pardon had protected Arpaio from punishment for his crime, but it "does not erase a judgment of conviction, or its underlying legal and factual findings," she wrote.

The former sheriff unsuccessfully appealed Bolton's ruling. He was bitter, still, about the way the pardon had played out. He'd spent two decades grooming his once-popular America's Toughest Sheriff persona and now, when he studied printouts listing how many times his name was tagged in

Google, he knew the reportage about him was overwhelmingly negative. Yet, he sensed his popularity was stronger than ever.

He decided to run as a Republican candidate in the United States Senate primary in 2018. That May, he staged a media event centered around delivering his nomination petitions to the secretary of state's office, which sat on the grounds of the Arizona State Capitol complex in Phoenix. Less than a decade had passed since thousands had protested Senate Bill 1070 there, but now the grounds were quiet. It was a sunny day, not yet hot. Wide-fronded date palms splotched the concrete sidewalks with shade. A small entourage of Arpaio supporters, including Kathryn Kobor and Barb Heller, gathered with a handful of reporters to witness Arpaio's nomination petition delivery.

Kobor told us Arpaio was redeemed by the Trump pardon. As a senator, he would fight against taking in too many refugees and asylees, just like the president. She didn't think Arpaio too old for the job. He was up to it. "Joe Arpaio is as strong as a bull. He's got good genes," she told us.

A young Puente activist, Maria Castro, pointed her phone video camera at the former sheriff and asked: "What makes you think that you're fit to be senator of Arizona?" Arpaio asked if Castro was a reporter.

No, Castro shot back, she was an activist. "You continuously hurt my people throughout my entire lifetime," she said; "what makes you think that it's okay for you to try to represent the people of Arizona?"

Arpaio replied he was writing a detailed report—what he believed to be Judge Snow's improper exercise of power and government entities colluding against him—and that might give her a "different viewpoint."

Castro retorted: "Viewpoint of what? You continuously violated people's rights."

She hadn't fallen for his bait, and he walked off. A few of his fans stayed back with Castro, an American citizen they called "illegal."

"How many identities have you stolen in your lifetime, ma'am?" asked Heller.

"Un-American, un-American, un-American!" another woman said, pointing at Castro. Kobor tried to intervene. "All blood runs red, okay? We don't care what color you are, what your eye color is, your hair color is—"

Castro interrupted her. "You might not. But Sheriff Joe racially profiled, and then violated the judge's orders."

Arpaio, meanwhile, thanked his fans and his two-man staff, then riffed about his plan to win so he could serve Donald Trump and the people of Arizona. There were a few polite claps. "Make Arizona Great Again!" some supporters chirped. Reporters pushed Arpaio on his fanboy-like attachment to the president. Did he *ever* disagree with the president, one asked.

"Uh, no," Arpaio answered. "I agree with him. From day one we were seeing that we were on the same highway . . . And I will say again, he will be reelected, and go down in history as one of our greatest, greatest presidents, as long as the media will let him alone."

Arpaio was running in the Republican primary against Martha McSally, a veteran and moderate by modern Trump-era Republican standards, and Kelli Ward, a far-right former state senator. Ward and Arpaio competed for the same voting block of Trump supporters. Kobor and Heller supported Arpaio. Other fellow restrictionist activists, like bikers Valerie Roller, George Sprankle, and Jim Williams, supported Ward.

"I have no idea why Joe would get in that race," Williams told us.

Arpaio said repeatedly he wanted to become a senator to support Trump and his policies. But being a senator would do more than just that. Being a senator would bring Arpaio closer to the president he heroized, as a political peer.

"I never went to his tower," Arpaio once told us. "I never went out, really, to eat with them you know, like his inner circle. But he was sure mentioning me many, many times in his speeches and I have a whole list of 'em . . . But I don't think he read my resume and all that, figure out who is this guy . . . So he and I, like I said before, travel the same highway."

Trump, meanwhile, had imposed a national "zero tolerance" policy in which all adult unauthorized border crossers were to be charged with criminal misdemeanors instead of civil violations. This caused the separation of parents and children at the border.

The president used increasingly dehumanizing restrictionist language to describe immigrants that spring. Immigrants were "animals." He claimed Democrats wanted "illegal immigrants" to "infest our country."

Arpaio stuck up for Trump and claimed the families themselves were to blame for being separated from their kids. "Why don't we blame the families, the adults, for taking the chance, violating the law coming across the border with these young kids?" Arpaio asked CNN's Chris Cuomo. "They are the ones that should be held responsible. If I get to Washington, I am going to make sure there is another law, a tougher law to go after these people."

A few days later, we asked Arpaio to elaborate on his thoughts regarding the president's new "zero tolerance" policy that had caused family separations. "I like it," he answered. "I've been saying it for years. You know? I'm not going to take any credit, but I've been saying and doing this stuff for years."

Then he added: "The only regret I have is I'm not still the sheriff. I'd have a lot of fun if I was still the sheriff. You know? It would be a little more exciting and easier to enforce those laws."

At the time, we were driving with Arpaio in his campaign car, a black Nissan Altima plastered with *Sheriff Joe for US Senate* signs. The former media relations director at the sheriff's office, Chris Hegstrom, was our chauffeur. Our destination: Wickenburg, a small conservative town on the northern edge of Maricopa County known for its cowboy ropers and its rehab centers.

Hegstrom pulled the campaign car into the parking lot of a county park near a sandy stream shaded with cottonwood trees. "What is this place? Is this the place we're supposed to be talking?" Arpaio asked. He seemed disappointed by the small group, a mix of older and younger right-wingers.

On the return trip, Arpaio couldn't figure out how to fasten his seatbelt. And for a moment, he couldn't remember how he'd celebrated his eighty-sixth birthday two days before. But when questioned about his time in office, he recalled the past easily.

On the evening of August 28, 2018, a group of about seventy-five Arpaio supporters gathered at Georgie's Diner in Fountain Hills, hoping Arpaio might win the Republican primary race for the Senate. A gray-haired troubadour on a small stage sang "The Gambler."

"You've got to know when to hold 'em / Know when to fold 'em / Know when to walk away / And know when to run," the singer crooned.

Outside, the setting sun tinted Arpaio's campaign bus tangerine orange. People lined up to sign the side of the bus with washable Sharpies. Kathryn Kobor, dressed in a blue shirt, jeans, and tennis shoes, wrote: "Strength Joe Arpaio, Never Give Up."

Kathryn Kobor signs Arpaio's campaign bus in Fountain Hills, Arizona on August 28, 2018—the day Arpaio lost the Arizona Republican primary for the United States Senate. (Authors' photo)

Arpaio, wearing a navy blazer with a comb in the front pocket, and Ava, in a red dress with a white sweater and sandals, arrived at 7:05 p.m. They settled into a table near the singer. Arpaio told us he hadn't enough campaign funds to pay for last-minute television ads, had been marginalized by the press, and discounted by his opponents.

It had been a year since the president had pardoned him. And yet Trump had not endorsed him or any of the other Arizona senate primary candidates. When a reporter asked Arpaio how he felt about not getting a Trump endorsement, he said: "I've known him for two years, we have a great relationship. Leave it at that."

The first returns were encouraging. He trailed McSally by only six points. But then he was down by twenty points. He settled at the bar, watching the returns on a local television station. During ads, he glanced at a different screen showing *Bachelor in Paradise.*

"Maybe after this is all over we can share a gyro or something," Ava told him.

"Hero?" he asked.

Around 8:40 p.m. it was clear McSally had won the primary. Arpaio came in dead last. He walked up to a podium with Ava. He congratulated McSally, said he'd hold her feet to the fire and make sure she supported Trump, then sang praises for Trump. He'd do everything he could to get him re-elected. "It took me 75 years to find a hero," he said, "and that hero is President Trump."

The singer launched into "Proud to be an American" as Arpaio and Ava walked outside to talk to television news reporters. It was 9:04 p.m. Ghostly jet contrails spiraled across the black sky. The parking lot smelled like cigar smoke. A thin aide in a red dress with a fake eyelash dangling from her left cheek fielded the interview requests. Ava held her husband's hand.

"I'm sad," Kobor told us as she stood in the parking lot. She had been prepared for Arpaio's defeat, but still felt an "empty spot."

"You kinda get your expectations up," she said, "but you know you kinda have to be realistic. He is eighty-six. But I think he'll go on to something . . . He's not done."

In the months that melted into 2019 and beyond, Joe Arpaio had time on his hands.

He sued *The New York Times* for more than one hundred forty-seven million dollars in a defamation suit alleging an opinion piece, "Well, At Least Sheriff Joe Isn't Going to Congress," cast him in a false light and would damage his chances of running for the Senate in 2020. With the help of the right-wing activist lawyer Larry Klayman, Arpaio also sued CNN, HuffPost, and *Rolling Stone Magazine* for more than three hundred million dollars for referring to him as a "felon" when he had only been found guilty of a misdemeanor.

These were long shot cases, since Arpaio as a public figure would have to prove actual malice, a high standard. But they did generate news coverage at a time when he fretted about his negative image in the media. He told us not even Fox News invited him on anymore.

Then Ava stepped on a rattlesnake that had somehow gotten in the house. The snake bit Ava, who was hospitalized. With the help of an assistant, Arpaio emailed reporters a few days later. "My wife Ava bit by rattle-snake in residence on 3-22-19. Ava was in intensive care at the hospital for several days. She has been recuperating at home the past 2 weeks. Now she is doing great. She is a fighter and won another battle. Thank you for all the support and prayers from thousands of people around the country. Ava and I are not retired, we will continue to face new and exciting challenges. I believe Ava is ready to do interviews."

He included his private cell phone number in the email, so reporters could call him.

Even though Arpaio was sidelined, his legacy continued to galvanize Latino voters. Activists who identified as Dreamers, Latinx, or Mexican American—and had come of age during Arpaio's sweeps in the heyday of Arizona restrictionism—had amped up Latino political power. From 2014 to 2018, Latino voter turnout jumped from 32 percent to 49 percent. In those four years, a few Latino activists who had opposed Arpaio and Arizona's restrictionist immigration laws, including former Somos America member Raquel Terán, won seats as Democrats in the Arizona statehouse, chipping away at the Republican majorities. The Latino vote helped Democrat Kyrsten Sinema defeat Republican Martha McSally for the senate seat that Arpaio had wanted.

It was heartening for Lydia Guzman. Shortly after her fifty-second birthday, in November 2019, we caught up with her and Tom Black at La Barquita restaurant, where they'd first met. But this time, they brought along their grandson Stanley, the son of Guzman's daughter, Ashley. As his grandmother chatted, Stanley, a preschooler dressed in a T-shirt imprinted with the words: "Reptile Expert," drew contentedly on a paper napkin and joked with Black.

Black had retired as a respiratory therapist and was recovering from unexpected quadruple bypass heart surgery. Guzman had nursed him through it, sitting with him and watching Harry Potter movies she'd never had time to see when she was answering the hotline or helping immigrants caught up in Arpaio's worksite raids or neighborhood sweeps.

Like many borderlands restaurants, La Barquita was decorated with a mishmash of Mexican and American cultural icons—a framed portrait of Pancho Villa, a paper Thanksgiving turkey, a painting of a Mexican hacienda, cutouts of autumn leaves and scarecrows. Over campechana, a jumble of seafood drenched in a lime-infused juicy red sauce, Guzman recalled so much had happened in the two years since Judge Bolton's decision to uphold the pardon. She remembered feeling defeated and marginalized as demonstrators had circled round her and shouted "USA! USA!" on the courthouse plaza. At the time, she'd thought Arpaio and his racist supporters had won. But as she'd watched the once-powerful sheriff plunge deeper into ignominy, she'd realized the movement had won, after all. And she felt blessed to have been a small part of it, despite the personal cost of divorce, financial stresses, and once-angry kids.

Guzman hoped Americans would reject Trump just as Maricopa County voters had rejected Arpaio. She was heartened that throughout the nation there was growing opposition to Trump and his restrictionist policies, and that the Latino-led movement in Arizona was a national model for resistance and organizing now. Still, she was a realist. She knew there was a possibility that yet another cycle of anti-Latino animus might wash over Arizona again. If that happened, she thought, the Latino resistance had learned how to fight it and could beat it down again. But it would not be easy, and activists would endure more pain, struggle, and sacrifice.

"I just don't want it to come back," she told us.

It all started with mystery billboards. Joe Arpaio insisted he didn't know who put them up or who paid for them. But the billboards, which appeared in Maricopa County in July 2019, had a flattering photograph of Arpaio grinning in his sheriff uniform. Next to the photo were the words: *Sheriff Joe One More Time 2020.*

Not long after, Joe Arpaio announced he was running once again for Maricopa County sheriff. Arpaio would later have a campaign bus plastered with a picture of him and Trump together, along with the slogan: *Make Maricopa County Great Again.*

The news of Arpaio's candidacy came as a shock to Jerry Sheridan, Arpaio's former chief deputy. Sheridan was running for sheriff, too. In February, several months before the mystery billboards had appeared, Sheridan said he'd sought Arpaio's support in his sheriff race. And Arpaio, in Sheridan's memory, had been enthusiastic, offering his endorsement, promising to help with fundraising, and being the first to sign Sheridan's petition to qualify him as a candidate in the Republican primary race for sheriff.

Months later, Sheridan told us, Arpaio had called him. He explained to Sheridan "somebody" had put billboards up, and the public response was so overwhelmingly in favor of Arpaio running for office, Arpaio just had to honor the public's call.

"I loved you like a father, and I can't believe you're doing this to me," Sheridan said.

"Jerry," Arpaio answered, "I never had any friends. I never looked at any of you as my friends at the sheriff's office."

"It opened my eyes as to things that bugged me about him when I worked for him," Sheridan later told us. "His ego led him around." In Sheridan's memory, Arpaio was deeply self-absorbed during the *Melendres* "crisis" when Judge Snow issued his 2013 orders and reforms. Arpaio, according to Sheridan, had checked out.

"I ran that organization. I did," Arpaio later told us. "And he [Sheridan] was supposed to do what I told him. And if things went wrong in the Snow case, don't always blame me for it. He was the one involved more on that than I was."

He dismissed Sheridan's feelings that his new bid for re-election amounted to a betrayal. He insisted he'd offered to endorse Sheridan at a press conference, but figured Sheridan didn't take him up on the offer because Arpaio was too politically radioactive.

"So when he's going to say I sabotage him, that's not true. But even if it was true, let me put it this way, he has said constantly through the career, I'm like a father to him . . . If I'm his father and I say, 'Son, do me a favor. I really want to run for sheriff. Will you help me?' The son should say to the father, 'Dad, if that's what you really want, do it.'"

On a different day, when we visited Arpaio in his Fountain Hills office with the framed presidential pardon and the nightstick, we asked Arpaio to respond to critics who said he'd betrayed his fiercely devoted ex-chief deputy. "Okay, what do you mean? What's loyalty mean? What do you mean loyal?" he shot back, adding "I'm in this to win."

"I'm telling you one thing," Arpaio said, "I'm not taking any prisoners."

Afterword

Lydia Guzman views her fifty-third birthday in November 2020 as one of her best. On that day, she and Tom Black had danced in front of their glowing widescreen television as they'd watched Americans of all ethnicities celebrating on city streets after media outlets had called the presidential election for Democrat Joe Biden. Once reliably red, Arizona had gone blue, and helped defeat Trump by sending its eleven electoral votes to Biden. Arizona voters had also elected a second Democratic senator, Mark Kelly.

In Maricopa County, precincts heavily populated by Latino voters had supported Biden with margins over 75 percent, helping the county flip for the first time in more than seventy years. Grassroots activists, many of whom had participated in the Adiós Arpaio and the Bazta Arpaio campaigns years before, had been key to the outcome. They'd knocked on over one million doors and had made nearly eight million phone calls to mobilize voters of color and young people throughout Arizona. As a result, Latino voters had broken turnout records in Arizona. They'd joined Black, Native American, independent, and young voters, along with John McCain Republicans, to give the Democrats their narrow victory.

Just like so many Americans isolated by the COVID-19 pandemic, Guzman had worked from home for months. If not for the coronavirus, she and her husband would have joined marches on the streets of Phoenix in the summer of 2020 to show solidarity with Black Lives Matter and protesters voicing outrage over the fate of victims of police brutality—including George Floyd Jr., who had died when a Minneapolis police officer pressed his knee on his neck.

Instead of marching, Guzman had doubled down on her work, jumping on Zoom to coordinate voter outreach, census participation, and COVID-19 assistance through her position at Chicanos Por La Causa. After the election, she began collaborating on redistricting efforts.

She hopes one day she and Black will be able to take their grandson Stanley to Disneyland.

Joe Arpaio has accepted his loss of the 2020 Republican primary race for Maricopa County sheriff to his former chief deputy, Jerry Sheridan. In the general election a few months later, Sheridan lost by nearly eleven points to the incumbent, Paul Penzone.

Arpaio feels certain he would have won the general election had he had a rematch with Penzone.

Arpaio's third book, *Sheriff Joe Arpaio An American Legend*, written with David Thomas Roberts, was published in late 2020. The book chronicles the "deep state" plot that Arpaio had long claimed led to his criminal contempt of court case. Roberts notes those "same forces" opposed Trump: "It's almost as if the unjust, unethical, and criminal political witch-hunt that tagged Sheriff Joe with criminal contempt was a dry run for President Trump." Arpaio says he had difficulty believing Trump lost the presidency. He hopes his hero will follow his lead. "I got beat, came right around and ran again," he says. "So I would like to see him run again."

Arpaio co-founded a foundation that solicits funds to "support and legally represent law enforcement." He sells personalized video greetings on Cameo for thirty dollars. He still seeks media attention and has appeared on left-leaning television shows where he's been pranked and mocked, but says it doesn't bother him as long as his name is spelled right.

Antonio Bustamante is a senior public defender for Yuma County, on the Arizona-Mexico border. He's thrilled with the results of the 2020 presidential election, and Arizona's role in it. But he frets about the country's deep divide, made all the more clear amid unproven post-election claims of voter fraud. "Half of the country is mean as hell. And un-American as hell," Bustamante says. "So I am worried."

Alfredo Gutierrez finds he's "incapable of withdrawal" from activism, and advocates for improved educational, workplace, and living conditions for marginalized people in rural and tribal communities. Now a Chicano elder, he sees the new generation of Latino activists and leaders as "the ideological and spiritual descendants of those young Chicanos so many years ago."

"They are the reason for hope."

In the 2020 election, as a protest vote on his ballot, Gutierrez had written in Lydia Guzman's name for Maricopa County sheriff. He says he couldn't vote for Sheriff Paul Penzone because, among other things, Penzone allows ICE to track deportable immigrant inmates in county jails.

Salvador Reza continues to pressure Penzone to ban ICE from his jails. "Arpaio is gone," he says, "but the racist institutions and systems of oppression that he created are alive and well."

Danny Ortega practices law in Phoenix. He sees the nation's cultural divide as a necessary step to achieving greater equality for marginalized Americans. When Trump garnered more than 74 million votes in the 2020 presidential election, Ortega took it to mean the country is far more racist, or at least more tolerant to racism, than he had thought when Trump won the presidency in 2016. But the last decade of Latino-led battles for civil rights in Arizona has taught him that when racism is revealed, it is easier to fight.

In early 2020, when Governor Doug Ducey, a Trump supporter, had floated a new immigration-themed legislative proposal, Ortega was encouraged when the movement had managed to defeat it. Ortega has total confidence in the new crop of Latino leaders. He says passing the baton to this generation is "nothing short of just absolutely exhilarating."

Carlos Garcia was elected a Phoenix city council member in 2019. He wears T-shirts with social justice slogans to city council meetings and pushes for accountability for Phoenix police officers accused of brutality.

In 2020, Alexis Aguirre, Garcia's wife, successfully ran as a write-in candidate for the Roosevelt school district's governing board. The district serves many students of color.

Garcia believes Maricopa County's political shift only matters if entrenched anti-immigrant policies are completely dismantled. "I've never stopped and I don't plan to stop fighting for human rights," he says. "Being an elected official is an extension of the work I've done before and will continue."

Chimal Garcia still plays chess. His four-year-old sister Yaretzi likes to play with the chess pieces.

Maria Castro had gone door to door to get out the vote on behalf of Living United for Change in Arizona (LUCHA). She had first canvassed voters in 2011 as a high schooler during the effort to recall state Senator Russell Pearce. This time, she says she wore a plastic face shield along with a mask that spelled "VOTE" in large orange letters. The year 2020 had marked the third presidential election cycle in which she'd knocked on many of these doors, but she says this time voters were more engaged. "This time around, people were like, 'Yes, we're ready to get rid of Trump,'" she says. "I think the defeat of Arpaio made it tangible that we can defeat the villains that haunt our dreams."

Dr. Angeles Maldonado and Ray Ybarra Maldonado run a prominent law firm in Phoenix that takes on immigrant and civil rights cases, among many others. They remain engaged in social justice issues and have close ties to community groups. They have two children.

Mary Rose Wilcox and her husband, Earl Wilcox, still own El Portal, which they had reopened only to close again amid the pandemic. The couple continues to advocate for the Latino community.

Jason LeVecke remains active in politics. Though his business had vetted restaurant workers with E-Verify, in 2014 ICE audited his company. He suspects the audit was retribution because he'd challenged immigration policies. He lost many workers, and his company ended up in bankruptcy. He is pursuing new ventures.

Kathryn Kobor stays active in restrictionist causes. An avowed Trump supporter, she had joined protesters who suspected election fraud and rallied outside the Maricopa County Elections Department. She continues rescuing cats in her neighborhood.

Barb Heller remains committed to supporting the military and law enforcement, and sends gift bags to Arizona police officers to thank them for their service. She is "sickened" by Trump's loss in an election she views as dishonest and worries about the fate of the nation.

Linda Bentley retired from the *Sonoran News* in 2018 and lives in Florida.

Kris Kobach lost his 2020 Republican primary bid for a U.S. Senate seat in Kansas. He still practices law, and aided efforts to prevent the certification of 2020 election results.

The Maricopa County Sheriff's Office is still implementing court-ordered reforms in the *Melendres* case. It will remain under court supervision until it achieves compliance with those orders for three consecutive years.

Judge G. Murray Snow became Chief Judge for the United States District Court, District of Arizona in 2018, and continues to preside over the *Melendres* case.

Maricopa County has so far paid 76,900 dollars split between eighteen people who were wrongfully detained by sheriff's deputies in violation of Judge Snow's 2011 order. The county's total *Melendres*-related expenses are projected to surpass 178 million in 2021.

Manuel de Jesus Ortega Melendres has not returned our phone calls since 2018. He'd grown bitter because he was not eligible for financial compensation in the famous lawsuit that bore his name. Melendres does not qualify because his arrest took place four years before Snow issued his 2011 order.

Samuel, who was wrongfully arrested in 2012, qualified for compensation but did not apply.

Daniel Magos supervises students at an elementary school in southwest Phoenix. More than a decade ago, after he had spoken to ACLU attorneys for the first time about the *Melendres* lawsuit, he had placed a large American flag on his house as a reminder of the nation's promise of freedom and justice. He still hangs the flag.

Acknowledgments

In the four years it took to research and write this book, dozens of people contributed their talents and time to these pages. We are especially thankful to those who patiently let us into their lives and shared their stories, insights, knowledge, perspectives, and time during interviews that sometimes lasted several hours.

We are beyond thankful to our diligent fact checker Matt Mahoney; to Diana Hume George, for brilliantly editing our first complete draft; to Tracy Greer for smart editorial insights and invaluable research; to Valeria Fernández, Dan Barr, Amy Silverman, Len Downie, Alfredo Corchado, Rick Rodriguez, and Tom Zoellner, who read our early writing and provided generous and instructive feedback; to Richard Just, for his encouragement and brainstorm sessions, to the scholars who reviewed the book proposal and manuscript for the University of California Press and offered helpful comments; and to Grace Clark, Garret Schwartz, and Rebekah Zemansky, who helped build our digital archive and timelines. Maddalena Marinari offered key historical advice.

Photographer José L. Muñoz tirelessly documented Maricopa County's troubled history and contributed important photographs to this book. Artist Maggie Keane captured the *Melendres* courtroom drama in her sketches, and we are thrilled to share her drawings in this book. Dr. Christine Marin, Joe Eddie Lopez, Rose Marie Lopez, and Nancy Godoy shared key historical photographs. We thank Nick Oza, our talented friend, for photographing us for the back cover.

We appreciate Dan Barr's astute legal advice and frequent moral support throughout this project. Gregg Leslie and Arizona State University's Sandra Day

O'Connor College of Law First Amendment Clinic students John Dragovits, Maxine Hart, Dylan Mileusnich, Bobby Niska, Lauren Norton, Olivia Otter, Noah Schultz-Rathbun, Sam Turner, Michael Uchrin, and Alexa Weber provided a thoughtful and thorough legal review of the final manuscript. Marcos Garciacosta supplied sound counsel that has guided us throughout this project. We are grateful to James Borelli and Mike Mansel for their pre-publication guidance.

We are indebted to University of California Press, and in particular Naomi Schneider, Summer Farah, Kate Warne, Teresa Iafolla, Katryce Lassle, Alex Dahne, Kate Hoffman, Kathleen MacDougall, and Virginia Baker for their hard work on this book. We thank our agent, Jill Marsal.

Support from the Center for the Future of Arizona, New America, the Russell Sage Foundation, and the Walter Cronkite School of Journalism at Arizona State University made this project possible. We extend our thanks to Chris Callahan, Kristin Gilger, Lattie Coor, Sybil Francis, Kristi Kappes, Peter Bergen, Konstantin Kakaes, Awista Ayub, and Sheldon Danziger. Thanks as well to the entire Cronkite faculty and staff, especially Allysa Adams, Marianne Barrett, Dawn Gilpin, Anita Luera, Andrés Martinez, Jacquee Petchel, Walter V. Robinson, Fernanda Santos, Miguel Sauceda, Bill Silcock, Leslie-Jean Thornton, and Julia Wallace. We are also grateful for the feedback we received from New America fellows and Russell Sage Foundation visiting scholars.

We are blessed to belong to a community of Phoenix journalists who helped us in many ways. Thank you Valeria Fernández, for sharing memories and stories, and for allowing us to review raw footage collected with Dan DeVivo for the excellent documentary film, *Two Americans*. We are grateful to Jacques Billeaud, Megan Cassidy, Joe Dana, Ryan Gabrielson, Daniel González, Michael Kiefer, Stephen Lemons, Morgan Loew, Richard Ruelas, Yvonne Wingett Sanchez, and Ray Stern for their shared insights and prior reporting.

FROM TERRY GREENE STERLING

Sara and Tina, you are honest, kind, smart, beautiful women and I love you beyond words and am so proud and happy to be your mom; Brooke, your love sustained me through rough patches and I hope mine does the same for you; Jack, I love you so and am sorry I was so zoned out and didn't have any food in the house when I was on deadline; Michael, you are a good man who sticks up for those whose voices are ignored, which informs my writing and makes me love you even more; Bard and Maile, I love you and thanks for rescuing me from my laptop with FaceTimes; Erich, thanks for getting completely why I write—I love you and will put your picture up; Hugh, the day you came into our lives we were all enriched and we love you; Kaia and Alec, love you and yayayayayaya; Walt, you are the love of my life and now that I'm no longer on deadline let's go to Antarctica.

FROM JUDE JOFFE-BLOCK

I likely would never have been involved in this project without editors Alisa Barba, Monica Campbell, Jason DeRose, Tracy Greer, Al Macias, and Peter O'Dowd first assigning me to cover the *Melendres* litigation and Arizona immigration fights for public radio audiences. A residential fellowship with the Logan Nonfiction Program was invaluable, and I'm thankful to Josh Friedman, Tom Jennings, Carly Willsie, and the fellows who continue to motivate me. Friends near and far, my sister Miriam, brother-in-law Andrew, the Mazurs, Karl Klare, and the Kay-Christensen family provided wise feedback and kept me in good spirits. Deva, through videos, gave much needed comic relief. Braden, your optimism, enthusiasm for this project and cooking have meant the world to me and made this possible. My parents, Carole and Fred, offered unwavering encouragement since the beginning. Thank you for sharing your curiosity and dedication to research. You two inspire me.

APPENDIX I Selected Arizona
Immigration Laws

Year passed	Title of law	Description	Current status
1988	Official English (Arizona English as the Official Language Amendment, or Proposition 106)	Forbids Arizona state employees from using a language other than English at work.	Struck down by the Arizona Supreme Court in 1998.
2004	Proposition 200 (Arizona Taxpayer and Citizen Protection Act)	Makes state officials verify the identity of all applying for public benefits. If unauthorized immigrants apply, state workers must report them to federal authorities or face criminal charges. Requires Arizonans to submit citizenship documents to register to vote, and show ID at the polls.	Arizona's then-Attorney General interpreted the scope to pertain to five state public benefits programs. Much of the law remains in effect, including the voter ID requirement. After a legal challenge, the United States Supreme Court ruled in 2013 the proof of citizenship requirement to register to vote could not be applied to federal elections.
2005	Human Smuggling Law (no official name, Senate Bill 1372)	Makes it a state felony to transport undocumented immigrants into Arizona for money. In Maricopa County, migrants who paid a smuggler were also prosecuted under this law for conspiring to smuggle themselves.	A federal judge stopped Maricopa County from prosecuting migrants for conspiracy to smuggle themselves in 2013. Another federal judge struck down the law in 2014 as part of litigation over Senate Bill 1070.
2006	Proposition 100 (Bailable Offenses Act)	Prevents state courts from setting bail for undocumented immigrants arrested on felony charges.	After a challenge by the ACLU known as *Lopez-Valenzuela v. Arpaio*, a Ninth Circuit en banc panel struck down the law in 2014.
2006	Proposition 102 (Standing in Civil Actions Act)	Prohibits unauthorized immigrants from receiving punitive damages in state lawsuits.	Still in effect.

Year	Law	Description	Status
2006	Proposition 103 (English as the Official Language Act)	Makes English the official language of Arizona.	Still in effect.
2006	Proposition 300 (Public Program Eligibility Act)	Makes unauthorized immigrants ineligible for in-state college tuition, financial aid, or adult education programs.	Still in effect.
2007	The Legal Arizona Workers Act (Employer Sanctions Law)	Requires Arizona employers check the immigration status of potential employees via the federal database E-Verify. Employers who knowingly hire unauthorized immigrants are vulnerable to fines and losing their business licenses. Also includes provisions that enable local law enforcement to arrest and prosecute undocumented workers on felony identity theft charges.	Still in effect. Employer sanctions provision upheld by the United States Supreme Court in 2011 after a legal challenge brought by business groups and immigrant/civil rights groups.
2010	Senate Bill 1070 (Support Our Law Enforcement and Safe Neighborhoods Act)	Omnibus immigration law. Bans "Sanctuary Cities." Creates new crimes committed by unauthorized immigrants, legal immigrants, or people who harbor or hire them. Section 2(B) requires local law enforcement, while enforcing other laws, to check immigration status of those stopped, detained, or arrested if there is reasonable suspicion they are in the country unlawfully.	The United States Department of Justice and immigrant rights groups challenged the law. Several provisions were struck down by the United States Supreme Court and lower courts, but other provisions remain in effect.

Selected Federal Lawsuits

Year filed	Case name	Description	Resolution
1978	Gonzales v. City of Peoria	Migrant farmworkers sued the city of Peoria, Arizona over unconstitutional policing—including arresting undocumented immigrants who had committed no crimes and turning them over to Border Patrol.	In 1983, the Ninth Circuit Court of Appeals ruled local police could not enforce the civil provisions of federal immigration law, such as arresting someone for being in the country without legal status (but could enforce the criminal provisions of federal immigration law).
2006	We Are America/ Somos America v. Maricopa County Board of Supervisors	Migrants and immigrant rights groups, including Somos America, sued the county for arresting and prosecuting migrants for conspiring to smuggle themselves under Arizona's human smuggling law.	In 2013, a federal judge struck down the county's policy of charging migrants with conspiring to smuggle themselves.
2007	Melendres v. Arpaio (later Melendres v. Penzone)	Latino motorists and Somos America challenged Arpaio's policing practices, including racial profiling and wrongful detentions of Latino motorists during traffic stops. The plaintiffs' legal team included ACLU, MALDEF and Covington and Burling.	Federal judge G. Murray Snow issued a preliminary injunction in 2011 that forbade Arpaio and the sheriff's office from arresting suspected unauthorized immigrants who had not committed any crimes. In 2013, Snow ruled the sheriff's office had discriminated against Latino motorists and ordered sweeping reforms. In 2016, Snow found Arpaio and others in civil contempt of court for violating his orders, and referred Arpaio and others for criminal contempt of court proceedings. [See United States v. Arpaio]
2007	U.S. Chamber of Commerce v. Whiting (previously Chamber of Commerce v. Candelaria)	Business groups challenged the Legal Arizona Workers Act. It later merged with another suit filed by ACLU, MALDEF, Somos America, and other civil rights groups.	In 2011, the United States Supreme Court held the employer sanctions provisions were not preempted by federal law and could remain in effect.

2010	*United States v. Arizona*	The United States Department of Justice contended the six main sections of Senate Bill 1070 were preempted by federal immigration law.	In 2012, the United States Supreme Court struck down three provisions, but allowed Section 2(B) to take effect. The provision requires local police to inquire about immigration status if they have a reasonable suspicion someone is in the country without legal status. Some additional sections of the law were later struck down by lower courts.
2010	*Valle del Sol v. Whiting*	Immigrant rights groups, civil rights groups, unions, churches, and ethnic business associations represented by the ACLU, MALDEF, Danny Ortega, and others challenged Senate Bill 1070 in its entirety for being discriminatory against Latinos.	The parties settled in 2016, and Arizona agreed to release an Attorney General opinion modifying how police could enforce Sections 2(B) and 2(D). Under the opinion, local police should not prolong a traffic stop, detention, or arrest in order to investigate immigration status. They are also not supposed to arrest unauthorized immigrants who are not suspected of committing crimes.
2012	*United States v. Maricopa County*	The United States Department of Justice Civil Rights Division sued Maricopa County for unconstitutional conduct by Arpaio and his office, including discrimination against Latinos in traffic stops, worksite raids and jails, and retaliation against perceived critics.	A federal judge in 2015 sided with the justice department that the sheriff's traffic stops had discriminated against Latinos. The parties then settled the remaining three issues. The justice department lawyers became intervenors in the *Melendres* lawsuit and weighed in on what reforms were necessary to remedy the agency.
2014	*Puente v. Arpaio*	Puente Arizona and undocumented workers challenged Arpaio's worksite raids. They were represented by UC Irvine School of Law Immigrant Rights Clinic, ACLU of Arizona, Ray Ybarra Maldonado, and others.	The sheriff's office disbanded its worksite raid unit shortly after the lawsuit was filed. A federal judge ruled Maricopa County officials could not use federal I-9 employment eligibility forms or documents submitted in the I-9 process to investigate or prosecute immigrants for ID theft.
2016	*United States v. Arpaio*	The United States Department of Justice Public Integrity Section prosecuted Arpaio for criminal contempt of court for violating Snow's order.	A federal judge found Arpaio guilty of criminal contempt of court in 2017. President Donald Trump pardoned Arpaio. In 2020, the Ninth Circuit Court of Appeals denied Arpaio's bid to vacate the guilty finding against him.

On Sources

All our major on-the-record interviews are listed in Author Interviews, immediately following the Notes below. Scenes that we witnessed ourselves are identified in citations as "authors' observations." The Bibliography of Unpublished Sources provides more detailed entries for the personal correspondence, public records, press releases, and court exhibits cited in the Notes. When we describe court hearings, we are relying on the actual transcripts of the hearings and our observations.

Notes

PROLOGUE

xxv n1 **The window shade was drawn:** This chapter draws from author interviews with Joe Arpaio at his office in Fountain Hills.

xxv n2 **He'd long branded himself . . . moldy food:** *Graves v. Arpaio,* 623 F.3d 1043 (9th Cir., 2010).

xxv n3 **As sheriff . . . tens of thousands of undocumented immigrants:** ICE records show the MCSO's 287(g) partnership identified more than 40,000 immigrants for deportation. According to MCSO, press release, December 21, 2011, the tally was 44,000. See U.S. Immigrations and Customs Enforcement, "287(g)-Identified Aliens for Removal," 287(g) Master Stats, October 31, 2010, via ICE FOIA Library, https://www.ice.gov/doclib/foia/reports /287g-masterstats2010oct31.pdf; U.S. Immigration and Customs Enforcement, "287(g) Removals/Voluntary Returns," FY 2011, 2013, via Muck-Rock, https://www.muckrock.com/foi/united-states-of-america-10/ices-statistics-on-deportation-through-the-287g-in-fy2011-fy2013–12227/; U.S. Immigration and Customs Enforcement, "ICE 287(g) Program Removal Statistics for FY2012," via MuckRock, https://www.muckrock.com/foi/ united-states-of-america-10/ices-statistics-on-deportation-removal-through-the-287g-in-fy2012–8942/.

xxvi **I'm the victim:** Arpaio interviews.

xxvii n1 **Trump, fourteen years..."never surrender":** Arpaio interviews.

xxvii n2 **He could take care of himself:** Arpaio interviews.

xxvii n3 **The president reportedly had asked:** Philip Rucker and Ellen Nakashima, "Trump asked Sessions about closing case against Arpaio, an ally since birtherism," *The Washington Post*, August 26, 2017.

xxviii n1 **The president read InfoWars:** Jim Rutenberg, "In Trump's volleys, echoes of Alex Jones's conspiracy theories," *The New York Times*, February 19, 2017.

xxviii n2 **The piece was headlined:** Jerome Corsi, "'Where is Trump?' Sheriff Arpaio asks," InfoWars, August 7, 2017.

xxviii n3 **The protesters included:** Libby Nelson, "'Why we voted for Donald Trump': David Duke explains the white supremacist Charlottesville protests," Vox, August 12, 2017.

xxviii n4 **"very fine people on both sides":** There is a full accounting of this quote in Robert Farley, "Trump has condemned white supremacists," FactCheck.org, February 11, 2020.

xxix n1 **Lydia Guzman stood with thousands of protesters:** This section draws from author interviews with Lydia Guzman, including at the August 22, 2017 protest.

xxix n2 **Recent polling showed:** Megan Cassidy, "Poll: Arizonans oppose Joe Arpaio pardon; ex-sheriff says he hasn't been invited to rally," *The Arizona Republic*, August 21, 2017.

xxxi **"he's going to say my name":** Arpaio interviews.

ONE. AN IMMIGRANT'S SON

3 **Ciro jumped aboard the *Presidente Wilson*:** U.S. Department of Labor Immigration Service, "List Six List or Manifest for Alien Passengers for the United States," *SS Presidente Wilson*, July 1, 1923.

4 n1 **beat the ten other ships:** "Immigration record broken as 11 ships race to enter port," *The New York Times*, July 2, 1923; Catherine G. Massey, "Immigration Quotas and Immigrant Selection," Center for Administrative Records Research and Applications, U.S. Census Bureau, February 2015.

4 n2 **When the *Presidente Wilson* arrived:** "The Nation's Immigration Laws, 1920 to Today," Pew Research Center, September 28, 2015.

4 n3 **swarthy-skinned invaders:** Francis A. Walker, "Restriction of immigration," *The Atlantic*, June 1896.

5 n1 **They feared eastern and southern European immigrants:** "Eugenists dread tainted aliens," *The New York Times*, September 25, 1921.

5n2 **foreign born again occupied over 13 percent:** Gustavo López and Jiynnah Radford, "2015, Foreign-Born Population in the United States, Statistical Portrait," Pew Research Center, May 3, 2017.

5n3 **Josephine had immigrated . . . Josephine died:** "Mrs. Ciro Arpaio dies; funeral on Monday," *Springfield Republican,* June 25, 1932.

5n4 **Ciro was thirty:** "Wedding ceremony at St. Ann's Church," *Springfield Republican,* June 28, 1931.

6n1 **Michael:** Joe Arpaio's half-brother did not respond to interview requests for this book.

6n2 **"the promotion rolls were backed up":** Joe Arpaio and Len Sherman, *Joe's Law: America's Toughest Sheriff Takes on Illegal Immigration, Drugs, and Everything Else That Threatens America* (New York: American Management Association, 2008), 136.

7n1 **Bill Mattingly:** The account of Arpaio's undercover work draws from William Mattingly and Joe Arpaio interviews.

7n2 **"Italian cutie":** Dolores Tropiano, "The woman behind the star," *The Arizona Republic,* May 6, 1997.

7n2 **Joe, go home to Ava:** Mattingly interview.

8n1 **"It's okay":** Ava Arpaio interviews.

8n2 **It was a prestigious post:** "The Early Years," Drug Enforcement Administration, https://www.dea.gov/documents/1919/12/17/dea-history-early-years.

8n3 **Ciro read a story:** The Associated Press, "Ton of opium seized in Turkey," *The Times Record,* April 2, 1963.

8n4 **In an interview with a Phoenix reporter:** Randy Collier, "Retiring 'narc' recalls exploits," *The Arizona Republic,* July 25, 1982.

9n1 **He referenced the shootout again:** "Statement of Joseph M. Arpaio," Transcript of Hearing Before the Caucus on International Narcotics Control of the United States Senate, April 19, 1989.

9n2 **In both books . . . "on one occasion":** Joe Arpaio and Len Sherman, *Sheriff Joe Arpaio, America's Toughest Sheriff: How We Can Win the War against Crime* (Arlington, TX: Summit Publishing Group, 1996), 185; Arpaio and Sherman, *Joe's Law,* 166–167.

9n3 **We asked . . . "I never killed anybody":** Arpaio interviews. The DEA refused our request for Arpaio's personnel records, and we could not independently verify Arpaio's account.

10n1 **In the nation's capital . . . "regaled" Nixon with "war stories":** Arpaio and Sherman, *Sheriff Joe Arpaio,* 217.

10 n2 In 1969, Nixon ordered . . . with herbicides: Richard B. Craig, "Operation Intercept: The International Politics of Pressure," *The Review of Politics,* vol. 42, no. 4 (October 1980), 556–580; https://www.jstor.org/stable/1406640.

11 n1 By that time the Arpaios had a second child: Sherry Arpaio Boas and her brother, Rocco Arpaio, live in the Phoenix area; both declined to be interviewed for this book. Sherry's husband, Phil Boas, the editor of *The Arizona Republic* editorial pages, also declined. Boas had long recused himself from participating in the newspaper's coverage of his father-in-law.

11 n2 The Nixon administration valued Arpaio: "Narcotics, Marijuana and Dangerous Drugs Findings and Recommendations," report from Narcotics, Marijuana and Dangerous Drug Task Force, June 6, 1969.

12 n1 As the new DEA agent . . . wouldn't confirm it, either: Phil Jordan and Arpaio interviews; Dan Barr, "Demotion of drug-enforcement official reversed," *The Arizona Republic,* June 30, 1981.

12 n2 Garcia . . . clashed with Arpaio: This account draws from author interviews with Laura Garcia and "Chemicals kept by agency moved from bank center," *The Arizona Republic,* August 2, 1979.

13 n1 Arpaio remembered the conflict: Arpaio interviews.

13 n2 He was feted: Dorothee Polson, "Pot au Feu," *The Arizona Republic,* July 21, 1982.

14 On the stump: "Ex-drug agent, teacher plan council races," *The Arizona Republic,* February 2, 1983.

15 n1 reservations for space flights: Dave Eskes, "Affordable bookings on space flights available," *The Phoenix Gazette,* May 5, 1985, and J. Martin McOmber, "Society Expeditions files for bankruptcy," *The Seattle Times,* July 1, 2004.

15 n2 The United States Census . . . or Other: "1990 Census of Population: General Population Characteristics Arizona," U.S. Department of Commerce, Economic and Statistics Administration, Bureau of the Census, 1990.

15 n3 He was endorsed: "Arpaio for sheriff," *The Arizona Republic,* November 1, 1992.

15 n4 Kobor . . . an Arpaio loyalist for decades: Kathryn Kobor interviews.

16 Ava began calling him: Joe and Ava Arpaio interviews.

TWO. THE VALLEY GIRL

17 never thought much about her ethnicity: The accounts of Guzman's childhood draw from Lydia Guzman and Rafaela Avila interviews.

20 n1 Soto had felt discriminated against: Nell Soto, interview by Carlos Vasquez, July 12 and August 25, 1988, Pomona, California, transcript,

California State Archives State Government Oral History Program, https://archives.cdn.sos.ca.gov/oral-history/pdf/oh-soto-nell.pdf.

20n2 **In the 1987 election:** Irene Chang, "Ruling upheld on Pomona elections: Appeals court backs decision that system doesn't dilute minority vote," *The Los Angeles Times*, August 27, 1989.

20n3 **Pomona voters approved city council districts:** Jeffrey Miller, "Voters to decide how council is elected," *The Los Angeles Times*, September 22, 1988.

22n1 **They both lost:** Phil Sneiderman, "Largest field in years seeks Palmdale race," *The Los Angeles Times*, March 28, 1994.

22n2 **The proposed law:** "Save Our State (SOS): Illegal Aliens. Ineligibility for Public Services. Verification and Reporting. Initiative Statute," California Proposition 187 (1994).

22n3 **Tanton didn't deny:** Terry Greene Sterling, "FAIRy tales," *Phoenix New Times*, December 2–8, 2010.

23n1 **"In California of 2030 . . . political San Andreas Fault?":** John Tanton, Memo to WITAN IV Attendees, "WITAN MEMO," Part III, October 10, 1986, published by Southern Poverty Law Center, https://www.splcenter.org/fighting-hate/intelligence-report/2015/witan-memo-iii (accessed June 12, 2020).

23n2 **Tanton's memo . . . was leaked:** Andy Hall, "English advocate assailed," *The Arizona Republic*, October 9, 1988.

23n3 **But Tanton's memo, widely viewed as racist . . . Linda Chavez:** Andy Hall, "2 in US English quit over charges of racism," *The Arizona Republic*, October 18, 1988.

23n4 **Walter Cronkite:** Andy Hall, "'English' drive takes two setbacks," *The Arizona Republic*, October 14, 1988.

23n5 **He told *The Arizona Republic*:** Andy Hall, "English advocate assailed," *The Arizona Republic*, October 9, 1988.

23n6 **"I've come to the point of view":** John Tanton, letter to Garrett Hardin, December 10, 1993, quoted in Southern Poverty Law Center, "John Tanton," Extremist Files, https://www.splcenter.org/fighting-hate/extremist-files/individual/john-tanton (accessed May 21, 2020).

24n1 **FAIR bankrolled:** "Both sides air ads on Prop. 187," *The Los Angeles Times*, November 6, 1994.

24n2 **marched with about seventy thousand people:** Patrick J. McConnell and Robert J. Lopez, "L.A. march against Prop. 187 draws 70,000: Immigration protesters condemn Wilson for backing initiative that they say promotes 'racism, scapegoating,'" *The Los Angeles Times*, October 17, 1994.

25n1 **Four hundred thirty-two undocumented immigrants:** Office of the Attorney General Grant Woods, "Results of the Chandler Survey," State of Arizona, 1997, 1.

25n2 **"Numerous American citizens":** ibid., 31.

26 **"I'm here to help":** Nancy Velasco interview.

27n1 **"a full scale attack":** Danny Ortega interviews.

27n2 **struck down Official English:** *Ruiz v. Hull*, 191 Ariz. 441, 957 P.2d 984 (1998).

THREE. WHAT MADE ARIZONA CHICANOS

28n1 **Joe Arpaio hadn't been sheriff long:** This section draws from author interviews with Lisa Allen.

28n2 **First . . . Arpaio erected "Tent City":** Frederick Bermudez and Richard F. Casey, "A place to put the bad guys," *The Arizona Republic*, August 3, 1993. The Tent City jail grew to seventy tents by 2017; see Fernanda Santos, "Outdoor jail, a vestige of Joe Arpaio's tenure, is closing," *The New York Times*, April 4, 2017.

29n1 **They shared:** George E. Sullivan, "Report of Corrections Consultant on the Use of Force in the Maricopa County Jails, Phoenix, Arizona," May 14, 1997, 42.

29n2 **"GOP Kingmaker":** Martin Van Der Werf, "Arpaio plays GOP kingmaker," *The Arizona Republic*, September 6, 1996.

29n3 **His approval rating:** Steve Yozwiak, "Arpaio at peak of popularity," *The Arizona Republic*, March 19, 1997.

30n1 **Inside the sheriff's office:** Allegations of troubles in the workplace were detailed in Deputy Chief Frank B. Munnell, memo, August 17, 2010.

30n2 **In the early years:** John Kleinheinz interviews; Allen interview.

30n3 **"I don't see anybody dying":** "60 Minutes footage shows Arpaio when he was ruthless 'Joe the Jailer,' *60 Minutes*, August 25, 2017 rebroadcast of the February 11, 2001 profile by CBS News.

31n1 **Inmates were subjected to excessive use of force:** F. Eugene Miller, "Expert Penologist's Report on the Use of Force in the Maricopa County Jail System," January 10, 1996.

31n2 **restraint chairs . . . violent guards:** Sullivan, "Report of Corrections Consultant on the Use of Force in the Maricopa County Jails, Phoenix Arizona," May 14, 1997, 22–24.

31n3 **Arpaio regularly showed up at El Portal:** The following section draws from author interviews with Mary Rose Wilcox and Earl Wilcox.

32 **In 1848:** See Library of Congress, "Treaty of Guadalupe Hidalgo," Primary Documents in American History, https://www.loc.gov/rr/program/bib/ourdocs/guadalupe.html (accessed July 5, 2020).

33 n1 **In a popular 1878 guidebook:** Richard J. Hinton, *The Hand-Book to Arizona: Its Resources, History, Towns, Mines, Ruins and Scenery* (San Francisco: Pavot-Upham and Company, San Francisco, 1878; republished Tucson: Arizona Silhouettes, 1954), 379–380.

33 n2 **"Phoenix" . . . code for the rebirth of the South:** Edmund Drago, *Confederate Phoenix: Rebel Children and Their Families in South Carolina* (New York: Fordham University Press, 2010), 2.

33 n3 **By 1870, 240 people:** Bradford Luckingham, *Minorities in Phoenix, a Profile of Mexican American, Chinese American and African American Communities 1860–1992* (Tucson: University of Arizona Press, 1993).

33 n4 **Anglo was a synonym for "white":** Katherine Benton-Cohen, *Borderline Americans, Racial Division and Labor War in the Arizona Borderlands* (Cambridge, MA: Harvard University Press, 2009), 6–15.

34 n1 **In 1912 . . . how many Anglos in the town viewed:** "This is the United States," *The Arizona Republican*, September 17, 1912.

34 n2 **The test disenfranchised:** Benton-Cohen, *Borderline Americans*, 170.

34 n3 **Gutierrez was born into the anti-"Mexican" climate:** This section draws from Alfredo Gutierrez interviews and his memoir, *To Sin Against Hope: How America Has Failed Its Immigrants, a Personal History* (New York: Verso, 2013).

34 n4 **President Herbert Hoover . . . "real Americans":** Quoted in Diane Bernard, "The time a president deported 1 million Mexican Americans for supposedly stealing US jobs," *The Washington Post*, August 13, 2018.

34 n5 **part of a gutsy labor movement:** David R. Berman, *Radicalism in the American West 1890–1920: Socialists, Populists, Miners, and Wobblies* (Boulder: University of Colorado Press, 2007).

35 n1 **The Eisenhower administration claimed:** Kelly Lytle Hernandez, "Largest deportation campaign in U.S. history is no match for Trump's plan," University of California Los Angeles Newsroom, March 23, 2017, https://newsroom.ucla.edu/stories/ucla-faculty-voice:-largest-deportation-campaign-in-u-s-history-is-no-match-for-trumps-plan (accessed June 12, 2020). See also Kelly Lytle Hernandez, *Migra! A History of the U.S. Border Patrol* (Berkeley: University of California Press, 2010), 189. Hernandez found deportations slowed after Operation Wetback began and likely accounted for fewer than 300,000 apprehensions.

36 **often gathered in the shade of a large tree:** Later generations of Chicano students would describe the iconic spot by its proximity to a nearby hedge.

37 **"I was like Mr. Mainstream":** Quotes in this section draw from Danny Ortega interviews.

39 n1 **"You are one of the smartest Mexicans":** Gutierrez interviews.

39 n2 **"I knew what was going on behind my back":** Gutierrez interviews.

39 n3 **He clashed with his mentor:** This section draws from Gutierrez interviews; Gutierrez, *To Sin Against Hope*, 102–103; Ted Hesson, "Cesar Chavez's complex history on immigration," ABC News, May 1, 2013.

41 n1 **A Mexican farmworker with a green card:** *Gonzales v. City of Peoria*, No. 78-cv-618, Pls' Mot. for Summ. J. at 9 (D. Ariz., June 2, 1981).

41 n2 **But the Peoria police chief figured:** Peoria Chief of Police Newlin E. Happersett, letter, August 10, 1978.

42 **The appellate court opinion established:** *Gonzales v. City of Peoria*, 722 F.2d 468 (9th Cir. 1983). The ruling also established that local police could enforce the criminal provisions of federal immigration law, including illegal entry, if they had evidence a migrant had crossed the border illegally.

43 **After serving as Cesar Chavez's bodyguard:** Antonio Bustamante interviews.

FOUR. RESTRICTIONISM TAKES ROOT

44 **Guzman thought . . . Avila confessed:** Lydia Guzman and Rafaela Avila interviews.

45 n1 **stop the "illegals" from their alleged thievery:** Russell Pearce interviews.

45 n2 **Proposition 200 was backed by FAIR:** Terry Greene Sterling, "FAIRy tales," *Phoenix New Times*, December 2–8, 2010.

46 n1 **Pearce told us he was patrolling Guadalupe late one night:** "Deputy shot in chest with his own revolver," *The Arizona Republic*, July 3, 1977. We requested county juvenile records from this incident but they were destroyed in 2002, so we could not independently verify Pearce's account of the shooting.

46 n2 **After a controversial tenure:** In 1999, Pearce was fired as director of the state Motor Vehicle Division, in part because he changed a drunk driver's record to allow her to keep her license, according to news reports. Pearce denied the allegation and told us he was let go for political reasons. His former boss contradicted his account. See David Parrish, "Ex-MVD head's son charged in fraud," *The Arizona Republic*, December 23, 1999, and Stephen Lemons, "Russell Pearce seems incapable of telling the truth, even about his own religion," *Phoenix New Times*, March 29, 2012.

47 **Lou Dobbs lamented:** Lou Dobbs, *Lou Dobbs Tonight*, CNN, October 13, 2004.

47 **O'Reilly said:** Bill O'Reilly, interview with Peter Sepp, *The O'Reilly Factor*, Fox News, May 2, 2002.

48n1 **Proposition 200 opponents advised their allies:** "Protecting Arizona," Episode 9 of *How Democracy Works Now*, DVD, directed by Shari Robertson and Michael Camerini, 2010 (in the scene "The Consultants").

48n2 **And a young restrictionist:** Andrew Thomas did not respond to our request for an interview for this book

49 **Even the local Spanish language newspaper . . . applauded:** "Bien, la ley anti coyotes," *La Voz*, March 16, 2005.

50 **One Latino state lawmaker warned:** See Ben Miranda's comments in Arizona House of Representatives, Committee on Judiciary, Minutes of Meeting, February 10, 2005.

FIVE. ARPAIO TRANSFORMED

51 ***The Fountain Hills Times* wrote:** Bob Burns, "Sheriff's Posse seeks volunteers," *The Fountain Hills Times*, December 7, 2005.

52n1 **Ava had long hoped to retire:** Dolores Trapiano, "The woman behind the star," *The Arizona Republic*, May 6, 1997.

52n2 **A sliver of moon lit the dark desert:** The Patrick Haab account draws from Deputy Don Hess, MCSO Supplemental Report DR#05–063171, April 11, 2005; Detective J. D. Clancy, MCSO Supplemental Report DR#05–063171, April 26, 2005; MCSO 911 Call Transcript DR#063171, April 10, 2005; *Haab v. County of Maricopa*, 219 Ariz. 9191, P.3d 1025 (Az. Ct. App., Div. I, 2008); Devin Browne, "The case of Patrick Haab," *The Sasabe Republic*, 2017.

52n3 **Border Patrol agents stopped. . . more than one million:** U.S. Department of Homeland Security, *Yearbook of Immigration Statistics: 2006* (Washington, D.C.: U.S. Department of Homeland Security, Office of Immigration Statistics, 2007), 93.

53n1 **Haab walked . . . so his black Labrador retriever:** Kristina Davis, "East Valley man defends detaining migrants," *East Valley Tribune*, April 14, 2005.

53n2 **At a jailhouse press conference:** Robert Anglen, "GI: I held migrants in self-defense," *The Arizona Republic*, April 14, 2005.

54n1 **Strangers sent Haab donations:** Robert Anglen, "Soldier overwhelmed by support since arrest," *The Arizona Republic*, April 16, 2005.

54n2 **Haab insisted he didn't have a clue:** Patrick Haab, interview by Sean Hannity and Alan Colmes, *Hannity & Colmes*, Fox News, April 18, 2006.

54 n3 **Following Haab's arrest, Arpaio condemned:** Nick Martin, "Mesan arrested in detaining of migrants," *East Valley Tribune,* April 12, 2005.

55 n1 **Angry county voters wrote letters to newspaper editors:** Charles A. Webb, letter to the editor, *The Arizona Republic,* April 14, 2005; Chris Perkins, letter to the editor, *The Arizona Republic,* April 16, 2005; John Barclay, letter to the editor, *The Arizona Republic,* April 16, 2005.

55 n2 **He proposed unconventional fixes:** Cited in Terry Carter, "The prosecutor on trial: Ex-Maricopa County attorney faces disbarment for political ads," *ABA Journal,* April 1, 2012.

55 n3 **Thomas's actions on such a high-profile case embarrassed:** Brian Sands interviews. Arpaio told us: "I didn't lose any sleep over it."

55 n4 **Acosta's former boyfriend and father of her two children:** Arpaio interviews and *Arizona v. Zavala,* No. CR-2004011514 (Maricopa Cty. Super. Ct., 2005).

56 n1 **"If critics want to complain I'm smuggling aliens":** Daniel Gonzalez, "Mom reunited with abducted kids in Mexico," *The Arizona Republic,* July 20, 2005.

56 n2 **"They're citizens of the United States":** Dennis Wagner and Susan Carroll, "2 Ariz. cases show 'tangled mess' U.S. immigration law has become," *The Arizona Republic,* July 21, 2005.

56 n3 **guest of honor at a consulate event:** Lydia Guzman and Danny Ortega interviews.

57 n1 **Thanks to his influence, the justice department reversed:** Kris Kobach interview; U.S. Department of Justice, Office of Legal Counsel, Memorandum for the Attorney General, Washington, D.C., April 3, 2002.

57 n2 **According to Kobach's interpretations . . . "inherent authority":** Kris W. Kobach, "The quintessential force multiplier: The inherent authority of local police to make immigration arrests," *Albany Law Review,* vol. 69, issue 1 (2006), 179.

58 **Thomas laid it all out in a legal opinion:** Andrew P. Thomas, September 29, 2005.

59 n1 **"I'm not going to go around on street corners":** Amanda Lee Myers, "Lawmakers: Maricopa prosecutor misinterpreting immigration law," The Associated Press, March 3, 2006.

59 n2 **Arpaio would claim in his second memoir:** Joe Arpaio and Len Sherman, *Joe's Law: America's Toughest Sheriff Takes on Illegal Immigration, Drugs, and Everything Else that Threatens America* (New York: American Management Association, 2008), 26.

60 **Even before the new law was passed:** U.S. General Accounting Office, *Border Control: Revised Strategy Is Showing Some Positive Results* (Washington, D.C.: U.S. General Accounting Office, December 29, 1994).

61 n1 Thousands died on the journey: U.S. Government Accountability Office, *Illegal Immigration: Border-Crossing Deaths Have Doubled Since 1995; Border Patrol's Efforts to Prevent Deaths Have Not Been Fully Evaluated* (Washington, D.C., U.S. General Accountability Office, August 15, 2006). The remains of more than 3,000 migrants found in southern Arizona were turned over to the Pima County Office of the Medical Examiner between 2000 and 2019. See Pima County Office of the Medical Examiner, *Annual Report* (2019), 31.

61 n2 As border crossings became more treacherous: Wayne A. Cornelius, "Impacts of Border Enforcement on Unauthorized Mexican Migration to the United States," Social Science Research Council: Insights from the Social Sciences (September 26, 2006), https://items.ssrc.org/border-battles/impacts-of-border-enforcement-on-unauthorized-mexican-migration-to-the-united-states/ (accessed May 31, 2020).

61 n3 surveyed six hundred Maricopa County residents: Behavior Research Center Rocky Mountain Poll, "Immigration debate coverage leads Arizonans to exaggerate the proportion of illegal aliens in the workforce; ignites hostile feelings toward businesses who hire them," news release, October 5, 2005.

SIX. THE MOVEMENT RISES UP

66 n1 Sensenbrenner bill sparked: Irene Bloemraad, Kim Voss, and Taeku Lee, "The Protests of 2006," in *Rallying for Immigrant Rights: The Fight for Inclusion in 21st Century America,* ed. Kim Voss and Irene Bloemraad (Berkeley: University of California Press, 2011).

66 n2 "biggest demonstration ever": Yvonne Wingett and Susan Caroll, "20,000 in Phoenix rally for migrants," *The Arizona Republic,* March 25, 2006.

66 n3 The April 10, 2006 marches: This section draws from author interviews with Carlos Garcia, Alfredo Gutierrez, Lydia Guzman, Martin Manteca, and Danny Ortega.

67 But Bermudez . . . served time in federal prison: *United States v. Tinoco,* No. 2:94-cr-00216 (D. Ariz., January 10, 1996).

69 Somos America raised more than sixty thousand: Somos America, budget, April 21, 2006; Manteca interview.

70 "electoral earthquake in America!": Alfredo Gutierrez, "Recapturing the American ideal," *The Arizona Republic,* April 11, 2006.

71 n1 voters in one poll believed: Daniel González and Mike Maddon, "Immigrant clamor has everyone's attention," *The Arizona Republic,* May 3, 2006.

71 n2 In the hours after the Phoenix march: This section draws from author interviews with Jim Williams.

SEVEN. HOPES AND LETDOWNS

73 **nine million dollars to the family of Charles Agster:** Michael Manning interviews and the following documents from *Agster v. Maricopa Cty.*, (D. Ariz.) No. 2:02-cv-01686: Document 44 (First Amended Complaint, April 14, 2003); Document 51 (Answer to Pls' First Amended Complaint, April 28, 2003). The original Agster verdict award was reduced to $6,650,000. See Document 810 (Order, December 20, 2006); Document 811 (Amended Judgment, December 20, 2006); Document 820 (Order, March 30, 2007).

74n1 **Arpaio . . . denied wrongdoing:** *Norberg v. Maricopa County*, No. 2:97-cv-00866 (D. Ariz.).

74n2 **settlement of over eight million dollars:** Jerry Kammer, "Norberg's death still a mystery," *The Arizona Republic*, January 17, 1999. Manning, email, March 29, 2020.

74n3 **he was sure Arpaio's deputies were tailing him:** This section draws from author interviews with Michael Manning.

74n4 **ambulance chaser:** JJ Hensley and Megan Boehnke, "Lovejoy files claim vs. Arpaio over prosecution in K-9 death," *The Arizona Republic*, September 11, 2008.

75n1 **Yet Steve Bailey:** Author interviews with Steve Bailey. As a captain of the special investigations division, Bailey briefly was given oversight of the Human Smuggling Unit in 2014. He told us at that time he ended all immigration-related enforcement. He later led internal investigations related to the unit.

75n2 **Some . . . felt conflicted:** When the sheriff's office trained deputies to be 287(g) certified in 2007, Jerry Sheridan, who ran Arpaio's jails at the time, said bilingual Latino deputies told him they had not volunteered to take the 287(g) training. "I was devastated when I found out from some of the Hispanic guys especially, that they were ordered to do that," Sheridan told us. "And I didn't think that was right, because they had to go home to their families and tell them what was going on." See also Paul Giblin, "Immigration arrests cause conflicting loyalties for Hispanic deputies," *East Valley Tribune*, July 11, 2008.

75n3 **covered the migrant hunts:** Randall C. Archibold, "Arizona County uses new law to look for illegal immigrants," *The New York Times*, May 10, 2006, and John Pomfret and Sonya Geis, "Sheriff's illegal-immigrant offer: Up to 2 years on a chain gang," *The Washington Post*, May 21, 2006.

75n4 **"supported" the effort:** Bruce Merrill, "Bush's Proposals for Immigration Reform Strongly Supported," Arizona State University/Arizona PBS KAET poll, May 23, 2006.

75n5 **"thousands of letters . . . all were positive":** MCSO, press release, May 24, 2006.

76n1 **Elias Bermudez . . . led a protest:** Details about the protest draw from author interviews with Joe Arpaio and Elias Bermudez; Mel Meléndez, "Rally puts the heat on sheriff, official," *The Arizona Republic*, July 15, 2006; Sara Lynch, "Immigration activists challenge Arpaio," *East Valley Tribune*, July 14, 2006.

76n2 **"You can't change my mind":** Lynch, "Immigration activists challenge Arpaio."

77n1 **Arpaio . . . had arrested:** MCSO, press release, June 23, 2006.

77n2 **thought the law was bad policy:** Valeria Fernández, "En la frontera de la ley," *La Voz*, June 4, 2006.

77n3 **shuttled fifty-three immigrants:** Michael Kiefer, "Coyote law still untested by a jury," *The Arizona Republic*, August 18, 2006.

77n4 **Thomas jumped in with a legal opinion:** Andrew P. Thomas, August 1, 2006.

78n1 **joined a lawsuit:** *We Are America/Somos America Coalition of Arizona v. Maricopa County Board of Supervisors*, No. 2:06-cv-02816 (D. Ariz. 2006).

78n2 **the women had crossed into Arizona:** MCSO, Continuation Report DR:06–156216, September 18, 2006.

79n1 **"I'm not a criminal":** Lydia Guzman interviews.

79n2 **a federal judge would finally rule:** *We are America/Somos America*, Document 137 (Order, September 27, 2013).

79n3 **arrested more than 2,300 people:** According to federal court records, Maricopa County Sheriff's Office arrested more than 1,800 migrants on conspiracy to smuggle themselves between 2006 and June 2011. Records we received directly from the sheriff's office to account for July 2011 to September 2013 show 570 arrests for violations of the Human Smuggling Law in that time frame, but did not distinguish between smuggler and smugglee arrests.

80n1 **only two thousand showed up:** Daniel González and Monica Alonzo-Dunsmoor, "Few at immigration rally," *The Arizona Republic*, September 5, 2006.

80n2 **Mexican flag . . . diaper:** Monica Alonso-Dunsmoor, "Counterprotest makes mark at migrant rally," *The Arizona Republic*, September 5, 2006.

81n1 **"best friend illegal aliens have":** Howard Fischer, "Governor kills GOP border measure," Capitol Media Services, *The Arizona Daily Star*, June 7, 2006.

81n2 **Operation Wetback:** Sarah Lynch, "Pearce calls on Operation Wetback for illegals," *East Valley Tribune*, September 29, 2006.

81n3 **frenzied hub of voter outreach:** Martin Manteca and Guzman interviews. SEIU was also mobilizing Latino voters to pass a union-backed ballot initiative to raise the minimum wage.

81n4 **Latino voters . . . in the 2004 election:** William C. Velasquez Institute,
"Arizona Latino Voter Statistics," Census Analysis.

82n1 **thousands of Latino voters:** Manteca interviews. Manteca said that year
they signed up 36,000 voters to vote by mail.

82n2 **reviewed by Kobach:** Kris Kobach interview.

83n1 **"self-deport":** Jessica Vaughan, "Attrition Through Enforcement: A Cost-
Effective Strategy to Shrink the Illegal Population," Center for Immigration Studies, April 1, 2006.

83n2 **reduce Arizona's crime rate:** Russell Pearce, interview by Greta Wodele,
Washington Journal, C-SPAN, August 30, 2007.

83n3 **The governor claimed:** Janet Napolitano declined our requests for an
interview.

EIGHT. CAVE CREEK

85n1 **Jenks, the church rector:** This section draws from author interviews with
Father Glenn Jenks.

85n2 **"a magnet, drawing . . . like manure attracts flies":** The Associated
Press, "Valley publisher criticized, hailed for immigration articles," *Arizona Daily Sun,* September 28, 2003. Quote verified by Don Sorchych to
authors on October 18, 2018.

85n3 **Bentley, Sorchych's like-minded reporter:** Linda Bentley, "Cave
Creek judge tired of being scammed," *Sonoran News,* December 13,
2006.

85n4 **Bentley told us her unease over unauthorized immigrants:** This section
draws from author interviews with Linda Bentley.

87n1 **Galeener, a retired producer of Wild West shows:** This section draws
from author interviews with Buffalo Rick Galeener.

87n2 **because it "facilitated" the hiring of unauthorized immigrants:** Tim
Rafferty interview.

88n1 **Polls showed:** A Behavior Research Center Rocky Mountain Poll found
Arpaio had 64 percent approval in March 2007, which the poll said made
him "just about the most popular guy around." Referenced in "Sheriff Joe
Arpaio still popular . . . but appears to have peaked; county attorney ratings slip," news release, December 4, 2007.

88 n2 **earliest 287(g) partnership agreements:** U.S. Immigration and Customs Enforcement, "Fact Sheet, the ICE 287(g) program: A law enforcement partnership," January 21, 2010.

89 n1 **ICE . . . flat out refused:** Daniel González, "New ICE agent must deal with smuggling, politics," *The Arizona Republic,* October 16, 2006.

89 n2 **cornered Peña with additional questions:** Richard Ruelas, "Arpaio stays silent on real ICE plan," *The Arizona Republic,* March 2, 2007, and Ruelas interview. We were unable to speak with Alonzo Peña before his death in 2019. He testified in 2012 that he was unaware the sheriff's office had violated its 287(g) agreement with ICE.

89 n3 **the local ICE office would conduct little oversight:** U.S. Government Accountability Office, *Immigration Enforcement: Better Controls Needed over Program Authorizing State and Local Enforcement of Federal Immigration Laws* (Washington, D.C.: U.S. Government Accountability Office, January 30, 2009).

90 n1 **Arpaio couldn't remember his uncle's name:** Joe Arpaio interviews; Joe Arpaio, interview by Glenn Thrush, *Off Message Podcast,* Politico, June 20, 2016.

90 n2 **didn't comport with immigration policy at the time:** Catherine Massey, "Immigration quotas and immigrant selection," *Explorations in Economic History* 60 (2016): 23. See also Emergency Quota Act (Washington, D.C., U.S. Government Printing Office, 1921); Marinari, email, July 26, 2020.

91 n1 **"look like they're from a foreign country":** Judi Villa and Yvonne Wingett, "Sheriff unveils migrant hotline," *The Arizona Republic,* July 21, 2007.

92 n1 **more than 150 messages:** Yvonne Wingett, "Sheriff's office to analyze immigration-hotline calls," *The Arizona Republic,* July 24, 2007.

92 n2 **"Legal taxpayers!":** Carol V. Barotholomeaux, letter, in Arpaio immigration file records, July 26, 2007, 562–563.

92 n3 **the list went on and on:** Arpaio, hotline notes, in Arpaio immigration file records, July 26, 2007, 510.

93 n1 **to inform on Jews:** Arpaio immigration file records, August 7, 2007, 698; Arpaio interviews.

93 n2 **Alonzo Peña . . . had no problem:** Peña, letter, August 14, 2007.

93 n3 **Arpaio kept notes:** Arpaio, immigration file records, August 2007, 525; Arpaio interviews.

93 n4 **Latino blowback . . . unintended consequence:** E. J. Montini, "Critics of illegal-immigration hotline forgot they can't beat Arpaio," *The Arizona Republic,* August 12, 2007.

93 n5 **simply to offer their praise and support:** Arpaio, immigration file records, August 2007, 389, 383–388.

93 n6 **staff had gotten a tip . . . to assassinate Arpaio:** MCSO, Supplemental Report, "Conspiracy to Commit Murder," DR#07–54071, 2007; Yvonne Wingett and Dennis Wagner, "Supposed plot to kill Arpaio is doubted," *The Arizona Republic,* October 7, 2007; Joe Arpaio and Len Sherman, *Joe's Law: America's Toughest Sheriff Takes on Illegal Immigration, Drugs, and Everything Else That Threatens America* (New York: American Management Association, 2008), 3–20.

93 n7 **placing me and my family in danger":** Arpaio, immigration file records, August 2007, 525.

94 n1 **ordinance passed easily:** Town of Cave Creek, Special Town Council Meeting minutes, September 24, 2007.

94 n2 **undercover Latino 287(g) deputies:** Ross, email, September 24, 2007.

94 n3 **From behind a sun visor:** Hector Lopez interview. He witnessed the events that morning. The description of Melendres's arrest draws from Melendres interviews; Madrid, email, September 27, 2007; MCSO, CAD Incident History, #MA07181873, September 27, 2007; and Louis DePietro and Carlos Rangel testimony in the *Melendres* case.

95 **valid Mexican tourist visa:** U.S. Department of Homeland Security, memo to S. House of Representatives Judiciary Committee, "Response to U.S. House of Representatives Inquiry Dated 2/12/09." This memo included the recollection of a Phoenix ICE agent who had spoken with Melendres while in ICE custody, and said Melendres had denied he was working, and had a valid tourist visa and I-94 entry form. In contrast, MCSO deputy Carlos Rangel testified in 2012 that Melendres did not have an I-94 entry form with him and had said he was en route to work.

96 n1 **"jack off":** *Melendres v. Arpaio,* No. 2:07-cv-02513, Document 1 (D. Ariz., Complaint, December 12, 2007).

96 n2 **joined by six more day laborers:** Madrid, email, September 27, 2007.

NINE. TENSIONS AT A PHOENIX FURNITURE STORE

97 n1 **claimed the day laborers ogled schoolchildren:** Deborah B., email, September 17, 2007; Jafari, email, October 12, 2007.

97 n2 **day laborers weren't accused:** *Melendres,* Document 579 (Findings of Fact, May 24, 2013).

98 n1 **Arpaio's commanders took matters into their own hands:** The description of the Fountain Hills operation draws from John Kleinheinz, Joe

Arpaio, and Jerry Sheridan interviews; Ross, email, October 22, 2007, and *Melendres*, Document 579 (Findings of Fact, May 24, 2013). When asked about this incident, Arpaio insisted the day laborers "were violating the law."

98 n2 **Minuteman group:** O'Connell, letter, November 20, 2005.

98 n3 **Phoenix police chief . . . to stop:** Mel Melendez, "Activists seek work center," *The Arizona Republic,* January 13, 2006.

98 n4 **"Want to see America unraveling?":** Lawrence Downes, "When mariachis and minutemen collide," *The New York Times,* December 10, 2007.

99 n1 **Garcia felt the spit:** This section draws from Carlos Garcia interviews.

100 n1 **Reza had spent the last several years:** Salvador Reza interviews.

100 n2 **Garcia had not seen such a high level of animus:** This section draws from Carlos Garcia interviews.

101 **Kobor was in her sixties:** This section draws from Kathryn Kobor interviews.

102 n1 **Childress . . . a prominent American nativist:** "Profiles of 20 Nativist Leaders," Intelligence Report, Southern Poverty Law Center, March 1, 2008.

102 n2 **Reza, widely regarded as the mastermind:** This section draws from Salvador Reza interviews.

103 **The *Phoenix New Times* owners were released:** Terry Greene Sterling, "Journalists briefly jailed in Arizona grand jury subpoena case," *The Washington Post,* October 20, 2007. The 3.75-million-dollar settlement Jim Larkin and Mike Lacey received from the county in 2013 was confirmed by Moseley, email, June 12, 2020. Terry Greene Sterling was a staff writer at *Phoenix New Times* for fourteen years. She left the paper in 2000. Years later, Mike Lacey, a co-owner of the newspaper, gave five thousand dollars to many of his former writers, including Greene Sterling, who donated the money to the Tia Foundation, a nonprofit serving health needs in rural Mexico.

104 n1 **He was arrested for trespassing:** MCSO, Incident Report, November 3, 2007; Dan Pochoda interviews.

104 n2 **Bustamante had tried to swear off activism:** This section draws from Antonio Bustamante interviews.

105 n1 **People who turned out to support Arpaio:** Author interviews with Buffalo Rick Galeener, Kathryn Kobor, Tim Rafferty, Valerie Roller, George Sprankle, and Jim Williams.

105 n2 **undocumented population had climbed:** Michael Hofer, Nancy Rytnina, and Christopher Campbell, "Estimates of the Unauthorized Immigrant Population Residing in the United States: January 2006, Office of Immigration Statistics, U.S. Department of Homeland Security, August 2007.

https://www.dhs.gov/xlibrary/assets/statistics/publications/ill_pe_2006 .pdf (accessed June 2020).

105 n3 **nonfarm jobs had disappeared:** Maricopa County Over-the-Year Numeric Change Produced by the Arizona Office of Economic Opportunity Using CES Data in Cooperation with the U.S. Department of Labor, Bureau of Labor Statistics, 2008.

106 **suffered flashbacks and unnerving bouts of fear:** This section draws from author interviews with Manuel de Jesus Ortega Melendres.

107 n1 *Chamber of Commerce v. Whiting:* Eventually Somos America and other legal challenges would merge with this challenge to the Legal Arizona Workers Act.

107 n2 **In court papers:** *Melendres,* Document 1 (Complaint, December 12, 2007).

108 n1 **When Joe Arpaio learned:** Arpaio, undated notes (circa December 2007).

108 n2 **enjoyed widespread popularity:** Daniel González, "Arpaio keeps heat on migrants," *The Arizona Republic,* October 17, 2007.

108 n3 **He denied wrongdoing:** *Melendres,* Document 12, Defendants Arpaio and Maricopa County's Rule 12(b)(6) Motion to Dismiss, January 3, 2008, and Document 13, Separate Answer of Defendants Arpaio and Maricopa County, January 4, 2008.

TEN. MAYONNAISE TACOS AND EASTER BASKETS

109 **Guzman opened the refrigerator door:** The story of the three teenagers draws from Lydia Guzman interviews; Polanco, email, April 19, 2008, and Daniel González, "Migrant arrests severing parents from kids," *The Arizona Republic,* July 6, 2008.

110 n1 **Her new boss was Jason LeVecke:** Guzman and LeVecke interviews.

110 n2 **LeVecke was the grandson:** LeVecke interviews. Details about his business at the time comes from a declaration he made in *Arizona Contractors Association v. Candelaria,* No. 2:07-cv-02496, Document 62–1 (D. Ariz., December 17, 2007), which was a legal challenge to the Legal Arizona Workers Act.

111 n1 **"There is a general lack of understanding":** Daniel González, "Sanctions law spurs racial profiling, lawyers say," *The Arizona Republic,* September 30, 2007.

111 n2 **"I see this as a golden opportunity":** Guzman, email, January 10, 2008.

112 n1 *The Arizona Republic* **contrasted:** Michael Kiefer, "Crime rate for migrants in line with population," *The Arizona Republic,* February 25, 2008.

112 n2 **Arpaio responded to the article:** MCSO, press release, February 27, 2008.

112 n3 **From what she heard on her hotline:** Guzman, letter to the editor, *The Arizona Republic,* March 8, 2008.

113 n1 **Arpaio told reporters the two-day crackdown:** MCSO, press release, January 18, 2008.

113 n2 **On the Saturday before Easter:** This scene draws from MCSO, Saturation Patrol Documents, March 21–22, 2008; Guzman interviews; and Guzman records including Guzman, emails, "Sheriff's operations begin today Bell Rd," March 27, 2008 and "Need a lawyer . . . ," March 31, 2008.

114 n1 **Arpaio's staff had erected:** This description of the two-day Good Friday-Holy Saturday sweep comes from video footage captured by Dennis Gilman and interviews with Gilman, Brian Sands, Lydia Guzman, Salvador Reza, Danny Ortega, and Alfredo Gutierrez.

114 n2 **The sheriff had alerted:** MCSO, press release, March 20, 2008.

115 **Guzman urged Somos America activists:** Guzman, email, March 22, 2008.

116 n1 **At the end of the two-day sweep:** MCSO, Saturation Patrol Documents, March 21–22, 2008, and *Melendres,* Document 579 (Findings of Fact, May 24, 2013).

116 n2 **"Arpaio's Easter Egg Hunt":** Guzman, email, March 23, 2008.

116 n3 **The next sweep:** Galeener interviews.

116 n4 **"This is just terrible":** Guzman, email, "Friendly House & CPLC," March 27, 2008.

116 n5 **Sometimes she found sticky notes:** Guzman and Ashley Torres interviews.

117 n1 **This saturation patrol was particularly tense:** The description of this sweep comes from Bustamante, Garcia, Guzman, Gutierrez, Roller, and Sprankle interviews; Valeria Fernández, "'Redadas' del sheriff se tornan peligrosas,' *La Voz,* April 2, 2008; and documentary footage in the possession of filmmakers Valeria Fernández and Daniel DeVivo.

117 n2 **"Illegals go home!"** Fernández, "Redadas."

117 n3 **"They locked up brown people":** Gordon, speech, March 28, 2008.

117 n4 **The child's mother, Maria Aracely Reyes:** The Reyes story draws from Fernández, "Redadas"; Fernández and DeVivo video footage; MCSO, Stats sheet for saturation patrol: Cave Creek & Bell, March 28, 2008; and Guzman, email, "Info for attorneys," March 31, 2008.

118 n1 **"You are the toughest sheriff":** Fernández and DeVivo video footage.

118 n2 **"Nah nah nah nah . . .":** George Sprankle interview, and Jaquelyn Stevens, "Round Up Part 6 of 7," video posted to YouTube, April 6, 2008, https://www.youtube.com/watch?v=v6fCe08n6ss&t=48s (accessed June 13, 2020).

118 n3 **Arpaio announced to the press:** MCSO, press release, April 3, 2008.

119 n1 **He didn't:** "The People's Sheriff," PBS, March 27, 2009, https://www.pbs
.org/now/shows/513/index.html.

119 n2 **In Guadalupe, parents kept seventy kids home:** Terry Greene Sterling,
Illegal, Life and Death in Arizona's Immigration War Zone (Guilford, CT:
Globe Pequot Lyons Press, 2010), 80–81.

119 n3 **When . . . Gordon heard about Guadalupe:** Gordon, letter, April 4, 2008.

119 n4 **She emailed the most egregious:** Guzman, email, May 5, 2008.

ELEVEN. PAYBACK

120   **wearing red T-shirts that said:** Maricopa County Board of Supervisors,
Special Meeting, June 19, 2008; Dennis Gilman, "Safety and Accountability
in Maricopa County," video posted to YouTube, July 20, 2008, https://www
.youtube.com/watch?v=B_7XXssAGAg (accessed June 17, 2020); Yvonne
Wingett, "Protesters demand crackdown on Sheriff Arpaio," *The Arizona
Republic*, June 19, 2008; Barb Heller, Lydia Guzman, and Mary Rose Wilcox interviews.

121 n1 **She had quietly lobbied Governor Janet Napolitano:** Wilcox interviews
and Howard Fischer, "Napolitano diverts 1.6M from Arpaio," *Arizona
Daily Star*, May 14, 2008.

121 n2 **The county was grappling:** Wingett, "Protesters demand crackdown."

122   **He accused Wilcox of conspiring:** Arpaio's allies in the state legislature
restored the funding. See Yvonne Wingett, "Supervisors OK $1.6M to
Arpaio for immigration enforcement," *The Arizona Republic*, September 1,
2010. Phil Gordon denied having spoken to Mary Rose Wilcox or Janet
Napolitano on this matter.

123 n1 **Sometimes, his deputies arrested:** *Parraz v. Maricopa County*, No. 2:10-
cv-01663, Document 95 (D. Ariz., Order, February 4, 2013).

123 n2 **Once, deputies marched critics:** Maricopa County Board of Supervisors,
Meeting, December 17, 2008, and Stephen Lemons, "Four MCSA/ACORN
members freed after being arrested for applauding," *Phoenix New Times*,
December 18, 2008.

123 n3 **Seven protesters eventually sued:** Moseley, email, January 2, 2020.

123 n4 **While the sheriff's office diverted resources:** Ryan Gabrielson and Paul
Giblin, "Reasonable doubt part I: MCSO evolves into an immigration
agency," *East Valley Tribune*, July 10, 2008; Ryan Gabrielson, "Reasonable doubt part II: Overtime led to MCSO budget crisis, records show," *East
Valley Tribune*, July 10, 2008; and Ryan Gabrielson, "Reasonable doubt

part IV: Public safety shortchanged throughout county," *East Valley Tribune*, July 12, 2008.

123n5 **The newspaper series detailed . . . violated federal racial profiling:** Ryan Gabrielson and Paul Giblin, "Reasonable doubt part III: Sweeps and saturation patrols violate federal civil rights regulations," *East Valley Tribune*, July 11, 2008.

123n6 **Arpaio discounted the series:** Joe Arpaio interviews.

124n1 **"That's what Arpaio was living on":** Steve Bailey interviews.

124n2 **Joe Sousa . . . later told:** Joseph Sousa, interview by Daniel Giaquinto, May 8, 2017. Sousa declined to be interviewed for this book. In his Giaquinto interview, he accused Executive Chief Brian Sands of this pressure. Sands disputed Sousa's account to us, and claimed Sousa was trying to please Arpaio.

124n3 **He relied on a provision in the state's new Legal Arizona Workers Act:** The law created a new aggravated identity theft crime for using the information of "another person, including a real or fictitious person, with the intent to obtain employment."

124n4 **Panicked workers:** Descriptions of worksite raids in this section draw from Guzman interviews.

125n1 **Arpaio's deputies would arrest more than four thousand immigrants:** MCSO, Human Resources Personnel File for Armendariz, Spreadsheet of worksite raid arrests, July 1, 2016.

125n2 **Guzman did her best to respond:** The information Guzman collected from worksite raids didn't help the *Melendres* case, which was focused on traffic stops. But Guzman gave information to ACLU lawyers, who filed a suit on behalf of a Latino father and son wrongfully detained during a worksite raid. Attorneys Annie Lai, Ray Ybarra Maldonado, and others later filed a 2014 lawsuit, *Puente v. Arpaio,* challenging worksite raids and identity theft prosecutions on behalf of Puente.

125n3 **Immigrant families began fleeing:** Magnus Lofstrom, Sarah Bohn, and Steven Raphael, "Lessons from the 2007 Legal Arizona Workers Act," Public Policy Institute of California, March 2011.

125n4 **Lydia Guzman's cell phone rang:** Guzman interviews. This raid happened on October 17, 2009.

125n5 **Sometimes when Guzman stood outside:** This section draws from Guzman interviews.

126 **LeVecke worried too:** Jason LeVecke interviews.

127n1 **Arpaio had already conducted a worksite raid:** Katie McDevitt, "Gascón praises officers, criticizes sweeps," *East Valley Tribune*, June 27, 2008.

127n2 **Arpaio responded:** Gary Nelson, Michael Kiefer, JJ Hensley, "Arpaio raids Mesa City Hall, mayor outraged," *The Arizona Republic,* October 17, 2008.

127n3 **But in 2008, Phoenix mayor Phil Gordon:** This section draws from Phil Gordon, Arpaio, Paul Charlton, and Rev. Jarrett Maupin interviews; MCSO Lt. Travis Anglin, letter, April 24, 2008; MCSO, press release, July 29, 2008; Paul Charlton, letter, April 25, 2008; Wendy Halloran, "Former Phoenix mayor confronts false child-sex-crimes allegation," Channel 12, June 24, 2016; JJ Hensley, "Activist is arrested on charges of filing false report on Gordon," *The Arizona Republic,* November 21, 2008; *United States v. Maupin,* No. 2:09-cr-00052, Document 21 (D. Ariz., Plea Agreement, signed April 9, 2009; filed with the court, April 28, 2009).

127n4 **The sheriff's tipster for the criminal investigation:** Rev. Jarrett Maupin had tried, and failed, to get on the ballot to challenge Gordon in an earlier election. Once Maupin admitted he had lied, the sheriff's office arrested him. Maupin admitted in his plea deal to attempting to smear Gordon. In 2020, he said the plea he signed was inaccurate. He claimed federal authorities had threatened to deport his wife if he didn't sign.

128n1 **"When you cross this guy":** Paul Charlton, interviewed by Morgan Loew on KPHO, October 29, 2009.

128n2 **had promised an immigration reform bill:** See Lukas Pleva, "No big push in first year," PolitiFact, August 13, 2010, https://www.politifact.com/truth-o-meter/promises/obameter/promise/525/introduce-comprehensive-immigration-bill-first-yea/.

129n1 **Somos America needed to build national momentum:** Chris Newman, Salvador Reza, and Lydia Guzman interviews.

129n2 **Mary Rose Wilcox promised to pressure:** Puente Arizona, "Parade of Injustice!!!!" YouTube video, uploaded February 5, 2009, https://www.youtube.com/watch?v=PP7AcZNwvhc&t=1s (accessed June 17, 2020).

129n3 **National immigrant rights organizations:** Chris Newman interviews; National Day Laborer Organizing Network, email and petition, April 2, 2009.

129n4 **The National Council of La Raza called it:** National Council of La Raza, "Sheriff Arpaio's Lunchtime March of the Shackled Immigrants," February 2009, http://www.wecanstopthehate.org.

131n1 **One of Carlos Garcia's photos of shackled immigrant inmates:** "Arpaio's America," *The New York Times,* February 5, 2009.

131n2 **The newspaper posted the video link:** Editorial, "Traumatizing children, to keep us 'safe,'" *The New York Times,* January 14, 2009.

131n3 **Four Democratic members:** Rep. John Conyers, Jr., Rep. Zoe Lofgren, Rep. Jerold Nadler, and Rep. Robert C. Scott, to U.S. Attorney Eric Holder and Secretary of the Department of Homeland Security Janet Napolitano, February 12, 2009.

131n4 **he rationalized the televised march of shackled immigrants:** Arpaio, letter, February 24, 2009.

131n5 **Less than three weeks later, the justice department notified:** U.S. Department of Justice Acting Assistant Attorney General Loretta King, to Maricopa County Sheriff Joe Arpaio, March 10, 2009. The Bush administration had begun the investigation quietly in 2008, the same year Gordon and others requested it, according to records and Perez interviews.

132n1 **They dispatched . . . to testify before Congress:** Carlos Garcia, Lydia Guzman, and Chris Newman interviews.

132n2 **the story of Katherine Figueroa:** Dennis Gilman, "Arpaio Raids Carwash," video uploaded to YouTube, June 14, 2009, https://www.youtube .com/watch?v=YwXvLQXo7hw (accessed June 22, 2020).

132n3 **"a badge of honor":** JJ Hensley, "D.C. Justice team pays official visit to sheriff's office," *The Arizona Republic*, May 1, 2009.

132n4 **"just for spite":** The Associated Press, "AZ Sheriff Played Probe for Laughs," KTAR, April 23, 2012.

133n1 **Arpaio grumbled . . . "I was a hero":** Arpaio interviews.

133n2 **Arpaio's staff created his Twitter account:** MCSO, press release, June 9, 2009.

133n3 **In a Fox News interview:** Joe Arpaio, interview with Glenn Beck, *Glenn Beck*, Fox News, October 9, 2009.

133n4 **Arpaio's press team issued a correction:** Brian Lee, MCSO, email, October 15, 2009.

133n5 **A sergeant, who had no legal training:** MCSO Sgt. Brian Palmer, email, July 15, 2009. See also *Melendres*, Brian Palmer trial testimony, July 25, 2012.

134n1 **made a series of training videos:** Kris Kobach, Maricopa County Sheriff's Office Training Videos, June 25, 2010.

134n2 **Some seemed to invite racial profiling:** David A. Selden, Julie A. Pace, and Heidi Nunn-Gilman, "Placing S.B. 1070 and Racial Profiling into Context and What S.B. 1070 Reveals about the Legislative Process in Arizona," *Arizona State University Law Journal*, vol. 43, issue 2 (2011): 523.

134n3 **"Washington obviously did not like my deputies":** MCSO, press release, February 8, 2010.

134n4 **A federal judge would later rule:** Findings of Fact and Conclusions of Law, *Melendres*, May 24, 2013.

134n5 **Wilcox knew Joe Arpaio was coming after her:** This section draws on author interviews with Mary Rose Wilcox.

135n1 **"nemesis":** MCSO, press release, May 20, 2009.

135n2 **Arpaio's chief deputy David Hendershott:** Hendershott did not respond to requests for an interview. See MCSO Deputy Chief Frank Munnell, memo, August 17, 2010.

135n3 **deputies knocked on the doors:** See *In The Matter of Thomas,* Opinion and Order Imposing Sanctions, April 10, 2012.

135n4 **Wilcox was terrified, but not surprised:** Yvonne Wingett, "Arpaio focuses on Wilcox's Sky Harbor lease in probe," *The Arizona Republic,* June 17, 2009.

136n1 **"The sheriff has a vendetta":** JJ Hensley and Yvonne Wingett, "Does MACE unit fight corruption or political foes?" *The Arizona Republic,* July 19, 2009.

136n2 **Wilcox's criminal case followed:** Terry Greene Sterling, "A rose by any name," *Phoenix Magazine,* March 3, 2008. The Wilcoxes had borrowed $177,500 from Prestamos, a subsidiary of CPLC, and by December 2009 had paid back $57,500, according to Yvonne Wingett, Michael Kiefer, and JJ Hensley, "Stapley, Wilcox hit with charges," *The Arizona Republic,* December 9, 2009. Wilcox told us she had paid back the entire loan by 2009.

136n3 **Even her grandsons:** Mary Rose Wilcox testimony, *In the Matter of Thomas,* September 21, 2011.

136n4 **to shutter the restaurant:** The Wilcoxes would keep El Portal closed until 2014, but during that time they held special events and press conferences in the building. The restaurant had received low marks from health inspectors before it closed. Amy Silverman, "Mary Rose Wilcox's El Portal: Eater beware," *Phoenix New Times,* July 28, 2010.

136n5 **a federal lawsuit against her and other county officials:** *Arpaio v. Maricopa County Board of Supervisors,* No. 2:09-cv-02492 (D.Ariz., Complaint, December 1, 2009).

137n1 **After a Maricopa County superior court judge disqualified:** This section draws from an interview with Gary Donahoe and *Donahoe v. Arpaio,* Document 1 (Maricopa Cty., Ariz., Super. Ct., Complaint, November 29, 2010).

137n2 **"I couldn't bring a grand jury":** Terry Goddard interview.

137n3 **The case against Wilcox was dismissed:** *Arizona v. Wilcox,* CR-2010-005423–001 (Pima Cty., Ariz., Super. Ct., order, February 24, 2010). The Stapley case was transferred to another prosecutor, who said there was probable cause to prosecute him for seven felony charges, but she would not pursue it because the investigation was so problematic.

137n4 **Wilcox and ten other county officials . . . won:** Moseley, email, December 17, 2019.

TWELVE. DROWNING IN A GLASS OF WATER

139 n1 **Guzman was about to lose her home:** This section draws from interviews with Lydia Guzman, Jason LeVecke, and Tony Wesley.

139 n2 **"I just feel like I'm drowning":** Guzman, email, February 9, 2010.

140 **Magos had jotted:** This section draws from interviews with Daniel Magos and from his journal; MCSO, CAD Incident History, December 4, 2009; and Magos's testimony in *Melendres*. Deputy Dan Russell did not testify in the *Melendres* trial. But attorneys for the sheriff's office wrote in a post-trial August 9, 2012 motion, "the testimony of Daniel Magos shows that he was stopped for race neutral probable cause for not having a license plate on a trailer he was towing."

142 **Even as Guzman kept running the hotline:** This section draws from Guzman interviews and her personal correspondence.

144 n1 **The proposed law . . . commanded all Arizona law enforcement officers:** Senate Bill 1070 went through multiple iterations. After it was signed into law and incited controversy, the legislature passed House Bill 2162 that narrowed 1070. The new version erased the word "solely" from a line that had said law enforcement may not "solely consider race, color or national origin." See David A. Selden, Julie A. Pace, and Heidi Nunn-Gilman, "Placing S.B. 1070 and Racial Profiling into Context and What S.B. 1070 Reveals About the Legislative Process in Arizona," *Arizona State University Law Journal,* vol. 43, issue 2 (2011).

144 n2 **purpose of Senate Bill 1070:** Gabriel (Jack) Chin, "An unfixable law, a careful judge," *The New York Times,* July 29, 2010.

145 n1 **illegal immigration had slowed:** Department of Homeland Security, Annual Report, "Immigration Enforcement Actions: 2009," August 2010.

145 n2 **cattle rancher, Robert Krentz, was gunned down:** Terry Greene Sterling, "Arizona's immigration law's origin: Who killed Robert Krentz?" The Daily Beast, July 7, 2010, updated July 14, 2017. By 2020, the Krentz murder was still unsolved.

146 **nine college students chained:** Antonio Bustamante interviews.

147 n1 **She would later single out Reza's ear-shattering drum beats:** Jan Brewer, *Scorpions for Breakfast: My Fight Against Special Interests, Liberal Media, and Cynical Politicos to Secure America's Border* (New York: HarperCollins, 2011), 3 (in Kindle edition).

147 n2 **Latino protesters screamed "racist" at her:** Valerie Roller interviews.

147 n3 **Kobor demonstrated in favor of the bill:** Kathryn Kobor interviews.

148 n1 **Kobor's friend Pam Pearson:** Pearson interview.

148n2 **Guzman looked forward to receiving an award from the Latino non-profit:** This section draws from authors observation and Lydia Guzman, Antonio Bustamante, Carlos Garcia, Salvador Reza, and Rafaela Avila interviews; Jan Brewer's recollections in *Scorpions for Breakfast;* and video of the Erica Gonzalez-Melendez speech on the Chicanos Por La Causa Facebook page.

149 **It was an excruciating evening for the governor:** Brewer, *Scorpions for Breakfast.*

150n1 **"Outside, there was a huge group":** Brewer, *Scorpions for Breakfast.*

150n2 **mailbox . . . sticky green relish:** The section on the damage to her mailbox and subsequent house break-in draws from Lydia Guzman, Tony Wesley, and Ashley Torres interviews; John Roth, Glendale Police Department Report, April 29, 2010; and Guzman, emails, April 26 and 29, 2010.

151 **arrested Reza again:** Moseley, email, June 29, 2020.

152n1 **Brewer . . . non-existent "beheadings":** Robert Farley, "Gov. Jan Brewer talks of beheadings in the Arizona Desert," PolitiFact, September 8, 2010.

152n2 **One email sent by Pearce:** *Valle del Sol v. Whiting,* No. 2:10-cv-01061 (D.Ariz., Declaration of Daniel Pochoda, July 17, 2012); Alia Beard Rau, "ACLU: Pearce e-mails prove SB1070 was racially motivated," *The Arizona Republic,* July 19, 2012.

152n3 **Pearce didn't deny their existence:** Russell Pearce interview.

152n4 **troubled former precinct committeeman . . . marched with neo-Nazis and white supremacists:** Terry Greene Sterling, "Jason Todd Ready, an Arizona white supremacist, kills four, then himself," The Daily Beast, May 3, 2012.

153n1 **Ready was a "Judas Iscariot":** Pearce interview.

153n2 **Shawna Forde linked herself:** This section draws from *State v. Forde,* No. CR-11-043-AP (Ariz. Opinion, January 17, 2014); Terry Greene Sterling, "Shawna Forde guilty of murder: Exclusive interview with Arizona Minuteman," The Daily Beast, February 14, 2011; Forde, letter, January 8, 2012. In 2020, Forde was still on death row.

153n3 **Forde worked briefly:** This relationship is detailed in Dave Neiwert, *And Hell Followed with Her, Crossing the Dark Side of the American Border* (New York: Nation Books 2013), 172 (in Kindle edition).

154n1 **Simcox was later arrested:** *Arizona v. Simcox,* No. CR2013–428563 (Maricopa Cty., Ariz., Super. Ct.).

154n2 **The Minuteman movement lasted about seven years:** Neiwert, *And Hell Followed with Her,* 277–278.

154n3 **estimated Arizona had lost more than 140 million dollars:** Marshall Fitz and Angela Kelley, "Stop the Conference: The Economic and Fiscal

Consequences of Conference Cancellations Due to Arizona's SB 1070," Center for American Progress, November 2010.

155 **sixty business leaders wrote a letter to Senator Russell Pearce:** Drew Brown et al., letter, March 14, 2011.

THIRTEEN. LICKING THEIR CHOPS

157n1 **Pace . . . told us she withdrew:** Julie Pace and David Selden interviews.

157n2 **After activists scrambled . . . David Bodney:** For a short time, attorney David Bodney was editor of *Phoenix New Times*, and edited Terry Greene Sterling in the early 1990s. He was also the attorney for KJZZ, the public radio station in Phoenix, when Jude Joffe-Block was reporter for the station.

157n3 **to collect lawyers' fees from Maricopa County:** The parties in *Melendres* initially agreed to include MCSO as a party and dismiss Maricopa County. The Arizona Court of Appeals held in 2010 that MCSO was not the proper entity to be sued. Based on that, the Ninth Circuit Court of Appeals ruled Maricopa County should be substituted in as defendant.

157n4 **The new legal team wanted to convert the case:** *Melendres*, First Amended Complaint, Document 18, July 16, 2008.

158n1 **In 2009 . . . Murguia, denied Arpaio's motion:** *Melendres*, Document 60 (Order, February 10, 2009).

158n2 **Murguia, "the 'token' Hispanic female":** The Class West, email, January 20, 2009.

158n3 **Arpaio's lawyers noted in court filings that Mary Murguia had a twin:** *Melendres*, Defendants' Motion for Recusal, Document 63, February 23, 2009.

158n4 **sheriff's attorneys called for Judge Mary Murguia:** MCSO, press release, February 25, 2009.

159n1 **Murguia recused herself:** *Melendres*, Document 138 (Order, July 15, 2009).

159n2 **Snow moved to Phoenix:** Phil Alvidrez interview; Michael Kiefer, "Judge Snow vs. Sheriff Arpaio," *The Arizona Republic*, June 5, 2015.

159n3 **sheriff's office had withheld documents:** *Melendres*, Document 261 (Order, February 12, 2010).

160n1 **Bodney would likely have to reveal:** David Bodney interview.

160n2 **But LeVecke's restaurants were still struggling:** Jason LeVecke interview.

160n3 **Pochoda, the legal director of American Civil Liberties Union Arizona, failed:** Dan Pochoda interviews.

161n1 **That file turned out to be a treasure:** Cecillia Wang, Annie Lai, and Stanley Young interviews.

161n2 **Wang had confronted Arpaio before:** Cecillia Wang interviews.

161n3 **paused their dramatic neighborhood sweeps:** Arpaio testified during the July 2012 trial that the final saturation patrol was in October 2011. *Melendres,* Joe Arpaio trial testimony, July 24, 2012.

162n1 **"LEAR protocol":** MCSO, memo, August 8, 2009.

162n2 **culture of ICE was slowly shifting:** John Morton, Director, U.S. Immigration and Customs Enforcement, "Exercising Prosecutorial Discretion Consistent with the Civil Immigration Enforcement Priorities of the Agency for the Apprehension, Detention, and Removal of Aliens," Memorandum to Field Directors, Special Agents in Charge and Chief Consul, June 17, 2011.

162n3 **Misspending upwards of one hundred million dollars:** Wilson and Bohn, MCSO Financial Review Update (PowerPoint), September 22, 2010.

162n4 **keep track of the two federal investigations:** The section on the justice department investigations draws from Thomas E. Perez. letter, December 15, 2011; transcript of Thomas Perez's speech on December 15, 2011; Perez interviews; authors' attendance at the December press conference; Terry Greene Sterling, "Sheriff Joe Arpaio of Arizona's other Justice Department problem," The Daily Beast, September 3, 2010; Terry Greene Sterling, "Sheriff Joe Arpaio slammed in federal civil rights probe report," The Daily Beast, December 16, 2011.

163 **had prodded the FBI:** Charlton. letters, April 25 and October 31, 2008; Paul Charlton, Terry Goddard, and Rick Romley interviews. Michael Manning also alerted the U.S. Attorney in Washington as well as authorities in Phoenix in 2008 about inhumane conditions in Arpaio's jails.

164n1 **"We find reasonable cause":** Perez remarks published in U.S. Department of Justice, "Assistant Attorney General Thomas E. Perez Speaks at the Maricopa County Sheriff's Office Investigative Findings Announcement," *Justice News,* December 15, 2011; Tom Perez interview.

164n2 **The justice department investigators found:** Perez, letter, December 15, 2011.

164n2 **more than four hundred sex abuse cases:** Jacques Billeaud, "Critics: 'Tough' sheriff botched sex-crime cases," The Associated Press, December 4, 2011.

165n1 **flagged 44,000 inmates for eventual deportation:** MCSO, press release, December 21, 2011.

165n2 **the sheriff faced his third setback:** *Melendres,* Document 494 (Order, December 23, 2011).

166n1 **the judge sanctioned Arpaio and his agency:** *Melendres,* Document 493 (Order, December 23, 2011).

166n2 **gone were the neighborhood sweeps:** *Melendres v. Arpaio,* Brian Sands, Testimony, April 21, 2015. Between 2008 and 2011, the sheriff's office conducted twenty large-scale sweeps and netted fifteen hundred arrests. More than half of those arrested were undocumented immigrants. See The Associated Press, "Arizona sheriff shows none of trademark swagger," *The Mercury News,* July 24, 2012.

167n1 **proposed Arizona "birther bill":** The bill never became law.

167n2 **Trump based his claim on an edited YouTube video:** Robert Farley, "Trump said Obama's grandmother caught on tape saying she witnessed his birth in Kenya," PolitiFact, April 2, 2011.

167n3 **asked Arpaio to launch an investigation of Obama's birth certificate:** This section draws from Joe Arpaio, Brian Reilly, and Jeff Lichter interviews; authors' observations; and Terry Greene Sterling, "Arizona Sheriff Joe Arpaio's birther brouhaha," The Daily Beast, July 19, 2012. Brian Reilly told us he was satisfied Obama's birth certificate was authentic when Arizona's secretary of state received verification from Hawaii in 2012. He felt Arpaio kept going with the investigation because he was using it as a fundraiser.

167n4 **Arpaio dug in, saying it would bring in campaign donations:** *The Joe Show,* directed by Randy Murray (Randy Murray Productions, 2014).

168n1 **Arpaio held a press conference claiming:** MCSO, press release, July 17, 2012.

168n2 **"We are licking our chops":** Tom Liddy quoted in Jude Joffe-Block, "Sheriff Joe Arpaio's tactics go on trial," KJZZ, July 18, 2012.

FOURTEEN. DRIVING WHILE BROWN

169n1 **Arpaio slumped in the witness box:** Courtroom scenes rely on authors' observations; testimony of Joe Arpaio, Detective Charley Armendariz, Douglas Beeks, Steven Camarota, Lydia Guzman, Deputy Michael Kikes, Daniel Magos, Velia Meraz, Manuel Nieto Jr., Diona Solis, Victor David Vasquez; and interviews with Cecillia Wang, Stanley Young, Lydia Guzman, Carlos Garcia, Alfredo Gutierrez, Andre Segura, Velia Meraz, Daniel Magos, Manuel de Jesus Ortega Melendres, and Joe Arpaio.

169n2 **how Arpaio . . . could appear so diminished:** Cecillia Wang later told us she believed Arpaio's feeble affect—claiming he had a touch of the flu—was "definitely a schtick."

171n1 **The high court's decision:** *Arizona v. United States,* 567 U.S. 387, 132 S. Ct. 2492, 183 L. Ed. 2d 351 (2012). It was a five to three vote. Justice Elena Kagan recused.

171n2 **Kennedy's opinion . . . misleading report:** Ryan Gabrielson, "It's a fact: Supreme Court errors aren't hard to find," *ProPublica*, October 17, 2017.

172 **while challenging Arizona's law that denied undocumented immigrant arrestees the right:** The Ninth Circuit Court of Appeals struck down the law in 2014 due to the challenge, known as *Lopez-Valenzuela v. Arpaio*.

173n1 **"like I was testifying in court":** "Joe Arpaio: Joe's Law," C-SPAN, June 21, 2008. Channel 12 News (KPNX-TV) reporter Joe Dana noted this 2008 quote at the time of the 2012 trial.

173n2 **racially charged letters to Arpaio:** Jack [last name redacted], letter, May 24, 2008.

174 **"Arrest Arpaio! Not the people!":** The section on Carlos Garcia and the Puente demonstration draws from authors' observations; Carlos Garcia and Salvador Reza interviews; Puente Arizona, "Undocumented Arizonans arrested for coming out at Arpaio's trial," YouTube video, July 24, 2012; Cassondra Strande, "4 arrested at Arpaio protest outside courtroom," *The Arizona Republic*, July 25, 2012.

176 **replacing the controversial 287(g) program nationwide:** After the Supreme Court ruling over Senate Bill 1070, the Obama administration discontinued all of Arizona's remaining 287(g) agreements.

178 **Judge Snow played darts:** Andrew Case interview.

181 **In his testimony, Armendariz unwittingly admitted:** After the lunch recess, presumably after Armendariz had spoken with his attorney, he suggested on the stand that he let passengers go even if he could not verify their identities. It would turn out not to be true.

182 **dozens of Latino teenagers stood outside:** The Adiós Arpaio scene draws from authors' observations and Guzman interviews.

FIFTEEN. WHY ARE YOU TREMBLING?

183n1 **Romney . . . "self-deport":** Lucy Madison, "Romney on immigration: I'm for "self-deportation," CBS News, January 24, 2012.

183n2 **That year the GOP's platform on immigration echoed Kobach:** University of California Santa Barbara, The American Presidency Project, "2012 Republican Party Platform," August 27, 2012.

184n1 **Fox News Latino interview:** "Joe Arpaio: Don't blame me if Latinos don't vote Republican," Fox News Latino, August 31, 2012.

184n2 **"unauthorized presence in the United States is not a crime":** *Melendres v. Arpaio*, 695 F.3d 990 (9th Cir., 2012).

185n1 **Arpaio's lawyer . . . later testified:** *Melendres*, Casey testimony in civil contempt of court proceedings, September 29, 2015. Tim Casey did not want to testify and asked Snow to quash the subpoena from plaintiffs' attorneys compelling him to testify. Snow denied the request. Casey declined to be interviewed for this book.

185n2 **detailed in a prominent story:** JJ Hensley, "Arpaio case: Latinos allowed to join class-action suit," *The Arizona Republic*, December 23, 2011.

185n3 **Sheridan . . . claimed he did not know:** Jerry Sheridan interviews; Giaquinto, investigative report for MSCO, August 7, 2017.

185n4 **"I kind of delegated that":** Joe Arpaio interviews.

186 **Later that fall, a white Chevy truck:** The scenes detailing the arrests of the brothers and the aftermath rely on author interviews with Samuel [name changed] and Arpaio; Jude Joffe-Block and Terry Greene Sterling, "Wrongfully detained," Arizona Center for Investigative Reporting, April 12, 2018; and various MCSO records related to the brothers' traffic stop; MCSO, press release, October 9, 2012.

188n1 **Arpaio trumpeted . . . in a press release:** MCSO, press release, October 9, 2012.

188n2 **Segura notified the sheriff's lawyer:** Andre Segura interviews; Segura, letter, October 11, 2012; *Melendres*, Timothy Casey testimony, September 29, 2015.

188n3 **Some pre-election polls:** JJ Hensley, "National focus on sheriff's race," *The Arizona Republic*, October 22, 2012.

189n1 **civil rights division of the justice department had sued:** *United States v. Maricopa County*, No. 2:12-cv-00981, Document 1 (D. Ariz., Complaint, May 10, 2012).

189n2 **"I am the constitutionally and legitimately elected Sheriff":** MCSO, press release, April 3, 2012.

190n1 **A top prosecutor announced:** U.S. Attorney's Office, District of Arizona, press release, August 31, 2012; Scheel, letter, August 31, 2012. Heavily redacted FBI records obtained through FOIA would later show agents investigating the case had found probable cause to recommend various felony charges against unspecified targets.

190n2 **"one of the most heartbreaking episodes in my legal career":** Michael Manning interviews.

190n3 **Penzone tried mightily:** Penzone for Sheriff, "$182 million . . . and counting," campaign ad, *The Arizona Republic*, November 3, 2012.

190n4 **Penzone had managed to raise:** Penzone for Sheriff, October 25, 2012; Re-elect Joe Arpaio 2012, November 2, 2012; Campaign for Arizona's Future PAC, November 2, 2012.

190n5 **On election night:** The 2012 election night scenes draw from the authors' observations, notes, and *The Joe Show* (Randy Murray Productions, 2014).

191 **Guzman turned forty-five:** The sections on Guzman's personal and financial struggles draw from Lydia Guzman and Tony Wesley interviews, and Maricopa County property records.

192 **thirty thousand new Latino voters:** Jude Joffe-Block, "Why the race for Maricopa County sheriff could be about more than sheriff," KJZZ, September 21, 2012.

SIXTEEN. "GANAMOS!"

195 **running three hotlines:** Lydia Guzman and Julie Pace interviews.

196n1 **GANAMOS!!:** Guzman post, Facebook, May 24, 2013.

196n2 **Snow's painstakingly detailed . . . ruling:** *Melendres,* Findings of Fact and Conclusions of Law, Document 579, May 24, 2013.

197 **"blood and tears":** *Melendres,* Status Conference, January 18, 2019.

198n1 **"violating constitutional rights of the plaintiff class":** *Melendres,* Status Conference, April 3, 2014.

198n2 **Arpaio responded to Snow's blistering:** Joe Arpaio, "Sheriff Arpaio responds to federal ruling on racial profiling," YouTube video, May 29, 2013.

198n3 **For years . . . Arpaio and his commanders would incorrectly insist:** Jude Joffe-Block, "Term 'racial profiling' sparks language debate in MCSO lawsuit," KJZZ, April 18, 2014; Arpaio and Sheridan interviews.

198n4 **after the judge responded by clarifying:** *Melendres,* Status Conference, April 3, 2014.

199n1 **Latino resistance triumphed in court again:** *We are America/Somos America,* Document 137 (D. Ariz., Order, September 27, 2013).

199n2 **"Was very emotional":** Guzman, email, September 27, 2013.

199n3 **Snow issued a fifty-nine-page order:** *Melendres,* Document 606 (Supp. Perm. Injunction J. Order, October 2, 2013).

199n4 **Arpaio by then had started marketing himself as a humanitarian:** JJ Hensley, "Ariz. sheriff suspends immigrant patrols—for now," *The Arizona Republic,* June 14, 2013.

200n1 **"Everybody is after the sheriff":** Arpaio interviews.

200n2 **"I have received a copy of the court order":** MCSO, press release, October 2, 2013.

200n3 **the sheriff announced a "crime suppression operation":** The account in this section of the sweep draws from authors' observations; Arpaio and

Sheridan interviews; MCSO, press release, October 16, 2013; MCSO, training video, October 2013; *Melendres*, Order, Document 656, March 17, 2014.

201n1 **"Some courts want community outreach":** Joe Arpaio, Channel 5 interview, October 19, 2013.

201n2 **Snow chose Robert Warshaw:** Warshaw and Associates, "Independent Monitor Technical Proposal," December 9, 2013.

202n1 **Warshaw discovered and handed over to Judge Snow:** *Melendres*, Order, Document 656, March 17, 2014, and Status Conference, March 24, 2014.

202n2 **The angry judge ordered the sheriff's office:** *Melendres*, Document 680 (Enforcement Order, April 17, 2014).

202n3 **he sent a letter . . . to Obama's attorney general:** Arpaio, letter, January 16, 2014.

203 ***The Joe Show:*** The section draws from authors' observations; Randy Murray, Arpaio, and Kathryn Kobor interviews; MCSO, press release, April 6, 2014; Terry Greene Sterling, "The handcuffing of Sheriff Joe," *National Journal Magazine*, August 8, 2014.

SEVENTEEN. CONSPIRACY THEORIES AND VIDEOS

205n1 **Guzman first started getting the text messages:** Lydia Guzman interviews and screenshots of text messages.

205n2 **She had first met the deputy:** Armendariz, email, February 28, 2013.

205n3 **where Armendariz began crying:** This section on Armendariz draws from Guzman and Miguel Brusuelas interviews; Phoenix Police 911 calls; MCSO, Incident Reports, April 30 and May 8, 2014; Phoenix Police Department, "Ramon-Charley Ramirez Armendariz," 2014; *State of Arizona v. Ramon Charley Armendariz,* 2014; Maricopa County Office of the Medical Examiner Report of Toxicological Examination, August 6, 2014; *Melendres*, Charley Armendariz trial testimony, August 1, 2012; Fax, memo, August 1, 2014; Vogel, MCSO Administrative Investigation 14–0542, April 16, 2015; *Melendres*, Sealed Proceedings Transcript, May 7, 2014; MCSO, Human Resources Personnel File for Armendariz: interview video, May 2, 2014; Alcantar, email, September 14, 2011; *Melendres*, Document 1677 (Findings of Facts, May 13, 2016); and Steve Bailey interviews.

206n1 **notified her justice department contacts:** Guzman, email, August 28, 2013.

206n2 **Guzman told a justice department contact:** Guzman, email, May 6, 2014.

208n1 **a coworker had gathered it all up:** An MCSO detention officer later acknowledged during an internal investigation that she brought some items, which may have included IDs, to Armendariz's residence, according to MCSO Sgt. David Tennyson (Human Resources Personnel File for Armendariz: undated memorandum).

209 **After the sheriff's lawyers alerted Judge Snow:** *Melendres,* Sealed Proceedings, Status Conference, May 14, 2014. The transcript was later unsealed.

210 n1 **migraine headache, fatigue and confusion:** *Melendres,* Evidentiary Hearing, April 24, 2015.

210 n2 **In June, the alternative weekly:** Stephen Lemons, "Joe Arpaio's investigating Federal Judge G. Murray Snow, DOJ, sources say, and using a Seattle scammer to do it," *Phoenix New Times,* June 4, 2014.

210 n3 **informant, Dennis Montgomery, a former contractor for the Central Intelligence Agency:** See Eric Lichtblau and James Risen, "Hiding details of dubious deal, U.S. invokes national security," *The New York Times,* February 19, 2011; Aram Roston, "The man who conned the Pentagon," *Playboy Magazine,* January/February, 2010.

211 n1 **he was too frightened to sue:** Elias Bermudez interview.

211 n2 **Throughout what was left of 2014, Warshaw:** This section draws from *Melendres,* Sealed Proceedings, Status Conference, May 7, October 28, and November 20, 2014; Evidentiary Hearing, December 4, 2014; Warshaw, memo, September 28, 2014.

212 n1 **One former Human Smuggling Unit deputy:** Knight, memo, June 12, 2014; Cisco Perez unemployment hearing testimony, June 5, 2014.

212 n2 **Perez had lost his job:** The wiretap targeted another deputy, Alfredo Navarrette, who was accused of assisting a drug and human smuggling ring. Prosecutors dropped charges when it was revealed they had not sought authorization for the wiretap. He maintains his innocence.

212 n3 **"Hopefully, I'll be able to pocket":** Knight, letter, March 12, 2012.

214 n1 **"I'm not going to talk":** Joe Arpaio interviews.

214 n2 **thanks to a 2014 federal lawsuit:** *Puente,* Complaint, June 14, 2014.

215 n1 **donate one hundred thousand dollars to a civil rights organization:** *Melendres,* Expedited Motion to Vacate Hearing and Request for Entry of Judgment, Document 948, Exhibit A, March 17, 2015.

215 n2 **Kathryn Kobor and Barb Heller sat stiffly:** This section draws from Kobor and Heller interviews.

216 n1 **Arpaio was already down one lawyer:** See *Melendres* records, including Reply to Plaintiffs' Response to Application to Withdraw as Counsel of Record for Defendants, Document 793, November 18, 2014, and Transcript of Evidentiary Hearing, April 21, 2015.

216n2 **Sergeant Brett Palmer:** *Melendres*, Evidentiary Hearing, April 21, 2015. Palmer declined to be interviewed.

217n1 **He told Fox News host:** Joe Arpaio, interview by Neil Cavuto, *Your World*, Fox News, June 25, 2012 (200A video exhibit in the trial).

217n2 **"Are you aware that I have ever been investigated?":** This courtroom scene draws from authors' observations; *Melendres*, Evidentiary Hearings, April 23–24, 2015; Arpaio and Guzman interviews.

219 **"the Grissom information":** Casey, letter, November 6, 2013.

220n1 **in May 2015, Snow announced:** *Melendres*, Status Conference, May 14, 2015.

220n2 **Court records would later unravel the odd story:** Mackiewicz, email, September 4, 2016; *Melendres*, Declaration of Cecillia Wang, Document 1166, June 12, 2015; *Melendres*, Evidentiary Hearing, Dennis Montgomery, undated "Whistleblower Chronicles"; Arpaio and Sheridan interviews; *Melendres*, Document 1677 (Findings of Facts, May 13, 2016).

220n3 **convoluted timelines . . . Stanley Young's law firm:** Young's firm, Covington and Burling, also employed Snow's brother-in-law in its Washington, D.C. office. In 2012, the parties agreed Judge Snow should remain on the case and Arpaio had waived "any and all appeal issues regarding only the Court's potential bias, impartiality, and/or conflict of interest."

220n4 **Experts hired by the sheriff's office:** Drake, undated email.

220n5 **"This is fiction":** Jerry Sheridan interviews.

221n1 **a quarter million dollars:** *Melendres*, Jerry Sheridan testimony, Evidentiary Hearing, September 25, 2015.

221n2 **Arpaio's lawyers argued Snow was too conflicted:** *Melendres*, Motion for Recusal or Disqualification of District Court Judge G. Murray Snow, Document 1117, May 22, 2015.

221n3 **was represented by the right-wing attorney:** Larry Klayman, a founder of Judicial Watch and a well-known litigator who represented Arpaio in some matters, boasted on his website he "was credited as being the inspiration for the Tea Party movement."

221n4 **Shortly after Snow announced . . . he found out:** See *Melendres*, Document 1677 (Findings of Fact, May 13, 2016) and Order Re Criminal Contempt, Document 1792, August 19, 2016.

222n1 **approval ratings had dropped again:** Sean Holstege, "Poll: Arpaio's popularity falling amid federal case," *The Arizona Republic*, May 28, 2015.

222n2 **"get it out to the whole world":** Lisa Allen interview.

222n3 **There was an air of forced frivolity:** The description of the party is from authors' observations.

EIGHTEEN. "BUILD THE WALL!"

223 n1 **Ava Arpaio was in her early eighties when she was diagnosed:** Ava Arpaio, Joe Arpaio, and Lydia Guzman interviews; Daniel González, "Immigration activist's Facebook post generates sympathy for Sheriff Joe Arpaio's ailing wife, Ava," *The Arizona Republic,* June 15, 2016.

223 n2 **case championed by Tom Perez, was finally settled:** *United States v. Maricopa Cty.,* Document 391, Exhibit 2 (Settlement Agreement, July 17, 2015).

225 n1 **In June 2015, Trump and his wife:** Ashley Parker, "'I'm going down the escalator': Inside the Trump Tower spectacle that launched a presidency," *The Washington Post,* June 17, 2019.

225 n2 **hung "Stolen Lives Quilt" banners:** Barb Heller interviews.

225 n3 **Many of the four thousand:** Jude Joffe-Block, "Trump's Phoenix rally draws crowds, protest," KJZZ, July 11, 2015; "Donal Trump's #StandWithTrumpAZ Phoenix speech," YouTube video, Fox News, July 11, 2015.

226 **Trump "fired up the crazies":** Ryan Lizza, "John McCain has a few things to say about Donald Trump," *The New Yorker,* July 16, 2015.

227 **three people chained themselves:** This discussion of the Puente roadblock draws from Carlos Garcia and Arpaio interviews; authors' observations; Fox News, Channel 10 Phoenix, "Protesters try to shut down Donald Trump rally in Arizona," video, March 19, 2016.

229 **papers on his desk did not bode well:** Arpaio interviews; *Melendres,* Document 1677 (Findings of Facts, May 13, 2016); Jude Joffe-Block, "10 key findings from the civil contempt ruling against Sheriff Joe Arpaio," KJZZ, May 20, 2016.

230 n1 **The judge also found Brian Sands:** Sands, who retired in 2013, had argued in court that he took steps to respond to the order, and had advocated for distributing it to the entire sheriff's office. He also said he directed others to implement an office-wide training. *Melendres,* Document 1012, April 20, 2015, and Document 1214, August 6, 2015.

230 n2 **Sousa would later say:** Sousa interview by Daniel Giaquinto, May 8, 2017.

230 n3 **After twenty-three years as Arpaio's media relations director:** MCSO, press release, January 20, 2016.

230 n4 **Wizard of Paws and Prose:** Stephen Lemons, "Arpaio recently 'retired' top flack now making $102 an hour working for, you guessed it, Sheriff Joe," *Phoenix New Times,* March 28, 2016. When questioned by Lemons about the contract, Lisa Allen replied, "Wrong again."

230 n5 **Sherman became disillusioned:** Len Sherman interviews; Len Sherman, "Joe Arpaio's days as America's Toughest Sheriff are numbered," *The Arizona Republic,* March 4, 2016.

231n1 **on the day in May 2016:** Arpaio interview on May 13, 2016.

231n2 **She had met Tom Black:** Guzman and Black interviews.

232n1 **came across a cardboard box full of Guzman's awards:** Ashley Torres interview.

232n2 **Black accompanied Guzman to court:** This courthouse scene draws from authors' observations; Guzman, Kobor, Black, and Garcia interviews; *Melendres,* Status Conference, May 31, 2016.

233n1 **no confidence in the Maricopa County Sheriff's Office:** Snow ordered a number of independent investigations into possible misconduct in the sheriff's office. We requested copies in early 2019 but the sheriff's office did not make them all available before the deadline of this book.

233n2 **agency personnel who'd violated his order:** *Melendres,* Status Conference, May 31, 2016.

235 **2016 Republican National Convention in Cleveland:** The GOP convention scenes draw from authors' observations and Arpaio interviews.

NINETEEN. BAZTA ARPAIO

238 **Joe Arpaio needed a shave:** The scene draws from authors' observations; Arpaio, Guzman, and Gutierrez interviews; *Melendres,* In-Court Hearing, July 22, 2016.

240n1 **detailed thirty-two-page ruling:** *Melendres,* Document 1792 (Order Re Criminal Contempt, August 19, 2016). In 2018, court-appointed independent investigator Daniel Giaquinto found Bailey had not been untruthful, and cleared him of two out of the three allegations against him for internal discipline. Giaquinto's report acknowledged Bailey was following the advice of counsel, but found he "failed to question the advice of counsel and/or ask for clarification regarding whether to delay or withhold the disclosure of the 1459 identifications." In a court filing, Michele Iafrate said she was researching whether the newly discovered IDs fell under the court's order for disclosure. In a court hearing, she said, "We did not lie to the monitors or keep that from the monitors." Bailey told us nothing nefarious had gone on. "If we were going to have to investigate these ID's, so be it. There was . . . never a discussion like we should bury these. Ever." See Giaquinto, investigative report, February 12, 2018; *Melendres,* Document 1752 (Memorandum re Michele M. Iafrate), July 20, 2016.

240n2 **"multiple intentional false statements":** Snow noted in his order that "it is not appropriate to prosecute as criminal contempt the multiple intentional false statements made by Sheriff Arpaio and Chief Deputy Sheridan."

He said it would be up to federal prosecutors to decide if other criminal charges were warranted.

240 n3 **When Guzman found out about the ruling:** The El Portal scene draws from authors' observations and Lydia Guzman interviews.

241 **A week later, nothing had been decided:** Before becoming U.S. Attorney for Arizona, John Leonardo was a Pima County Superior Court judge who had dismissed the criminal case against Mary Rose Wilcox, pushed forward by Sheriff Joe Arpaio and Maricopa County attorney Andrew Thomas.

242 **Arizona Republican Party headquarters:** The primary election night scene draws from authors' observations, and Joe Arpaio and Kathy Hedges interviews.

243 n1 **Arpaio opened once again for his friend Donald Trump:** Authors' observations.

243 n2 **quoted questionable FAIR data:** Michelle Ye Hee Lee and Glenn Kessler, "Fact-checking Donald Trump's immigration speech," *The Washington Post,* August 31, 2016.

243 n3 **Trump did not acknowledge:** Ana Gonzalez-Barrera, "More Mexicans Leaving Than Coming to the U.S.," Pew Research Center, Hispanic Trends, November 19, 2015.

243 n4 **Border Patrol apprehensions:** U.S. Border Patrol, "Total Illegal Alien Apprehensions by Month, FY 2000–2016."

244 n1 **From the beginning of the Trump-Arpaio alliance:** The section on Bazta Arpaio draws from Carlos Garcia, Alejandra Gomez, and B. Loewe interviews; authors' observations; and Jude Joffe-Block, "Immigrants in Arizona are campaigning to oust a controversial sheriff," The World (Public Radio International), October 26, 2016.

244 n2 **Bazta Arpaio:** The campaign's name was a combination of the Spanish word *basta,* meaning "enough," and AZ, an abbreviation for Arizona.

245 n1 **The number of eligible Latino voters:** Daniel González, "In an Arizona county, anger at Trump spurs Latinos to vote," *USA Today,* September 26, 2016.

245 n2 **a group of Republican business people gathered:** The fundraiser scene draws from authors' observations and Beau Lane interview.

246 n1 **54 percent of Arizonans:** *The Arizona Republic,* Morrison Institute for Public Policy, and Cronkite News, "Arizona Republic/Morrison/Cronkite News Poll Finds Arizona Up for Grabs in Presidential Election," September 7, 2016.

246 n2 *The Arizona Republic* **hadn't endorsed Arpaio:** Editorial, "Our View: Elect Paul Penzone not Sheriff Showboat," *The Arizona Republic,* October 12, 2016.

246n3 **Soros started a political action committee:** Maricopa Strong, Maricopa County Campaign Finance Report, November 4, 2016.

246n4 **Arpaio emphasized his birther credentials:** The Surprise Tea Party scene draws from authors' observations; Arpaio interviews; Jude Joffe-Block, "A local Sheriff's race is drawing national attention and a hefty price tag," NPR, October 1, 2016.

246n5 **raised close to thirteen million dollars:** Elect Sheriff Joe Arpaio, November 4, 2016; Penzone for Sheriff, November 4, 2016.

247n1 **would prosecute Arpaio for at least one criminal count:** *United States v. Arpaio*, Status Conference, October 11, 2016; see also Jude Joffe-Block, "What you need to know about the criminal case against Sheriff Joe Arpaio," The World, October 12, 2016.

247n2 **the justice department would decline:** *United States v. Arpaio*, No. 2:16-cr-01012, Document 49 (Response to Defs.' memoranda on statute of limitations under 18 U.S.C. 3285, November 4, 2016).

247n3 **Arpaio believed . . . amounted to political retaliation:** Arpaio interviews. Court records show the prosecutors had requested an earlier hearing date but Arpaio's counsel preferred an October hearing.

247n4 **Bazta Arpaio threw a street-fair-like . . . "retirement party":** Authors' observations; Joffe-Block, "Immigrants in Arizona are campaigning," October 26, 2016.

247n5 **On election night, Arpaio and Ava did not show up:** The scene draws from authors' observations and Kathryn Kobor, email, November 11, 2016.

248 **Guzman stood with Tom Black . . . the ballroom floor:** The Democratic watch party scene draws from authors' observations and Guzman interviews.

249n1 **For the young Bazta Arpaio activists:** The Bazta celebration draws from Carlos Garcia and Alfredo Gutierrez interviews, photos and notes gathered by Garrett Schwartz, and Terry Greene Sterling, "The fall of Joe Arpaio, America's most controversial sheriff," *Newsweek*, November 9, 2016.

249n2 **We dialed Arpaio's cell phone several times:** Arpaio interviews and Sterling, "The Fall of Joe Arpaio," November 9, 2016.

TWENTY. THE NATIONAL ARPAIO

253 **Guzman and Tom Black married:** Wedding scene draws from Lydia Guzman and Tom Black interviews.

254n1 **admirers all over the country had called:** Amy Lake interview.

254n2 **Arpaio staged one of his last media events:** Arpaio interviews and authors' observations.

255 **Arpaio held his final press conference:** Authors' observations.

256 **Sheriff's office employees . . . packed the large restaurant to say good-bye:** The party scene draws from authors' observations.

258n1 **On inauguration evening:** The inaugural ball scene draws from Arpaio interviews; ABC News, "Trump inaugural balls: All the highlights," YouTube video, January 21, 2017; Katie Rogers, "Inaugural balls: Trump's first dance," *The New York Times*, January 20, 2017.

258n2 **Chimal Garcia:** This account draws from Chimal and Carlos Garcia interviews.

260 **joined hundreds . . . to protest the president's travel ban:** Guzman and Black interviews; ABC News, "Protests continue at Sky Harbor for second day," YouTube video, January 29, 2017.

261n1 **In her view, that road led to constitutional abuses:** This section about Trump's restrictionist advisors draws from Jason Zengerle, "How America got to 'zero tolerance' on immigration: The inside story," *The New York Times Magazine*, July 16, 2019; Julie Hirschfield Davis and Michael D. Shear, *Border Wars: Inside Trump's Assault on Immigration* (New York: Simon and Schuster, 2019), 37–38; Josh Harkinson, "The dark history of the White House aides who crafted Trump's 'Muslim Ban,'" *Mother Jones*, January 30, 2017; and Alfredo Gutierrez interviews.

261n2 **Paul Penzone was sworn into office by Judge Mary Murguia:** This section draws from Danny Ortega interviews and authors' observations.

262n1 **negotiate a settlement over . . . Senate Bill 1070:** *Valle del Sol*, Document 1297 (Joint Case Disposition, September 15, 2016).

262n2 **Guadalupe Garcia de Rayos:** The account draws from Carlos Garcia, Lydia Guzman, and Antonio Bustamante interviews; authors' observations; Marcela Valdes, "Is it possible to resist deportation in Trump's America?" *The New York Times Magazine*, May 23, 2017; and Richard Ruelas and Yihyun Jeong, "Arrest while working at fun park led to Arizona woman's deportation," *The Arizona Republic*, February 10, 2017.

263 **By then, Arizona immigration lawyers had highlighted:** Delia Salvatierra interview.

TWENTY-ONE. THE RESCUE

265n1 **Guzman was comforted:** This section draws from Lydia Guzman, Antonio Bustamante, and Alfredo Gutierrez interviews and authors' observations.

265n2 Attorney General Jeff Sessions had refused: Philip Rucker and Ellen Nakashima, "Trump asked Sessions about closing the case against Arpaio, an ally since 'birtherism,'" *The Washington Post,* August 26, 2017.

266n1 had energetically fundraised: Radley Balko, "Why should taxpayers subsidize Joe Arpaio's legal defense?" *The Washington Post,* July 27, 2017; Tom Jackman, "How ex-sheriff Joe Arpaio wound up facing jail time before Trump pardoned him," *The Washington Post,* August 25, 2017.

266n2 National Center for Police Defense: In 2016, NCPD received $388,952 in contributions. In 2017, the year Arpaio faced his criminal trial and solicited donations to his legal fund through NCPD, the organization received $3,370,172 in contributions and issued hundreds of thousands of dollars in legal assistance grants to unknown individuals as well as to a legal fund in California. The following year, after the pardon, contributions declined to $882,682, according to NCPD federal forms 990.

267n1 "for the rest of his life": Laurie Roberts, "Arpaio's latest fundraising plea? Give so he won't go to jail for life," *The Arizona Republic,* June 6, 2017.

267n2 A few months before his criminal trial: *United States v. Arpaio,* Document 105 (Motion Requesting a Voluntariness Hearing, March 24, 2017).

267n3 The closing arguments were the last chance: *United States v. Arpaio,* Trial, July 6, 2017; authors' observations.

268n1 After closing arguments ended: The post-trial scene draws from authors' observations and Arpaio and Guzman interviews; Terry Greene Sterling and Jude Joffe-Block, "Will Trump's DOJ send America's Toughest Sheriff to prison?" *Newsweek,* July 1, 2017.

268n2 busy taking care of North Korea: Agence France-Presse, "Trump declares 'patience is over' with North Korea," *The Guardian,* July 1, 2017.

269n1 Guzman pulled up Judge Bolton's fourteen-page ruling: *United States v. Arpaio,* Document 210 (Findings of Fact and Conclusions of Law, July 31, 2017).

269n2 For years, Guzman had smarted: Post-verdict reactions draw from authors' observations; Guzman, Salvador Reza, Alfredo Gutierrez, and Daniel Magos interviews; Magos journal; Cecillia Wang, "How the people of Maricopa County brought down 'America's Toughest Sheriff,'" blog, ACLU.org.

270 fifty or so people gathered for a feast: The party scene draws from video captured by Valeria Fernández.

271 Arpaio's supporters were dismayed: Reactions drawn from Arpaio, Kathryn Kobor, and Linda Bentley interviews; Linda Bentley, "Federal judge finds Arpaio guilty of criminal contempt," *Sonoran News,* August 1, 2017.

272n1 Arpaio's lawyer Mark Goldman delivered an envelope: Arpaio interviews.

272 n2 **he talked to Fox News:** Joe Arpaio, interview by Sean Hannity, "President Trump pardons former AZ Sheriff Joe Arpaio," Fox News, August 25, 2017.

272 n3 **The president later revealed:** President Donald Trump, "Remarks by President Trump and President Niinistö of Finland in Joint Press Conference," The White House, August 28, 2017.

TWENTY-TWO. I DON'T WANT IT TO COME BACK

274 **Guzman was at home:** This section draws from Lydia Guzman, Tom Black, and Carlos Garcia interviews; and Puente Human Rights Movement, "Tonight Trump sent a clear message that it's ok to break the law," Facebook video, https://www.facebook.com/watch/live/?v=1637157116309132&ref=watch_permalink.

275 **Guzman and Black slipped away:** The El Portal scene draws from authors' observations and Guzman, Black, Danny Ortega, Antonio Bustamante, and Mary Rose Wilcox interviews.

277 n1 **In Arizona, the once reliably conservative:** Editorial, "Our View: Donald Trump just resurrected Joe Arpaio from irrelevance," *The Arizona Republic*, August 25, 2017.

277 n2 **We called Arpaio several times:** Authors' observations, Arpaio interviews.

278 n1 **He told us he'd gotten two or three death threats:** Anonymous, letter, August 30, 2017.

278 n2 **An emailer called him "Sicko":** Arpaio interviews; [name withheld], email, August 27, 2017.

278 n3 **Danny Ortega and Antonio Bustamante joined about two hundred attorneys:** The demonstration scene is based on authors' observations.

279 n1 **Sheriff Paul Penzone took steps early:** Paul Penzone, once sheriff, refused to be interviewed or allow anyone on his staff to be interviewed for this book.

279 n2 **The new sheriff also ended:** Megan Cassidy, "Maricopa County Sheriff's Office: No more 'courtesy holds' for federal immigration agents," *The Arizona Republic*, February 21, 2017; MCSO, press release, February 24, 2017.

280 n1 **Arizona State University researchers had recently published an audit:** Danielle Wallace, Ph.D., et al., "Yearly Report for the Maricopa County Sheriff's Office, Years 2015–2016," Arizona State University Center for Violence Prevention and Community Safety, July 28, 2017.

280n2 **"It was four years ago":** *Melendres,* Status Conference, September 27, 2017.

280n3 **Wang remained active:** Cecillia Wang interviews.

281n1 **On a sunny October morning:** This section draws from authors' observations; Guzman, Daniel Magos, and Joe Arpaio interviews.

281n2 **"encroachment by the Executive on the independence of the Judiciary":** *United States v. Arpaio,* Document 239 (D. Ariz., Proposed Memorandum of Amici Curiae Certain Members of Congress, September 27, 2017).

282n1 **"I have concluded that the pardon is valid":** *United States v. Arpaio,* Motion Hearing, October 4, 2017.

283 **Judge Bolton allowed the guilty verdict to stand:** *United States v. Arpaio,* Document 25 (Order, October 19, 2017). It was upheld by the Ninth Circuit: *United States v. Arpaio,* 951 F.3d 1001 (9th Cir., February 27, 2020).

284 **He decided to run as a Republican candidate:** Arpaio's petition delivery scene draws from authors' observations and Kathryn Kobor interviews.

285n1 **supported Ward:** Valerie Roller, George Sprankle, and Jim Williams interviews.

285n2 **Immigrants were "animals":** Julie Hirschfield Davis, "Trump calls some unauthorized immigrants 'animals' in rant," *The New York Times,* May 16, 2018.

285n3 **"infest our country":** Betsy Klein and Kevin Liptak, "Trump ramps up rhetoric: Dems want 'illegal immigrants' to 'infest our country,'" CNN Politics, June 19, 2018.

285n4 **Arpaio stuck up for Trump:** Joe Arpaio interview by Chris Cuomo, *Cuomo Prime Time,* CNN, June 14, 2018.

286n1 **A few days later, we asked Arpaio to elaborate:** The Wickenburg scene draws from authors' observations and Arpaio interviews.

286n2 **On the evening of August 28, 2018:** The watch party scenes draw from authors' observations, and Arpaio and Kobor interviews.

288n1 **He sued *The New York Times:*** *Arpaio v. Cottle* (D.D.C., October 16, 2018); *Arpaio v. Zucker* (D.D.C., December 10, 2018).

288n2 **Then Ava stepped on a rattlesnake:** Arpaio, email, April 17, 2019.

289 **Latino voter turnout:** U.S. Census Bureau, "Voting and Registration in the Election of November 2014," Table 4b, July 2015, and "Voting and Registration in the Election of November 2018," Table 4b, April 2019.

290 **Joe Arpaio announced he was running once again:** This section draws from Arpaio and Sheridan interviews.

AFTERWORD

293 n1 **Lydia Guzman views:** The quotes and reflections in this section draw from author correspondence in November 2020.

293 n2 **margins over 75 percent:** Analysis by University of California Los Angeles Latino Public Policy Initiative. Diaz, email, November 16, 2020.

293 n3 **knocked on over one million doors:** Mi AZ Coalition, press release, November 11, 2020. The 2020 Mi AZ coalition included Living United for Change in Arizona (LUCHA), Mi Familia Vota, Chispa Arizona, CASE Action, UNITE HERE Local 11, and Our Voice, Our Vote.

294 **Arpaio's third book:** Joe Arpaio and David Thomas Roberts, *Sheriff Joe Arpaio An American Legend: The Fascinating and Untold True Life Story of America's Most Beloved Crime Fighter* (Conroe, Texas: Defiance Press and Publishing, 2020), 153.

297 n1 **aided efforts to prevent the certification:** Jonathan Shorman, "Kris Kobach aiding Michigan official who wants to take back vote certifying election," *The Kansas City Star*, November 20, 2020.

297 n2 **Maricopa County has so far paid 76,900 dollars:** Moseley, email, November 20, 2020.

297 n3 **to surpass 178 million in 2021:** Jacques Billeaud, "Taxpayer bill from Arpaio's profiling case will reach $178M," The Associated Press, May 22, 2020.

Author Interviews

What follows is a list of key interviews that informed this book. The list does not include short interviews, text messages, emails, short phone conversations with sources, press conference comments, or off-the-record and background interviews.

Paul Penzone refused to give an interview or allow anyone on his staff to talk with us about Joe Arpaio's tenure, *Melendres* litigation, and related issues.

Lisa Allen—October 13, 2017
Phil Alvidrez—May 6, 2014
Sheriff Joe Arpaio—May 12, August 14, 2009; July 23, 2013; April 22, April 26, 2014; May 13, July 4, July 18, July 19, July 21, July 22, August 3, August 30, September 20, November 28, December 12, 2016; April 3, August 8, September 12, October 9, 2017; June 16, August 28, December 4, 2018; June 13, August 30, October 23, 2019; June 19, November 11, 2020
Sheriff Joe Arpaio and Ava Arpaio—April 13, 2017; May 15, 2018
Rafaela Avila—May 24, 2020
Captain Steve Bailey—September 19, September 24, September 27, 2020
Linda Bentley—June 1, July 27, 2017
Elias Bermudez—September 22, 2018
Tom Black—July 12, 2017; August 28, November 17, 2019
David Bodney—April 6, 2017

Clint Bolick—2014
Miguel Brusuelas—December 8, 2014; August 4, 2016
Antonio Bustamante—May 5, May 11, 2017; January 13, 2018; May 28,
    November 16, 2020
Andrew Case—September 1, 2017
Maria Castro—November 10, 2020
Paul Charlton—July 25, 2016; May 9, September 7, 2017; January 17, 2018
Richard DeUriarte—December 17, 2019
Gary Donahoe—August 2, 2016
Ryan Gabrielson—March 8, November 20, 2017
Buffalo Rick Galeener—June 30, 2018; June 12, 2020
Carlos Garcia—April 21, April 25, 2017; May 10, 2018; June 12, 2020
Chimal Garcia—May 10, 2018
Laura Garcia—April 9, 2017
George Gascón—January 1, 2019
Dennis Gilman—October 4, 2017; June 13, 2020
Terry Goddard—May 27, 2017
Alejandra Gomez—August 1, 2019
Phil Gordon—May 1, 2017; June 14, 2020
Alfredo Gutierrez—April 3, April 20, May 11, 2017; February 10, 2018;
    February 2, 2019; May 5, 28, November 17, 2020
Lydia Guzman—June 6, 2012; July 31, 2015; January 2, 2016; April 7, May 10,
    June 9, August 5, 22, October 4, November 12, December 27, December 28,
    2017; January 20, January 26, February 9, March 16, March 17, April 7, May
    11, June 21, June 29, July 14, October 14, October 23, November 2, 2018;
    January 4, January 7, April 18, May 10, May 15, May 20, June 22, August 18,
    September 30, November 17, 2019; May 16, May 17, November 11, 2020
Kathy Hedges—August 30, 2016
Barb Heller—May 11, June 17, November 16, 2020
Father Glenn Jenks—August 11, 2016; February 20, 2018
Phil Jordan—February 13, 2017
John Kleinheinz—August 10, August 16, September 11, September 28, 2017;
    May 13, 2020
Kris Kobach—June 11, 2013; May 13, 2020
Kathryn Kobor—June 19, 2009; June 9, 2014; August 2, 2017; June 13, 2019;
    May 25, November 16, 2020
Andy Kunasek—November 22, 2019
Annie Lai—July 13, 2016; April 12, April 27, 2017, January 19, 2018; August
    1, 2019
Amy Lake—November 15, 2019
Beau Lane—September 7, 2016
Jason LeVecke—August 1, 2016; August 11, 2017; June 13, 2020

Jeff Lichter—September 20, 2016
Tom Liddy—2012; 2014; 2015; November 20, 2020
B. Loewe—August 7, 2019
Hector Lopez—January 6, 2017; February 20, 2018
Daniel Magos—February 20, March 1, March 25, August 16, October 10, 2017;
    June 10, 2020
Dr. Angeles Maldonado—2014
Michael Manning—July 14, July 20, 2016; January 4, 2018; July 1, 2020
Martin Manteca—January 25, 2018
William Mattingly—February 28, 2017
Rev. Jarrett Maupin—June 16, 2020
Manuel de Jesus Ortega Melendres—February 11, March 24, 2017
Stephen Montoya—February 5, 2018
Randy Murray—February 10, 2017
Chris Newman—October 25, 2017; July 24, 2018
Jason Odhner—June 20, 2017
Danny Ortega—May 4, 10, June 3, 2017; April 16, October 24, 2018; August
    22, 2019; June 1, November 16, 2020
Julie Pace—July 7, 2016; May 15, 2017; June 12, 2020
Russell Pearce—May 13, May 28, 2020
Pam Pearson—August 28, 2018
Tom Perez—September 20, 2017
Dan Pochoda—July 1, 2016; April 27, 2017
Monica Ramirez—March 10, 2017
Tim Rafferty—June 30, 2018
Brian Reilley—August 13, 2016; June 29, 2020
Roberto Reveles—June 6, 2017; January 21, 2018
Salvador Reza—July 31, 2015; August 10, 2016; February 22, 2017;
    September 25, 2018; June 7, 2020
Robert Robb—January 22, 2018
Valerie Roller—July 5, 2018; June 12, 2020
Rick Romley—July 10, 2020
Richard Ruelas—November 7, November 10, 2017
Brian Sands—December 22, 2017; September 22, 2018
Delia Salvatierra—June 29, 2019
Samuel—October 11, 2017; March 5, March 26, 2018
Kenneth Schorr—January 10, 2018
Andre Segura—October 20, 2016; April 18, 2017
David Selden—August 9, 2016; May 15, 2017
Jerry Sheridan—April 26, 2017; May 21, 2020
Len Sherman—February 22, 2017
Don Sorchych—June 1, 2017

George Sprankle—July 5, 2018

Roberto Suro—February 26, 2019

Ashley Torres—June 12, 2017

Nancy Velasco—July 8, 2017

Ronald Wakabayashi—July 6, 2020

Cecillia Wang—May 7, 2014; June 9, 2016; September 27, 2017; August 14, August 15, 2019

Mike Watkiss—January 12, 2018

Tony Wesley—December 27, 2019

Sean Whitcomb—July 4, 2018

Earl Wilcox—January 8, 2018

Mary Rose Garrido Wilcox—May 5, May 29, 2017; December 28, 2019; May 27, 2020

Jack Wilenchik—June 23, October 4, 2017

Chad Willems—October 5, 2017

Jim Williams—March 12, March 21, 2019; June 12, 2020

Sandra Wilson—November 20, 2019; July 2, 2020

Stanley Young—June 6, 2016; May 9, 2017

Bibliography of Unpublished Sources

Items with an asterisk were court exhibits in the *Melendres* litigation or in the criminal contempt of court case against Joe Arpaio. All items are arranged alphabetically, except for MCSO documents, which are arranged chronologically.

Alcantar, Herman. Email, "Release of funds for [Name witheld]," September 14, 2011.

Anglin, Travis, MCSO Lt. Letter to Phoenix City Manager Frank Fairbanks, April 24, 2008.

Anonymous. Letter to Joe Arpaio, August 30, 2017.

Armendariz, Charley. Email, "Thank you," February 28, 2013.

Arpaio, Joe. Immigration File records:

———— Barotholomeaux, Carol V. Letter to Arpaio, July 26, 2007, 562–563.*

———— Hotline Notes, July 26, 2007, 510.

———— Immigration file, 389, 383–388.

———— Immigration file, 525.

———— Immigration file, 698.

Arpaio, Joe. Undated notes, circa December 2007.*

———— Letter to Chairman John Conyers, U.S. House of Representatives, Committee on the Judiciary, February 24, 2009.

———— Letter to Attorney General Eric Holder, January 16, 2014.

———— Email. "Ava Arpaio Snake bite recovery," April 16, 2019.

B., Deborah. Email. "Corner of Queen Creek & Ellsworth," September 17, 2007.*

Brown, Drew, et al. Letter to Senator Russell Pearce, March 14, 2011.

Campaign for Arizona's Future PAC, Campaign Finance Report, November 2, 2012.

Casey, Timothy J. Letter to Hon. Joseph M. Arpaio, November 6, 2013.*

Charlton, Paul. Letter to FBI Special Agent in Charge John Lewis, "Re: Tampering with a Witness," April 25, 2008.

—— Letter to FBI Special Agent in Charge John Lewis, "Re: Meeting with Attorney General Terry Goddard, Former County Attorney Rick Romley and Chief George Gascon, Mesa Police Department," October 31, 2008.

Clancy, J. D., MCSO Detective. Supplemental Report DR#05-063171, April 26, 2005.

Class West, The. Email to Joe Arpaio et al., January 20, 2009.*

Diaz, Sonja. Email to the authors, "Latino vote analysis from UCLA LPPI shows Latinos were a decisive factor in 2020 election," November 16, 2020.

Drake, Thomas. Email, "Response," Undated.*

Elect Sheriff Joe Arpaio. Maricopa County Campaign Finance Report, November 4, 2016.

Fax, Stephen, MCSO Sergeant, Professional Standards Bureau. Memo to Captain Steve Bailey, August 1, 2014.*

Fernández, Valeria and Daniel DeVivo. Video archive for the making of "The Two Americans," 2013.

Forde, Shawna. Letter to Terry Greene Sterling, January 8, 2012.

Giaquinto, Daniel G., Independent Investigator, MCSO. Investigative Report IA#2016-0687, August 7, 2017.

——Investigative Report IA#2017-0163, February 12, 2018.

Gordon, Phil. Cesar Chavez Luncheon Speech, March 28, 2008.

—— Letter to Honorable Michael B. Mukasey, Attorney General of the United States, "Re: Request for Civil Rights investigation of the Maricopa County Sheriff," April 4, 2008.

Guzman, Lydia. Email, "Questions About Levecke," January 10, 2008.

—— Email, "Volunteers needed today," March 22, 2008.

—— Email, "News articles," March 23, 2008.

—— Email, "Friendly House & CPLC," March 27, 2008.

—— Email, "Sheriff's operations begin today Bell Rd," March 27, 2008.

—— Email, "Info for attorneys," March 31, 2008.

—— Email, "Need a lawyer . . . ," March 31, 2008.

—— Email, "Racial Profiling Incidents by Sheriff Arpaio's Operation," May 5, 2008.

—— Email, "I need some help," February 9, 2010.

—— Email, "Some one vandalized my mailbox," April 26, 2010.

—— Email, "I'm back on line, whoo whooo!!!," April 29, 2010.

—— Email, "MCSO deputy contact," August 28, 2013.

—— Email, "FW: Judge: MCSO can no longer charge with 'Conspiracy to Smuggle yourself,'" September 27, 2013.

—— Email, "Charley paperwork," May 6, 2014.

Happersett, Newlin E., Peoria Chief of Police. Letter to City Attorney Calvin Brice, Subject: Raul Gonzales vs City of Peoria, August 10, 1978. [Exhibit in *Gonzales v. City of Peoria*]

Hess, Don, MSCO Deputy. Supplemental Report DR#05–063171, April 11, 2005.

Jack [Last name redacted]. Letter to Arpaio, May 24, 2008.*

Jafari, Melody. Email, "36th St. & Thomas Rd. Dr. Dr. Jafari," October 12, 2007.*

Knight, Bill, MCSO Deputy Chief. Letter to Deputy Cisco Perez, March 12, 2012.

—— Memo to Captain Steve Bailey, "Statements made by Cisco Perez during unemployment hearing . . . ," June 12, 2014.*

Kobach, Kris. Maricopa County Sheriff's Office Training Videos, retrieved from *The Arizona Republic*, "Arpaio's immigration-enforcement videos for deputies," June 25, 2010. [Video has since been disabled, but authors have maintained a recording]

Kobor, Kathryn. Email, "My input on Sheriff Joe–win or lose," November 11, 2016.

Lee, Brian, MCSO. Email, "News Conference Update," October 15, 2009.

Mackiewicz, Brian, MCSO Detective. Email, "elmers case summary.docx," September 4, 2016.*

Madrid, Manuel, MCSO. Email, "Cave Creek day labors and tip line," September 27, 2007.*

Manning, Michael. Email to the authors, March 29, 2020.

Maricopa County, Office of the Medical Examiner. Report of Toxicological Examination 14–03122, August 6, 2014.

Maricopa County Sheriff's Office (MCSO). 911 Call Transcript DR#063171, April 10, 2005.

—— "Continuation Report DR:06–156216, Human Smuggling/Conspiracy," September 18, 2006.

—— Traverse, Mike, MCSO Det. Supplemental Report, "Conspiracy to Commit Murder," DR#07–54071, 2007.

—— CAD Incident History MA07181873, September 27, 2007.*

—— Incident Report 07–205617, Trespassing, November 3, 2007.

—— Saturation Patrol Documents, 32nd Street and Thomas, March 21–22, 2008.*

—— "Stats sheet for saturation patrol: Cave Creek & Bell," March 28, 2008.*

——Memo, Subject: ICE LEAR Protocol, August 8, 2009.*

—— CAD Incident History, MAO9222294, December 4, 2009.

—— Training Video, October, 2013.*

—— After Action Report: Enforcement Operation, October 18 and 19, 2013.

———— Incident Reports 14–009988, April 30, 2014 and 14–010581, May 8, 2014.

Maricopa County Sheriff's Office, Human Resources Personnel File for Armendariz:

———— Internal Affairs Administrative interview of Charley Armendariz, Video, May 2, 2014.*

———— Spreadsheet of worksite raid arrests, Document 520–9, July 1, 2016. [Exhibit in *Puente v. Arpaio* lawsuit]

———— Sgt. David Tennyson, "Memorandum of Concern Regarding IA #14–295," Undated.*

Maricopa County Sheriff's Office, Press Releases:

———— "Arpaio refuses to be intimidated . . . ," May 24, 2006.

———— "Sheriff's crackdown on illegal immigration nets 4 more illegals," June 23, 2006.

———— "Sheriff Mobilizes Posse In Central Phoenix," January 18, 2008.*

———— "Illegal alien 'serious' crime escalating," February 27, 2008.

———— "North and central valley businesses cry for help from sheriff's office," March 20, 2008.

———— "Sheriff's Crime Suppression Operation Moves to Guadalupe," April 3, 2008.*

———— "Mayor's Racial Profiling Charge Sent to U.S. Attorney General Totally False, July 29, 2008.

———— "Arpaio Demands Judge to Step Aside," February 25, 2009.

———— "Arpaio appreciates to board members who approved $1.6 million for sheriff's illegal immigration enforcement," May 20, 2009.

———— "The real Sheriff Joe joins Twitter," June 9, 2009.

———— "Sheriff Arpaio Dedicates More Resources To Illegal Immigration Fight," February 8, 2010.*

———— "Department of Homeland Security Strips Arpaio's Office of its Federal Immigration Status," December 21, 2011.

———— "DOJ to Sheriff Arpaio: 'Monitor Absolutely Mandatory' Arpaio to DOJ: 'I Will Not Surrender My Office to the Federal Government,'" April 3, 2012.

———— "Sheriff's Investigators: "President's Long Form Birth Certificate Is Undoubtedly a Fraud," July 17, 2012.

———— "Second Time ICE Refuses to Accept Illegal Alien From Sheriff's Deputies since September," October 9, 2012.*

———— "Sheriff Arpaio's Statement Regarding Todays Melendres Ruling," October 2, 2013.

———— Sheriff Arpaio Orders a Crime Suppression Operation In West Valley," October 16, 2013.

———— "'The Joe Show' Premier Has Come to a Close," April 6, 2014.

———— "Lisa Allen: Announcement," January 20, 2016.

—— "Statement From Sheriff Paul Penzone Regarding Ice Detainers," February 24, 2017.

Marinari, Maddalena. Email to the authors, July 26, 2020.

Maricopa Strong. Maricopa County Campaign Finance Report, November 4, 2016.

Mi AZ Coalition. Press Release, "Flipping Arizona blue: The 2020 grassroots victory a decade in the making," November 11, 2020.

Montgomery, Dennis. "Whistleblower Chronicles," Undated.*

Moseley, Fields, Maricopa County Communications Director. Email to the authors, December 17, 2019.

—— Email to the authors, January 2, 2020.

—— Email to the authors June 12, 2020.

—— Email to the authors, June 29, 2020.

—— Email to the authors, November 20, 2020.

Munnell, Frank B., MCSO Deputy Chief. Memo to Joseph M. Arpaio, August 17, 2010.

[Name withheld]. Email to Joe Arpaio, (no subject), August 27, 2017.

National Day Laborer Organizing Network. "Take Action to End Racial Profiling! It's Time to Stop Sheriff Joe," Email and petition, April 2, 2009.

O'Connell, Stacey. Letter to Joe Arpio, Re: Minutemen Project/Illegal Immigration Maricopa Co., November 20, 2005.

Palmer, Brian, MCSO Sgt. Email, "Title 8," July 15, 2009.*

Peña, Alonzo. Letter to State Rep. Ben Miranda, Phoenix, Arizona, August 14, 2007.*

Penzone for Sheriff. Maricopa County Campaign Finance Report, October 25, 2012.

—— Maricopa County Campaign Finance Report, November 4, 2016.

Perez, Tom, Assistant Attorney General of the United States. Letter to Maricopa County Attorney Bill Montgomery, December 15, 2011.

Phoenix Police Department. "Ramon-Charley Ramirez Armendariz (Prior MCSO Deputy)," 2014–00743051, 2014–00766881, 2014–00776029.

Polanco, Reyna. Email, "Needs Your Help, Necesitan de su ayuda," April 19, 2008.

Re-elect Joe Arpaio 2012. Maricopa County Campaign Finance Report, November 2, 2012.

Ross, Sean, MCSO. Email, "Good Sheppard of the Hills (Cave Creek Church)," September 24, 2007.*

—— Email, "Fountain Hills Detail," October 22, 2007.*

Roth, John. Glendale Police Department Report 10–053756, April 29, 2010.

Scheel, Ann Birmingham, United States Attorney. Letter to Bill Montgomery, "Re: MCSO Financial Review & Related Matters," August 31, 2012.

Segura, Andre. Letter to Timothy J. Casey, October 11, 2012.*

Somos America. Budget, April 21, 2006.

Sousa, Joseph. Interview by Daniel Giaquinto. "Case #17–0163," May 8, 2017.

Thomas, Andrew P., Maricopa County Attorney. "Criminal Justice-Sheriff-Human Smuggling Enforcement Opinion No. 2005–002," September 29, 2005.

——— "Regarding the Authority of County Law Enforcement Officers to Arrest Illegal Aliens for Violations of State Criminal Laws or Federal Immigration Laws and Transfer Such Aliens to the Custody of the U.S. Border Patrol," Phoenix, August 1, 2006.

U.S. Attorney's Office District of Arizona. Press Release, "U.S. Attorney's Office Announces Closing of Criminal Investigation Into Conduct of the Maricopa County Sheriff's Office and the Maricopa County Attorney's Office," August 31, 2012.

U.S. Department of Homeland Security. Memo to U.S. House of Representatives Judiciary Committee, "Response to U.S. House of Representatives Inquiry Dated 2/12/09" (redacted copy), February 12, 2009.*

U.S. Department of Labor Immigration Service. "List Six List or Manifest for Alien Passengers for the United States," SS Presidente Wilson, July 1, 1923.

Vogel, Don. MCSO Administrative Investigation 14–0542, April 16, 2015.*

Wallace, Danielle, Ph.D., et al., "Yearly Report for the Maricopa County Sheriff's Office, Years 2015–2016," Arizona State University Center for Violence Prevention and Community Safety, July 28, 2017.*

Warshaw and Associates, Inc., "Independent Monitor Technical Proposal," December 9, 2013.*

Warshaw, Robert S., Monitor. Memo to G. Murray Snow, "Update and Assessment of MCSO's Armendariz and Related Investigations," September 28, 2014.*

Wilson, Sandi, Deputy County Manager and Lee Ann Bohn, Deputy Budget Director. MCSO Financial Review Update (PowerPoint), September 22, 2010.

Index

Page numbers in *italics* denote images. Page numbers appended with "n" indicate a note (e.g., 315n). The name "Guzman" refers to Lydia Guzman. The abbreviation "MCSO" stands for Maricopa County Sheriff's Office.

Chin, Jack, 144
citizenship: of Mexican Americans in the Arizona Territory, 33; as no protection from
deportation, 34; pathway to, for undocumented immigrants, 65, 66; Proposition
200 requiring proof of for voter registration, 306. *See also* citizens, Latinos as
citizens, Latinos as: as plaintiffs in the *Melendres* case, 115, 157, 181; poll showing
significant underestimation of the
number of, 61; as targets of traffic stop/
neighborhood sweeps, 115, 119
civil contempt of court evidentiary hearing
(2015): overview of, 223; admission of
civil contempt by Arpaio and Sheridan,
214–15, 239, 267; Arpaio and chief deputy Sheridan found to intentionally disobey Snow's 2011 order, 229–30; Arpaio's
investigations of Judge Snow in attempt
to remove Snow from the case, 210–11,
217–22, 229, 349n; Arpaio's testimony,
216–18, *218*; contempt of court sanctions provided as remedy in *Melendres*
orders, 199; continued violation of
Snow's 2011 order found in, 229–30;
criminal contempt of court referral ruling
stemming from, 230, 235, 238–40, 258,
351–52n; defense lawyers, 216, 267;
deputy testifying to lack of training in
Snow's 2011 order, 216; Finding of Facts
for, 229–30; independent investigations
into MCSO ordered by Snow, 233, 351n;
Latino activists present for, 215–16, 217,
220, 232–35, 238, 239–40; media and,
215, 231, 233; offer of settlement from
Arpaio and Sheridan rejected by the Latino plaintiffs, 214–15; protesters of, 215,
232, 233, *234*, 238; time required for,
221; video evidence of failure to comply
with 2011 order, 216–17
civil rights investigation. *See* federal justice
department, civil rights investigation of
Arpaio (2012)
Civil War, and the Arizona Territory, 32–33
Clinton, Bill: immigration crackdown under,
60–61, 325n; U.S. Immigration and
Nationality Act (1996), 60–61, 88
Clinton, Hillary, 243, 248
CNN, 47
CNN, Arpaio suing for defamation, 288
Code Pink demonstrators, 236
Community Legal Services (legal aid), 41–43
community raids. *See* sweeps

conspiracy theories pushed by Arpaio: overview of, 211; assassination plots, 93, 211;
and background as federal drug enforcement agent, 58; birth certificate of
Obama (birtherism), 166–68, 211, 246,
247, 255–56, 343n, 353n; Facebook tip
investigation in attempt to remove Judge
Snow from *Melendres* case, 217–19, 221;
origins of criminal contempt of court
charge, 255, 284, 294; "Seattle Investigation" in attempt to remove Judge Snow
from *Melendres* case, 210, 211, 216, 218,
220–21, 229, 247; as victim of liberal
news media, x; as victim of Obama holdovers in the federal government, x, xxvi,
247, 249, 255, 273, 294, 353n
contempt of court: ordered as sanctions for
MCSO failure to cooperate with reforms,
199. *See also* civil contempt of court evidentiary hearing (2015); criminal contempt of court trial (*United States v.
Arpaio*)
Conyers, John, 131
CopWatch, 116, 259
Cornejo, Carmen, 269
Corsi, Jerome, xxvii–xxviii, 167
courts: Guzman's faith in, 24, 154, 156–57,
175, 189–90, 220, 266, 269–70, 276,
282–83. *See also* federal justice department; lawsuits; *specific courts*
Court Tower Project, 135, 137
COVID-19 pandemic, 293–94, 296
Covington and Burling: Arpaio conspiracy
theory involving, 220, 349n; pro bono
legal services in *Melendres v. Arpaio*/
Stanley Young, 160, 161, 169, 172–74,
216–17, 220, 349n. *See also Melendres v.
Arpaio*
coyotes, 53
crime: inflation of statistics for, by counting
immigration violations as felonies, 112,
171; neglect of duty to police sex crimes,
due to Arpaio's focus on immigration,
123, 164; by undocumented immigrants,
as restrictionist narrative, 122, 225, 243,
260; by undocumented immigrants, as
Trump narrative, 225, 243; by undocumented immigrants, Obama administration and focus on prosecuting and deporting for, 162, 176, 186, 262–63; violent
crime wave, ebbing of, 15; by violent racists, 153, 154. *See also* violence
crime suppression operations. *See* sweeps

Sprankle, George, 54, 102, 154, 285
Springfield, Massachusetts, 5–6, 8
Stapley, Don, 135, 338n
Starbucks, day-old pastries donated by, 85
Starworld Travel Agency (Scottsdale), 12,
    13–15, 16, 52, 224
"Stolen Lives Quilt," 225
Superior, Arizona, 36–37
Support Our Law Enforcement and Safe
    Neighborhoods Act. *See* Senate Bill 1070
Surprise, Arizona, 167, 246, 255
sweeps: overview of, xvi–xvii; defined as term
    in the text, xvii. *See also* day laborers; traf-
    fic stop sweeps as immigration enforce-
    ment strategy; worksite raids as immigra-
    tion enforcement strategy

Tanton, John, 22–24, 45. *See also* FAIR
Tea Party movement, 133, 166–67, 246,
    349n; and Arpaio final press conference,
    255–56
Tempe, Arizona, ASU campus, 36
Tent City jail: as backdrop for press confer-
    ences, 91; chain gangs, 29; as "concentra-
    tion camp," Arpaio reference to, 278; con-
    ditions in, 29; establishment of, 28–29;
    food, 29; media attention and, 29,
    30–31; Penzone and shutdown of, 279;
    pink underwear, autographed versions of,
    29; pink underwear requirement, 29;
    protests of conditions in, 236; tours of,
    29, 56; undocumented immigrants
    paraded to special section of, 129, *130*,
    131
Terán, Raquel, 289
Thomas, Andrew: 2004 campaign for Mar-
    icopa County attorney, 48; and "anti-cor-
    ruption" task force, 135–38; as disbarred,
    138; dropping charges against vigilante
    Patrick Haab, 55; and "inherent author-
    ity" of MCSO to enforce civil violations of
    federal immigration law, 77–78; inter-
    view request refused by, 323n; lawsuit
    filed with Arpaio against Wilcox and
    other county officials, 136–37, 279,
    352n; and prosecution of migrants who
    paid smugglers as conspiring to smuggle
    themselves, 57–58; as restrictionist, 55,
    56–57. *See also* U.S. Attorney's Office in
    Phoenix, abuse of power investigation of
    Arpaio and Thomas
Tia Foundation, 331n
Tonatierra, 192, 232, 270

Torres, Ashley (daughter of Lydia Guzman):
    birth and early childhood of, 21, *26*; and
    Tom Black (stepfather), 232; and family
    dog, 193; Guzman's worry about retalia-
    tion by MCSO against, 126; resentment
    of her mother's busy schedule, 47, 116;
    respect for her mother's activism, 232;
    son of (Stanley), 289, 294; and Tony Wes-
    ley (stepfather), 82
traffic stops: audit taken of, and racial dispar-
    ities of treatment in, 280; deputy training
    for, 200–201, 202; for gangs, guns, and
    drugs (October 2013), 200
traffic stop sweeps as immigration enforce-
    ment strategy: anti-Arpaio protesters and,
    117, 118, 119; and arrest and transport
    to Border Patrol for deportation, 187–88;
    and arrests and transport to ICE custody
    for deportation by 287(g) officers, 113,
    114; bullhorns/shouting used to inform
    the arrestees of their rights, 115, 254,
    264; child victims of, 113–14, 117–18,
    120; continuation of, despite Judge
    Snow's preliminary injunction forbidding,
    186–88; continuation of, despite revoca-
    tion of 287(g) authority, 142; documen-
    tation/filming of, 115, 131; end of, 166;
    "Good Friday" sweeps (2008), 113–16;
    Guzman meeting potential plaintiffs for
    Melendres case, 115, 142, 143; Guzman's
    warnings about on live television, 115;
    legal services in aid of those impacted
    (Los Abogados), 114; Macehualli Work
    Center area sweep, 116–18; Daniel
    Magos traffic stop, 140–42, 339n; as
    media event, 114, 115–16; minor viola-
    tions used as pretext to check identifica-
    tion, 113; numbers and demographics of
    those arrested, 116, 343n; Phoenix
    mayor Phil Gordon condemning, 117;
    posse members and, 113, 119; Pruitt's
    furniture store sweeps, 112–13; record-
    ings made by deputies, 209–10; restric-
    tionist/pro-Arpaio supporters and, 114,
    117, 118; suspension of (fall 2011), 161,
    342n. *See also* day laborers; federal justice
    department, civil rights investigation of
    Arpaio (2012); *Melendres v. Arpaio*
Trujillo, Alejandro, *35*
Trump, Donald: 2016 election win, 247–48,
    295; 2020 election fraud claims by, 297;
    2020 election loss, 293–97; accused as a
    fake conservative by Grant Woods, 279;

Founded in 1893,
UNIVERSITY OF CALIFORNIA PRESS
publishes bold, progressive books and journals
on topics in the arts, humanities, social sciences,
and natural sciences—with a focus on social
justice issues—that inspire thought and action
among readers worldwide.

The UC PRESS FOUNDATION
raises funds to uphold the press's vital role
as an independent, nonprofit publisher, and
receives philanthropic support from a wide
range of individuals and institutions—and from
committed readers like you. To learn more, visit
ucpress.edu/supportus.